Jesus Christ

Source of Our Salvation

Source of Our Salvation

Michael Pennock

ave maria press • notre dame, indiana

Engaging Minds, Hearts, and Hands **for Faith**

"An education that is complete is one in which the hands and heart are engaged as much as the mind. We want to let our students try their learning in the world and so make prayers of their education."

—Bl. Basil Moreau
Founder of the Congregation of Holy Cross

In this text, you will find:

 methods for investigating and understanding all that God has done for us through his Son, Jesus Christ—the story of our Redemption that is accomplished through the Paschal Mystery.

 suggestions for answering God's call to each of us for an intimate relationship with him through our deepening practice of prayer.

 ways to practice discipleship, including adherence to all that Christ taught, service to the poor and marginalized, and fulfilling the responsibility for the mission of evangelization.

Contents

1

GOD'S GOOD CREATION: THE BEGINNING OF SALVATION HISTORY

God created man in his image;
in the divine image he created him;
male and female he created them.

—Genesis 1:27

- **Model of Compassion**

  The saving deeds of our Lord in the Paschal Mystery reveal God's love, forgiveness, and compassion.

- **Origins of the World and Humankind**

  Natural questioning about the existence and meaning of life leads us to answers from Divine Revelation, God's free gift of self-communication by which he makes known the mystery of the divine plan.

- **How Scripture Is Interpreted**

  Special attention to the literary forms and the intention of the sacred authors are among the ways we can understand the meaning of Scripture.

- **The First Creation Account (Gn 1:1-2:4a)**

  The first creation account contrasts with ancient creation myths by expressing the inspired belief in the one, true God— Yahweh—who entered human history in a radical new way.

- **The Second Creation Account (Gn 2:4b-25)**

  The second creation account was written by the Yahwist author who portrays God as anthropomorphic, that is, with human qualities.

- **The Theme of Creation in Theology and Scripture**

  God's creation is the foundation of his saving plans.

Model of Compassion

Professional golfer Roberto De Vicenzo is perhaps best known for a mistake he made in signing a scorecard. In the final round of the 1968 Masters Tournament De Vicenzo signed an incorrect scorecard that had been prepared for him by his caddie. The scorecard incorrectly stated that he made a par on the seventeenth hole when, in fact, he birdied it, that is, shot one under par on the hole. His birdie would have tied him with the eventual champion, Bob Goalby. However, under the Rules of Golf, when a player signs an incorrect scorecard, the score stands. Due to this error, De Vicenzo came in second. A lesser man would have been embittered by this mistake and the unbending rules of golf, but not Roberto De Vicenzo. He accepted full responsibility for not checking the accuracy of his scorecard before signing it. He simply said, "What a stupid I am."

Roberto De Vicenzo continued his career by playing superb golf. Worldwide, he won a remarkable 230 tournaments, including the prestigious British Open. Along the way, he garnered many honors including the Bob Jones Award for distinguished sportsmanship in golf.

The mark of his character shines forth in an incident that happened late in his career. As De Vicenzo left the clubhouse after winning another tournament, a young woman approached him and congratulated him on his victory. She then began to cry and tell him that she was jobless and had a baby who was near death. She said that she could not afford a doctor or hospital bills. De Vicenzo paused a moment and then asked, "May I help your little girl?" He endorsed his winning check, handed it to the woman, and wished her and her sick baby well.

A week later, a Professional Golfers' Association official told De Vicenzo that the lady in the parking lot had defrauded him. She was childless and told her sad story to fleece him out of his money. De Vicenzo asked the official, "You mean there is no dying baby?" The golf official said, "That's right." De Vicenzo face lit up with a huge smile, "Well, that's the best news I've heard all year."

Roberto De Vicenzo's relief and compassion in the face of an evil that had befallen him reminds

The Goodness of Creation

Genesis 1–3 reveals important theological truths about the origins of creation, humans, and sin. Among these truths is that God creates a good and orderly world (Gn 1:31). This includes the natural world: the sky and sun, the moon and the stars; lakes and rivers, waterfalls and rainbows; trees and flowers, fields and mountains; all kinds of animals; and human beings most of all. "God willed creation as a gift addressed to man, an inheritance for and entrusted to him" (*CCC*, 299). Many times the Church has had to defend God's gift of creation, including that of physical creation. Related to the teaching of the goodness of creation, complete the following assignment and reflection.

Assignment

With a digital camera, take five photos that represent the goodness of creation. Print out your favorite photo and adhere it in your journal. Write a paragraph explaining how this picture makes you feel.

Reflection

- How happy are you with the way that God made you?
- What is the best thing about you?
- If Jesus were to tell someone about you, what might he say?

us how God deals with us. He forgives us time and again despite our dishonesty, deception, and sinfulness. God's forgiveness and compassion come to us most completely in the Person of Jesus Christ, our Lord and our Savior. He is the Good News of our Salvation.

The subject of this book is Jesus the Savior. In examining his compassion, you will be studying in greater depth those saving actions of our Lord known as the Paschal Mystery. The *Catechism of the Catholic Church* highlights the importance of the Paschal Mystery:

> The Paschal Mystery of Christ's cross and Resurrection stands at the center of the Good News that the apostles, and the Church following them, are to proclaim to the world. God's saving plan was accomplished "once for all" by the redemptive death of His Son Jesus Christ. (*CCC*, 571)

At the heart of the Paschal Mystery are Christ's redemptive Death on a cross and his glorious Resurrection, which have won for us the forgiveness of sin and eternal life with the Blessed Trinity. The story of God's redeeming activity in human history, which reaches its completion in our Lord's Passion, Death, and Resurrection, starts at the very beginning of human history with the creation of the first humans, named in Genesis as Adam and Eve. Their fall from grace, known as Original Sin (see Chapter 2), ruptured their relationship with God. But God did not abandon them or their human descendants to sin. This is the story of Salvation History, a history that reaches its peak in Jesus Christ, our Savior.

For Reflection

What do you think about Roberto De Vicenzo's decision to give the woman money and his later reaction when he found out that there was no sick child?

Origins of the World and Humankind

Think back to when you were a three-year-old, perhaps taking a walk with your beloved grandfather. You were outside enjoying the beauties of the natural world, chatting about this and that. As all young children do, you asked your grandfather things about the world around you. Likely the most frequent questions you asked began with a simple "why?" "Why are things like they are, Granddad?" You needed to know then, and you need to know now.

One of the most basic thought processes for humans is questioning. We want to figure out the meaning of our own lives and the larger scope of what it means to be human. We are meant to seek and to know the truth. We want reality to make sense, so we ask questions in our search for answers and meaning. Albert Einstein (1879–1955), had this to say about natural human inquiry:

> The important thing is not to stop questioning. Curiosity has its own reason for existing. One cannot help but be in awe when he contemplates the mysteries of eternity, of life, of the marvelous structure of reality. It is enough if one tries merely to comprehend a little of this mystery every day. Never lose a holy curiosity.

Einstein was not a particularly religious man, but he saw questioning as something that can lead us to seek the God who made us to seek truth.

Think back again to an earlier time in your life. As you grew older, you began to ask even more questions—very personal ones that had to do with your origins. For example: How did Mom and Dad meet? Where did they come from? Why did they settle here? Why was I born in this time, in this place, with these relatives? What does life have in store for me? Why do I have to die? What is the

philosophy
The investigation of truths and principles using human reason.

pantheism
The belief in opposition to Christian doctrine, that God and nature are one and the same.

polytheism
The belief, in opposition to Christian doctrine, that there are many gods.

Redemption
A word that literally means "ransom." Jesus' Death is ransom that defeated the powers of evil.

Salvation History
The story of God's saving actions in human history.

Divine Revelation
The way God communicates knowledge of himself to humankind, a self-communication realized by his actions and words over time, must fully by his sending us his divine Son, Jesus Christ.

meaning of life—of my life? Where did everything come from?

You are in good company if you ask questions like these because you are indeed engaged in a holy activity—that of thinking and searching for truth. Through the ages, men and women have tried to make sense out of reality, to seek meaning in the world around them. This helps explain the existence of **philosophy**, the name for the systems of thought that try to provide rational explanations of why things are the way they are and how we know and should conduct our lives. Most of these systems of thought have concluded that behind the life we see and experience there must be a source of all life—something or someone greater than we are who brought life into existence and sustains it. When asked whether he believed in God or not, Albert Einstein replied,

I am not an atheist. . . . We are like a little child entering a huge library filled with books in many languages. The child knows someone must have written those books. It does not know how. It does not understand the languages in which they are written. The child dimly suspects a mysterious order in the arrangement of the books but doesn't know what it is. That, it seems to me, is the attitude of even the most intelligent human being toward God. We see the universe marvelously arranged and obeying certain laws but only dimly understand those laws.

Down through the centuries, various religions and cultures have tried to discern the origin of the world and all creation. Using only human reason, different religions have come up with many diverse, and often conflicting, theories. For example, Hinduism holds that the universe is the same as the force that created it. This is known as **pantheism**, the religious belief that the material world and God are one and the same. Other ancient religions (e.g., Zoroastrianism) held that there are two equal spirits in the universe, one evil and the other good, who are constantly engaged in a cosmic struggle. Still other religions are based in **polytheism**, that is, they believe there are many gods who are responsible for the creation of the world.

Although by studying his works by the natural light of human reason we can come to know the one true

God with certainty, it is not the whole story, because human reason is limited. Various philosophies based on human reason and other religions are limited too. Catholics respect the beliefs of these other religions about God and the origins of the world. The Church's perspective on these life questions is unique and unequaled. Catholics and other Christians believe that the Divine Author is a loving Father who has sent his only Son to live among us, to teach us about the Father, to show us how to live, and to redeem us so that we can one day go to a blessed home of happiness and joy in Heaven. The Second Vatican *Council's Declaration on the Relation of the Church to Non-Christian Religions* taught:

> The Catholic Church rejects nothing that is true and holy in these religions. She regards with sincere reverence those ways of conduct and of life, those precepts and teachings which, though differing in many aspects from the ones she holds and sets forth, nonetheless often reflect a ray of that Truth which enlightens all men. Indeed, she proclaims, and ever must proclaim Christ "the way, the truth, and the life" (John 14:6), in whom men may find the fullness of religious life, in whom God has reconciled all things to Himself. (*Nostra Aetate,* No. 2)

While the Church does respect other religions, she has been entrusted with the truth of the Gospel of Jesus Christ. She must share with others the Good News that he is the "way, the truth, and the life." St. Ambrose (340–397) explained the Gospel message this way:

> When we speak about wisdom, we are speaking of Christ. When we speak about virtue, we are speaking of Christ. When we speak about justice, we are speaking of Christ. When we speak about peace, we are speaking of Christ. When we speak about truth and life and Redemption, we are speaking of Christ.

St. Ambrose understood that all that is important in life is the Person of Jesus Christ. This text focuses especially on Ambrose's last point—**Redemption**. Jesus is our Redeemer. He is the one who will make it possible for us share in God's own life:

> It pleased God, in his goodness and wisdom, to reveal himself and to make known the mystery of his will. His will was that men should have access to the Father, through Christ, the Word made flesh, in the holy Spirit, and thus become sharers in the divine nature. (*CCC,* 51, quoting the *Dogmatic Constitution on Divine Revelation*, 2)

Understanding Divine Revelation

Out of God's infinite mercy and love, he stepped into human history to disclose who he really is. He did this through the events of **Salvation History**, that is, the account (of both deeds and words) of God's saving activity for humankind. In other words, God *revealed* himself to the world.

Deposit of Faith

"The heritage of faith contained in Sacred Scripture and Tradition, handed on in the Church from the time of the Apostles, from which the Magisterium draws all that it proposes for belief as being divinely revealed" (*CCC*, Glossary).

Sacred Tradition

The living transmission of the Church's Gospel message found in the Church's teaching, life, and worship. It is faithfully preserved, handed on, and interpreted by the Church's Magisterium.

Sacred Scripture

The inspired Word of God; the written record of God's Revelation.

inspiration

The guidance of the Holy Spirit that enabled the human authors to record faithfully, and without error, what God wanted revealed to us for our beliefs.

Magisterium

The official teaching office of the Church. The Lord bestowed the right and the power to teach in his name to Peter and the other Apostles and their successors. The Magisterium is the bishops in communion with the successor of Peter, the Bishop of Rome (Pope).

Recall that **Divine Revelation** is God's free gift of self-communication by which he makes known the mystery of the divine plan. God's divine plan is to communicate his own divine life to the men he freely created, in order to adopt them as his sons in his only-begotten Son. In brief, this is the answer to the ultimate question of why we are here. We are here because God created us to know him, to love him, and to be called in communion with him (*CCC*, 27). Jesus reveals most fully what that communion means: adoption as sons and daughters into the divine family.

How do we know what God has revealed? Divine revelation is contained in a single **Deposit of Faith**, which Christ turned over to the Apostles after his Ascension into Heaven. The Apostles, under the inspiration of the Holy Spirit, handed on this deposit, or "heritage of the faith," to the Church. They did this through their oral preaching and their writings, both done under the inspiration of the Holy Spirit. This is why all generations since the Apostles can hear about God's love for us in Jesus Christ until he returns in glory at the end of time. We find the single Deposit of Faith in Sacred Tradition and Sacred Scripture.

The word *tradition* means "handing on." **Sacred Tradition** is the living transmission or "handing on" from one generation to the next of the Church's Gospel message. **Sacred Scripture**, consisting of the Old and New Testaments, is the written record of Revelation. It is "the speech of God as it is put down in writing under the breath of the Holy Spirit" (*Dogmatic Constitution on Divine Revelation*, No. 9, *CCC*, 81). Jesus Christ is the unique Word of Sacred Scripture, both its starting and ending points. His presence is revealed in human words of both the Old Testament and New Testament. The Scriptures tell us that the Word of God became man and saved us from sin.

We can rely on the truth of Sacred Scripture because it is inspired. God used the human authors and their unique talents to put into writing exactly what he wanted written, and nothing more. Likewise, we can only understand the meaning of Scripture when it is "read and interpreted in the light of the same Spirit by whom it was written" (*CCC*, 111, quoting *Dei Verbum*, 12 § 3). This is the meaning of **inspiration**.

> The books of the Scripture firmly, faithfully, and without error teach that truth which God, for the sake of our salvation, wished to see confided in Sacred Scriptures. (*Dogmatic Constitution on Divine Revelation*, No. 11, *CCC*, 107)

When Christ entrusted the Deposit of Faith to the Apostles, he authorized them to interpret God's Word authentically. This authority keeps the Church free from error and guarantees that Christ's Gospel is passed down authentically to future generations. Jesus gave this teaching authority to the Apostles' successors—the Bishop of Rome (the pope) and the bishops in communion with him.

ST. IRENAEUS
OF LYONS

The life of the Christian is essentially knowing Jesus Christ. It is also in being known yourself. No one is intended to live life in isolation. You must both know Christ and his Father and be known by them. These essential insights of our faith were gleaned by St. Irenaeus, a Father and Doctor of the Church, who was bishop of Lyons in Asia Minor in the late second century.

Irenaeus was born around the year 125 in a seaside province in Asia Minor. He likely had the chance to hear the Gospel directly from one of the Apostles or their immediate disciples. Irenaeus was ordained a priest and served under the bishop, St. Ponthinus. In 177, Irenaeus was sent to Rome. While he was gone, the Church in Lyons faced severe persecutions. St. Ponthinus and other Church leaders were martyred. Eventually Irenaeus was sent home to replace Ponthinus as bishop.

Irenaeus was left to face another challenge in the region that was affecting the entire Church, the heresy of Gnosticism. This was the name for movements in the second century that claimed secret, revealed knowledge of God had been transmitted to either the Apostles or the leader of a Gnostic sect.

St. Irenaeus answered the Gnostics in his treaty *Against Heresies*. He also highlighted the importance of Church Tradition for arriving at religious truth. He wrote that the source of right teaching and belief resides with the Roman Church because the Church was founded by Jesus and entrusted to St. Peter.

It was in *Against Heresies* that Irenaeus wrote about the glory of God being witnessed in the person who is fully alive:

> The glory of God gives life; those who see God receive life. For this reason God, who cannot be grasped, comprehended or seen, allows himself to be seen, comprehended and grasped by all, that he may give life to those who see and receive him. It is impossible to live without life, and the actualization of life comes from participation in God, while participation in God is to see God and enjoy his goodness.

Faithful Disciple

This authority is known as the **Magisterium**. The Holy Spirit guides the pope and bishops so that they can serve the Word of God, listen to it faithfully, preserve it through the ages, and explain it to the Church so that we can live according to Christ's teachings.

The first eleven chapters of Genesis are vital in the story of Salvation History because they reveal important truths about the creation of the world and of humans, of the relationship between males and females, of God's intentions for us, of Original Sin and the fall from grace, and of God's promise of a future Redeemer. This next section focuses on the first two chapters of Genesis. Before Genesis 1–11 are discussed as a whole, it is necessary to first address the figurative, symbolic language used by the authors of Genesis so that we can correctly interpret what religious truths God wants us to learn from this opening book of the Bible—a book that answers many important *why* questions about human existence.

For Review

1. What questions are humans naturally conditioned to ask?
2. What does philosophy attempt to do?
3. Define *pantheism* and *polytheism*.
4. What is unique about the Christian belief about Revelation?
5. Define *Salvation History* and *Divine Revelation*.
6. Briefly state God's divine plan of Salvation for human beings.
7. Define the *Deposit of Faith*.
8. What is the relationship between Sacred Scripture and Sacred Tradition?
9. What special role does the Magisterium play in relationship to the Deposit of Faith?

QUESTIONS AND ANSWERS ABOUT CREATION

- **Why did God create?**
  God did not have to create. He is complete perfection in himself. He created the world to manifest his glory. God did not create to increase his glory, which is impossible, but to show forth and communicate his goodness, truth, and beauty.

- **What does the glory of God mean?**
  "Glory" is the recognition and praise of someone's excellence. Applied to God, it means recognizing God's absolute goodness, love, beauty, power, majesty, holiness, and perfection.

- **Why did God create humans?**
  God created us out to share his love and goodness and "to be his sons through Jesus Christ," that is, to adopt us into the divine family and share his eternal life with us.

- **How do we humans glorify God?**
  St. Irenaeus said, "The glory of God is man fully alive." We are fully alive when we know, love, and serve God; when we offer back to him in thanksgiving all of creation in this world; and when we are raised up to eternal life with him in Heaven. We are truly human when we become other Christs, the perfect Man, the Son of God, who is the perfect image of God.

For Reflection

- What questions about the meaning of life do you have? List some steps you can take to find some answers to these questions.

- The typical human cell has forty-six chromosomes. A single human chromosome contains twenty billion bits of information, the equivalent of about three billion letters or five hundred million words. Assume further that there are three hundred words on a page of written text; this would correspond to about two million pages of text on one chromosome! Imagine how rich a library of information goes into making one human being. Discuss one other phenomenon from the natural world that would lead you to believe there is a Creator-God.

How Scripture Is Interpreted

The inclusion of *two* creation stories in the first two chapters of Genesis presents a quandary. You might question why there are two accounts of the same event. You might also wonder how these stories came to be since there was no one around at the time of creation to record them! Similarly, in Genesis 3, we have the story about a serpent (Satan) talking to Eve in the Garden of Eden, tempting her to eat the fruit of a tree. It is certainly valid to ask: could a snake really talk in the Garden?

Reading the Bible with understanding requires us to recognize that it deals with a time, people, and culture that are foreign to us. To interpret it correctly requires that we gather some background information on the text, including being able to distinguish between figurative and symbolic language and what should be taken literally.

The Second Vatican Council offered guidelines on how to interpret Sacred Scripture:

> However, since God speaks in Sacred Scripture through men in human fashion, the interpreter of Sacred Scripture, in order to see clearly what God wanted to communicate to us, should carefully investigate what meaning the sacred writers really intended, and what God wanted to manifest by means of their words.
>
> To search out the intention of the sacred writers, attention should be given, among other things, to "literary forms." For truth is set forth and expressed differently in texts which are variously historical, prophetic, poetic, or of other forms of discourse. The interpreter must investigate what meaning the sacred writer intended to express and actually expressed in particular circumstances by using contemporary literary forms in accordance with the situation of his own time and culture. For the correct understanding of what the sacred author wanted to assert, due attention must be paid to the customary and characteristic styles of feeling, speaking and narrating which prevailed at the time of the sacred writer, and to the patterns men normally employed at that period in their everyday dealings with one another (*Dei Verbum*, 12).

Note the meaning of this teaching of the Second Vatican Council. First, God used humans and human language to communicate his message. Therefore, we must first figure out what the authors of the texts really meant

by their written words. To do so requires that we pay close attention to literary forms, that is, the different kinds of literature (literary genres) that appear in the Bible. For example, we would interpret a fable differently than a piece of news reporting. The fable might present an important lesson on how we should behave using an imaginative story, whereas a news story would present "just the facts" as they occurred. We could learn the truth about some aspect of human behavior from the lesson the fable is trying to teach without having to believe the story took place as written.

Also, we should pay attention to the customs and ways of speaking, feeling, and passing on information that took place at the time the sacred author was writing. For example, a teaching of the creation stories is that the human person, created in God's image and likeness, is a being with both corporal (bodily) and spiritual aspects. The way the biblical author drew out this point in the second creation account was to say that "the Lord God formed man out of the clay of the ground and blew into his nostrils the breath of life, and so man became a living being" (Gn 2:7). In these words the biblical author revealed this truth: "Man, whole and entire, is therefore *willed* by God" (*CCC*, 362).

After identifying the literary form, we must ask the further question: What did God want to teach by way of these words, that is, by using these literary forms? To answer this question, we must read the text in the spirit in which it was written. *The Constitution on Divine Revelation* continues:

> But, since Holy Scripture must be read and interpreted in the sacred spirit in which it was written, no less serious attention must be given to the content and unity of the whole of Scripture if the meaning of the sacred texts is to be correctly worked out. The living tradition of the whole Church must be taken into account along with the harmony which exists between elements of the faith. (12)

What this means is that the Holy Spirit has inspired the sacred writers to reveal the truths of our religion in both the Old and New Testaments. Together, they are a unity and express the speech of God in human words. Finally, the Magisterium of the Church has the task of drawing on Sacred Tradition as it "carries out the divine commission and ministry of guarding and interpreting the word of God."

More on Literary Forms

The teaching of the Second Vatican Council that "Sacred Scripture must be read in light of the same Spirit by whom it is written" (*Dei Verbum*, 3) is an essential starting point for the interpretation of biblical texts. Also, it is important to interpret Scripture from two main senses—the literal and spiritual. These two ways for looking at and interpreting Scripture shape the way the Bible is to be understood.

The first way is to look at the literal sense of Scripture. The literal sense refers to the literal meaning conveyed by the words and discovered by **exegesis**. The goal of exegesis is to lead or bring out the biblical author's intentions, purpose, and meaning related to the writings. The precise literal sense refers to what the written words mean as they are written. There are several types of literary forms in the Bible. Examples from the Old Testament include:

- *Anthem.* An anthem is a joyful song or hymn. The beginning of Psalm 27 is an example of an anthem:

  The Lord is my light and salvation;
  > whom should I fear?
  The Lord is my life's refuge;
  > of whom should I be afraid? (Ps 27:1–2)

- *Census.* A census is an official numbering of the people of a country or district. See Numbers 1–14.

- *Debate.* A debate discusses a problem in a back-and-forth way. The debate in Job 4–30 starts with his curse and includes discussions with his friends. The debate ends when God intervenes.

- *Epigram.* An epigram is a short poem, often making a caustic point at the end. Note the example in Proverbs below. The first two verses give advice; the third verse tells what will happen if you do not follow it.

  Hear, my son, and be wise,
  > and guide your heart in the right way.
  Consort not with winebibbers,
  > nor with those who eat meat to excess;
  For the drunkard and the glutton come to poverty,
  > and torpor clothes a man in rags.
  (Prv 23:19–21)

- *Etiology.* An etiology is a story that gives the cause of something. In Genesis 32:23–33, for example, an explanation is given for why "the Israelites do not eat the sciatic muscle that is on the hip socket."

- *Genealogy.* A genealogy provides a list of ancestors and their descendants. Genesis 5 gives the descendants of Adam up to the time of the sons of Noah.

- *Maxim.* A maxim is similar to a proverb. It states a brief practical principle for daily living. For example: "Two are better than one: they get a good wage for their labor."

- *Parable.* A parable is a vivid short story told to convey religious truth, usually with a surprise

ending. For example, Isaiah 5:1–6 tells the story of a vineyard that yielded only wild grapes, so it was destroyed. Verse 7 interprets the parable by comparing the vineyard to the nation of Israel.

There are many other literary forms in both the Old and New Testaments. One starting point for understanding the biblical text is to be able to identify the form and how the sacred author wanted his words understood by his audience. A second way of interpreting Scripture involves not just looking at the words themselves, but also at what the words signify. The spiritual sense can be divided into three subdivisions:

1. Allegorical, that is understanding Scripture by recognizing its connection and significance with Christ. For example, the story of Jonah in the belly of the large fish references the three days Christ spent in the tomb.
2. Moral, or how the Scripture ought to lead us to act more justly. For example, Ruth teaches us the importance of loyalty in our relationships.
3. Anagogical (Greek for "to lead"), reminding us that the sacred words are intended to lead us to eternal life.

It is the task of everyone from biblical scholars to everyday Christians to judge, interpret, and read a biblical literary form according to these senses of Scripture and to do so ultimately subject to the judgment of the Church, "which exercises the divinely conferred commission and ministry of watching over and interpreting the Word of God" (*Dei Verbum 12 § 3, CCC*, 119). Only then will we know the truths God wished to convey through the human authors and their literary styles.

exegesis
A Greek word meaning "to lead." It is the study or the explanation of a biblical book or passage.

For Review

1. Why is it important to pay attention to literary forms when reading the Bible?

2. Name and explain three examples of literary forms found in the Old Testament.

For Reflection

Share an important truth for living from a childhood fable or story that you find meaningful.

The First Creation Account (Gn 1:1-2:4a)

Both creation accounts are part of the **primeval history** of Genesis 1–11. These stories are drawn from an ancient literary form known as **myth**. The myths of ancient peoples tried to express spiritual truths and basic cultural beliefs in the form of stories or narratives. Many of these ancient folktales use common themes and symbols like creation near or from water, battles between heavenly powers, and the creation of humans from the earth.

In their primeval accounts of creation, the Israelites borrowed some of the traditional elements, symbols, and stories from the myths of their neighbors, many of whom believed in many gods controlling life here on earth. In the first Genesis creation account, the author shows great knowledge of the Babylonian creation myth known as *Enuma Elish*,

More Examples of Literary Forms in the Bible

In the first text in this series, you learned about some of the literary forms used in the Bible, including allegory, biography, creed, etiology, fable, history, law, and prophecy. Below are five other literary forms from the Old Testament. Read the examples. Write how the particular example fits the definition of the form.

- *Anthropomorphisms* attribute human characteristics or experiences to God. Example: 2 Chronicles 16:9.
- *Chronicles* are accounts of events in the order of time. Example: Ezra 1.
- *Contracts* are binding legal agreement between two parties. Example: Ruth 4:1-12.
- *Hyperboles* are deliberate exaggerations as a figure of speech to make a point. Example: Psalm 119:136.
- *Riddles* are thought-provoking questions or statements; a conundrum. Example: Judges 14:12-18.

Assignment

Read 2 Samuel 12:1-4. Identify its literary form.

though the Genesis story does not accept its view of many gods, all springing from the gods of fresh and salt water. Marduk emerged as the hero in the story as he created the heavens out of the carcass of the goddess Tiamet whom he slayed. He also created humans out of the blood of another god to be slaves so that the gods could rest. The Israelites, inspired by the Holy Spirit, changed these traditional stories and symbols to convey their belief in the one true God—Yahweh—who entered their history in a radical new way.

Contrast this Babylonian myth with the forceful, stately, and grand style of Genesis 1:1–2:4a where creation is the result of an awesome, dramatic act by a glorious and majestic God. The intention of the author was to show the Jews who were in captivity in Babylon, or had just recently returned to Jerusalem, that their God is the only true God. Yahweh is the God who creates only goodness. He is totally unlike the false gods of Babylon, who were believed to have created humans to be slaves to the gods. A clear telling of the first creation account to the Israelites was: "God has selected *you* as his Chosen People. He has been faithful to *you*. Therefore, *you* must be faithful to him."

In composing the story of the origins of the world, the author may have drawn on the Israelites' tradition of a seven-day week, in which the seventh day, the Sabbath, was a day of rest and prayer. Creation takes place in six days, with each day representing a higher level of creation. Humans are

at the peak of God's design. The refrain "God saw how good it was" delineates each day. It also stresses the goodness of everything God made, in contrast to the Babylonian and other ancient myths that held that some creatures were evil.

The author seems to have used a brilliant parallel construction to distinguish between separation and decoration: God divides on the first three days, he decorates or "adds to" on the next three days:

Separation	Decoration
Day 1: light from darkness	Day 4: bodies of light—sun, moon, stars
Day 2: sky from water	Day 5: birds and fish
Day 3: land from water	Day 6: life on land—animals and humans

Note how in this first creation account both males and females are created at the same time. God creates both man and woman in the divine image:

> Then God said: "Let us make man in our image, after our likeness. Let them have dominion over the fish of the sea, the birds of the air, and the cattle, and over all the wild animals and all the creatures that crawl on the ground."
>
> God created man in his image;
> > in the divine image he created him;
> > male and female he created them. (Gn 1:26–27)

By saying God rested on the seventh day, the biblical author reminds the Jews of their own obligation to

primeval history
Stories or myths about the origins of the earth, humans, other creatures, languages, and cultures.

myth
Symbolic stories that express a spiritual truth or a basic belief about God.

AN OVERVIEW OF THE PENTATEUCH

To understand the Book of Genesis, it is necessary to understand how it fits within the entire Pentateuch. The Pentateuch (meaning "five scrolls" in Greek) contains the Torah, that is, the Law of the Jewish people. The other four books of the Pentateuch are Exodus, Leviticus, Numbers, and Deuteronomy. The Pentateuch is also known as the "Book of Moses," or the "Five Books of Moses," because ancient Judaism and early Christianity believed that Moses authored them. Even the New Testament assumes this, for example, when Jesus refers to the Pentateuch as "the Book of Moses" (Mk 12:26).

However, the Church understands that the first five books of the Bible only took their final form after centuries of telling, retelling, adapting, and reinterpreting the many stories of Yahweh's dealings with the Chosen People. It is true that Moses is the central figure of the Pentateuch since God delivered the Ten Commandments to him on Mount Sinai and he led the Israelites out of Egypt. The Israelites naturally looked to him as the source of the laws and traditions recorded in the Torah. However, Moses certainly could not have written *everything* in the Pentateuch. For example, Deuteronomy 34:5-12 gives an account of Moses's death.

Pentateuch

A Greek word meaning "five scrolls." It is used to refer to the first five books of the Bible— Genesis, Exodus, Leviticus, Numbers, and Deuteronomy. The books contain the Jewish Law, the Torah.

Torah

The Law handed down to the Chosen People by God that they were to live in response to his covenant with them. A summary of the Torah is found in the Ten Commandments.

The Pentateuch was likely composed in stages, probably proceeding this way:

- *Stage 1:* The core incident in the Pentateuch is the strong personality of Moses, the lawgiver, and the events of the Exodus, God's deliverance of the Israelites from Egypt.

- *Stage 2:* Various laws, speeches, stories about human origins and the patriarchs, reflections, liturgical celebrations, and so forth, were handed down orally from generation to generation. Some of these were committed to writing as well.

- *Stage 3:* Authors and editors began to collect their sources into a continuous narrative.

- *Stage 4:* Sometime during the fourth and fifth century BC under the leadership of the priestly scribe Ezra, the various traditions were brought together into the five-volume document we know as the Pentateuch.

Most scholars believe there were at least four major sources that went into the composition of the Pentateuch. Because the Pentateuch (including Genesis) is a composite work, later authors and editors did not always try to reconcile all the differences in the stories and traditions that came down to them. They simply included their stories right along with the stories of other authors. A most notable example of this is the two creation accounts that appear right after each other in the first three chapters of Genesis.

The four major traditions or sources that are behind the Pentateuch are:

- *Yahwist (J).* This tradition originated around 950 BC in the southern kingdom of Judah. Its name comes from its frequent use of "Yahweh" (or "Jahweh" in German) for God's name. This source emphasizes the divine promises made to the patriarchs and provides the basic outline for the Pentateuch: human origins, patriarchs, slavery in Egypt, the Exodus, the desert wanderings, the covenant on Mount Sinai, and entrance to the Promised Land.

- *Elohist (E).* Traceable to the northern kingdom of Israel, which uses "Elohim," a generic name for "god" in Hebrew, this source came about one hundred years after the Yahwist. The E source emphasizes prophecy (especially the message of Elijah and Elisha) and the theme of covenant. It is more abstract than the J tradition. Abraham is a central figure in the Elohist narrative. Additionally, many scholars believe that around 750 BC an editor combined J and E into one narrative without bothering to drop repetitions or contradictions.

- *Deuteronomist (D).* The name Deuteronomist is derived from a Greek word meaning "second law." First composed in the northern kingdom at the shrine at Shechem in approximately 650 BC, it may have been completed in Jerusalem. This source refers to God as "Yahweh" and emphasizes morality and living the Law. "Listen, Israel" is a constant refrain. Central also are several long speeches by Moses.

- *Priestly (P).* This source originated during the Babylonian Exile and was likely completed around 400 BC. The Priestly account refers to God in the formal "Elohim," like the Elhoist, and is interested in census lists, genealogies, numbers, dates, liturgical procedures, Temple ceremonies, ritual cleanliness, and so forth. It also emphasizes worship because it sees God's action in the history of Israel as a liturgy. Because P was the last tradition, it gave a coherent framework to the Pentateuch. Priestly editors under Ezra gave the first five books of the Bible their final form.

worship God on the Sabbath (from sundown on Friday to sundown on Saturday). Sabbath observance helped captive Jews maintain their identity as God's Chosen People among a foreign people with pagan beliefs. They believed they should offer thanks and praise to God each week because he is the source of all that is good.

Religious and Theological Truths of the First Creation Account (CCC, 290-373)

This first creation account is not a scientific explanation of the beginning of the universe. Rather, God inspired its author to draw on the knowledge of the people of his time to construct a story that reveals important *religious* and *theological* truths about creation, including these:

1. *There is only one God.* The biblical authors wrote that God is eternal and gave a beginning to all that exists outside of himself. The priestly author of this first creation story firmly rejects the vindictive false gods of the Babylonians portrayed in their creation myth, Enuma Elish.

2. *God planned creation.* Creation did not result from anything else like chaotic forces, warring gods, fate, or chance. God created the world in an orderly way to share his being, wisdom, and goodness with us. God creates by his Word, decreeing what is to be and establishing limits.

3. *God created an ordered and good world out of nothing.* Material creation is good and not the result of magic or the workings of false gods. The Babylonian creation story told how humans emerged from the rotting corpse of a god. Ancient peoples believed that much of material reality is evil and constantly at war with the spiritual elements in the universe. In contrast, Jews and Christians see in Genesis a positive view of created reality. The biblical

author tells us that God was pleased with everything he made, especially human beings made in God's own image and likeness and entrusted with responsibility for the rest of creation.

4. *God creates man in his own image, male and female.* We are unique because:

   - We possess great dignity, value, and worth. Man is "the only creature on earth that God has willed for its own sake" (*CCC*, 356, quoting *Gaudium et Spes*, 3). We are able to know and love God. We are predestined to share in the eternal goodness of God himself by reproducing in our own lives the image of Jesus Christ, God's Son made man, the "image of the invisible God" (Col 1:15).

   - Human nature unites both the spiritual and material worlds. Humans are endowed with bodies and souls, the spiritual principle in us.

   - God created males and females as perfect in equality as human persons, with inalienable dignity. They are privileged to share in God's great gift of creation by being given the power to procreate life, to "be fertile and multiply" (Gn 1:28).

5. *God gave humans a place of honor in creation, making them stewards over what he created.* We are responsible for taking care of and developing the many gifts of creation God entrusted to us.

6. *God blessed the Sabbath and made it holy.* The priestly writer tells how God rested on the seventh day. Obviously, God does not need to rest. But we, God's creatures, need to take time to be renewed by ceasing from ordinary activities one day out of the week. Furthermore, we need to recognize a kind and loving God as the source of our existence and worship him in prayer and thanksgiving. Catholics keep Sunday holy, the first day of the week and the day of Christ's Resurrection by participating at Mass and refraining from unnecessary work.

These six truths emerge from the magnificent first creation story. They highlight our belief in the one, powerful, good, wise, and loving God who shares his life with his creatures.

 ## For Review

1. Define: *Pentateuch* and *Torah*.

2. Summarize the stages involved in composing Genesis and the other books of the Pentateuch.

3. Briefly identify the four sources that are behind the Pentateuch.

4. What is the purpose of the ancient literary form known as *myth*?

5. Discuss at least three religious and theological truths that emerge from the first creation account.

Keeping Sunday Holy

In commemoration of the day of our Lord's Resurrection, Catholics are obligated to gather to celebrate the Eucharist to thank God for all the good gifts he has bestowed on us, especially the gift of Salvation won for us by Jesus Christ, our Savior. Catholics also rest from regular work and activity on Sundays. Analyze how you spent the past two Sundays. In your journal, note what activities you engaged in that showed you take "Sabbath rest" and the "Sunday obligation" seriously. If your review shows that you have neglected to "keep holy the Lord's day," write out some resolutions on how you might observe it more faithfully this coming weekend.

For Reflection

- What does it mean to you to have been created in God's image?

- How has your understanding of God been enhanced by reading and praying with the Book of Genesis?

The Second Creation Account (Gn 2:4b-25)

The second creation account is written in a more down-to-earth style and portrays God as *anthropomorphic*, that is, with human qualities. Some scholars attribute the second account to the Yahwist (J) author and have dated it some time in the tenth century BC.

The account images God as a potter who molds Adam's body like a delicate sculpture. Into this form Yahweh breathes his spirit, the breath of life. This intimate picture reveals the loving relationship between Yahweh and the first human being. In the first creation account, humans are created last by God. In this second account, Yahweh creates humans before any other creatures and shares his own life (breath) with them. This image of this closeness between human and divine radically contrasts with the beliefs of most ancient peoples who thought God was distant and to be feared.

The author describes a compassionate God who cares for Adam by making him a garden and sending him animals for companionship. God puts Adam in charge of creation by permitting him to name the animals. (In the ancient world, the power to name gave one control over what was named.) However, animals do not fulfill Adam's basic human need for companionship.

This is why the author gives a further story, the creation of Eve from Adam's rib. This highlights a rich image of the dignity of women and their equality with men. This second story provides an etiology of marriage, that is, why men and women leave their parents to form their own family. The story reveals that Yahweh wants the couple to "become one

Preserving the Earth

There is rightful concern today about ecology and the degradation of God's good creation. The challenge is to be part of the solution and not part of the problem. You can do a lot to make people aware of the need to conserve precious resources. Try one of the following recycling projects. Advertise your project on an approved Internet network. Consider the following examples for projects:

- Begin a paper-recycling contest between classes at your school. (Recycling one ton of paper saves seventeen trees, 380 gallons of oil, three cubic yards of landfill space, 4,000 kilowatts of energy, 7,000 gallons of water, and sixty pounds of air pollutants.)

- Recycle Styrofoam cups and trays.

- Establish stations around the school for recycling batteries.

- Start a campaign to eliminate drinking bottled water. Encourage people to refill their personal bottles or cups from a tap or other common water dispenser.

Original Holiness and Original Justice

The state of man and woman before sin. "From their friendship with God flowed the happiness of their existence in paradise" (*CCC*, 384).

body," to enter into a close relationship that mirrors God's own relationship with them. Man and woman are equal and complementary, intended by God to be true companions.

The author who is sometimes associated with the Yahwist or "J" understanding tells us that Adam and Eve felt no shame, even though they were naked. Their natural condition of intimacy with God and each other was one of total openness. Only when sin entered the picture did human beings feel ashamed and want to hide.

After examining these two creation accounts, we can better understand why the final editor of Genesis was inspired by God to include two different creation accounts. Together they reveal something very important about our God: *Yahweh, the awe-inspiring sole creator of the universe (story 1) is intimately concerned with the man and woman he made the jewels of his creation (story 2).*

Truths of the Second Creation Account (CCC, 369-379)

The second creation account emphasizes both the equality and differences between man and woman that are willed by God. It teaches that God created humans in friendship with his Creator and in harmony with themselves and all the creation around them.

The second creation account also teaches that Adam and Eve were born in a state of **Original Holiness and Original Justice**.

The Church, interpreting the symbolism of biblical language in an authentic way, in the light of the New Testament and Tradition, teaches that our first parents, Adam and Eve, were constituted in an original "state of holiness and justice." This grace of Original Holiness and Original Justice was "to share . . . divine life." (*CCC*, 375)

Original Justice and Original Holiness involved the inner harmony of the human person, the harmony between man and woman, and the harmony between our first parents and all of creation. As long as the first humans remained in intimacy with God, they would not have to suffer or die. Work was not a burden but a share in perfecting God's visible creation.

Man and woman were created for each other, for companionship, to be helpmates to each other, and to share in God's work of creating new life. Furthermore, they were to love everything God created for them and to responsibly care for the world he entrusted to them.

For Review

1. Name at least one difference between the two creation accounts.

2. Name three anthropomorphisms in the second creation account.

3. Name a religious and theological truth revealed in the second creation account.

 **For Reflection**

How do you imagine the Garden of Eden before sin? Describe in detail.

The Theme of Creation in Theology and Scripture

The first three chapters of Genesis are foundational because they reveal important truths about creation—"its origin and its end in God, its order and goodness, the vocation of man, and finally the drama of sin and the hope of salvation" (*CCC*, 289). The theme of creation is very important in Christian theology and in Sacred Scripture. *The Catechism of the Catholic Church* puts it this way:

> Creation is the foundation of "all God's saving plans," the "beginning of the history of salvation" that culminates in Christ. Conversely, the mystery of Christ casts conclusive light on the mystery of creation and reveals the end for which "in the beginning God created the heavens and the earth": from the beginning God envisaged the glory of the new creation in Christ. (*CCC*, 280)

The next sections highlight the theme of creation elsewhere in the Old Testament and New Testament.

Creation in the Book of Isaiah

The Book of Isaiah was written to comfort and encourage a disheartened people who were in captivity in Babylonia in the sixth century BC. The complete Book of Isaiah is a collection of poems composed chiefly by the great prophet but also by his disciples, some of which were written years after his life. Included in chapters 40–55, sometimes called Deutero-Isaiah or "Second Isaiah" are links to the theme of creation and Salvation that assured Israel that God controls all nations and events:

> I am the Lord, who made all things,
> who alone stretched out the heavens,
> when I spread out the earth, who was
> with me? (Is 44:23)

> Who has cupped in his hand the waters of
> the sea,
> and marked off the heavens with a span?
> Who has held in a measure the dust of the
> earth,
> weighed the mountains in scales
> and the hills in balance? . . .
> Do you not know
> or have you not heard?
> The Lord is the eternal God,
> creator of the ends of the earth.
> (Is 40:12, 28)

The poet intended for a discouraged people to know that God is in charge. He is both almighty Creator and Savior. He will renew the face of the earth by creating rivers in the desert and making crooked paths straight. The passage is intended to let the people know that just as God delivered the Israelites from slavery in Egypt, made a covenant with them, and created them as a people, he will rescue the captives from the Babylonians. Also, God will renew the people just as he renews creation:

> I am the Lord, there is no other;
>> I form the light, and create the darkness. . . .
>
> Let justice descend, O heavens, like dew from above,
>> like gentle rain let the skies drop it down.
>
> Let the earth open and salvation bud forth;
>> let justice spring up!
>
> I, the Lord, have created this.
> (Is 45:7–8)

Creation in the Book of Psalms

The Psalms are "songs of praise" to God. The book of Psalms is a source of inspiration, instruction, hope, consolation, and instruction for both Jews and Christians. Creation is a central theme in many Psalms, stressing God's uniqueness, power, and majesty, while reminding us that we should worship God. Psalm 8 is an example of a hymn of praise that highlights God's greatness. The psalmist is awestruck at God's creative activity and especially at God's marvelous creature—humans: "You have made him little less than the angels, and crowned him with glory and honor" (Ps 8:6).

Another example of the theme of creation is found in Psalm 104, a majestic hymn that praises God's creative wisdom and power. The psalmist's heart leaps to the heavens, praising God's majesty:

> Bless the Lord, my soul!
>> Lord, my God, you are great indeed!
>
> You are clothed with majesty and glory,
>> robed in light as with a cloak.
>
> You spread out the heavens like a tent;
>> you raised your palace upon the waters.
>
> You make the clouds your chariot;
>> you travel on the wings of the wind.
>
> You make the winds your messengers;
>> flaming fire, your ministers. . . .
>
> How varied are your works, Lord!
>> In wisdom you have wrought them all;
>> the earth is full of your creatures.
> (Ps 104:1–4, 24)

Creation in the Book of Proverbs

All wisdom has its source in God. Wisdom is an expression of God's own nature. The Book of Proverbs personifies wisdom and praises it as God's helper in the act of creation. Specifically, Proverbs 8 stresses the role of divine wisdom at the beginning of creation. God's wisdom was responsible for an orderly, intelligent, and joyful creation:

> "The Lord begot me, the first-born of his ways,
>> the forerunner of his prodigies of long ago; . . .
>>
>>> When he established the heavens I was there,
>>
>> when he marked out the vault over the face of the deep;
>
> When he made firm the skies above,

when he fixed fast the foundations of
the earth;
When he set for the sea its limit,
so that the waters should not transgress
his command;
Then was I beside him as his craftsman."
(Prv 8:22, 27–30)

Christ and Creation

With the coming of Jesus Christ, the Son of God, we have access to the fullness of Divine Revelation. We learn from St. Paul that "Christ [is] the power of God and the wisdom of God" (1 Cor 12:24). The Letter to the Colossians proclaims the identity of Jesus Christ:

He is the image of the invisible God,
the firstborn of all creation.
For in him were created all things in heaven
and on earth,
the visible and the invisible,
whether thrones or dominions or princi-
palities or powers;
all things were created through him and
for him.
He is before all things,
and in him all things hold together.
He is the head of the body, the church.
He is the beginning, the firstborn from the
dead,
that in all things he himself might be
preeminent.
For in him all the fullness was pleased to
dwell,
and through him to reconcile all things
for him,
making peace by the blood of his cross
(through him), whether those on earth or
those in heaven. (Col 1:15–20)

These remarkable verses, perhaps originally an early Christian hymn, proclaim our Lord to be:

- the *Agent of Creation* ("in him were all things created"),

- the *Wisdom of God* ("the firstborn of all cre-ation," as in Proverbs 8:22),

- the *Sustainer* ("in him all things hold together"),

- and the *Savior* (God reconciles everything through him).

The Gospel of John tells us Christ is also the Word of God who spoke creation into existence. Everything was created through him:

In the beginning was the Word,
and the Word was with God,
and the Word was God.
He was in the beginning with God.
All things came to be through him,
and without him nothing came to be.
What came to be through him was life,
and this life was the light of the human
race;
the light shines in the darkness,
and the darkness has not overcome it.
(Jn 1:1–5)

The Holy Trinity and Creation (CCC, 290-292)

New Testament passages like Colossians 1:15–20 and John 1:1–5 reveal very clearly that God created everything by the eternal Word, the Son of God. In addition, the Church professes belief in the creative activity of the Holy Spirit. He is the "giver of life" and "the source of all good" as proclaimed in the Catholic creeds.

The Old Testament Hebrew word for spirit is *ruah*, which can be translated as both "wind" and "breath." Recall the mighty wind in Genesis 1:2 that swept over the waters when God created the heavens and earth. This image powerfully points to the creative activity of the Holy Spirit from the very beginning. In the New Testament, the Holy Spirit came to the Apostles on Pentecost Sunday in a strong driving wind (Acts 2:2). His descent on them emboldened Christ's disciples and formed them into the Church that would proclaim the Resurrected Lord to the ends of the earth.

"Breath" is also an apt image for the creative activity of the Holy Spirit. To live, we must breathe. Thus, the Holy Spirit is a life-giver. The psalmist knew this well when he wrote about God's creative activity:

> When you send forth your breath, they are created,
>> and you renew the face of the earth.
>> (Ps 104:30)

This image of God sending his Spirit to bring life also reminds us how the Spirit was present at the creation of the first man, when God breathed life into Adam (Gn 2:7).

In conclusion, then, we must understand that when God said, "Let us make man in our image, after our likeness" in Genesis 1:26, the words suggest the activity of all Three Persons of the Blessed Trinity. Only God alone can reveal himself as Father, Son, and Holy Spirit. This is the teaching of the Church—that creation is the work of Father, Son, and Holy Spirit.

> The Old Testament suggests and the New Covenant reveals the creative action of the Son and the Spirit, inseparably one with that of the Father. This creative co-operation is clearly affirmed in the Church's rule of faith: "There exists but one God . . . he is the Father, God, the Creator, the author, the giver of order. He made all things by himself, that is, by his Word and by his Wisdom," "by the Son and the Spirit" who, so to speak, are "his hands." Creation is the common work of the Holy Trinity. (*CCC*, 292)

This chapter presented an overview of the biblical accounts of God's creation. Creation is the first stage of Salvation History, revealing God's glory and his existence. The psalmist said it so well when he proclaimed, "The heavens declare the glory of God; the sky proclaims its builder's craft" (Ps 19:2).

And in the words of the famous poet Gerard Manley Hopkins, "The world is charged with the grandeur of God." As the astronaut Frank Borman observed, "The more we learn about the wonders of our universe, the more clearly we are going to perceive the hand of God."

God's hand is in creation. He is the master builder who made human beings in his image to share life with him. God's creation is very good. From the beginning, humans were meant to be in communion and harmony with our loving God. However, the tragic consequences of Original Sin remain with us. But God did not abandon us. He promised a Savior who would redeem us from sin and death. We turn to that promise and God's fidelity to it in Chapter 2.

For Review

1. Share one example of how the creation theme is present in an Old Testament book other than the Book of Genesis.

2. What role does Christ have in creation?

3. How is the Holy Spirit involved in creation?

4. Why do Catholics believe that creation is the work of the Blessed Trinity?

5. What does the Church believe about evolution?

For Reflection

• Write your own song of praise to God for the gift of creation. Read Psalm 148 as inspiration.

• "The glory of God is man fully alive." Given your own talents, write how you might use them to glorify God.

EXPLAINING THE FAITH

What does the Church teach about evolution?

The word *evolution* means many things to different people. The term has been applied to the origin of the universe, to the origin of life, and to the origin of humans.

A popular definition of evolution found in a typical biology text might define it as "change over time." This definition applies to any sequence in the events of nature. Another common understanding of the term refers to the idea that a group of organisms are descended from a common ancestor. Some people would hold that all organisms have come from a common ancestor. People explain these changes in various ways. For example, atheistic scientists might explain them by way of an unguided, materialistic process of random variation and natural selection. Believers, however, will view what some people see as mere chance in nature as God's ongoing, providential action in his creation of life and of human beings.

In light of Divine Revelation, what can Catholics believe about evolution? The Church teaches that scientific truth and truths of the faith that come from Divine Revelation do not contradict each other. They are complementary paths to the one Truth. The *Catechism of the Catholic Church* tells us:

> Though faith is above reason, there can never be any real discrepancy between faith and reason. Since the same God who reveals mysteries and infuses faith has bestowed the light of reason on the human mind, God cannot deny himself, nor can truth ever contradict truth. (*CCC*, 159, quoting *Dei Filius* 4:DS 3017)

Concerning the origin of the universe, Genesis teaches that God created the entire universe, both material and spiritual aspects of it, out of nothing at the beginning of time. The Church does not take a position on whether the stars, nebulae, and planets were all created at once or developed over time. However, if they did develop (evolve)—and are developing (evolving)—over time, it is according to God's plan.

Turning to biological evolution, the Church has not taken an official position on whether life forms developed over the millennia. Once again, however, if various life forms did develop over time, it is because God has guided their development because he is the One who ultimately created them.

Concerning human evolution, the Church would permit belief that the human body *might* have developed from previous life forms but that God creates each human soul. The human soul, our spiritual nature, does not evolve from matter, nor is it inherited from our parents like our bodies are. Rather, God creates each individual human soul:

> The Church teaches that every spiritual soul is created immediately by God—it is not "produced" by the parents—and also that it is immortal: it does not perish when it separates from the body at death, and it will be reunited with the body at the final Resurrection. (*CCC*, 366)

However we interpret the "six days of creation," either literally or symbolically, the biblical text requires that we hold that the universe did not always exist. God is infinite and eternal. He created the universe and that is when time began. The *Catechism* puts it this way:

> *Nothing exists that does not owe its existence to God the Creator.* The world began when God's word drew it out of nothingness; all existent beings, all of nature, and all human history are rooted in this primordial event, the very genesis by which the world was constituted and time begun. (*CCC*, 338)

Main Ideas

- The story of Redemption begins at the beginning of human history, at creation. (pp. 2–3)

- Human reason can come to know God by studying his works, though that is not the whole story, because human reason is limited. (pp. 3–5)

- God disclosed who he is through the events of Salvation history. (pp. 5–6)

- We know what God has revealed through the gift of the Deposit of Faith, Sacred Tradition, and Sacred Scripture working together. (pp. 5–6)

- The Deposit of Faith is entrusted to the Magisterium. (pp. 6–8)

- To read the Bible with understanding, we must recognize that it deals with a time, people, and culture that is foreign to us. (pp. 9–10)

- There are dozens of literary forms in the Bible, including anthem, epigram, etiology, parable, and more. (pp. 10–12)

- The Book of Genesis is part of the Pentateuch that contains the Torah, that is, the Law of the Jewish people. (pp. 12–15)

- Both Genesis creation accounts are part of primeval history recorded in Genesis 1–11. (pp. 12–15)

- The first creation account changed traditional stories and symbols of ancient myths to convey the Chosen People's belief in one, true God—Yahweh. (pp. 15–16)

- The second creation account portrays God as anthropomorphic, that is, with human qualities. (pp. 17–18)

- The second creation story also highlights the fact that the first humans were born in a state of Original Holiness and Original Justice, the grace of which was to share the divine life. (p. 18)

- The theme of creation is present in Catholic theology and Sacred Scripture as the foundation of all of God's saving plans and the beginning of Salvation History. (pp. 19–22)

- With the coming of Jesus Christ, we have access to the fullness of Divine Revelation. (pp. 20–21)

- Creation is the work of the Holy Trinity—Father, Son, and Holy Spirit. (pp. 21–22)

- The Church teaches that scientific truth and the truths of faith that come from Divine Revelation do not contradict each other. (p. 23)

Terms, People, Places

Match the following terms with the definitions below.

A. inspiration

B. polytheism

C. Deposit of Faith

D. Divine Revelation

E. philosophy

F. Magisterium

G. myth

H. Torah

I. Original Holiness and Original Justice

J. Redemption

1. The official teaching office of the Church.

2. The guidance of the Holy Spirit to help in the recording of Sacred Scripture

3. A word that means "ransom."

4. A summary is found in the Ten Commandments.

5. God's self-communication.

6. Symbolic stories that express a spiritual truth or a basic belief about God.

7. The state of man and woman before Original Sin.

8. Contained in both Sacred Scripture and Sacred Tradition.

9. A false belief that there are many gods.

10. The investigation of truth and principles using human reason.

Primary Source Quotations

Our Creator God
The Trinity is our maker. The Trinity is our keeper. The Trinity is our everlasting lover. The Trinity is our endless joy.
—Bl. Julian of Norwich

In God alone there is primordial and true delight, in all our delights it is this delight that we are seeking.
—St. Bonaventure

The Lord Lives in Our Life
Invisible in his own nature God became visible in ours. Beyond our grasp, he chose to come within our grasp.
—St. Leo the Great

Poor creature though I be, I am the hand and foot of Christ. I move my hand and my hand is wholly Christ's hand, for deity is become inseparably one with me. I move my good and it is aglow with God.
—St. Simeon the New Theologian

Search for the poem "God's Grandeur" by Gerard Manley Hopkins, S.J. Prepare a dramatic reading of the poem. Consider setting the reading to music. Share the poem with your classmates.

Ongoing Assignments

As you cover the material in this chapter, choose and complete at least three of these assignments.

1. Research various theories on the probable location of the Garden of Eden. Present your findings in a PowerPoint presentation.
2. Conduct and record interviews on the subject of belief in God with one of the following audiences:
   - Five children under the age of ten on what they believe about God. Identify any statements they make that reveal wisdom that goes beyond their years.
   - Five believing adults on why they believe in the existence of God. Note any common reasons they might give.
3. Research a Native American religion. Find answers to these questions:
   - What is its concept of the Almighty?
   - What do they believe about how humans came to be?
   - How do they view the reason for human existence?
   - What are their beliefs about human destiny and concepts of the afterlife?
4. Prepare a PowerPoint presentation on how humans have abused the environment. Show how thoughtlessness is contrary to the biblical concept of good stewardship.
5. Prepare a PowerPoint presentation on Psalm 104. Use pictures from nature to accompany the words. Choose suitable background music.
6. Report on George Sim Johnson's article, "How to Read the First Chapter of Genesis" *Lay Witness* (September 1998). Report on the story of the Catholic priest behind the "big bang theory" of the origin of the universe. See Mark Midbon, "'A Day Without Yesterday': Georges Lemaitre & the Big Bang" *Commonweal* (March 24, 2000): 18–19.
7. Research and report on the subject of science and creation.
8. Research and report on the creation myth from a religion and culture other than Christianity.
9. Report on what three early Church Fathers and theologians taught about Genesis.
10. Research the topic "Ecological Footprint." Take one of the quizzes you discover to see how much of the earth's resources you consume.

Chapter 1 Quick View

Prayer

St. Francis of Assisi (1182–1226) is one of the most popular Catholic saints. He is the patron saint of ecology due to his great love of God's beautiful creation. He wrote the following prayer toward the end of his life. It is a wonderful hymn of praise to God the Creator and Father of us of all.

Canticle of Brother Sun

Most High, all powerful, good Lord,
Yours are the praises, the glory, the honor,
and all blessing.
To You alone, Most High, do they belong,
and no man is worthy to mention Your
  name.
Be praised, my Lord, through all your
  creatures,
especially through my lord Brother Sun,
who brings the day; and you give light
  through him.
And he is beautiful and radiant in all his
  splendor!
Of you, Most High, he bears the likeness.
Praise be You, my Lord, through Sister
  Moon
and the stars, in heaven you formed them
clear and precious and beautiful.
Praised be You, my Lord, through Brother
  Wind,
and through the air, cloudy and serene,
and every kind of weather through which
You give sustenance to Your creatures.
Praised be You, my Lord, through Sister
  Water,
which is very useful and humble and precious and chaste.
Praised be You, my Lord, through Brother
  Fire,
through whom you light the night and he is
  beautiful
and playful and robust and strong.
Praised be You, my Lord, through Sister
  Mother Earth,
who sustains us and governs us and who
  produces

varied fruits with colored flowers and herbs.
Praised be You, my Lord,
through those who give pardon for Your
  love,
and bear infirmity and tribulation.
Blessed are those who endure in peace
for by You, Most High, they shall be
  crowned.
Praised be You, my Lord,
through our Sister Bodily Death,
from whom no living man can escape.
Woe to those who die in mortal sin.
Blessed are those whom death will
find in Your most holy will,
for the second death shall do them no harm.
Praise and bless my Lord,
and give Him thanks
and serve Him with great humility. AMEN.

- *Reflection*: What is it in God's creation that you are most grateful for?

- *Resolution*: In the coming days, focus on each of the five senses in turn. For example, one day choose the gift of sight. Several times a day, stop and concentrate on this gift of sight and all the beautiful things it enables you to see. Recite a short prayer of praise and thanksgiving to God for this gift. On subsequent days, focus on the other senses in turn, praising and *thanking* God for what they enable you to perceive.

THE FALL AND THE PROMISE OF A SAVIOR

*I will make of you a great nation,
and I will bless you;
I will make your name great,
so that you will be a blessing.
I will bless those who bless you
and curse those who curse you.
All the communities of the earth
shall find blessing in you.*

—Genesis 12:2-3

Creation and De-creation
The consequences of Original Sin remain a part of our lives today.

The Effects of Original Sin
The pains of childbirth, back-breaking work to eke out a living, shame as a result of nakedness, and death are some of the effects of Original Sin.

Was Original Sin a Historical Event?
The Fall of Adam and Eve in Genesis does not have to be interpreted in a literal way, but we must believe that there was a real historical event behind it.

God Remains Faithful in Times of Sin
Cain and Abel, the Great Flood, and the Tower of Babel are three Scripture stories that tell us that the spread of sin was immediate and with dire consequences for humanity.

Covenants in the Old Testament
The covenant between God and Noah was the first covenant of three other major covenants in the Old Testament. In biblical covenants between men, God is the witness to the agreement.

God Remains Faithful to His Promises
The time of the Israelite monarchy showed how God remained faithful to his promises, in spite of the continued sinful behavior of the leaders and the people.

Creation and De-creation

An anonymous satirical poem titled "De-creation" graphically contradicts the beautiful creation accounts in the Book of Genesis by showing how sin is destroying the world:

> In the beginning was the earth,
> and the earth was beautiful.
> But the people on the earth said,
> "Let us build skyscrapers and
> expressways."
> So they paved the earth with concrete and
> said, "It is good!"
> On the second day,
> the people looked at the rivers and said,
> "Let us dump our sewage into the waters."
> So they filled the waters with sludge
> and said, "It is good!"
> On the third day,
> the people looked at the forest and said,
> "Let us cut down the trees
> and build things."
> So they leveled the forests
> and said, "It is good!"
> On the fourth day,
> the people saw the animals and said,
> "Let us kill them for sport and money."
> So they destroyed the animals
> and said, "It is good!"
> On the fifth day,
> the people felt the cool breeze and said,
> "Let us burn our garbage
> and let the breeze blow it away."
> So they filled the air with carbon
> and said, "It is good!"
> On the sixth day,
> the people saw other nations on earth and
> said,
> "Let us build missiles
> in case misunderstandings arise."
> So they filled the land with missile sites
> and said, "It is good!"
> On the seventh day,

> the earth was quiet and deathly silent,
> for the people were no more.
> And it was good!

This poem is a sad, if not accurate, view of creation today. "De-creation" takes place because human beings have turned from God and put their own self interests above those of their Creator, other humans, and the beautiful world God has entrusted to us. De-creation takes place because of human pride and sin, causing alienation from self, others, God, and creation itself. It all started with the **Original Sin** of Adam and Eve described in Genesis 3:1–24. However, God never abandoned sinful humanity. From the beginning, God promised a Savior, a Redeemer, who would make all things new. In the midst of the story of the fall of humanity, God promised that he would "strike" at the tempter from then on. Likewise, the prophet Isaiah told the Chosen People to remain hopeful. Why? Because the Lord is coming. He will make all things new:

> Say to those whose hearts are
>   frightened:
>   Be strong, fear not!
> Here is your God,
>   he comes with vindication;
> With divine recompense
>   he comes to save you.
> Then will the eyes of the
>   blind be opened,
>   the ears of the deaf be
>   cleared;
> Then will the lame leap like
>   a stag,

> then the tongue of the
>   dumb will sing.
> Streams will burst forth in the
>   desert,
>   and rivers in the steppe.
> The burning sands will be-
>   come pools,
>   and the thirsty ground,
>   springs of water. . . .
> (Is 35:4–7)

The topic of this chapter is Original Sin and its consequences for human beings. From there it reminds us how God did not abandon sinful humans but rather entered into covenants with them and promised to redeem them by sending a Savior. Ultimately, this is what God did: he sent us his own Son in whom he has established his covenant forever.

Original Sin
The fallen state of human nature into which all generations of people are born. Christ Jesus came to save us from Original Sin.

The Root of All Sin

The *Catechism of the Catholic Church* reminds us that sin leads to more sin that "results in perverse inclinations which cloud conscience and corrupt the concrete judgment of good and evil. Thus sin tends to reproduce itself and reinforce itself, but it cannot destroy the moral sense at its root" (*CCC*, 1865). The *Catechism* goes on to list the seven capital sins, that is, sins that are at the root of all other sins and vices (bad habits). For each capital sin (listed below), write a corresponding virtue (good habit). For example, diligence and hard work counteract sloth. Be as specific as you can with each example.

- *Pride*: inordinate self-esteem
- *Avarice*: greed; inordinate love of earthly things
- *Envy*: sadness at another's success
- *Wrath*: anger or emotional violence
- *Lust*: disordered sexual desire
- *Gluttony*: excessive preoccupation over food or drink
- *Sloth*: laziness in regard to one's responsibilities

Assignment
Which capital sin seems to be the biggest problem in your life right now? Write of something you can do in the next week to counteract it by practicing one of the virtues.

⦿ For Reflection

How would you define "de-creation"?

The Effects of Original Sin

Genesis 3 describes Original Sin and its effects. From it, we learn important truths about the human condition. Recall that God created us good from the start; we were meant to be happy. Adam and Eve enjoyed Original Holiness and Original Justice with God. The grace of original holiness meant human beings were created to share in God's own life. Adam and Eve were meant to be in friendship with God, living in harmony with him, with each other, and with all other creatures. Being in the state of original justice meant that humans would not die or experience suffering or pain.

After losing the state of Original Holiness and Original Justice, human beings suffer many effects of the loss. Women now suffer the pains of childbirth, men (and women) do back-breaking work to eke out a living, nakedness causes shame, and death is the fate of humans. All of these sad outcomes are the result of Original Sin. By disobeying God's commands, the first humans chose themselves and their own wills rather than submit themselves to the will of a loving God. Friendship with God required them to respond to him. By asserting their own wills instead of responding to the Lord in friendship and obedience, Adam and Eve sinned: "Sin is an abuse of the freedom that God gives to created persons so that they are capable of loving him and loving one another" (*CCC*, 387).

Was Original Sin a Historical Event?

Did the Fall of Adam and Eve take place as depicted in Genesis 3? The *Catechism of the Catholic Church* teaches:

> The account of the fall in Genesis 3 uses figurative language, but affirms a primeval event, a deed that took place at the beginning of the history of man. Revelation gives us the certainty of faith that the whole of human history is marked by the original fault freely committed by our first parents. (*CCC*, 390)

We are not required to interpret the story about the Fall of Adam and Eve in Genesis in a literal way, but we must believe that there was a real historical event behind it. After all, where did sin and evil come from? God, who is all-good, cannot be the source of sin. Yet, human wickedness, moral evil, and sin are here. The great Catholic writer, G. K. Chesterton, said that you could prove the truth of the doctrine of Original Sin by simply reading the daily newspaper. Sin is part of the human condition from the beginning. "Sin is present in human history; any attempt to ignore it or to give this dark reality other names would be futile" (*CCC*, 386).

As Divine Revelation unfolded throughout history, it reached its fulfillment in the Life, Death, and Resurrection of Jesus Christ. Only then could God's People understand the full meaning of Original Sin.

> [T]his story's ultimate meaning . . . is revealed only in the light of the death and Resurrection of Jesus Christ. We must know Christ as the source of grace in order to know Adam as the source of sin. (*CCC*, 388)

Temptation Leads to Original Sin

Temptation is defined as "an attraction, either outside oneself or from within, to act contrary to right reason and the commandments of God." Genesis uses the symbol of the serpent to tell us about the seductive influence of a fallen angel who tempted Adam and Eve to choose themselves over their God. This fallen angel is known as **Satan**. Like all angels, Satan and other demons were created good by a loving God. They became evil by their own design by making a free choice. They:

radically and irrevocably rejected God and his reign. We find a reflection of that rebellion in the tempter's words to our first parents: "You will be like God." The devil "has sinned from the beginning"; he is "liar and the father of lies." (*CCC*, 392)

Satan, in the guise of a serpent, did great harm by seducing and tempting Adam and Eve. Created good in God's image and likeness, man was deceived into letting his trust in his Creator die in his heart and, abusing his freedom, disobeyed God's command. This is what man's first sin consisted of. All subsequent sin would be disobedience toward God and lack of trust in his goodness (*CCC*, 397).

Genesis 2:16–17 mentions the tree of knowledge of good and evil and God's command not to eat its fruit on pain of death. The serpent distorted the truth and deceived Adam and Eve. He promised that if they ate of the forbidden fruit, they would be like God. The forbidden fruit symbolizes knowledge only God should have—the knowledge of good and evil. Through their own willful choice, both by disobeying and defying God, Adam and Eve tried to make themselves gods. They sinned by preferring themselves to God. In so doing, they scorned God and did not recognize that they were creatures. They wanted to be like God but not in accord with his own plans for them (*CCC*, 398).

Satan
A fallen angel or the devil; the Evil One (CCC, 391, 395, 2851).

Consequences of Original Sin

The sin of Adam and Eve did in fact bring them new knowledge, namely the knowledge of shame and guilt. They realized they were naked and sewed fig leaves together to make loincloths to cover their nakedness. This action symbolized how their sin caused alienation between them. More importantly, their sin led to their alienation from God, the loss of Original Holiness. They tried to hide from God because they were "afraid of the God of whom they have conceived a distorted image—that of a God jealous of his prerogatives" (*CCC*, 299). The Yahwist author uses intimate language when talking about the Lord God who walks in the Garden looking for the man and the woman "in the breezy time of the day" (Gn 3:8). When questioned about why he ate the forbidden fruit, Adam blamed Eve. When Eve was questioned, she also made an excuse for her behavior: "The serpent tricked me into it, so I ate it" (Gn 3:13). Blaming and making excuses does not negate what Adam and Eve really did—freely and defiantly choosing to contradict God's command.

The *Catechism* lists the following outcomes that resulted from the Original Sin:

> The harmony in which they had found themselves, thanks to original justice, is now destroyed: the control of the soul's spiritual faculties over the body is shattered; the union of man and woman becomes subject to tensions, their relations henceforth marked by lust and domination (Gn 3:7–16). Harmony with creation is broken: visible creation has become alien and hostile to man (Gn 3:17, 19). Because of man, creation is now subject "to its bondage to decay" (Rom 8:21). Finally, the consequence explicitly foretold for this disobedience will come true.... Death makes its entrance into human history (Rom 5:12). (*CCC*, 400)

All humans are implicated in the sin of Adam and Eve. Through Original Sin, we have inherited a fallen human nature, are deprived of Original Holiness and Original Justice, and are subject to death. St. Paul taught that, "through one person sin entered the world, and through sin, death, and thus death came to all, inasmuch as all sinned" (Rom 5:12).

Exactly how does Original Sin affect all of humanity? St. Thomas Aquinas observed that the human race is in Adam "as one body of one man." There is a unity of the human race that results in our sharing in Adam's sin, just as we all share in Christ's Salvation. The transmission of Original Sin is fundamentally a mystery, but Divine Revelation does make it clear that Original Holiness and Original Justice was given to Adam not only for himself but also for all humans to follow. By giving into temptation, Adam and Eve committed a *personal*

Protoevangelium

A term that means "the first gospel," which is found in Genesis 3:15, when God revealed he would send a Savior to redeem the world from its sins.

New Adam

Announced in the Protoevangelium, a name for Jesus Christ who through his obedience in Life and Death makes amends for the disobedience of Adam.

wars in which nations are bent on destroying other nations; abortions that snuff out the lives of innocent children; prejudice that denies people basic human rights; marital discord that leads to broken families; lust that results in sexual perversion and life-threatening diseases; the list is truly endless. Something is wrong with human nature. Things were not meant to be this way. Human beings are seriously wounded and in need of help.

The Protoevangelium

God did not abandon Adam and Eve and their descendants after the Original Sin. Immediately after Adam and Eve offered their excuses for their disobedience, the Lord God revealed his plan of Salvation. This plan would conquer evil and death, restore humanity from the Fall, and bring into harmony once again all relationships, especially the relationship between humans and their loving God.

The announcement of God's plan of Salvation appears in Genesis 3:15. God speaks to the serpent (Satan), who had deceived Adam and Eve and led them into sin:

> I will put enmity between you and the woman,
>   and between your offspring and hers;
>   He will strike at your head,
>   while you strike at his heel. (Gn 3:15)

This verse is known as the **Protoevangelium** (translated "first gospel"). It predicts a future Messiah and Redeemer, a battle between the serpent and the woman, and a final victory of a descendant of hers. Christian Tradition sees in this passage the announcement of the **New Adam**. The New Testament tells us "the Son of God was revealed to destroy the works of the devil" (1 Jn 3:8). Jesus Christ did this by "becoming obedient unto death, even death on a cross." His obedience made up in a superabundant way for Adam's disobedience. Church Fathers have identified the woman in this passage as the Blessed Mother, the new Eve. Her offspring, of course, is Jesus Christ.

sin. This personal sin of theirs "affected the *human nature* that they would then transmit *in a fallen state*" (*CCC*, 404). The wounded human nature is passed on through propagation to all succeeding generations. We are deprived of Original Holiness and Original Justice, lost by the sin of our first parents. The *Catechism* teaches that Original Sin is "'contracted' and not 'committed'—a state and not an act" (*CCC*, 404).

Adam and Eve's sin did not totally corrupt human nature. However, it weakened it. This means that we are subject to the temptations of Satan. Our wounded human nature also subjects us to ignorance, suffering, and death. Moreover, it inclines us to sin, a condition known as concupiscence. St. Paul knew this condition well when he wrote, "What I do, I do not understand. For I do not do what I want, but I do what I hate" (Rom 7:15).

The effects of Original Sin are obvious to anyone who has eyes to see. Think of all the problems that exist in the world: greed that leads to exploitation of the poor and destruction of the environment;

Jesus' Death on the cross won for us Salvation and Redemption. It atoned for the Original Sin of Adam and Eve and all the sins people have committed down through the centuries. Mary was the first person to benefit in a unique way from Christ's victory over sin. She, the Mother of God, "was preserved from all stain of original sin and by a special grace of God committed no sin of any kind during her whole earthly life" (*CCC*, 411).

Christ's Death is the source of our Salvation. St. Paul writes, "But God proves his love for us in that while we were still sinners Christ died for us" (Rom 5:8). Christ is God's instrument for the great reversal. He is our Salvation: "For just as through the disobedience of one person the many were made sinners, so through the obedience of one the many will be made righteous" (Rom 5:19). It is through the Church that we receive the gift of Salvation. All Salvation comes through the Body of Christ, the Church, from Christ. As Christians, we enter into the life of Christ when we receive the Sacrament of Baptism. The water symbolizes death to an old life of sin, cleansing, and rebirth into a new life, the life of Christ. The Holy Spirit guides our new life in Christ.

God has raised us up through Jesus Christ—the Good News of Salvation History. "The doctrine of original sin is, so to speak, the 'reverse side' of the Good News that Jesus is the Savior of all men, that all need salvation and that salvation is offered to all through Christ" (*CCC*, 389). Good can come out of bad. Victory can be won out of defeat. No greater good and no greater victory could possibly happen to humanity than the coming of Jesus Christ, the Redeemer.

> But why did God not prevent the first man from sinning? St. Leo the Great responds, "Christ's inexpressible grace gave us blessings better than those the demon's envy had taken away." And St. Thomas Aquinas wrote, "There is nothing to prevent human nature's being raised up to something greater, even after sin; God permits evil in order to draw forth some greater good. Thus St. Paul says, 'Where sin increased, grace abounded all the more'; and the Exultant sings, 'O happy fault, . . . which gained for us so great a Redeemer!'" (*CCC*, 412)

The Protoevangelium is the first announcement of the Gospel of Jesus Christ. Reading the Old Testament in this way—discerning persons, events, or things that prefigure and serve as a prototype of the fulfillment of God's plan in the Person of Christ—is known as *typology*. This type of reading of the Old Testament is practiced in many examples that will be introduced both in this chapter and in Chapter 3. However, for God's plan to unfold, he first had to form a nation—Israel—from whom the Savior would be born. God entered into covenants with his

Origins of Names, Types of Sins

- Read Genesis 2:7 and Genesis 3:20 to guess the meanings of the names Adam and Eve. Then research to find out if you were right. Also, check the meaning of your baptismal name. Does the description fit your personality in any way? You may wish to check your middle name as well.

- There are several examples in the Old Testament of how the Chosen People "missed the mark" in keeping their covenant with God. The prophets had a special role in the history of the Chosen People to call people away from their sins. Speaking for God, they told of the offenses the people had committed. Read these four passages from the prophets Isaiah, Jeremiah, and Hosea and identify the sin that is being criticized: Isaiah 1:2; Jeremiah 2:29; Hosea 7:13; Hosea 8:1.

Damaging Effects of Original Sin

The effects of Original Sin are evident in today's world. Every sinful act naturally leads to a repetition of itself. "This results in perverse inclinations which cloud conscience and corrupt the concrete judgment of good and evil" (*CCC*, 1865). The evil of sin is almost unimaginable. Sin is a very personal act; however, we have a responsibility for the sins committed by others when we cooperate in them (see *Catechism of the Catholic Church*, 1860).

Consider the true story of Megan Meier, a thirteen-year-old girl from Missouri. Megan was overweight, emotionally vulnerable, and suffered with bouts of depression. She had been friends with another girl through seventh grade, but eventually they broke off the relationship, or so Megan thought.

Sometime after the relationship ended, a guy name Josh showed up on Megan's MySpace page asking to be added as a friend. He began to chat with her, saying she was cute and saying other nice things about her. This, of course, helped Megan's self-image. For a time, things went well. But then Josh started to say he didn't want to be friends with Megan anymore. He claimed that Megan talked behind the backs of her friends and that no one liked her. Obviously, Megan was very upset by this turn of events. What could possibly have happened to bring this on?

Josh continued to send mean notes. Moreover, he had been sharing other nasty messages with others online—messages that called Megan the most derogatory of names. Megan was devastated, especially when one night Josh wrote that everyone hated her and the world would be better off without her.

Tragically, Josh got his wish; later that night Megan hanged herself.

Weeks later the truth of the whole affair came out. There was never a "Josh." Lori Drew, the forty-nine-year-old mother of Megan's ex-friend, was accused of fabricating Josh and creating a false identity on MySpace in order to seek revenge on Megan for ending the friendship with her daughter.

Reflection Questions

- How did this story make you feel?
- Where does such evil come from?
- Have you heard other examples like this?
- What should the law do about the parents?

Assignment

Research more about the life of Megan Meier. Use her life as an inspiration to find ways to eliminate cyberbullying among your peers. Propose a list of dos and don'ts for Internet use that addresses this problem.

people and never abandoned his promise to bring humanity a Savior, even though the people fell into their sins time and again.

⬤ For Review

1. What did it mean for Adam and Eve to have been created with Original Holiness and Original Justice?
2. Define *Original Sin*.
3. Define *sin*.
4. How was Adam and Eve's sin also a personal sin?
5. How did Satan tempt Adam and Eve?
6. List three effects of Original Sin for Adam and Eve.
7. How does Original Sin affect all humans?
8. Define *concupiscence*.
9. What is the Protoevangelium?
10. Who are the woman and her offspring alluded to in Genesis 3:15?

⬤ For Reflection

- How has your personal sinfulness resulted from the abuse of freedom?
- Cite several examples of the tendency to blame one's sins on something or someone else.

God Remains Faithful in Times of Sin

Humanity's sinful behavior expanded after the personal sin of Adam and Eve. Once Original Sin entered human history, it spread like a virus. The effects of sin on human beings are harmful and destructive, yet God never abandoned the creatures he made. This point is made in three other stories in Genesis. The Yahwist stresses God's judgment on sinners but also his mercy. This theme is brought to fulfillment in Jesus' attitude toward sinners.

Cain and Abel (Gn 4:1–16)

The story of the first offspring of Adam and Eve reveals how sin leads to fratricide, the murder of a brother. Out of jealousy toward Abel, whose offering was more pleasing to the Lord, Cain killed his brother. Beforehand, God told Cain that he could master his sinful urges, but Cain, like all sinners, did not resist the temptation (Gn 4:7).

Sin deserves punishment, so the Lord banished Cain from the land and condemned him to a life of wandering. He also "put a mark on Cain, lest anyone should kill him at sight" (Gn 4:15). God's punishment is swift and just, but even the commission of such an evil crime as the murder of one's brother did not mean abandonment by the Lord. Faithful and loving to his beloved creatures, the Lord wished to refashion humanity, a humanity that will be redeemed in the fullness of time by the New Adam, Jesus Christ.

The Great Flood (Gn 6:5–9:29)

A careful reading of the account of the Great Flood reveals many repetitions and discrepancies. A possible explanation may be that the story interweaves both the so-called Yahwist (J) and Priestly (P) versions. Compare Genesis 6:19–20 to Genesis 7:2–3 for an example of this repetition. Also note in these verses a major discrepancy in the number of animals Noah is to take onto the ark. The P version (6:19–20) tells how God ordered Noah to take *one pair* of every species onto the ark, while J's instruction (7:2–3) is to take *seven pairs* of clean animals and one pair of unclean animals.

By including both versions, the biblical authors were stressing the importance of the flood story in Salvation History, for by means of the flood, God entered into his first great covenant with humanity. Though the story contains many symbolic elements, it may be rooted in a real natural catastrophe at the dawn of history. Babylon and Syria also had flood stories similar to the Noah story. The most famous parallel is the Sumerian Epic of Gilgamesh where the gods instruct the hero to build an ark and take animals on it before they destroy the world. There are other similarities in these ancient stories.

Genesis reveals that the purpose of the flood was to cleanse the world of human wickedness and depravity. God blessed Noah and instructed him and his family to repopulate the earth. Bringing to mind the creation of Adam, Noah is instructed to be fertile, multiply, be master of the animals, and subdue the earth. God's love for Noah is reflected in the first biblical account. Here God pledged that a flood would never again destroy the earth or the entire human race. The rainbow, a symbol of the Lord's presence to humanity, symbolized the covenant. It is a reminder to everyone that God continues to love humanity despite its sinful nature, which demands correction and punishment:

I set my bow in the clouds to serve as a sign of the covenant between me and the earth. When I bring clouds over the earth, and the bow appears in the clouds, I will recall the covenant I have made between me and you and all living beings, so that the waters shall never again become a flood to destroy all mortal beings. (Gn 9:14–15)

Later, God himself would enter into history by sending his only Son to save humanity, not from a flood, but from sin and death.

The sign of this covenant with Noah is the rainbow. Every time we see a rainbow, we should remember God's presence. God's love for us is steadfast, regardless of our sin and weakness. The rainbow symbolizes God's promise to bless us abundantly.

Tower of Babel (Gn 11:1-9)

The history of sin continues its saga in the Tower of Babel story. Here the biblical authors tell the story about the building of a ziggurat, a Mesopotamian-type temple that the Babylonians constructed to worship their god, Marduk. This story is combined

Guardian Angel

Angels are messengers with free will and naturally superior intellect to humans. Since the third century, the Church has maintained, thought not officially, that all the baptized have Guardian Angels who personally watch out for them. The Feast of Guardian Angels is October 2.

with a second story that describes humanity's attempt to build a civilization in defiance of God's command to disperse and populate the earth.

The sin involved in this story is the people's ambition to "make a name" for themselves by creating a culture independent of God. This resulted in alienation from God and discord among people. As the Book of Genesis teaches over and over, the sin of "going it apart from God" ultimately leads to punishment and separation.

In the Babel story, the Yahwist author uses a play on the Hebrew word *balal*, meaning "confusion," to explain the etiology of different languages among the world's diverse people. *Babel* (the Hebrew word for

EXPLAINING THE FAITH

What do Catholics believe about angels? (CCC, 325-336; 350-352; 391-395, 414)

The Nicene Creed proclaims that God created all that is seen and unseen. This includes pure spirits known as angels. Sacred Scripture and Sacred Tradition attest to their existence. Angels are those personal, immortal, invisible, and spiritual beings who lovingly worship God. Angels, like humans, have an opportunity to love and accept their loving Creator or reject him out of prideful self-interest. Satan and the other devils were angels who freely, radically, and irrevocably rejected God's reign.

The word *angel* means "messenger." Scripture describes the main functions of angels as servants and messengers of God. They are mediators between God and humans. The New Testament tells how angels are active during critical times of Salvation History. For example, the angel Gabriel is present at the Annunciation and angels are at the birth of Jesus. Angels are also present during Jesus' trials in the desert and Garden of Gethsemane, at the Resurrection, and at the Lord's Ascension into Heaven. Jesus Christ is the Lord of the angels because they were created through and for him.

Catholics believe that each of us has a Guardian Angel to watch over us. The Church encourages devotion to our Guardian Angels, asking for their spiritual help, especially in times of temptation. St. John Bosco (1815-1888) gave good advice when he wrote, "When tempted, invoke your angel. He is more eager to help you than you are to be helped! Ignore the devil and do not be afraid of him: He trembles and flees at the sight of your Guardian Angel."

The feast day of Sts. Michael, Raphael, and Gabriel, the only angels specifically named in the Bible, is September 29. The feast day of Guardian Angels is October 2.

Prayer to Guardian Angel
Angel of God,
my Guardian dear,
to whom His love
commits me here,
ever this day (or night)
be at my side,
to light and guard,
to rule and guide.
Amen.

Babylon) is the place where human pride caused the Lord to confuse the speech of the world. Defying God brings about indescribable consequences such as difficulty in human communication and cooperation.

However, with all of God's punishments comes some good. The people scattered around the earth, which was one of God's commands. Eventually, after Jesus' Resurrection, various pilgrims gathered in Jerusalem on Pentecost Sunday. Even though all spoke different languages, they understood Peter's proclamation of the Gospel of Jesus Christ (see Acts 2:5–13). The coming of the Holy Spirit, who guides Christ's Body, the Church, unites all people in Jesus, the Son of God.

The Babel story ends Genesis's treatment of prehistory. As we will see in the covenants to come, God does not abandon humanity. The genealogy given after the Babel story begins with Noah's son, Shem, and ends with the patriarch Abraham. Through Abraham and his descendants, God forms a Chosen People and blesses all generations to the end of time.

For Review

1. What is a main lesson of the Cain and Abel story? What is the "mark of Cain"?
2. How did the biblical authors understand the purpose of the Flood?
3. What covenant did the Lord make with Noah? What is its sign?
4. Why were the people punished for building the Tower of Babel?

For Reflection

A rainbow is a symbol of God's abiding presence and love. What symbol is a sign of God's love and presence in your life? Explain this symbol or depict it graphically.

Covenants in the Old Testament

The covenant between God and Noah was the first Old Testament covenant. It is described from prehistory. Three other major covenants are part of the historical record of God's Chosen People. The Hebrew word for covenant is *berith*. In the ancient world, covenants between persons were solemn agreements to do, or refrain from doing, something. In some covenants, for example, the superior party (like a monarch) would unconditionally promise to do something without imposing conditions on the people. A typical covenant involved a statement of the terms of the covenant, an oath by which each party promised to observe the terms of the agreement, and a formal ratification involving some external ritual. In biblical covenants between men, God is the witness to the agreement. An example of this is the pact made between Laban and Jacob (Gn 31:44, 50).

As witnessed in the covenant with Noah, Sacred Scripture reveals that God entered into solemn covenants with humans. Biblical covenants were so important that the concept of covenant is central to Sacred Scripture. The word *testament* is a synonym for covenant. Thus, the Hebrew Scriptures are termed the Old Testament while we name the Christian Scriptures, the New Testament. The covenants in Scripture had two sacred parts: the promise made and the conditions attached to the promise.

The three other major Old Testament covenants are:

- *The Covenant with Abraham*, where God blessed Abram's family, promising to give them the land of Canaan and making them a blessing to the nations (Gn 15:18).
- *The Covenant with Moses on Mt. Sinai*, where God selected Israel as his Chosen People (Ex 19:5, 6).

New Covenant

The climax of Salvation History, the coming of Jesus Christ, the fullness of God's Revelation.

Gentiles

A term that means "non-Jews."

- *The Covenant with David*, where God promised that the Messiah and Savior would come from David's dynasty (2 Sm 23:5).

The Old Testament prophet, Jeremiah, foretold a **New Covenant** (Jer 31:31–34). This covenant would be written in the hearts of humankind and, as promised by the prophet Isaiah, would center in a person (Is 42:6; 49:8).

Jesus Christ is the New Covenant between God and his people. His covenant is sealed in his blood; his sacrifice is what saves and redeems us.

Covenant with Abraham (CCC, 59-61)

Abram was a nomadic herder who was born around four thousand years ago in Ur, in what is today present-day southern Iraq. God called him to journey to Shechem in the land of Canaan. God promised that he would give the new land to Abram and his progeny:

> "I will make of you a great nation,
>   and I will bless you;
> I will make your name great
>   so that you will be a blessing.
> I will bless those who bless you
>   and curse those who curse you.
> All the communities of the earth
>   shall find blessing in you." (Gn 12:2–3)

God eventually changed Abram's name to Abraham, which meant "father of a multitude of nations."

Abraham heard God's call, believed it, and obeyed. Hearing, believing, and obeying God comprise the elements of the virtue of faith. Abraham is often referred to as "father of faith," not only for Christians and Jews, but for Muslims as well. He dramatically prefigured the humble Virgin Mary who heard God's call that she was to be the Mother of the Redeemer. She heard, believed, and obeyed God's will by saying, "Behold, I am the handmaid of the Lord. May it be done to me according to your word" (Lk 1:38). Through her child, Jesus Christ, all people of the earth are indeed blessed.

Genesis 12–22 records six different times God appeared to Abraham to make or reinforce his promises. The covenant God made with Abraham extended to his descendants—blessing humanity through the patriarchs: Isaac (son of Abraham and Sarah) and Jacob (son of Isaac and Rebekah). Jacob would become Israel, which became the name of a great nation. One of Israel's sons—Judah—would be given the scepter as ruler, and Jesus, the Messiah, would come from Judah's line. Jesus' mission was to save and renew all humanity, both Jews and **Gentiles**:

> The people descended from Abraham would be the trustee of the promise made to the patriarchs, the chosen people, called to prepare for that day when God would gather all his children into the unity of

the Church. They would be the root on to which the Gentiles would be grafted, once they came to believe. (*CCC*, 60)

Among the provisions of the covenant with Abraham are these:

- a great nation would descend from him (Israel)
- Abraham and his family would be given a land (Canaan)
- Abraham would be blessed and his name would be revered
- the entire earth would ultimately be blessed through him
- Abraham and his wife Sarah would parent a child even though both were old (Gn 15:1–4; 17:16–21)

God also told Abraham that his descendants would be held as slaves in a foreign land (Gn 15:13–14), something that transpired when the Israelites were captive in Egypt.

The sign of the covenant was that boy babies should be circumcised on the eighth day after birth. "That shall be the mark of the covenant between you and me" (Gn 17:11).

Genesis reveals that "Abram put his faith in the Lord, who credited it to him as an act of righteousness" (Gn 15:6). In the Sacrament of Baptism, through the power of the Holy Spirit, we become members of Christ's Body, the Church. Our membership and participation in the Church is an extension of the covenant God made with Abraham. Christ's saving Death on the cross has justified us before God, bringing about righteousness:

Justification is conferred in Baptism, the sacrament of faith. It conforms us to the righteousness of God, who makes us inwardly just by the power of his mercy. Its purpose is the glory of God and of Christ, and the gift of eternal life. . . . (*CCC*, 1992)

The remaining chapters of Genesis relate the story of the patriarchs and matriarchs, that is, the fathers and mothers of our faith, including stories about Isaac and his wife Rebekah, Jacob (Israel) and his wives Leah and Rachel, and Jacob's sons, most notably Joseph. Betrayed by his brothers, Joseph won favor with the pharaoh and was an instrument of his brothers' salvation by finding them a home in Egypt during a time of famine. The Book of Exodus tells how a new Egyptian king enslaved the Israelites for fear that they might side with his enemies and leave the country. The Egyptians "dreaded the Israelites and reduced them to cruel slavery, making life bitter for them with hard work" (Ex 1:12–13). This experience of slavery led God to carve a path that would lead the Israelites to freedom and eventually a return to the Promised Land of Canaan.

Covenant with Moses (CCC, 62-63)

After two hundred years of suffering under the Egyptians, God appointed Moses to lead the Israelites out of slavery. This event is known as the Exodus (from a Greek word for "departure") from Egypt. The pharaoh's stubbornness required God to send ten plagues to force him to let the Israelites depart Egypt. However, the pharaoh regretted his decision and he pursued the departing Israelites. God thwarted his efforts by miraculously allowing the Israelites safe passage through the Red Sea and destroyed the pursuing Egyptian army.

Then began the Israelites' forty-year sojourn in the Sinai desert, a journey that brings to mind Abraham's trek to Canaan, the land promised by God. By means of the Exodus and his instructions to them while in the desert, God formed Israel as his people:

He established with them the covenant of Mount Sinai and, through Moses, gave them his law so that they would recognize him and serve him as the one living and true God, the provident Father and just judge, and so that they would look for the promised Savior. (*CCC*, 62)

The covenant God made with the Israelites is stated simply in the Book of Deuteronomy:

> For you are a people sacred to the Lord, your God; he has chosen you from all the nations on the face of the earth to be a people peculiarly his own. It was not because you are the largest of all nations that the Lord set his heart on you and chose you, for you are really the smallest of all nations. It was because the Lord loved you and because of his fidelity to the oath he had sworn to your fathers, that he brought you out with his strong hand from the place of slavery, and ransomed you from the hand of Pharaoh, king of Egypt. Understand, then, that the Lord, your God, is God indeed, the faithful God who keeps his merciful covenant down to the thousandth generation toward those who love him and keep his commandments. (Dt 7:6–9)

The events of the Exodus proved again that God was faithful to his promises to Abraham: he preserved them as a people, freed them, and promised a future Savior. In the covenant with Moses, known as the Sinai Covenant, the Lord entered into a personal union with them, revealing his special love and mercy. In return, the Israelites "shall therefore carefully observe the commandments, the statutes and the decrees which I enjoin on you today" (Dt 7:11). These are known as the Law of Moses, the Torah, or simply the Law.

The **Decalogue** summarizes the Law. It expresses what humans know in their hearts, and deduce by reason, to be right or wrong. This is known as the **natural law**, the principles of morality, of right living, that extend to the human race in all places and at all times. As the revealed expression of the natural law, the Ten Commandments are unchangeable and permanent throughout history. They correspond to basic human drives and needs:

- preservation of life ("Do not kill")
- the development of individuals and communities ("Worship God alone, honor his name, and

keep holy the Lord's Day"; "Honor your father and mother"; "Do not steal"; "Do not bear false witness"; "Do not covet your neighbor's goods")

- sharing life with others ("Do not commit adultery" and "Do not covet your neighbor's wife")

By worshipping the Lord alone as the true God, and by living a life conformed to the Ten Commandments, the Chosen People were to be a beacon of God's revelation to the whole world. This understanding has helped to define the Church's relationship to the Jewish people through today. As the *Catechism of the Catholic Church* teaches, the "Jewish faith, unlike other non-Christian religions, is already a response to God's revelation in the Old Testament" (*CCC*, 839). However, a study of the Old Testament also reveals how the people would turn their backs on God. They fell into **idolatry** by worshipping false gods. The Israelites' neglect of the Law deserved punishment, and, at times, throughout their history, God did punish them: "I will be your God and you shall be my people" (Jer 7:23 [see also, Ez 11:20 and Hos 2:25]).

Covenant with David

The First and Second Books of Samuel contain stories about some of the most prominent people in the Old Testament: among them Samuel, the prophet; Saul, Israel's first king; and David, Israel's greatest king. This era followed the period of the **Judges**, tribal chieftains who helped defend Israel against its enemies, settle disputes, and call Israel back to God.

Although 1 and 2 Samuel are among the historical books, history is reported from a theological perspective. The writers saw the Lord's hand in choosing David as king and in making Jerusalem the religious capital of the nation. The key promise of God's covenant with David was that Israel would be a royal dynasty, a promise that led to the belief of a Messiah (God's "anointed one"), who would save the Chosen People from their enemies. Jesus is the Christ, the Messiah, the Son of David. He is the King of Peace who came to save both Jews and all mankind. Nathan tells David:

> The Lord also reveals to you that he will establish a house for you. And when your time comes and you rest with your ancestors, I will raise up your heir after you, sprung from your loins, and I will make his kingdom firm. It is he who shall build a house for my name. And I will make his royal throne firm forever. I will be a father to him, and he shall be a son to me. (2 Sm 7:11–12)

To this good news, David replied:

> Great are you, Lord God! There is none like you and there is no God but you, just as we have heard it told. . . . You have established for yourself your people Israel as yours forever, and you, Lord, have become their God. . . . Your name will be forever great, when men say, "The Lord of hosts is God of Israel," and the house of your servant David stands firm before you. (2 Sm 7:22, 24, 26)

The Davidic covenant specified in more detail the covenants God had made with Abraham and Moses. God not only blessed Abraham and his descendants but he formed a people from them, gave them the Law to guide them, and asked them to worship him in truth and love. God further promised that the future Messiah, the Savior of all humanity, would descend from the house of King David. For their part, the Chosen People were to live the Law as a beacon to the nations of the one true, saving God. Despite the infidelities of the people and even kings like David, God always remained faithful to his promises. In his own good time, he sent his Son to be born of the Blessed Virgin Mary. Jesus—a name that means "Savior"—is the Redeemer of all humanity. David's expression of joy and praise is a right one: "Great are you, Lord God! There is none like you."

Decalogue
Literally, "ten words," it describes the Ten Commandments given by God to Moses on Sinai.

natural law
God's plan for human living that is written in the very way he created things. Binding on all people at all times, it is the light of understanding that God puts in us so we can discover what is good and what is evil.

idolatry
Worshipping something or someone other than the true God.

Judges
In ancient Israel, those who acted as temporary military leaders, as well as arbiters of disputes within and between tribes. The judges were also expected to remind people of their responsibilities to God.

For Review

1. Describe provisions of the covenant God made with Abraham.

2. Why is Abraham the "father of faith"?

3. How is Mary a perfect model of faith?

4. What was the sign of the covenant with Abraham?

5. What was the Exodus?

6. What is the summary of the Torah?

7. What is the natural law?

8. What are the three basic human needs or drives addressed by the Decalogue?

9. Why did the people make the golden calf? Why did Moses break the stone tablets (read Exodus 32)?

10. Who were the judges in the Old Testament?

11. Who was Israel's first king?

12. Summarize the Davidic covenant.

For Reflection

- How can you connect Abraham's plight as an immigrant to the experience of immigrants in the world today?

- How do you feel connected to the covenants of the Old Testament?

God Remains Faithful to His Promises

In many ways, the kingship of David was a golden period in the monarchy of Israel. He had united the kingdom with Jerusalem as its capital. For a time, he brought peace, culture, and prosperity to the land.

David, though, was a flawed figure. A notable example is how he had an affair with Bathsheba, the married wife of one of his soldiers. He then contrived to have her husband killed after she had become pregnant with David's child. When confronted by the prophet Nathan, David repented (2 Sm 11–12). However, his future reign was beset with various rebellions.

A Divided Kingdom and Captivity

David's son Solomon succeeded his father as king. Known for his wisdom, he built the Temple in Jerusalem, a center of worship and pilgrimage for the Chosen People. Unfortunately, more idolatry followed, and under Solomon's sons the kingdom divided into two: the northern kingdom of Israel, consisting of ten tribes and centered in Samaria; and the southern kingdom of Judah, consisting of the tribes of Benjamin and Judah and centered in Jerusalem.

The northern kingdom fell to Assyria in 722 BC, and the southern kingdom was overrun by Babylonia in 587 BC. During the time of political turmoil and religious backsliding, prophets in both the north and the south reminded people of God's covenant. They proclaimed the need for the Chosen People to worship the one true God in fidelity and truth and to live according to the Law, especially by looking out for the needs of the poor and powerless. As the vehicles to share God's Word, prophets were often unpopular because they challenged corrupt rulers and the status quo. They felt impelled by God to preach his message—worship the one true God and repent sinfulness. To this essential message, later prophets added reassuring words that, despite present appearances, God would never abandon his promises to them.

Prophets Preach Repentance and Hope

An example of a prophet who preached to the northern kingdom was Amos. Around 750 BC, he proclaimed that true worship of God required concrete deeds manifested to the weak and poor. He also chided the Israelites on their many sins: genocide, cruelty, anger, sexual excess, violence, pride, and the like. He warned that unless people repented, the nation would be destroyed. Amos offered timeless advice:

> Hate evil and love good
> and let justice prevail at the gate.
> (Am 5:15)

The prophet Jeremiah echoed the theme of repentance. He preached at the time of Babylonia's assault on the southern kingdom. He used props in dramatic scenes to try to get the attention of the people. For example, he shattered a jug in front of the elders and priests to serve as a warning that God would destroy those who had abandoned him. Another time, he walked through the streets of Jerusalem with a wooden yoke on his shoulders to emphasize to the people that only by submitting to Babylon could the kingdom of Judah be spared destruction. Jeremiah also balanced his dire warnings with a message of hope for the people. To the captives in Babylon, he preached:

> The days are coming, says the Lord, when I will make a new covenant with the house of Israel and the house of Judah. It will not be like the covenant I made with their fathers. . . . I will place my law within them, and write it upon their hearts; I will be their God, and they shall be my people. No longer will they have need to teach their friends and kinsmen how to know the Lord. All, from least to greatest, shall know me, says the Lord, for I will forgive their evildoing and remember their sin no more. (Jer 31:31, 33–34)

This passage is hopeful because it reminded the Chosen People that God will take the initiative by giving them new hearts so that they will be obedient to the Lord. Knowledge of God will be internal and personal. It will no longer only be written on tablets of stone or in law books. Rather, God will touch a person's heart so that the Lord may live within.

Christians understand in Jeremiah's words a prophecy of the New Covenant established by Jesus Christ. The Savior's life, Death, and Resurrection inaugurated a covenant of God's grace that heals and conquers sin. It is a covenant of new life and the outpouring of the Holy Spirit who guides us from within.

Another prophet who preached both repentance and hope was Ezekiel. For example, before Jerusalem fell to the Babylonians, Ezekiel had strongly censured the People of God for their sinful conduct and warned them of imminent destruction. However, after the fall of Jerusalem, the once highly critical Ezekiel offered a demoralized and defeated nation a message of hope. As recorded in Ezekiel 33–39, the prophet promised that a new shepherd king would make a covenant of peace with the people. He also predicted a time when God would restore the nation. He told of a prophetic dream he had where he stood in a field of dry bones:

> These bones are the whole house of Israel. They have been saying, "Our bones are dried up, our hope is lost, and we are cut off. . . ." Thus says the Lord God: O my people, I will open your graves and have you rise from them, and bring you back to the land of Israel. Then you shall know that I am the Lord, when I open your graves and have you rise from them, O my people! I will put my spirit in you that you may live, and I will settle you upon your land; thus you shall know that I am the Lord. I have promised, and I will do it, says the Lord. (Ez 37:11–14)

Ezekiel's vision prophesied that the people would return to the Promised Land. Their despair will be turned to hope. God will bring them back to life!

Coming of the Messiah

The Book of Isaiah actually consists of three main parts, probably composed by three different authors. Each prophesized about the future of God's People and the coming of a Messiah. Chapters 1–39 come from the original prophet, Isaiah of Jerusalem, who preached during the time of the collapse of the northern kingdom and the moral breakdown of the southern kingdom. His ministry spanned the period from 742 to 700 BC. He preached a powerful message of repentance to a sinful nation, criticizing idolatry, empty sacrifice, human pride, and cruelty to the poor. He also prophesied that God would give a sign: "The virgin shall be with child, and bear a son, and shall name him Immanuel" (Is 7:14). The child who will be born is a son upon whom God will rule:

> They name him Wonder-Counselor,
> God-Hero,
>> Father-Forever, Prince of Peace.
> His dominion is vast and forever peaceful.
> (Is 9:5–6)

Christians see in Isaiah's prophecy of Immanuel (a name meaning "God is with us") a reference to the promised Messiah, the Son of God, Jesus of Nazareth.

Isaiah 40–55, sometimes called Deutero-Isaiah or Second Isaiah, is generally attributed to an anonymous poet. It may have been written around 550 BC during the Babylonian exile. The author foretold to the captive people that Babylonia was on the verge of collapse. In fact, he was correct. Cyrus of Persia defeated the Babylonians and in 538 BC permitted exiles to return home. At this time a remnant of the Jewish people returned to Jerusalem and, under leaders like Ezra and Nehemiah, rebuilt and rededicated the Temple (516 BC).

Deutero-Isaiah had many consoling words for his people. The prophet proclaimed that God is coming to save his people and that his love is enduring, like that of a mother for her baby:

> Can a mother forget her infant,
>> be without tenderness for the child of her womb?
> Even should she forget you
>> I will never forget you.
> See, upon the palms of my hands I have
>> written your name. (Is 49:15–16a)

Besides the message of consolation, hope, and deliverance, Deutero-Isaiah also teaches that God is the one, all-powerful, creator God. Everything that exists comes from, depends on, and is subject to God: "I am the first and I am the last; there is no God but me" (Is 44:6). "I am the Lord, there is no other" (Is 45:6b).

The prophet reminds the Israelites that God called them to serve as a light to attract other nations to the worship of the one true God. As God used Cyrus of Persia to do his work, so the Lord's love for the Israelites should illuminate the way for other nations.

> I will make you a light to the nations,
>> that my salvation may reach the ends of
>> the earth. (Is 49:6)

WHO WAS THE SUFFERING SERVANT?

Second Isaiah's words about the "Suffering Servant" had meaning both when they were written and five hundred years later at the time of the birth of Jesus Christ.

At the time of the writing, the prophet believes that at least one possible identity of the Suffering Servant is the Jewish people themselves, due to their experience in exile. They are collectively called the "Servant of God" (see Is 41:8-10).

While many other identifications of the Suffering Servant have been proposed (e.g., the prophet himself, or another prophet living at that time), the Church is clear in its pronouncement that the Suffering Servant prophecies are fulfilled in Jesus Christ. The *Catechism* teaches:

> The Scriptures had foretold this divine plan of salvation through the putting to death of "the righteous one, my servant" as a mystery of universal Redemption, the slavery of sin. Citing a confession of faith that "Christ died in accordance with the scriptures." In particular, Jesus' redemptive death fulfills Isaiah's prophecy of the suffering Servant. (*CCC*, 601)

Deutero-Isaiah also contains four important pieces known as the "Servant Songs." These describe an individual, "the servant," whom God will use to usher in a glorious future. Christians see in these songs prophetic images of Jesus, the servant whose sufferings redeemed all people. Jesus was familiar with these passages and applied them to himself. He interpreted the messianic way to Salvation as a path of suffering and service and not the easy road of glory and domination.

Finally, a disciple or disciples of the great prophet composed Isaiah 56–66 some time after the Jews returned from exile. One of the themes that emerges from these chapters is a promise that in a coming day God's light would shine brightly on the Jewish nation and attract all people to God (see Is 60:15). Another theme is the belief that God's Salvation is meant for all, not just the Chosen Ones. Worship of the one true God and the Lord's Salvation are a universal call and gift:

> For my house shall be called
> a house of prayer for all peoples. (Is 56:7)

Approaching the Birth of Christ

The centuries prior to the birth of Christ saw Persian rule give way to the Greeks under Alexander the Great, then to the Seleucid Dynasty, and finally to the Romans. God's People fought the efforts of some of the foreign rulers to *Hellenize* them, that is, to impose Greek culture on their way of life and religion. Faithful Jews kept their religion alive through Temple worship and by meeting in prayer houses called synagogues.

The Seleucid ruler, Antiochus Epiphanes, tried to obliterate Judaism. In 165 BC, he desecrated the Temple, an action that led to a revolt by the Maccabean family who helped preserve the Jewish religion from the influence of the pagans. For a time, Israel had a degree of political independence, but internal squabbles among leaders and priests led to the formation of sects. In 63 BC, the Romans imposed their rule on Israel. They appointed Herod the Great, a half-Jew, to govern. Herod was a great builder and was responsible for the reconstruction of the Temple. But he was also a cruel and vindictive ruler who governed with an iron hand. It was shortly before his death, in 4 BC, that the Prince of Peace, Jesus Christ, was born. All the prophecies concerning the Messiah would come true. In him, God's covenant with the Jews and all humanity would reach its perfect fulfillment in his Passion, Death, and Resurrection. Chapter 3 focuses on the events around Christ's birth and discusses how his life fulfilled the Old Testament prophecies.

☀ For Review

1. Explain King David's central role in Salvation History.

2. When did the northern kingdom fall to the Assyrians? When did the southern kingdom fall to the Babylonians?

3. Who were the prophets? What was their essential message?

4. Summarize the prophetic message of Amos.

5. What did Jeremiah preach about the new covenant?

6. What was the meaning of Ezekiel's dry bones vision?

7. What important Messianic prophecy does Isaiah of Jerusalem make in Isaiah 7:14?

8. What is the meaning of the title *Immanuel*?

9. How do the Servant Songs apply to Jesus Christ?

☀ For Reflection

- Prayerfully read Isaiah 52:13-53:12. Note three ways this passage applies to Jesus Christ.

- Read and briefly describe the following Old Testament passages referring to the coming of the Messiah: Psalm 22:19, 35:11, 41:9; Isaiah 11:2, 35:56; Hosea 11:1; Micah 5:2; Zechariah 9:9, 11:12-13; Malachi 3:1.

Main Ideas

- At creation, Adam and Eve were gifted with Original Holiness and Original Justice. (p. 32)

- Among the effects of Original Sin were the loss of Original Holiness and Original Justice. (p. 32)

- The Fall of Adam and Eve is told using figurative language, though there was a real historical event that was behind the occasion of the Original Sin. (pp. 32–33)

- Temptation lead to the Original Sin; Adam and Eve sinned by preferring themselves to God. (p. 33)

- Because of Original Sin, humans have inherited a fallen human nature, are deprived of Original Holiness and Original Justice, and are subject to death. (pp. 34–35)

- Original Sin weakened human nature, but it did not totally corrupt it. (p. 35)

- The Protoevangelium, recorded in Genesis 3:15, announces God's plan for a future Messiah and Redeemer and a final victory over sin and death. (pp. 35–36)

- It is Christ's Death that is the source of our Salvation. (p. 36)

- Sin spread exponentially after the Original Sin, and occasions of sin in the Old Testament include those connected to Cain and Abel, the Great Flood, and the Tower of Babel. (pp. 38–39)

- God formed covenants with his people in the Old Testament. The first covenant was with Noah. Covenants between God and the Chosen People were those with Abraham, Moses, and David. (pp. 38–41)

- The Covenant with Abraham promised land to Abraham and his progeny. (pp. 42–43)

- The Covenant with Moses formed the Chosen People and gave them a Law, summarized in the Ten Commandments. (pp. 43–44)

- The Davidic Covenant specified in more detail that a Messiah, the Savior of all humanity, would be a descendant of King David. (pp. 45–46)

- The prophets of the Old Testament preached repentance and hope. (pp. 47–48)

- The Book of Isaiah prophesizes about the future of God's People and the coming of the Messiah. (pp. 48–50)

Terms, People, Places

Complete each sentence by choosing the correct answer from the list of terms below. You will not use all of the terms.

Decalogue
Gentiles
Guardian Angel
idolatry
Judges
Natural Law
New Adam
New Covenant
Original Sin
Protoevangelium
Satan

1. The full meaning of _____ is only revealed in the Death and Resurrection of Jesus Christ.
2. Time and again the Chosen People would turn their backs on God and fall into the sin of _____ by worshipping false Gods.
3. The _____ were tribal chieftains who helped defend Israel against its enemies, settle disputes, and call Israel back to God.
4. Jesus' mission was to save all humanity, including the _____.
5. Your _____ is meant to watch over you and help to shield you from temptation.

6. The _____ is principles of morality that extend to the human race in all places and at all times.

7. The _____ summarizes the Law.

8. Literally, the _____ is translated as the "first gospel."

9. By becoming obedient even to Death on a cross, Jesus fulfilled his role as the

   _____.

10. The fallen angel who tempted Adam and Eve is known as _____.

Primary Source Quotations

Sin and Evil

The whole of man's history has been the story of our combat with the powers of evil, stretching, so our Lord tells us, from the very dawn of history until the last day. Finding himself in the midst of the battlefield man has to struggle to do what is right, and it is at great cost to himself, and aided by God's grace, that he succeeds in achieving his own inner integrity.

—*Gaudium et Spes*, 37

God did not make death, nor does he rejoice in the destruction of the living.

—Wisdom 1:13

I do not trust myself as long as I am in this body of death. . . . The hostile flesh always draws me toward death, that is toward enticements unlawful to indulge in.

—St. Patrick

To sin is human, but to persist in sin is devilish.

—St. Catherine of Siena

Reserve some time to pray before the Blessed Sacrament for people in your family who have gone before you to eternal rest. Pray for them by name.

Ongoing Assignments

As you cover the material in this chapter, choose and complete at least three of these assignments.

1. Prepare a PowerPoint presentation with a collection of various depictions of the creation and the fall.

2. Prepare a PowerPoint presentation on how Satan has been portrayed in Christian art.

3. Prepare a report on the seven capital sins. Use practical examples to show how the capital sins have a detrimental effect on your life.

4. Prepare a report on the three angels mentioned in the Bible: Gabriel, Michael, and Raphael. Reproduce a photo of how one of them has been depicted in art or on holy cards.

5. Report on the "hierarchy of the angels."

6. Examine some Old Testament covenants by reading the selected passages. Answer the questions that accompany each passage.

   1 Samuel 18:1–5
   • Who are the subjects of the covenant?

   • Why was it made?

   • What was the sign of the agreement?

   Ezra 10:1–5
   • What was the agreement made?

   • How was it made?

   Hebrews 9:11–22
   • Who is the mediator of the covenant?

   • What brings about forgiveness?

7. Report on the efforts of some scholars to search for the location of Noah's ark.

8. Read the following passages in Genesis where God appears to Moses. Note what God promises in each particular passage: 12:1–3; 12:7; 13:14–18; 15:4–5, 13–18; 17:1–8.

9. Report on one of the Old Testament matriarchs of the faith—Sarah, Rebekah, Rachel, and Leah—and their relationship to Mary.

10. After reading a description of the Ark of the Covenant, do one of the following:

    •   Draw a sketch of its probable appearance.

    •   Report on what happened to it, including some modern theories.

11. Read Isaiah 40–44. Transcribe in your journal at least five verses that speak of God's mercy and tenderness to the Chosen People.

Prayer

Pope Leo XIII introduced the following Prayer to St. Michael the Archangel to be recited at the end of Mass. Though it is no longer recited as part of the Eucharistic liturgy, later popes encourage us to recite it frequently. Pope John Paul II urged us to pray it "to obtain help in the battle against forces of darkness and against the spirit of this world."

> *Prayer to St. Michael the Archangel*
> St. Michael the Archangel,
> defend us in battle.
> Be our protection against the wickedness
>   and snares of the devil.
> May God rebuke him, we humbly pray;
> and do Thou, O Prince of the Heavenly
>   Host—
> by the Power of God—
> cast into Hell, Satan and all the evil spirits,
> who roam throughout the world seeking the
>   ruin of souls.
> Amen.

•   *Reflection*: What is a "snare" that is tempting you to be less than the beautiful child of God you are called to be?

•   *Resolution*: During the coming two weeks, recite this prayer each time you are tempted to sin.

3

THE COMING OF THE MESSIAH

*"For today in the city of David a savior has been born for you
who is Messiah and Lord. And this will be a sign for you:
you will find an infant wrapped in swaddling clothes
and lying in a manger." And suddenly there was a multitude
of the heavenly host with the angel, praising God and saying:
"Glory to God in the highest and on earth peace
to those on whom his favor rests."*

—Luke 2:11-14

● Jesus: Our Hope and Salvation

Through his Paschal Mystery, Jesus Christ has won Salvation for humanity.

● Gospel Portraits of Christ's Origins

Taken together, the four Gospels paint the most complete picture of the saving deeds of Jesus, beginning with the events surrounding his origins and birth.

● Learning from the Life of Christ

The events at the beginning of Jesus' public ministry set the stage for communicating the mysteries that form a foundation for our Salvation.

● The Beginning of Jesus' Ministry

The central theme of Jesus' preaching from the beginning is that the Kingdom of God is at hand.

Jesus: Our Hope and Salvation

A college president once remarked to his student body that the world contains three kinds of people: the few who make things happen; the many who watch things happen; and the vast majority of people who are clueless about what is happening. He went on to point out that the world desperately needs more people who "make things happen."

Jesus Christ is definitely someone who made things happen. Born over two thousand years ago in a land far removed from the center of power, he changed history forever. Through his Life, Passion, Death, and Resurrection, he has won eternal Salvation for humanity. Because of this, Jesus is the most important Person to walk the face of the earth. Do an Internet search of the name Jesus, and you will find upwards of 259 million references! Search Amazon.com for books written about him, and you will find more than 275,000 at recent count!

Even nonbelievers recognize his importance. For example, the British author H. G. Wells (1866–1946) wrote, "I am a historian. I am not a believer. But I must confess as a historian that this penniless preacher from Nazareth is irrevocably the very center of history. Jesus Christ is easily the most dominant figure in all history."

Put more succinctly, Jesus is our hope and our Salvation. He is our guide and our mentor. St. Thomas Aquinas said it well, "If, then, you are looking for the way by which you should go, take Christ, because he himself is the way."

For Reflection

Describe someone you know who "makes things happen" in the name of Jesus Christ.

Gospel Portraits of Christ's Origins

St. Paul wrote in his letter to the Galatians: "But when the fullness of time had come, God sent his Son, born of a woman, born under the law, to ransom those under the law, so that we might receive adoption" (Gal 4:4–5). The coming of Jesus Christ, the Son of God who is Lord, is the Gospel, the good news of our Salvation. After centuries of preparation in the Old Testament, God himself came to his people, thus fulfilling the promises he made to Abraham and his descendants.

Son of a Jewish mother, Jesus was born in Bethlehem sometime around 4–6 BC at the time of King Herod the Great and during the reign of the Roman emperor, Caesar Augustus. Jesus' family returned to Nazareth, a small town in the northern province of Galilee. There he learned the trade of carpentry from his foster father, Joseph. After his baptism as an adult, he embarked on a preaching and healing ministry. Eventually, he ran into resistance from the authorities. Thus, he was crucified under the Roman procurator Pontius Pilate during the reign of the emperor Tiberius, either in the year AD 30 or 33.

Death is not the final chapter in the life of Jesus. Rather, his Resurrection is the "crowning truth of our faith in Christ" (*CCC*, 638). It confirms all of his works and teachings and proves his divinity. Along with the Passion and Death of Jesus, his Resurrection constitutes the Paschal Mystery of our Salvation. Through his Death, Jesus Christ frees us from sin; by his Resurrection, he opens us to a new life.

After appearances to his disciples over forty days, Jesus ascended into Heaven where he is seated at the right hand of the Father. With God the Father, he sent the Holy Spirit to guide his followers. We, like the first disciples, confess that Jesus is "Lord," a title that indicates our belief in his divine sovereignty. The Holy Spirit enables us to proclaim our

Jesus as Our Guide

There is a story about Michelangelo, who was working in his studio one day. A young boy entered the studio and saw the famed sculptor hammering away at a large, shapeless block of granite. The boy asked what he was doing. Michelangelo picked up the child, stood him on his workbench, and said, "Can't you see? There is an angel hidden in this rock. I am chipping away all the pieces that are not the angel to set it free."

God sees hidden beauty in each of us. He has sent his instrument—his Son, Jesus Christ—to free us, to unleash our hidden possibilities. Our Lord's chisel is his Gospel that frees us and calls us to be what he created us to be. Receiving Jesus in friendship is the key to true freedom. John 6 is known as the "Bread of Life" discourse. Read John 6 and then take the following personal inventory. From the statements below, determine how much you look to the Lord as the source of your life:

- **Possessions:** I enjoy the good things that come my way, but I know that they can never be the true source of my happiness.
- **Scripture:** I derive spiritual nourishment from the Scriptural Word of God, which I read regularly.
- **Eucharist:** I attend Mass every Sunday and Holy Day of Obligation and frequently receive Holy Communion.
- **Prayer:** I ask the Lord for help when I need it, talking to him as my best friend.
- **Gratitude:** I take time to thank the Lord for the life he has given me, for my family, friends, health, education, and talents.
- **Bread for Others:** Just as the Lord is bread for me, I try to be a source of life for others. For example, I try to listen to their needs and respond to them.

Assignment

Reflect on one of the areas above. Which needs most improvement? Write out a specific plan of action for the next two weeks on what you can do to improve. Check every night on your progress.

infancy narratives
Stories in the Gospels of Matthew and Luke about the early life of Jesus.

Son of God
In the Old Testament, a title used for angels, kings, and others who had an intimate relationship with God. In the New Testament, through his actions and teachings, the title reveals the divinity of Jesus as the only Son of God.

Emmanuel
A name for Jesus that means "God is with us." Quoting Isaiah 7:14, Matthew uses Emmanuel to show that God's promise of deliverance is fulfilled in the birth of Jesus.

Son of David
A title for Jesus that indicates his ancestry can be traced to King David, as foretold in Scripture.

faith in the divinity of the Lord Jesus, to live Christ-like lives, and to spread the Gospel message of Salvation in Jesus Christ to the rest of the world.

Four Gospel Portraits of Jesus

The four Gospels are our primary source of knowledge about the birth, Life, Death, and Resurrection of Jesus Christ. They are the heart of the New Testament. Drawing on the testimony of eyewitnesses, they recount the saving deeds of our Lord. It is from them we learn that Jesus is the only Son of God, that he is the Lord God, our Savior, and the Messiah.

Each of the four Gospels begins the story of Jesus in a different way. The Gospel of Mark, the first Gospel written around the year AD 70, does not mention the birth of Jesus or any facts about his childhood or family life. Rather, Mark's Gospel begins by referring to a prophecy from Isaiah about a messenger coming to prepare the way of the Messiah. This messenger is John the Baptist, a distant relative of Jesus. John the Baptist preached that "One mightier than I is coming after me. I am not worthy to stoop and loosen the thongs of his sandals. I have baptized you with water; he will baptize you with the holy Spirit" (Mk 1:7–8). The opening of Mark's Gospel bridges the promises of the Old Testament with the commissioning of Jesus at his baptism in the Jordan River: "And a voice came from the heavens, 'You are

my beloved Son, with you I am well pleased'" (Mk 1:11).

In contrast to how Mark's Gospel begins with an adult Jesus, the Gospel of John, written between AD 90 and 100, begins before the creation of the world:

> In the beginning was the Word,
>   and the Word was with
>   God,
>   and the Word was God.
>   (Jn 1:1)

This verse hearkens back to the opening verse of the book of Genesis and the account of creation. The prologue in John's Gospel teaches that the Word of *God* is God and that "all things came to be through him, and without him nothing came to be" (Jn 1:3). Jesus is clearly divine, the Son of God, who took on human flesh to accomplish our Salvation.

The Gospel of Matthew (written around AD 80–85) and the Gospel of Luke (written around AD 85), both begin their Gospels with **infancy narratives**. Yet there are differences between the two. For example, Matthew reports Mary and Joseph living in Bethlehem at the time of Jesus' birth. He tells the story of the magi, Herod's killing of the baby boys, and the Holy Family's flight to Egypt. Matthew's Gospel also describes how Joseph returned with his family to Nazareth out of fear of the brutality of Herod's son, Archelaus, who was ruling in Judea at the time.

In contrast, Luke reports how Mary and Joseph were already living in Nazareth when they came to

Bethlehem to register for a Roman census. It was during this journey to Bethlehem that Jesus was born in a manger. After performing required religious duties in Jerusalem, the Holy Family peacefully returned to Nazareth.

The infancy narratives of Matthew and Luke have differences, but they also agree on several different points:

- Both Matthew and Luke use the infancy stories to highlight Jesus' identity.

- An angel foretold Jesus' birth in both accounts.

- Jesus is conceived by the action of the Holy Spirit. Thus, he is the **Son of God**. He is **Emmanuel**, "God is with us."

- He was born of the Virgin Mary, as was prophesied.

- Joseph, Jesus' foster father, was his legal father. Joseph was of the House of David; therefore, Jesus was truly a **Son of David**, as was promised.

- Jesus was born in Bethlehem, as prophesied in Micah 5:1.

The next sections provide an overview of the infancy narratives of Matthew and Luke and the prologue of John's Gospel.

The Infancy Narratives in Matthew's Gospel (Mt 1-2)

Matthew wrote his Gospel for a predominantly Jewish-Christian audience. One of his major concerns was to show how Jesus fulfilled God's promises to the Jews. His infancy stories accomplish this aim.

Genealogy (Mt 1:1-17)

The genealogy in Matthew links Jesus' ancestry to Abraham, the father of the Jews, and to King David, from whose dynasty the promised Messiah would come. This is meant to tell the reader how Jesus is the fulfillment of the Jewish hopes.

There are other lessons to be gleaned from the genealogy. For example, in his list of patriarchs

(from Abraham to David), Matthew includes cheaters and liars (Jacob and Judah). This reminds us how Jesus himself associated with sinners in his adult life. Matthew also mentions several women in his genealogy with questionable backgrounds. He lists Tamar (Gn 38) who had children by her father-in-law, Judah; Rahab, a prostitute in Jericho who helped Jewish spies (Jo 2); Ruth, a Moabite woman who made the God of her mother-in-law her own; and Bathsheba (2 Sm 11), Solomon's mother with whom David had earlier committed adultery.

By including sinners in the genealogy, Matthew is making the point of the marvelous way that God accomplishes his plan of Salvation. Later in the Gospel, John the Baptist would identify Jesus as God's Chosen One who would separate sinners from the just, as a farmer separates wheat and chaff with a winnowing fan (see Matthew 3:12). From his very origins, Jesus is the Suffering Servant "who silently allows himself to be led to the slaughter and who bears the sin of the multitudes, and also the Paschal Lamb, the symbol of Israel's redemption at the first Passover" (*CCC*, 608).

Birth of Jesus (Mt 1:18-25)

Jesus' birth is the result of divine action, the power of the Holy Spirit. He is both divine and human. Moreover, Isaiah prophesied his divine birth:

> "Behold, the virgin shall be with child and bear a son, and they shall call him Emmanuel," which means "God is with us." (Mt 1:23)

This is the first of five Old Testament prophecies that Matthew quotes in his infancy narratives. As mentioned, Matthew 2:6 cites the prophet Micah's prediction saying that the Messiah is to be born in Bethlehem. Also, Matthew 2:15 refers to Hosea's prophecy about being called out of Egypt; Matthew 2:18 recalls Jeremiah 31:15 and Rachel's weeping over her exiled descendants, a reference to Herod's slaughter of the infants; and Matthew 2:23 connects the town of Nazareth to prophetic statements in the Old Testament.

Joseph plays a key role in Matthew's genealogy. A descendant of David, he accepts the angel's message that Mary conceived by God's power. Joseph, a righteous man, takes Jesus as his own son, making him legally a Son of David. Finally, Joseph

gives his child the name Jesus. This is a most appropriate name because in Hebrew *Jesus* means "God saves." In the Person of the Son of God, God redeems us from sin.

Matthew's Jewish-Christian audience would have been familiar with the Old Testament patriarch Joseph, the son of Jacob. He was a famous interpreter of dreams who saved his family from famine in Egypt. Jesus' foster father, another Joseph, serves as an important link in the story of Salvation History. St. Joseph receives God's revelation about Jesus' origins in a dream and saves his family by taking them to Egypt.

Visit of the Magi (Mt 2:1-12)

The magi were visitors from the East, perhaps astrologers, who are meant to represent the Lord's willingness to accept Gentiles among those who worship him. They brought royal gifts of gold, frankincense, and myrrh. This scene at the beginning of Matthew's Gospel also foreshadows the end of the Gospel when the Risen Lord commands the Apostles to preach the Gospel to all nations, including the Gentiles (Mt 28:19). The visit of the magi "means that pagans can discover Jesus and worship him as the Son of God and Savior of the world only by turning toward the Jews and receiving from them the messianic promise as contained in the Old Testament" (*CCC*, 528). The Feast of the **Epiphany** celebrates the time when Jesus is manifested as the Messiah, the Son of God, and Savior of the world.

Epiphany
The feast that celebrates the mystery of Christ's manifestation as Savior of the world.

Flight into Egypt and Massacre of the Infants (Mt 2:13-18)

Matthew presents Jesus as the new Moses, the new Lawgiver. God used Moses to lead his people to freedom and to give the Law to the people on Mt. Sinai. God's Son, Jesus Christ, is the true liberator, the Savior who gives the New Law to his disciples in the Sermon on the Mount (Mt 5–7). Jesus' narrow escape from death as an infant at the hands of cruel leaders symbolizes Jesus' own future.

The incident in which Jesus escapes from the powers of evil brings to mind Moses' own narrow brush with death as an infant when a cruel pharaoh wanted to kill him (Ex 1–2). Herod's slaughter and the Holy Family's flight into Egypt reveal that from the beginning of Jesus' life, the forces of darkness were opposed to him—the "light of the world."

Jesus' "whole life was lived under the sign of persecution" (*CCC*, 530). No independent historical record reports King Herod's ordering such an atrocity at the time of Jesus' birth. However, it was very much in character for him to have done such a deed. Intensely jealous of his own power and authority, Herod did in fact kill some of his own children for fear that they would usurp his throne.

Investigating Jesus' Ancestry

1. Read Luke's version of Jesus' genealogy in Luke 3:23-38. Note at least two differences between it and Matthew's account (Mt 1:1-17).

2. Read and report on the story of one of these women mentioned in Matthew's version of Jesus' genealogy:

- Tamar—Genesis 38

- Rahab—Joshua 2

- Bathsheba—2 Samuel 11

Return to Nazareth (Mt 2:19-23)

At the Exodus, God delivered the Chosen People from Egypt. "Jesus' departure from Egypt recalls the exodus and presents him as the definitive liberator of God's people" (*CCC*, 530). As commanded by the angel, Joseph settles his family in the small town of Nazareth in Galilee, a northern province in the Holy Land that pious Jews considered to be contaminated by Gentile influence. It is from this territory that Matthew records Jesus embarking on his mission of proclaiming God's Kingdom.

The Infancy Narratives in Luke's Gospel (Lk 1-2)

Luke was a skilled writer and careful historian. Luke also wrote the Acts of the Apostles as a "part two" of his Gospel. He dedicated both of them to Theophilus, a name meaning "beloved of God." This person might have been a prominent Christian convert or Luke's patron. Some suggest the name might even be a symbol for any Christian who will read or hear Luke's Gospel.

Luke 1:1–14, the prologue to the Gospel, reveals that others had previously written about Jesus and that Luke is checking with eyewitnesses to write his own orderly account. Like Matthew's Gospel, one of Luke's likely sources was the Gospel of Mark. Luke and Matthew also drew on a common source of sayings called "Q" (from the German word *Quelle*, meaning "source"). This material represents both written and oral traditions. In addition, Luke had a source unique to him (often designated "L"), while Matthew had a source unique to him (often designated "M").

Luke and Matthew, writing in the same decade, probably did not know of each other's effort. This helps explain why they have different stories about the events surrounding Jesus' birth.

Announcement of John the Baptist's Birth (Lk 1:5-25)

Luke masterfully interweaves the announcement and births of Jesus and his cousin John the Baptist. Yet, in his narrative, Luke clearly shows that Jesus is the Messiah, not John. It is Jesus whose origins are divine.

John the Baptist's parents were Zechariah and Elizabeth, an older, childless couple. When Zechariah was in Jerusalem for his annual two-week duty as a priest, the angel Gabriel told him that his wife would conceive a child and that he was to name the child John. Zechariah was struck speechless for expressing doubt at the angel's revelation and asking for proof. He would later regain his speech when asked what his child should be named (Lk 1:64).

John the Baptist was a bridge person between the Old Testament and the New Testament. He was a New Elijah, announcing the coming of the promised Messiah. He was the immediate precursor and forerunner of Christ, the one to "prepare the way." John first recognized the coming of the Messiah when he leaped in his mother's womb when in the presence of the Blessed Mother who was pregnant with the Savior (Lk 1:44).

Announcement of the Birth of Jesus (Lk 1:26-38)

Six months after announcing the birth of John the Baptist, the angel Gabriel appeared to Mary, a virgin who was engaged to Joseph of the house of David. The angel greeted Mary with the words "Hail, favored one! The Lord is with you" (Lk 1:28). When informed that she was to conceive a child, a child who would be great, the Son of the Most High, Mary told the angel that she had not had sexual relations. The angel then told Mary she would conceive Jesus by the power of the Holy Spirit. With great humility and faith, Mary believed the angel and said, "Behold, I am the handmaid of the Lord. May it be done to me according to your word" (Lk 1:38). This event is known as the **Annunciation**.

Mary's yes to the angel's announcement thus began the time of the fulfillment of God's promises and preparations. She, a humble daughter of Israel, was the instrument God used to bring Christ into the world. The mission of many Old Testament holy women prepared the way for Mary. For example, Eve, despite her disobedience, was promised that a descendant would conquer Satan. Sarah conceived her child Isaac in old age. And God chose other powerless women to advance his salvific work: Hannah, Deborah, Ruth, Judith, Esther, and many others.

Mary, the Blessed Mother, is above them all. She cooperated with God's plan, even knowing that her yes might bring her ridicule and condemnation. God singled out Mary among women and gave her the graces necessary to cooperate with his plan. For example, Mary was conceived without Original Sin by virtue of the merits of her son, Jesus Christ, the Savior of the human race. This is known as the **Immaculate Conception**. This freedom from the effects of Original Sin and any personal sin, a total gift from God to his chosen one, enabled Mary to give the free assent of her faith to the announcement of her becoming truly the Mother of God.

Mary Visits Elizabeth (Lk 1:39-56)

Mary's compassionate concern for her aged relative prompted her to visit Elizabeth in a town in the province of Judah. After being greeted by Mary, Elizabeth immediately recognized the miracle of God's love that had taken place. With a heart bursting with joy, Elizabeth acknowledged that Mary is indeed the Mother of God:

> "Most blessed are you among women, and blessed is the fruit of your womb. And how does this happen to me, that the mother of my Lord should come to me?" (Lk 1:42–43)

Mary's response to Elizabeth is the famous canticle, the **Magnificat**. Her words echo those of Hannah, the mother of the prophet Samuel, who recited them after his birth due to God's intervention. In humility, Mary praises God as the source of blessedness. She praises his mercy for reversing normal human expectations, for raising up the lowly and overthrowing prideful and powerful people:

> The hungry he has filled with good things;
>> the rich he has sent away empty. (Lk 1:53)

Birth of John the Baptist (Lk 1:57-80)

When Zechariah is given his speech back at the time of his son's birth, the Holy Spirit inspired him to sing God's praises in a prayer known as the *Benedictus*. In it, Zechariah praises God for remembering the promises he made to David for the Salvation of the Jews. In the last part of the prayer, Zechariah speaks to his newborn son:

> And you, child, will be called prophet of the Most High,
>> for you will go before the Lord to prepare his ways,
> to give his people knowledge of salvation
>> through the forgiveness of sins. (Lk 1:76–77)

Birth of Jesus (Lk 2:1-20)

Bethlehem, the birthplace of David and Jesus, is about six miles south of Jerusalem. Because it was his ancestral home, Joseph took the expectant Mary there to enroll in a census. Jesus was born in a manger because of the lack of suitable lodgings; he was also wrapped in swaddling clothes. While Jesus' clothing emphasizes his humility and poverty, it might also suggest his royalty since Solomon, David's son, was wrapped in swaddling clothes (Wis 7:4–5).

The expression "first-born son" is a legal designation for a child who had special rights under the Law of Moses. It does not mean that Mary had other children.

The first people to visit Jesus are poor shepherds who were considered not respectable by the standards of pious Jews. The angels announce to them the coming of the Savior who is both Messiah and Lord. He will bring "peace to those on whom his favor rests" (Lk 2:14).

Annunciation
The announcement of the birth of Jesus that takes place when the angel Gabriel tells Mary that God has chosen her to be the Mother of the Lord.

Immaculate Conception
The belief that Mary was conceived without Original Sin. The Feast of the Immaculate Conception is on December 8.

Magnificat
The Latin title for the Canticle of Mary in Luke 1:46—55 that begins *Magnificat anima me Dominum* ("My soul proclaims the greatness of the Lord").

A major theme of Luke's Gospel is how Jesus came to preach to the lowly and outcast. These lowly shepherds are the first to broadcast news of Salvation to the Jews. Luke's Gospel later reports how Jesus uses humble fishermen and other outsiders to spread his Good News.

When Mary heard all the good things that were said about her son, she kept them in her heart, reflecting on their meaning. Her heartfelt reflection on God's Word is a model for Christians who want to learn how to pray.

Jesus' Circumcision and Presentation in the Temple (Lk 2:21-38)

Jesus' **circumcision** signified his incorporation into the Jewish people. It prefigures Jesus' lifelong submission to the Law and his willingness to worship in the faith of his ancestors. It is also prefigures Baptism, the sacrament that incorporates Christians into the Body of Christ.

After forty days, Mary and Joseph took the infant Jesus to the Temple for the rite of purification as specified by the Mosaic Law (see Leviticus 12). A sign of his family's poverty is that his parents offered a sacrifice of two turtledoves or young pigeons as the Law specified; these were the gift of poor people who could not afford the gift of a year-old lamb.

At his presentation in the Temple, the prophets Simeon and Anna recognize Jesus to be the long-expected Messiah, the first-born Son who belongs to the Lord. They bless God for being allowed to see him. They also predict the perfect sacrifice that the adult Jesus will endure for the Salvation of humanity ("the sword of sorrow that will pierce Mary's heart").

Finding of Jesus in the Temple (Lk 2:39-52)

Luke ends his infancy narrative by reporting how Jesus returned to Nazareth with Mary and Joseph where he lived in obedience to them. His obedience contrasts with Adam's disobedience to God. His living an ordinary life as a Jew of his time reveals the mystery of how the God-made-man identifies with us humans, especially in our ordinariness.

 Aiding the Homeless

The description of the Holy Family having to leave the Holy Land in search of a safe home and the boy Jesus being lost in the Temple reminds us to consider the plight of the homeless in our midst today. Consider doing one of the following:

- Locate a homeless shelter in your city. (Check with Catholic Charities in your diocese.) Volunteer your services, for example, by preparing or distributing meals or helping to organize a food drive to help stock the pantry.

- Contact the St. Vincent de Paul Society at your parish to ask for ways you can help.

- Sponsor a school or parish drive to collect personal hygiene items (for example, toothpaste and brushes, soap, shaving cream, etc.) to distribute at a homeless shelter.

- Investigate the work of the Covenant House, an agency that offers support to homeless youth, and ways you can get involved in its ministry.

When Jesus was twelve years old, he went to the Temple in Jerusalem with his parents for the Passover feast. When he was found missing on the caravan home, his distraught parents eventually found Jesus astounding the teachers in the Temple by his brilliant response to their questions. This prefigured the future day when he would again confound the learned scribes and rabbis, some of whom would plot his death.

When questioned by Mary as to why he remained in the city, Jesus replied, "Did you not know that I must be in my Father's house?" (Lk 2:49). Mary and Joseph did not fully understand the meaning of Jesus' words, but again Mary kept his words in her heart, prayerfully reflecting on their significance.

Luke's focus on both Temple and Jerusalem is another way his Gospel bridges the Old Testament with the New Testament. It is in the Temple that Simeon proclaims that Jesus would be the Savior for Jews and Gentiles alike. As a twelve-year-old, Jesus instructs the learned men in the Temple, and then, as an adult, he teaches in the Temple (Lk 19:47). And after Jesus' Resurrection, the disciples continue to worship there (Lk 24:53; Acts 3:1). Throughout his Gospel, Luke highlights Jesus' journey to Jerusalem, the holy city that "kills its prophets." It is in Jerusalem where Jesus' Passion, Death, and Resurrection accomplish our Salvation. And in this same city on Pentecost Sunday, the Holy Spirit descends on the Apostles and sends them to the ends of the world to proclaim Jesus as Lord and Savior.

The Incarnation in the Prologue to John's Gospel (Jn 1:1-18)

Matthew and Luke begin their Gospels with the birth of Christ. John, on the other hand, starts his Gospel from before the beginning of the world. He brilliantly retells the Genesis story about creation by clearly showing how creation came about through the Word of God:

> All things came to be through him,
>> and without him nothing came to be. (Jn 1:3)

The Word of God *is* God (Jn 1:1) and

> What came to be through him was life,
> and this life was the light of the human race.
> (Jn 1:3–4)

John's Gospel then offers the earth-shaking truth: this very Word of God became man in the Person of Jesus Christ. This is known as the **Incarnation**. John chose this word to emphasize that at the appointed time, the only Son of the Father, the eternal Word, assumed our human nature—both body (flesh) and soul—and became man in order to accomplish our Salvation in that same human nature.

The Incarnation is a **dogma** of our faith. Its source is in Divine Revelation; we know it to be true because God revealed it to us:

circumcision
A sign of incorporation into Judaism. Jesus is circumcised on the eighth day after his birth as a sign of his submission to the Law.

Incarnation
The dogma that God's eternal Son assumed a human nature and became man in Jesus Christ to save us from our sins. The term literally means "taking on human flesh."

dogma
A central truth of Revelation that Catholics are obliged to believe.

> And the Word became flesh
>   and made his dwelling among us,
>   and we saw his glory,
>   the glory as of the Father's only Son,
>   full of grace and truth. (Jn 1:14)

The Incarnation reveals to us that Jesus Christ, who is the Son of God and the second Person of the Blessed Trinity, is both true God and true man. "He is truly the Son of God who, without ceasing to be God and Lord, became a man and our brother" (*CCC*, 469).

John's prologue tells us that John the Baptist came to testify to Jesus Christ, the Messiah, who was the light that came into the world. Though he came into the world, and the world came to be through him, many, including his own people, failed to recognize him (Jn 1:10–11). But to those who did recognize him, he enabled them to become children of God (Jn 12) and gave them grace and truth (Jn 17). Jesus Christ came to save us and to reveal his Father to us: "The only Son, God, who is at the Father's side, has revealed him" (Jn 1:18).

The Purpose of the Incarnation (*CCC*, 456-460)

The masterful prologue to the Gospel of John includes many marvelous truths of our faith. The *Catechism of the Catholic Church* explains more fully what the Gospel reveals about the Word of God. The Word became flesh:

- "*To save us by reconciling us with God*, 'who loved us and sent his Son to be the expiation for our sins'" (*CCC*, 457). Jesus came to be our Savior, to take away our sins.

- "*So . . . we might know God's love*" (*CCC*, 458). In one of the most famous verses in the entire Bible, John proclaims:

> For God so loved the world that he gave his only Son, so that everyone who believes in him might not perish but might have eternal life. (Jn 3:16)

EXPLAINING THE FAITH

Why is Jesus' birth celebrated on December 25?

Neither the infancy narratives in the Gospels of Matthew or Luke name the date of Jesus' birth. There is no way to be exactly sure the date on which he was born. However, by AD 336, the Church officially marked the birth of Christ on December 25. It may have been celebrated on that date for years before. The tradition certainly spread after 336 throughout the Church and the world.

How did December 25 become the date chosen for Christ's birthday? One reason is that December 25 is near the winter solstice. The Romans observed a holiday for that occasion called Saturnalia from December 17 to 23. December 25 offered a good chance to counter this pagan festival with an important religious celebration.

Also, by the fourth century, March 25 had already been established as the date of the Annunciation, the conception of Jesus. Celebrating the birth of Jesus nine months later was a logical next step.

This verse has been called the "Gospel in miniature," since it tells us that our God is a God of love. God shows this love by sending us his Son to save us. If we believe in him, we will not perish. But he will give us eternal life! Indeed this is good news—truly great news!

- "*To be our model of holiness*" (*CCC*, 459). By taking on flesh, Jesus, the Second Person of the Blessed Trinity, gives us the opportunity to imitate and become more like him, God who is all holy. Again, John's Gospel gives us an important saying of Jesus: "I am the way and the truth and the life. No one comes to the Father except through me" (Jn 14:6). By Jesus' life, Death, and Resurrection, he has shown us the very meaning of what love is. And he instructs us to imitate him:

> Love one another as I love you. No one has greater love than this, to lay down one's life for one's friends. You are my friends if you do what I command you. (Jn 15:12–14)

- *To make us "partakers of the divine nature"* (*CCC*, 460). Christ became man to adopt us into the divine family by the power of the Holy Spirit. St. Athanasius expressed it this way: "For the Son of God became man so that we might become God."

Finally, recall the Protoevangelium where God promised that a descendant of Adam and Eve will crush the head of the serpent, that is, destroy the power of Satan.

> I will put enmity between you and the woman, and between your offspring and hers; He will strike at your head, while you strike at his heel. (Gn 3:15)

On two occasions in John's Gospel, Jesus addresses his mother as "Woman," a reference to the Protoevangelium (see Jn 2:1–5 and 19:26). He is the offspring of the Woman who is the new Eve—Mary. It is he who came to destroy the power of the devil. The Paschal Mystery of his Death and Resurrection

accomplished this very thing: "Indeed, the Son of God was revealed to destroy the works of the devil" (1 Jn 3:8).

For Review

1. When was Jesus likely born?
2. What is "the crowning truth of our faith in Christ"?
3. What is the primary source of our knowledge about Jesus Christ?
4. Give the approximate dates for the writing of the four Gospels.
5. Contrast the beginnings of Mark's and John's Gospels.
6. List elements that the infancy narratives in Matthew and Luke have in common.
7. Discuss how three Old Testament prophecies are fulfilled in Matthew's infancy narrative.
8. Discuss two things that Jesus' genealogy in Matthew's Gospel reveals about him.
9. How is St. Joseph like the Old Testament patriarch of the same name?
10. What is the meaning of the name Jesus?
11. How is Jesus the New Moses?
12. What Old Testament event is recalled in the Holy Family's return to Nazareth from Egypt?
13. What sources did Luke use in the writing of his Gospel?
14. Identify Theophilus.
15. What can we learn from Mary's response to Gabriel's announcement that she was to be the Mother of God?
16. What is evidence that Jesus was born in humility and poverty?
17. What is the meaning of Jesus' circumcision and Presentation in the Temple?

18. Identify Simeon and Anna.

19. What is the significance of Jesus' experience at the Temple at age twelve?

20. According to the prologue of John's Gospel, what role did the Word of God play in creation?

21. Discuss at least three reasons for God becoming man in Jesus Christ.

For Reflection

• Write a short personality sketch about any two of your ancestors. Comment on how you might be like them.

• What do you think Jesus might have been like as a teenager? Include some insights on how he might be like *you*. Mention some other qualities he would have that might set him apart from his peers.

• What do each of the elements of John 3:16 mean to you?

Learning from the Life of Christ (*CCC*, 512–518)

Modern biographies seem to treat every imaginable aspect of a person's life story. The Gospels are not like that. For example, the Gospels do not tell us what Jesus looked like—how tall he was, the color of his hair or eyes, a description of his face or his smile, the length of his hair. Furthermore, the Gospels reveal little about Jesus' hidden life, that is, the years from his birth until he came on to the public scene at his baptism. Except for this one incident when Jesus was twelve years old, all the Gospels focus on Jesus' public ministry, which began when he was around thirty years of age.

Even though the public ministry of Jesus forms the primary focus of the Gospels, there are even events in his life in those years that are not treated: "But these are written that you may [come to] believe that Jesus is the Messiah, the Son of God, and that through this belief you may have life in his name" (Jn 20:31).

The Evangelists' belief in Jesus moved them to want to share their faith with others. Knowing who Jesus is as the Son of God and Savior of the world, they saw and were able to help others see how the mystery of Salvation takes place in every aspect of Jesus' life. "His deeds, miracles, and words all revealed that 'in him the whole fullness of deity dwells bodily'(Col 2:9)" (*CCC*, 215). Jesus' humanity pointed to the invisible mystery of who he is as God's Son and the reason he came—to redeem us.

Therefore, every aspect of Christ's earthly life—his words and deeds, silences and sufferings, his way of being and speaking—is a Revelation of the Father. As God the Father instructed Peter, James, and John on the mountain at the time of Jesus' Transfiguration, "This is my chosen Son; listen to him" (Lk 9:35). Or as Jesus told Philip at the Last Supper, "Whoever has seen me has seen the Father"

(Jn 14:9). Because Jesus is God's Revelation, *everything* about Christ's life reported in the Gospels has profound meaning. From the smallest detail to the most awe-inspiring miracles, we learn about God's great love revealed to us in his Son, Jesus Christ.

The *Catechism of the Catholic Church* reiterates that Christ's whole life is a mystery of Redemption. Although Christ redeems us above all else through his sacrifice of blood on the cross, the mystery of Redemption takes place throughout our Lord's entire life. For example,

- in his Incarnation through which by becoming poor he enriches us with his poverty;
- in his hidden life we learn how his obedience to his parents atones for our disobedience;
- in his preaching he tells us of the ways of God and purifies our consciences;
- in curing the sick and driving out demons, he fulfilled the prophecy of Isaiah who said about the Messiah: "He took away our infirmities and bore our diseases" (Mt 8:17 quoting Is 53:4);
- through his Cross and Resurrection he justifies us (*CCC*, 517).

Every aspect of Christ's life: his words, his deeds, his sufferings had one purpose: to restore humanity to the original vocation that God had for us—intimacy with God as his children. The next sections address some of the mysteries of the early part of Christ's ministry—his baptism and temptations in the desert—to learn how they help reveal the mystery of Salvation. Chapter 4 presents some of the saving actions and words of Jesus during the rest of his public life up to the time of his arrest.

The Baptism of Jesus (Mk 1:2-11; Mt 3:1-17; Lk 3:1-20; Jn 1:19-34)

Jesus' baptism is linked to the figure of John the Baptist, a relative of Jesus. John the Baptist was also a prophet and a precursor of Jesus, the Messiah. John the Baptist came on the scene around AD 28 (the fifteenth year of the reign of the emperor, Tiberius, see Lk 3:1) to preach a message of repentance in preparation for God's judgment on a sinful humanity. John instructed his hearers to share with the poor; he told tax collectors to be fair in their dealings; he challenged soldiers to be gentle and content with their salaries. And he warned sinners of God's coming judgment, calling on them to repent and be baptized as a sign of their turning away from sin.

The Gospels compare John the Baptist to the Old Testament prophet, Elijah. Like Elijah, John wore a garment of camel skin and a leather belt and ate grasshoppers and wild honey for food. Jesus himself identified John the Baptist as the new Elijah, the one prophesied to usher in the Messianic age (Mt 11:14). John the Baptist attracted many followers. They asked him if he was the Messiah. John's response was, "I am baptizing you with water, but one mightier than I is coming. I am not worthy to loosen the thongs of his sandals. He will baptize you with the holy Spirit and fire" (Lk 3:16). This someone, of course, was Jesus Christ, the true Messiah.

John the Baptist was a forceful, charismatic person. Many people came from all over Palestine to hear his message. John baptized in the Jordan River, a symbol of Jewish freedom and the point of entry into the Promised Land after forty years of wandering and suffering in the Sinai desert after the Exodus. Through baptism in the Jordan, John's followers showed that they were willing to walk the path of their ancestors in the faith. They were willing to turn from self-centered sinfulness to hear once again and obey God's word. John's baptism was a public sign of repentance in preparation for the coming of the Messiah.

Jesus himself heard of John's preaching and traveled from Galilee to the Judean wilderness to hear John for himself and to be baptized by him. By doing so, he took on the identity of his people. By submitting to John's baptism, Jesus permitted himself to be numbered among sinners, identifying with us in our spiritual need. Above all else, the mystery of Jesus' baptism displays his humility. From the beginning of his mission of preaching and healing, the Lord accepted the role of God's Suffering Servant.

In one form or another, all four Gospels include the following phenomena that took place at Jesus' baptism:

- *The sky opens*, thus revealing that God has come to meet his people through his Son, Jesus Christ. Our Lord's mission is about to begin.

- *A dove descends from the sky.* The dove signifies the coming of the Holy Spirit. It is a symbol of joy, innocence, freedom, power, and peace. In this new era, the presence of the Holy Spirit will be with Jesus as he launches his public ministry.

- *A voice proclaims, "You are my beloved Son"* (Mk 1:11). Thus two Old Testament prophecies are fulfilled. Psalm 2:7 promised the coming of the anointed-king, the Messiah; and the prophet Isaiah told about the Servant who will suffer on our behalf:

  I will proclaim the decree of the Lord,
      who said to me, "You are my son;
      today I am your father." (Ps 2:7)

  Here is my servant whom I uphold,
      my chosen one with whom I am pleased,

  Upon whom I have put my spirit;
      he shall bring forth justice to the nations.
      (Is 42:1)
  Yet it was our infirmities that he bore,
      our sufferings that he endured. (Is 53:4)

The baptism of Jesus reveals the following important theological truths by:

- showing Jesus' perfect submission to his Father's will,

- foreshadowing Jesus' death for the remission of our sins, and

- serving as a model for our own baptism.

Christ's baptism reveals his identity and his mission. He is about his Father's work of Salvation,

which is accomplished by the power of the Holy Spirit. His baptism also foreshadows Christian Baptism, which is done in the name of the Father, and the Son, and the Holy Spirit. Our own Baptism enables us to participate in our Lord's work of healing and reconciliation. The Sacrament of Baptism also joins us to the Catholic Church by plunging us into the waters with Christ so that we may rise with him, be reborn in the Holy Spirit, and be adopted into God's family.

The Temptations of Jesus (Mt 4:1-11)

The three Synoptic Gospels—Matthew, Mark, and Luke—all report that Jesus retreated to the Judean wilderness after his baptism and before embarking on his public ministry. As Mark's Gospel states, "At once the Spirit drove him out into the desert, and he remained in the desert for forty days, tempted by Satan. He was among wild beasts, and the angels ministered to him" (Mk 1:12–13). Matthew and Luke fill in the details of Mark's brief statement by telling us Satan tempted Jesus three times. The three temptations of Jesus recall the temptations of the Chosen People when they wandered in the desert for forty years. By undergoing a similar three-fold test, Jesus Christ was able to bring the history of his people to a perfect conclusion.

First Temptation

Satan first tempts Jesus to turn stones into loaves of bread. This brings to mind the Chosen People's desire to turn back to the safety of slavery in Egypt because they were hungry while wandering in the desert. Though free, they longed for security and safety. In Jesus' case, his hunger would not turn him away from doing God's will. He did not have a divided heart. His steadfastness in pursuing his mission was rooted in "every word that comes forth from the mouth of God" (Mt 4:1).

ST. JOHN THE BAPTIST

St. John the Baptist, the forerunner of Jesus and his relative, lived an **ascetic** life and preached in the Jordan region that Israel's judgment was at hand. He stripped the message of his Jewish ancestors to the basics, proclaiming a baptism for the repentance of sins. He offered his followers a baptism in water that was intended as a symbol of the washing away of their sins. When Jesus arrived at the banks of the river for baptism, John humbled himself and acknowledged Jesus as the Messiah. Jesus counted John as the last and among the greatest of the prophets. Though most of John's followers became disciples of Jesus, some continued independently. Disciples of John are cited in Acts of the Apostles 19:1–4, as Paul ministered in Ephesus.

What were the origins of John's ministry? At the time of Christ there were several branches of Judaism that were apart from the Sadducees and Pharisees, two branches mentioned often in the Gospels. The Dead Sea Scrolls, for example, helped to shed information on an apocalyptic group known as the Essenes, who believed that God would usher in his Kingdom through a dramatic, even catastrophic event. The Essenes withdrew from life to the Qumran area near the northwest shore of the Dead Sea. As celibates who did not marry, they shared goods in common and tried to be ritually pure by frequent washings throughout the day. There is a possibility that John the Baptist was part of the Essene community or another similar group of Judaism.

For certain, John the Baptist understood his role in relationship to Christ. When he saw Jesus coming toward him at the river John said,

> Behold, the Lamb of God, who takes away the sin of the world. He is the one of whom I said, "A man is coming after me who ranks ahead of me because he existed before me." I did not know him, but the reason why I came baptizing with water was that he might be made known to Israel. (Jn 1:30)

ascetic
A form of strict self-denial as a means of spiritual discipline. Christian ascetics imitate Christ's life of self-sacrifice in order to live the Gospel more faithfully.

John had already told his disciples that he would be "unworthy to untie" Jesus' sandal straps. The respect between John and Jesus was mutual. Jesus said of him: "Among those born of women there has been none greater than John the Baptist; yet the least in the kingdom is greater than he" (Mt 11:11).

Herod Antipas had John arrested and imprisoned at Machaerus Fortress on the Dead Sea when John spoke against Herod's adulterous marriage. John was beheaded at the request of Salome, the daughter of Herodias, Herod's wife.

The Feast Day of St. John the Baptist is June 24. The feast of his beheading is on August 29.

Faithful Disciple

Second Temptation

Next, Satan challenges Jesus to throw himself down from the Temple's pinnacle, thus endangering his life. Here Jesus is tempted to preserve himself from destruction, to test God's love for him while pursuing his mission. At the heart of Jesus' temptation is whether he would continue to love God even at the risk of death. Would he stay faithful to his mission despite suffering and pain that will come his way? Jesus' faithful answer to the devil was, "You shall not put the Lord, your God, to the test" (Mt 4:7). Trust in God's love, despite obstacles, will be the hallmark of Jesus' ministry.

Third Temptation

The third temptation is to power and wealth. The devil offers Jesus the kingdoms of the world if he will worship him. Jesus rejects the easy, pleasurable, popular way. He is committed to be faithful to God at all times. Only God is worthy of our worship. Jesus rebukes Satan by saying, "The Lord, your God, shall you worship and him alone shall you serve" (Mt 4:10).

Jesus' temptations in the desert prefigure certain temptations he would face in his public ministry. His heart was undivided in preaching the Gospel, despite the temptation to settle down and live a life of leisure. He was willing to offer his life for all humans rather than to flee from suffering and a cruel death. He put his Father's will above everything as he lived a life of poverty and rejected every effort to make him a worldly king.

Jesus undoubtedly related his temptations to his disciples, telling them that they would also be tempted. Temptation is not a sin but a trial or a test. Temptation forces us to respond, to show what we will do in a given situation. In his letter to the Galatians, St. Paul warns us to be watchful and avoid temptations. In the Lord's Prayer, Jesus instructs us to ask God that we not be led into temptation. The reason is simple, "The spirit is willing but the flesh is weak" (Mk 14:38).

However, the truth is that as Christ's followers, we *will* be tempted. We will be asked to take the easy way out, to seek pleasure rather than to do God's will. Society will tempt us to worship money or power or prestige or sex outside of marriage rather than to serve God and obey his Law. We will be tempted to look out for ourselves first and neglect the needs of the ones we love or the weak and helpless in our midst.

We can turn to Jesus when we are tempted because he can identify with us. Jesus, our Suffering Servant, has conquered Satan, the tempter, for us and for our Salvation. The Letter to the Hebrews reminds us,

---

 True Values

By resisting Satan's temptations, Jesus revealed his true values. Examine how well you share two of his values by reading the Scripture quotations below and responding to the questions.

1. *Every person is sacred.* Jesus stayed true to his mission. He offered his life for every human being. He teaches that God cares about everything (Mt 10:29-31). Our loving God does not want a single person to be lost (Mt 18:10-14).

   • How do you treat others when you meet them—more as strangers or as brothers and sisters in Christ?

2. *Know what is important.* Jesus came to do God's will. Nothing would deter him (Lk 9:62 and Mt 6:19-24).

   • Rate your commitment to do God's will on a scale of 1 to 10, with 10 being "most committed." Explain your rating.

For we do not have a high priest who is unable to sympathize with our weaknesses, but one who has similarly been tested in every way, yet without sin. So let us confidently approach the throne of grace to receive mercy and to find grace for timely help. (Hb 4:15–16)

Jesus' fidelity to the Father in the desert contrasts with the Chosen People who gave into sensuality in the desert and worshipped false gods in the form of statues. Jesus is the New Israel. He is also the New Adam. Unlike our first parents, he ignored the enticements of the devil. Decisively conquering Satan, Jesus' victory in the desert foreshadowed the ultimate victory he won through the Paschal Mystery of his Passion, Death, and Resurrection.

Jesus faced temptation and set his ministry on the path of gentle, compassionate service of others. Jesus kept on the path of truth and love and invites his friends to believe in him and walk with him. His way of love and obedience to God is tough and demanding. It contrasts with Satan's easy enticements, but it is the only way to proceed in truth and righteousness.

For Review

1. What was the main criterion the Evangelists used in including certain details of Christ's life in the writing of their Gospels?

2. Why is everything in the life of Christ significant?

3. What is significant about John the Baptist baptizing in the Jordan River?

4. What were the three events that took place at Jesus' baptism? What did each mean?

5. What theological truths are revealed at Jesus' baptism?

6. What happens when Christians receive the sacrament of Baptism?

7. How do Jesus' temptations reveal him as the New Israel and the New Adam?

For Reflection

- Jesus asked "Who do the crowds say that I am? (Lk 9:19)." Why do you believe they may have made this identification?

- Think of temptation in the terms of this formula:

  temptation = desire + opportunity
  For example, when taking a test, you want to do well (the desire) and you sit next to a smart classmate (opportunity). The temptation to cheat from your classmate is not a sin, but it can turn into sin if you follow this formula:

  sin = desire + opportunity + action
  Analyze three common temptations to sin that have troubled you in the past. Write out your temptations as in the formula above. Discuss one way you can resist each of the temptations you diagrammed.

The Beginning of Jesus' Ministry (CCC, 541-546; 567)

Both Mark 1:14–20 and Matthew 4:12–25 report that Jesus began to preach after John the Baptist was arrested. His preaching took place in Galilee, and its theme is summarized in this simple verse: "This is the time of fulfillment. The kingdom of God is at hand. Repent, and believe in the gospel" (Mk 1:14–15). This chapter concludes with a brief treatment of how the Gospels report the beginning of Jesus' public ministry. Chapter 4 will then review the major themes of Jesus' preaching ministry, discuss his miracles, and explain why the authorities plotted his Death.

Coming of God's Kingdom

The central theme in Jesus' preaching is simply the coming of the **Kingdom of God.** This important expression refers to God's rule or reign, "of righteousness, peace, and joy in the holy Spirit" (Rom 14:17). Jesus is the principal agent of the Kingdom. He ushers in the Kingdom with his words and deeds, and by sending out his disciples to call people to himself. The Paschal Mystery of the Lord's Death and Resurrection accomplishes once and for all the coming of God's Kingdom. Today, the Kingdom remains in our midst in the Eucharist. And the Holy Spirit forms God's people into the Church, in which the Kingdom of God is mysteriously present. It will be fully established at the Second Coming of Jesus Christ who will hand it over to his Father.

As Chapter 4 points out in more detail, Jesus demonstrated in word (including in his parables) and in deed (including his miracles) that the Kingdom of God is that of a loving, merciful Father who embraces everyone, including poor people and sinners. God's Kingdom is a free gift that we cannot earn. However, to gain entrance into the Kingdom, we must repent of our sins, believe in Jesus Christ, and respond to others in love by imitating the Lord himself and following the inspirations of the Holy Spirit.

From the very start of his ministry he chose Apostles—Simon (Peter) and his brother Andrew and two other brothers, James and John, the sons of a man named Zebedee to preach God's Kingdom. Jesus would form these men to carry on his work after his Ascension into Heaven. He would build his Church on them and give them and their successors—the Holy Father and the bishops—the authority to forgive sins in his name, to teach in matters of doctrine, and to guide God's People in morality and Christian living. The Church Jesus would later found is the Body of Christ and the Temple of the Holy Spirit. It is the seed and beginning of God's Kingdom.

Teaching with Authority

Luke reports that Jesus began his public life by teaching in the synagogues of Galilee. At the beginning of his ministry, Jesus went to his own **synagogue** in Nazareth. He did one of the Sabbath readings, the one from Isaiah 61:1ff, which prophesied the coming of the Messiah:

"The Spirit of the Lord is upon me
   because he has anointed me
   to bring glad tidings to the poor.
He has sent me to proclaim liberty to captives
   and recovery of sight to the blind,
     to let the oppressed go free,
   and to proclaim a year acceptable to the Lord." (Lk 4:18–19 quoting Is 61 ff.)

At first, his townsfolk marveled at Jesus' dramatic reading of this famous prophecy. However, when he applied it to himself by saying that he was the fulfillment of the passage, the people became irate. They wondered aloud how could the Messiah be so ordinary, the son of a neighbor, the carpenter Joseph. Jesus remarked that a prophet is honored everywhere but in his own hometown. So incensed were the people, they tried to lead him to a cliff and throw him off. This passage foreshadows the rest of Jesus' public life: At first, people accept him. However, later, Christ is rejected and killed in Jerusalem.

Call of Disciples

Coming immediately after the prologue, John 1:19–2:12 also presents deep theological insight into the Person of Jesus. John the Baptist is named as a primary witness to Jesus' identity: "Behold, the Lamb of God, who takes away the sin of the world" (Jn 1:29). John's Gospel also reveals that some

Kingdom of God
The reign of God proclaimed by Jesus and begun in his Life, Death, and Resurrection. It refers to the process of God's reconciling and renewing all things through his Son and his will being done on earth as it is in Heaven. The process has begun with Jesus in the Church and will be perfectly completed at the end of time.

synagogue
A meeting place for study and prayer.

of Jesus' earliest disciples were originally followers of John the Baptist. Andrew and another disciple heard John call Jesus the "Lamb of God." When Andrew's brother Simon went to see Jesus, the Lord changed his name to Cephas, which means Peter.

When Jesus returned to Galilee, he met Philip and asked him to be a disciple. Philip joyfully told his friend, Nathanael, that Jesus, the son of Joseph, from Nazareth, was the promised Messiah. Nathanael sarcastically responded, "Can anything good come from Nazareth?" He, like many of his contemporaries, did not expect God to come to them through an ordinary carpenter from a small, insignificant place like Nazareth.

When Jesus met Nathanael and told him that he had seen him sitting under a fig tree, Nathanael was startled but inspired to proclaim, "Rabbi, you are the Son of God; you are the King of Israel" (Jn 1:49). The Lord said,

> Do you believe because I told you that I saw you under the fig tree? You will see greater things than this. . . .You will see the sky opened and the angels of God ascending and descending on the Son of Man. (Jn 1:50–51)

Wedding at Cana

John's Gospel is organized around seven "signs" or miracles that reveal who Jesus is. The first took place at a wedding feast in Cana, before Jesus began his public preaching. Mary, Jesus' mother, informed him the hosts had run out of wine. Mary was likely sensitive to the virtue of hospitality and the great shame that would befall the hosts if they were unable to provide refreshment for their guests.

Mary displayed here simple and confident faith that Jesus would help the host family, even though he told his mother that his time to manifest himself openly had not yet come. "My hour has not yet come" refers to Jesus' Passion, Death, Resurrection, and Glorification when his real glory would be

manifested. The sign he would perform at Cana, the changing of water to wine, like all the other signs in John's Gospel, point to the Paschal Mystery, the climax of his heavenly mission of surrendering his life so that all humanity might gain eternal life (Jn 3:16).

In this first sign, there are clear references to three sacraments. Jesus' attendance at a wedding feast shows that he was in touch with ordinary people and enjoyed a good celebration. But this celebration is a wedding, which celebrates human love and new life. The Lord's attendance at this wedding blesses marriage as a sacrament of divine love. The Sacrament of Matrimony signifies the union of Christ and the Church and it gives spouses the grace to love each other with the love Christ has for the Church. The miracle Christ performed at Cana involved transforming jugs of water. The water in them was used for cleansing oneself before eating the meal. They symbolize the waters of the sacrament of Baptism, the purifying waters that cleanse us of sin and bring us new life in Christ. Finally, wine—which, at the Last Supper, Jesus changes into his own blood—points to the Eucharist. It brings spiritual life, that is, communion with Jesus, our Lord and Savior.

John's first sign also reveals a caring Jesus, who has power over nature. It also shows the influence of his mother who intercedes on behalf of others. His loving response to his mother's request shows that he is in touch with people and is willing to act with authority as the situation demands.

For Review

1. Define Kingdom of God.

2. What did Jesus proclaim in the synagogue in Nazareth? Why did people reject him?

3. Explain three ways the prophecy of Isaiah quoted in Luke 4:18–19 applies to Jesus Christ.

4. Summarize John the Baptist's testimony about Jesus.

5. What does Jesus tell Nathanael that he will witness? What does it mean?

6. What is the meaning of the miracle at Cana?

For Reflection

At first, Nathanael misjudged Jesus. When was a time when you made a false judgment about someone because of some external detail? Comment on how you were able to come to a proper judgment about the person.

Main Ideas

- The four Gospels are the primary source of knowledge about the birth, Life, Death, and Resurrection of Jesus Christ. (p. 56)

- The Gospels of Matthew and Luke begin with infancy narratives. Mark's Gospel begins with the adult ministry of Jesus. John's Gospel begins before the creation of the world. (pp. 58–59)

- Matthew's and Luke's infancy narratives have differences and similarities, with much of their perspectives based on the audiences they were writing for. (p. 59)

- Matthew, writing for a Jewish audience, links Jesus' ancestry to Abraham, the father of the Jews, and other parts of the infancy narrative to events in Jewish history. (p. 59)

- Luke's infancy narrative begins through the eyes of Mary, who is greeted by the angel Gabriel with the announcement that she will conceive and bear God's Son. (pp. 61–63)

- A major focus of Luke's Gospel, including his infancy narrative, is how Jesus came to preach to the lowly and outcast. (pp. 63–64)

- Another theme common to Luke's infancy narrative and the rest of his Gospel is Jesus' journey to Jerusalem, the city where his Passion, Death, and Resurrection accomplish our Salvation. (pp. 64–65)

- The prologue of John's Gospel teaches that the Word of God *is* Jesus in the flesh. (p. 65)

- The purpose of the Incarnation is for Jesus to win our Salvation so that we might know God's love, to be our model of holiness, and to make us "partakers of the divine nature." (pp. 66–67)

- The entirety of Christ's life is worthy of our study because he is the Revelation of God the Father. (pp. 68–69)

- The mysteries of the early part of Christ's ministry—including his baptism and temptations in the desert—help to reveal more about the mystery of our Salvation. (pp. 69–70)

Terms, People, Places

Use complete sentences to answer the following questions.

1. According to the infancy narratives, what are two possible ways that Mary and Joseph came to Bethlehem for Jesus' birth?

2. Why was it important for Matthew to document in his Gospel that Jesus is the Son of David?

3. What does the Feast of the Epiphany celebrate?

4. How do the Annunciation accounts differ between Matthew's and Luke's Gospels?

5. How does the prologue of the Gospel of John highlight the purpose of the Incarnation?

Primary Source Quotations

Birth of the Lord
The Virgin today brings into the world
the Eternal
And the earth offers a cave to the
Inaccessible.
The angels and shepherds praise him
And the magi advance with the star,
For you are born for us,
Little Child, God eternal!
  —*Kontakion* of Romanos the Melodist

The Way of Salvation
To become a child in relation to God is
the condition for entering the kingdom.
—*Catechism of the Catholic Church*, 526

By a Carpenter humankind was
made, and only by that Carpenter can
humankind be remade.
                    —Desiderius Erasmus

Instructions from the Wedding at Cana
His mother said to the servers, "Do
whatever he tells you."
                    —Mary, Mother of God,
                      quoted in John 2:5

Read Simeon's prophecy about Jesus' destiny (Lk 2:34–35). Discuss how this prophecy would eventually be fulfilled.

Ongoing Assignments

As you cover the material in this chapter, choose and complete at least three of these assignments.

1. Research ten quotations about Jesus spoken by famous people. Reproduce them in an attractive format and present them to the class.

2. Create a PowerPoint presentation on some aspect of one of these biblical places mentioned in the Bible.
   - Bethlehem
   - Capernaum
   - Nazareth
   - Cana

3. Write a report on what Josephus, the Jewish historian, said about the death of John the Baptist.

4. Write a commentary on the essay "Jerusalem at the Time of Jesus" (St. Anthony Messenger Press) by Fr. Jerome Murphy-O'Connor.

5. Report on some aspect of daily life in the time of Jesus.

6. Where did Jesus travel in the early years of his ministry? Research the issue and draw a map that depicts the footsteps of Jesus.

7. Prepare a report on scientific theories that attempt to explain the star of Bethlehem at the time of Jesus' birth.

8. Read the following passages from John's Gospel. Make a list of what Jesus reveals about himself. John 6:35, 41, 48–51; 8:12; 9:5; 10:7, 9; 10:11, 14; 11:25; 14:6; 15:1, 5.

9. Report on Jewish wedding customs at the time of Jesus.

10. Report on the death of John the Baptist by reading Mark 6:17–29 and Matthew 14:3–12. Who did Herod think Jesus was (Mt 14:1–2; Mk 6:16)? Include with your report a classical painting that depicts John the Baptist's death.

11. Research and report on information about the National Shrine of the Immaculate Conception. Include a sample of some Marian prayers. Name and explain your favorite prayers.

Prayer

When Mary heard the news that she was to be the Mother of God, she prayed the following prayer, the Magnificat. This prayer teaches the true meaning of humility and doing God's will. Pray it with confidence and faith in God's goodness.

Magnificat
My soul proclaims the greatness of
   the Lord,
My spirit rejoices in God my Savior,
for he has looked with favor on his
   lowly servant.
From this day all generations will
   call me blessed:
the Almighty has done great things
   for me,
and holy is his Name.
He has mercy on those who fear him
in every generation.
He has shown the strength of
   his arm,
he has scattered the proud in
   their conceit.
He has cast down the mighty from
   their throne,
and has lifted up the lowly.
He has filled the hungry with
   good things,
and the rich he has sent away empty.
He has come to the help of his
   servant Israel
for he has remembered his promise
   of mercy,
the promise he made to our fathers,
to Abraham and his children forever.
Glory to the Father and to the Son
   and to the Holy Spirit,

as it was in the beginning, is now,
    and will be forever. Amen.

- *Reflection*: Jesus has exalted you, too. You are great in his eyes.

- *Resolution*: Think of one thing you can do for Jesus this week to thank him for the gift of his friendship. Be sure to follow through on your promise.

THE MINISTRY AND MESSAGE OF JESUS CHRIST

As for you, do not seek what you are to eat and what you are to drink, and do not worry anymore. . . . Instead, seek his kingdom, and these other things will be given you besides. Do not be afraid any longer, little flock, for your Father is pleased to give you the kingdom.

—Luke 12:29, 31-32

What Is Really Important

William Randolph Hearst, the early-twentieth-century newspaper tycoon, was fabulously wealthy and a famed patron of the arts. One day he found a description of a piece of art that he greatly desired to purchase for his collection. He sent an art dealer to Europe to find it and secure it for his collection. After months of tedious inquiries, the art dealer reported to Hearst that he had located the desired object. "Where is it?" inquired the tycoon. "In your own warehouse," the dealer replied. It was still in a crate with many other priceless treasures that Hearst had purchased over the years. The wealthy newspaper publisher had been looking for a treasure that was already in his possession.

The danger of too much wealth is that it can blind us to the treasures we already have. Jesus' wise teachings often warn against amassing worldly possessions and ignoring our spiritual well-being. For example, in the parable of the rich fool (Lk 12:16–21), Jesus told about a farmer who had a great harvest and so planned to tear down his old barns and build new ones to hold the grain for future years. The farmer's plan was to live off of his good fortune and "rest, eat, drink, and be merry" (Lk 12:19). But the man was foolish. He thought *he*

was in control of his future; he ignored the truth that God is in charge of our lives. Everything God gives to us is a gift of his goodness; it is not something we earn or deserve. And God can call us to himself at any time. This is exactly what happened to the rich man who died the very night he was making plans about how to handle his newfound wealth.

NOTING THE GOSPEL OF LUKE

This chapter will highlight some important teachings of Jesus, especially as they appear in the Gospel of Luke. As you begin Chapter 4, read Luke 4:31–21:38. Make note in your journal of the following:

- the most *challenging* verse for you
- the verse that *encourages* you the most
- your *favorite* verse
- the most *informative* verse
- the most *difficult* verse to understand
- your favorite *parable*
- the *miracle* of Jesus that most impresses you

When you finish making these notes, go back over the list and explain why you chose the verses you did.

Jesus' message is that we should grow rich in the sight of God. This is what is important: "For where your treasure is, there also will your heart be" (Lk 12:34). Our society often preaches the message that wealthy people are more successful and more important than poor people, but this is not the case. Jesus clearly teaches that "one's life does not consist of possessions" (Lk 12:15). He came to tell us that God loves all of us and that our focus in life should not be on what we have but who we are as God's beloved children.

This chapter reviews other important teachings of Jesus and unique elements of his ministry, including: the announcement of God's Kingdom, his use of parables and miracles to help us to witness the Kingdom, and his gift of Eucharist as a pledge of love.

 **For Reflection**

What do you think are dangers in accumulating too much wealth?

Jesus Announces the Kingdom of God (*CCC*, 541-545)

In the Old Testament, God's kingly rule referred to his justice and judgment over the Israelites. After the Babylonian Exile and the oppressive rule of the Persians, Greeks, and Romans, the Jews looked to God's kingship as taking place in the future with some great event in which God would deliver his

 ## Paradox in Jesus' Teaching

A paradox is a statement that, at first glance, seems self-contradictory, but in reality expresses a possible truth. Several of Jesus' teachings are thought-provoking paradoxes that contain important truths. Reflect on the following teachings of Jesus. Then respond to the questions given.

"For whoever wishes to save his life will lose it, but whoever loses his life for my sake will save it" (Lk 9:24).

"For the one who is least among all of you is the one who is the greatest" (Lk 9:48).

"Some are last who will be first, and some are first who will be last" (Lk 13:30).

"For everyone who exalts himself will be humbled, but the one who humbles himself will be exalted" (Lk 14:11).

- What do you think Jesus meant by each of these sayings? Do they fit the definition of paradox?
- Research the context for each of these verses. To whom is Jesus speaking? How might his teaching apply to all his followers?
- Choose one of the teachings above. In your own life, how have you observed it to be true?

not only announced the coming of the Kingdom of God, but he inaugurated it in his own person. As God's Son, Jesus Christ gathers all human beings into the family of God. His preaching and the signs he performed invite all people to gather around him. Especially in the Paschal Mystery of his Death and Resurrection, Jesus accomplished the coming of the Kingdom. Jesus announced the Kingdom of God from the beginning of his public ministry. In Galilee, Jesus preached, "This is the time of fulfillment. The kingdom of God is at hand. Repent, and believe in the gospel" (Mk 1:15).

Jesus' contemporaries understood the expression "Kingdom of God" to be a time in the future when God would show his power, pass judgment, and establish his divine rule over all of creation. At that time, every creature would recognize the one true God—the God who revealed himself to the Chosen People. When this future day would come, that is, when God's Kingdom is fully established, God's will would be accomplished on earth just as it is in Heaven.

The Kingdom of God has many unique characteristics, explained in the sections that follow.

The Kingdom Has a Present and Future Dimension

Matthew 13 contains a number of short parables where Jesus teaches about the "Kingdom of Heaven." Writing for a Jewish-Christian audience, Matthew used the expression "Kingdom of Heaven" rather than "Kingdom of God." He did this as a sign of reverence because Jews typically avoided saying the holy name of God. The parables in Matthew 13 (for example, the parables of the mustard seed and the yeast in Matthew 13:31–33) also point out that the Kingdom has both a present and future dimension. The Kingdom begins small, for example, in the preaching of Jesus, but it will bring about great results. The small mustard seed will grow into a large bush; the yeast will cause the dough to rise.

People. For example, the Book of Daniel tells of a cosmic battle led by the Archangel Michael, a great tribulation, and the vindication of the righteous in the resurrection to eternal life. Other Jewish writings spoke of God bringing a new Heaven and a new earth ruled by justice, peace, and goodness. Some thought that God would send a Messiah, an anointed one, to usher in the Kingdom.

Jesus *is* the Messiah. He is God's only Son, Emmanuel—"God-with-us." He is the one who announced the coming of God's Kingdom, God's reign of peace, justice, truth, and goodness. He asked people to prepare for God's rule by turning from their sins and believing in the Gospel. Jesus

The Kingdom is present now, but it will flourish in the future.

Additionally, Matthew 13 reveals in the parables of the hidden treasure and the pearl of great price (Mt 13:44–46) that the Kingdom is extremely valuable; it requires our total commitment. The coming of the Kingdom also indicates that God will separate the good from the bad and reward the faithful and punish evildoers. This is the theme of the parable of the wheat and weeds (Mt 13:24–30, 36–43) and the fishing net (Mt 13:47–50).

The Kingdom Is Meant for All, Especially the Poor

God's Kingdom is open to everyone. Although it is first announced to the Chosen People, Christ invites all people to enter the Kingdom. The parable of the sower (Mt 13:1–9, 18–23) teaches that we must hear Jesus' words, take them to heart, and put them into practice. The Kingdom does not take root in some people because of their lack of understanding and being tempted by the devil; others are superficial, easily giving up on Jesus' Word when tempted by trials or persecutions; still others do not let the Word take root in them because of worldly concerns and the lure of wealth. But for those who hear Jesus' Word and properly understand it, the results will be amazing.

Although the Kingdom is open to everyone, Jesus announces it in a special way to the poor and the lowly. The Beatitudes in Luke's Gospel begin this way:

Blessed are you who are poor,
for the kingdom of God is yours.
Blessed are you who are now hungry,
for you will be satisfied.
Blessed are you who are now weeping,
for you will laugh. (Lk 6:20–21)

Jesus himself shared the life of the poor, from his humble birth to his Death on the cross, stripped of his clothes. He knew hunger and thirst. He had no possessions. "Foxes have dens and birds of the sky have nests, but the Son of Man has nowhere to rest his head" (Mt 8:20).

Jesus taught that we must respond to the needs of the poor by feeding the hungry, giving drink to the thirsty, welcoming the stranger, clothing the naked, caring for the sick, visiting the imprisoned (Mt 25:31–46). These are the conditions that he set for us to enter his Father's Kingdom at the time of judgment. In the parable of the great feast, Jesus says, "Blessed is the one who will dine in the kingdom of God" (Lk 14:15). A special invitation is extended to "the poor and the crippled, the blind and the lame" (Lk 14:21), that is, those whom society ignores— the helpless ones, the overlooked, the lost and powerless. God's Kingdom is open to them.

The Kingdom Is Open to Sinners

"Christ Jesus came into the world to save sinners" (1 Tm 1:15). He preached and ministered to sinners, including Levi and Zacchaeus. Levi and Zacchaeus were tax collectors or, in other words, public sinners in the eyes of the Jews because of their alignment with the Romans.

The Gospel of Luke describes how Levi gave a great banquet for Jesus at his house. The Pharisees and scribes thought that if you ate with sinners you showed approval of them. They scrupulously avoided table fellowship with tax collectors and sinners, fearing that they would be contaminated by their immorality. When they grumbled to Jesus' disciples about his association with sinners, Jesus said, "Those who are healthy do not need a physician, but the sick do. I have not come to call the righteous to repentance but sinners" (Lk 5:31–32).

Luke gives another example of a tax collector who followed Jesus—Zacchaeus (Lk 19:1–10). Jesus stayed at the house of Zacchaeus, again evoking the criticism of observers. But Zacchaeus won the praise of Jesus because he did what Jesus required— repented of his sins. To prove that he really did turn from a life of sin, Zacchaeus told the Lord that he gave away half of his possessions to the poor and repaid four times over anyone he had defrauded of money. Jesus assured the reformed sinner that he was saved, "For the Son of Man has come to seek and to save what was lost" (Lk 19:10).

By his association with sinners and his care for their welfare, Jesus showed forth God's mercy, a sign of the coming of the Kingdom.

The Beatitudes Model the Kingdom

Because a new age has dawned and God's reign is here, Jesus expects his followers to live in such a way that they will attract others to God's Kingdom. The **Beatitudes** preached in the Sermon on the Mount (Mt 5–7) instruct his followers on how to live to be able to enter the Kingdom of God (Mt 5:20). In Luke's Gospel, the Beatitudes are presented in the Sermon on the Plain (Lk 6:17–49), about a third of the length of the Sermon on the Mount. Luke's Beatitudes correspond to the first, fourth, second, and eighth of Matthew's Beatitudes, but with some differences. The fourth Beatitude in Luke is essential because it shows that Jesus' disciples have identified with the Lord, who has suffered rejection:

> Blessed are you when people hate you,
>   and when they exclude
>   and insult you,
>   and denounce your name
>   as evil
>   on account of the Son of
>   Man. (Lk 6:22)

The Beatitudes teach that wealth can blind us to the truth that God is the source of all gifts, which we should share with others. Jesus compares wealthy and well-fed people to false prophets who spoke flattering words to get people to think highly of them. What Jesus requires of us is to love, even our enemies:

> But to you who hear I say, love your enemies, do good to those who hate you, bless those who curse you, pray for those who mistreat you. (Lk 6:27)

The Kingdom of God requires high standards. Not only must we live by the Golden Rule—"Do to others as you would have them do to you" (Lk 6:31)—but we must do even more. We must imitate God himself by being kind to ungrateful and wicked people. As Jesus teaches, we must "Be merciful, just as [also] your Father is merciful" (Lk 6:36). Imitating the Father requires that we not judge or condemn others. Rather, we must be generous. We must give without counting the cost because God himself is so generous. He will shower his blessings on us, his children:

> Give and gifts will be given to you; a good measure, packed together, shaken down, and overflowing, will be poured into your lap. For the measure with which you measure will in return be measured out to you. (Lk 6:38)

Like a good tree bearing good fruit (see Lk 6:43–45), disciples will bring about good results only if they listen to the words of Jesus and make them

Beatitudes

Beatitude means "supreme happiness." The eight Beatitudes preached by Jesus in the Sermon on the Mount respond to our natural desire for happiness.

prejudice

An unsubstantiated or preformed judgment about an individual or group.

come alive in their lives. Words are not enough: "Why do you call me, 'Lord, Lord,' but not do what I command?" (Lk 6:46). A person who comes to Jesus, listens to his words, and acts on them is like a person who builds his house on a foundation of rock so as to withstand the floods of a river. The foundation of a Christian life, of working for God's Kingdom, requires both listening and action, hearing Jesus and obeying him.

 ## For Review

1. What two things did Jesus ask people to do when he announced the coming of the Kingdom of God?

2. How do the parables of the mustard seed and yeast (Mt 13:31–33) stress both the present and future dimensions of the Kingdom of God?

3. What is the meaning of the parable of the wheat and weeds (Mt 13:24–30, 36–43)?

4. According to the parable of the sower (Mt 13:1–9, 18–23), name two situations that keep people from entering the Kingdom of God.

5. Identify Levi and Zacchaeus. Why did Jesus associate with tax collectors?

6. List three things from the Sermon on the Plain (Lk 6:17–49) that the Lord requires of his followers.

Examining Prejudice

When Jesus said to "stop judging and you will not be judged" (Lk 6:37), he was talking about the prejudicial judgments that people make about others, that is, judgments made with insufficient evidence. Prejudice diminishes people and results in behaviors like talking against people, avoidance, discrimination, and even violence.

Examine the prejudices that might be exhibited in your school toward the following groups of people. Discuss any stereotypes ("oversimplified generalizations about persons or groups without regard for individual differences") attached to this group. (For example, "All rich people are selfish.") Then devise a concrete plan of action that you and your classmates can take to combat the prejudice directed toward one or more of the groups you discussed.

- overweight girls
- overweight boys
- a particular ethnic group
- a particular racial group
- non-Catholic students
- star athletes
- elderly teachers
- add to this list

For more information on the topic, review the booklet, *101 Ways to Combat Prejudice*, a joint project of Barnes and Noble and the Anti-Defamation League, for some ideas on how to fight prejudice.

For Reflection

Think about three different people, for example, a sibling, a classmate, a parent, a teacher, or a teammate. For each person, write a few sentences on how you would like them to treat *you*. Then, in light of what you wrote, list a specific thing you can do for each of the persons you wrote about.

Jesus Teaches about the Kingdom of God in Parables (*CCC*, 546)

In teaching about the Kingdom of God, Jesus often told stories to reveal what the Kingdom was like. He drew from images that were familiar to his audience, including illustrations from farming, fishing, and everyday life. Jesus told stories in the form of a **parable**. In general, a parable is an analogy where one reality is compared to something that is better known. Jesus' parables teach about some aspect of the Kingdom of God. Jesus wanted his hearers to think about what living in the Kingdom requires of us right now and how cooperating with God's reign looks to a glorious future of eternal life with our loving Father.

The subject of Jesus' parables ranged from fishing and farming to wedding celebrations and joyful meals celebrated with friends. He talked about planting seeds, baking bread, and winemaking. His stories involved characters like an unjust judge, good servants, a wayward son, a persistent widow, a good shepherd, and a loving father. The elements in his stories include ordinary objects like lost coins, weeds, bread, and withered trees.

Jesus' parables are important for many reasons:

1. *They convey the heart of his message.* To learn from them is to learn much about the major theme of his preaching about the Kingdom of God.

2. *They show that Jesus was an outstanding teacher.* Parables like the Good Samaritan and the Prodigal Son are among the most famous stories ever told. They are easy to remember and therefore easily bring to mind important points in Jesus' teaching.

3. *They give us a good idea of how Jesus was able to defend himself against opponents.* For example, when questioned why his disciples do not fast the way the disciples of John the Baptist or the Pharisees did, Jesus compared himself to a bridegroom at a wedding. Because he is present, it is a time for celebration. He also told why it is unwise to sew new cloth on old cloth and pour new wine in old wineskins (Lk 5:33–39). The point of these parables is that the Gospel is new and revolutionary. The

parable

A favorite teaching device of Jesus in which he told a short story with a striking, memorable comparison that taught a religious message, usually about some aspect of God's Kingdom.

THREE PARABLES FROM LUKE'S GOSPEL

Read each of the following parables:

- The Prodigal Son (Lk 15:11-32)
- The Pharisee and the Tax Collector (Lk 18:9-14)
- The Tenant Farmers (Lk 20:9-16)

Write your own interpretation of their meaning. Then consult a biblical commentary to see if your interpretation is correct.

The Prodigal Son (Lk 15:11-32)

This famous parable tells the story of a father who had two sons. The younger son asked for and got his share of his inheritance. His selfish request was equivalent to wishing that his father were dead. Nevertheless, out of love, the father honored his son's wish. The son then went to a distant land and squandered his money on wasteful living. He ended up in the bleak position of having to feed pigs in order to survive. He eventually came to his senses and returned to his father, requesting to be treated as a slave. Instead of being angry, his father joyfully welcomed his younger son back into the family. He gave him the best robe (a sign of honor), a ring, and sandals (the sign of a free man), and threw a banquet in his honor. The older brother complained about his father's treatment of his wayward brother, reminding his father that he had always been faithful. Instead of rebuking his elder son for his pride, the father gently told his son that everything he had belonged to him. "But now we must celebrate and rejoice, because your brother was dead and has come to life again, he was lost and has been found" (Lk 15:32).

Jesus told this parable to challenge people who criticized him for associating with sinners. Jesus wished to show that God, represented by the father in the story, is compassionate and loving. God will forgive repentant sinners, represented by the younger brother. Jesus calls those who are judgmental and self-righteous, like the older brother in the story, to reconsider their attitude. He challenges them also to repent and accept that God is compassionate and forgiving. Although the parable has traditionally been called the "Prodigal Son" to emphasize the wasteful extravagance of the younger son in his spending habits, the one who is truly extravagant in his love is the father. Therefore, a better title for the parable might be "The Loving Father and the Two Brothers." God is indeed lavishing in his love of all repentant sinners.

(continued on next page)

The Pharisee and the Tax Collector (Lk 18:9-14)

A Pharisee and a tax collector went to the Temple to pray. The Pharisee, who strictly upheld the Law, arrogantly thanked God that he was not a sinner like other people—greedy, dishonest, an adulterer. He proudly listed all the good things he did like fasting and tithing. In contrast, the tax collector humbly admitted that he was a sinner and in need of God's forgiveness. His prayer was, "O God, be merciful to me a sinner" (Lk 18:13).

Jesus told this parable to attack those who think of themselves as virtuous and superior to others. The Lord taught that God is not impressed by prideful people but welcomes with open arms the humble sinner. Jesus taught, "Everyone who exalts himself will be humbled, and the one who humbles himself will be exalted" (Lk 18:14).

The Tenant Farmers (Lk 20:9-16)

Jesus tells of a vineyard owner who traveled to another country and left his property in the care of tenants. When the harvest came, the owner successively sent three servants to collect his share of the produce from the harvest. However, the tenants attacked the fist servant, beat and insulted the second servant, and killed the third. Finally, in the hope that the tenants would change their behavior, the vineyard owner sent his own son to the vineyard. However, the tenants did not respect the son's authority. They killed him, too, thinking that they would then inherit the vineyard for themselves.

The parable of the tenants is an **allegory**. Jesus told this story against the scribes and chief priests who did not accept his authority. In the story, God is the vineyard owner, the vineyard is Israel, and the servants are the prophets who are put to death by the leaders (the tenants). The son, of course, is Jesus who will be crucified. The others to whom the vineyard is passed are the Gentiles who will be grafted onto Israel. Jesus' opponents knew the story was addressed to them, but they failed to heed its warnings and continued to plot Jesus' Death.

allegory

A story involving a sustained comparison in which people, things, and events symbolically represent something else.

Jesus summarized the parable by quoting Psalm 118:22: "The stone which the builder rejected has become the cornerstone" (Lk 21:17). He also tells how this stone will destroy its opponents: "Everyone who falls on that stone will be dashed to pieces; and it will crush anyone on whom it falls" (Lk 20:18). The message is that because of the rejection of Jesus' teaching, the Kingdom of God (the vineyard) will be taken away from those to whom it had been entrusted (religious leaders).

Kingdom of God is an entirely new way of believing and living.

The Message of the Parables

The Gospels remind us that Jesus "taught them at length in parables" (Mk 4:2). Listed on the next page are the parables of Jesus recorded in the Gospels of Mathew, Mark, and Luke.

The forty-one parables contain the heart of the Good News. A short summary of the primary messages of the parables (with references) follows:

- *Salvation is here!* Jesus ushers in the Kingdom of God just as spring brings leaves to the fig tree (Mt 24:32–35). Like a mustard seed, the Kingdom begins small but will grow (Mk 4:30–32). God makes it grow by his own design (Mk 4:26–29) and eventually it will reach a great harvest (Lk 8:5–8).

- *The Kingdom of God is a pure gift.* Jesus invites everyone into the Kingdom, even people we might consider unworthy (Lk 14:15–24). The heavenly banquet is for everyone (Mt 22:1–14). God is like a vineyard owner who freely dispenses his gifts, far beyond what one has earned (Mt 20:1–16). For our part, we are servants who can only joyfully and gratefully accept God's love (Lk 17:7–10).

- *God loves sinners.* The essence of the Good News is God's love for sinners. He is the Good Shepherd who seeks out the lost sheep (Lk 15:3–7) or the woman who searches frantically for her lost coin and rejoices when she finds it (Lk 15:8–10). He is the merciful father who welcomes back the lost son and deals gently with another son who harshly judges his brother (Lk 15:11–32). God's joy over the returned sinner is great. He only asks in return that we forgive others as we have been forgiven (Mt 18:23–35).

- *The Good News about the Kingdom of God requires an urgent response.* The time for decision is now. We must be ever watchful for God's return (Lk 12:35–40). The Bridegroom (Jesus) can come at any time (Mt 25:1–13).

Some people will refuse to respond to him, like tenants in a vineyard who refuse to give the owner his proper share (Mt 21:33–46). They will complain like little children who are acting like spoilsports (Lk 7:29–35). In the end, they will be judged. Wheat will be separated from the weeds (Mt 13:24–30), and bad fish will be tossed out of the net (Mt 13:47–50). If the Kingdom is found, one must be wily like a crafty businessman in order to gain it (Lk 14:25–35). It is like finding a pearl or a hidden treasure; one must give all to gain it (Mt 13:44–46).

- *The Good News of God's Kingdom demands repentance.* Having accepted the gift of the Kingdom, we must be prepared for the feast (Mt 22:1–14). We must be faithful (Mt 21:28–32). We must ask for God's forgiveness, as did the sinful tax collector (Lk 18:9–14). We must forgive others (Mt 5:25–26) and pray without ceasing, like the friend begging for bread at midnight (Lk 11:5–8) or the woman badgering the unjust judge (Lk 18:1–8). Above all else, we must love everyone, even our enemies, following the example of the Good Samaritan (Lk 10:25–37). Finally, Jesus' followers must put the goods of this world into proper perspective; for example, money is a means to Heaven, not an end in itself (Lk 12:13–21; 16:1–12).

- *Following Jesus may bring suffering.* Those who suffer for Jesus will be rewarded while those who take advantage of others will be punished (Lk 16:19–31). If we respond to the "least of these," we respond to Jesus and will enter into the fullness of God's Kingdom for eternity (Mt 25:31–46).

For Review

1. What is a parable?

2. What is the general message of Jesus' parables?

3. What is the meaning of the parable of the Prodigal Son?

(continued on page 95)

Parable	Matthew	Mark	Luke
A Lamp Under a Bushel	5:15–17	4:21–22	8:16–18
New Cloth on Old Garments	9:16	2:21	5:36
New Wine in Old Wine Skins	9:17	2:22	5:37
The Sower	13:3–23	4:2–20	8:4–15
The Mustard Seed	13:31–32	4:30–32	13:18–19
Yeast	13:33		
The Tenant Farmers	21:33–45	12:1–12	20:9–19
The Budding Fig Tree	24:32–35	13:28–32	21:29–33
A House Built on a Rock	7:24–27		6:47–49
Wayward Children	11:16–19		7:31–35
Leaven	13:33		13:20–21
Lost Sheep	18:12–14		15:3–7
A Treasure Hidden in a Field	13:44		
A Pearl of Great Value	13:45–46		
Dragnet	13:47–50		
The Unmerciful Servant	18:23–25		
Laborers in the Vineyard	20:1–16		
A Father and Two Sons	21:28–32		
The Marriage Feast for the King's Son	22:1–14		
The Wise and Foolish Maidens	25:1–13		
The Servants and Their Talents	25:14–30		
Separating Sheep from Goats	25:31–46		
A Seed Growing Silently		4:26–29	
The Doorkeeper on Watch		13:34–37	
Two Debtors			7:41–43
The Good Samaritan			10:25–37
A Friend at Midnight			11:5–10
The Rich Fool			12:16–21
Watchful Servants			12:35–38
The Wise Steward	24:45–51		12:42–48
The Barren Fig Tree			13:6–9
Dinner Guests			14:16–24
A Lost Coin			15:8–10
The Prodigal Son			15:11–32
The Dishonest Steward			16:1–13
The Rich Man and Lazarus			16:19–31
Useless Servants			17:7–10
The Persistent Widow			18:1–8
The Pharisee and the Tax Collector			18:9–14
Ten Pounds			19:11–27

4. Why did Jesus tell the parable of the Pharisee and the tax collector (Lk 18:9-14)?

5. Explain how the parable of the Tenant Farmers (Lk 20:9-16) is an allegory that applies to Jesus himself.

For Reflection

The basic message of the parable of the Good Samaritan (Lk 10:25-37) is that we need to love our neighbors, which includes our enemies. But this parable has a richer meaning as well. For example, St. Augustine saw this parable as an allegory and interpreted it this way:

Jerusalem	=	Heaven
Jericho	=	the world
robbers	=	Satan and the bad angels
wounded man	=	Adam
priest	=	the Law (Torah)
Levite	=	prophets
Samaritan	=	Jesus
the inn	=	the Church
Samaritan's return	=	Jesus' return at the end of time

Using the allegorical elements from St. Augustine, write a paragraph explaining what the parable means.

Jesus' Miracles: Signs of the Kingdom of God (*CCC*, 547-550)

Jesus' miracles were signs that the Messianic age had dawned. They attest that the Father had sent him. They also invite people to believe in him. And Jesus responds to their faith by granting what they ask. Miracles, therefore, can strengthen faith in Jesus as God's Son, doing his work. Miracles are defined as observable events that the laws of nature cannot explain. They happen as the result of God's action. Scripture calls Jesus' miracles "works, wonders, and signs," which accompany his words. They reveal that the Kingdom of God was present in his very person. They prove that he is the promised Messiah, the Son of God.

However, the marvelous signs Jesus performed did not automatically cause people to believe. His opponents could not deny that he healed people and performed other miracles. But they questioned the source of his power; sometimes they even said that it came from Satan. For example, this happened when he drove a demon out of a mute person who was then able to speak. Some attributed this to the power of Satan; others wanted a clear sign from Heaven. But Jesus knew that their charge was absurd. His miracles always resulted in a great good, revealing the defeat of evil and God's power over Satan. Jesus challenged his critics by saying:

> Every kingdom divided against itself will be laid to waste and house will fall against house. And if Satan is divided against himself, how will his kingdom stand? (Lk 11:17–18)

Jesus clearly showed how his works and signs point to the coming of God's Kingdom. He asked his critics to consider the truth of following: "But if it is by the finger of God that [I] drive out demons, then the kingdom of God has come upon you" (Lk 11:20). Jesus' miracles were clear signs of the coming of the Kingdom of God.

Jesus performed miracles to free people from earthly problems and the evils of hunger, injustice, illness, and even death. However, Jesus' mission was not to abolish all human sufferings here on earth, but to free us from the worst slavery, that of sin. Furthermore, Jesus' exorcisms (see below) offered freedom from the power of demons. They prefigured the victory of his Paschal Mystery, which

blasphemy

Any thought, word, or act that expresses hatred or contempt for Christ, God, the Church, saints, or holy things.

would abolish the power of Satan, defeat sin and death, and win for us eternal life with God.

Kinds of Miracles

Jesus performed various signs, all of which pointed to the coming of the Kingdom of God in Christ's very life. The four examples discussed below are from the Gospel of Luke.

Physical Healings

Physical healings demonstrate Jesus' power over sin and reveal that the coming of God's Kingdom brings wholeness and true happiness. They also reveal who Jesus is.

In Luke's Gospel, there are a variety of healings. For example, Jesus healed Simon Peter's mother-in-law. He also healed a leper who approached him with faith, "Lord, if you wish, you can make me clean" (Lk 5:12). Jesus stretched out his hand and touched the leper and cured him.

Jesus also responded to the faith of a Gentile—a centurion—who pleaded with Jesus to cure his slave (Lk 7:1–10). Jesus was amazed at the man's faith and granted his wish.

On another occasion, Jesus cured a blind beggar who shouted at him as he walked by: "Jesus, son of David, have pity on me!" (Lk 18:38). Jesus then asked the man, "'What do you want me to do for you?' He replied, 'Lord, please let me see'" (Lk 18:41). Jesus granted the blind man his wish. The man immediately followed Jesus and praised God. This miracle teaches how Jesus wants us to approach him and to ask him directly for what we need. He responds to our faith.

Another time, Jesus cured a man with a withered hand on the Sabbath (Lk 6:6–11). Some of the religious leaders thought that healing on the Sabbath was forbidden by the Law, but Jesus asked them, "Is it lawful to do good on the Sabbath rather than to do evil, to save life rather than to destroy it?" (Lk 6:9). Jesus healed the man, thus proving that he is Lord of the Sabbath while teaching that the Son of God came to do good works.

In Luke 5:17–26 one of Jesus' healings revealed his identity as God's Son. A paralyzed man was lowered through the roof tiles into the crowded room where Jesus was teaching. After Jesus saw the faith of those who helped their friend, he said, "As for you, your sins are forgiven" (Lk 5:20). This outraged some scribes and Pharisees who were present. They believed Jesus committed the sin of **blasphemy** because only God could forgive sins. However, to demonstrate that he had the authority to forgive sin and that he was indeed the Son of God, Jesus ordered the paralyzed man to rise, pick up his stretcher, and go home. The man did so, which astonished the onlookers. They were awestruck as they began to glorify God and say, "We have seen incredible things today" (Lk 5:26).

Exorcisms

Exorcisms are the expulsion of evil spirits from a person. Jesus performed them to establish his power over Satan and the demons who war against God's purposes and tempt humans to do evil.

One of the exorcisms recorded in Luke takes place in a synagogue in Capernaum (Lk 4:31–37). After driving a demon out of a man, Jesus' action caused amazement, "What is there about his word? For with authority and power he commands the unclean spirits and they come out" (Lk 4:36).

When Jesus encountered the Gerasene demoniac in Luke 8:26–39, the demons recognized Jesus as the Son of God and feared him. Jesus sent the demons into a herd of pigs, an unclean animal for the Jews. The pigs rushed down the steep cliff and were drowned in the sea. When the people learned how the man was cured, they were afraid to be in the presence of one so mighty. Therefore, they asked Jesus to leave their territory. The man whom Jesus freed from the demons wished to follow him, but

Jesus told him to return to his own home to recount how God delivered him.

Nature Miracles

Nature miracles attest to Jesus' power over the forces of nature, since all creation came about through him. As John's Gospel puts it, "In the beginning was the Word . . . and the Word was God. All things came to be through him, and without him nothing came to be" (Jn 1:1, 3).

Among the nature miracles is Jesus' calming of the storm at sea in Luke 8:22–25. As God's Son, Jesus has power over creation. When he demonstrates this power, even his disciples ask the question, "Who then is this, who commands even the winds and the sea, and they obey him?" (Lk 8:25).

Another dramatic nature miracle is the multiplication of the loaves and fishes (Lk 9:10–17), a miracle recorded in all four Gospels. The miracle recalled God's feeding the Chosen People in the desert. It also continues to remind Church leaders to feed God's people with Gospel and the Holy Eucharist. In fact, the wording of Luke 9:16—"Then taking the five loaves and the two fish, and looking up to heaven, he said the blessing over them, broke them, and gave them to the disciples to set before the crowd"—brings to mind the Last Supper and Jesus' institution of the Eucharist, the sacrament of Holy Communion with the Lord who gives eternal life.

Raisings from the Dead

Jesus' raising people from the dead bears witness that he has mastery over life and death.

The three raisings from the dead recorded in the Gospels include Jesus' raising of his friend Lazarus in John 11:1–44, the raising of the synagogue leader's daughter reported in all the Synoptic Gospels, and the raising of the son of the widow of Nain in Luke 7:11–17. These examples foreshadow Jesus' own Resurrection. They are clear signs that God is in our midst, that the Messiah has come, a time when Isaiah prophesied:

The blind regain their sight, the lame walk, lepers are cleansed, the deaf hear, the dead are raised, the poor have the good news proclaimed to them. (Lk 7:22)

In the miracle of the raising of the son of the widow Nain, Jesus reveals his great compassion: "He was moved to pity for her" (Lk 7:13). As a widow, she was powerless; her dead son was her only means of support. Jesus' heart went out to her. He touched the coffin and ordered the dead youth to get up. The youth obeyed and began to speak. This miracle brings to mind the Old Testament prophet Elijah who also performed an act of mercy for a mother whose son stopped breathing (see 1 Kings 17:17–24). The power of God exhibited in Jesus, his Son, at first made the people afraid. But soon, they began to glorify God. They recognized what had taken place: "A great prophet has arisen in our midst. . . . God has visited his people" (Lk 7:16).

In total, Jesus' miracles accomplish many things:

- They show that God's power has broken into human history through the coming of his Son.

- They show that Jesus Christ has dominion over Satan and the forces of darkness and evil. God's Kingdom is here; Satan's reign is ending.

- They reveal that because he is God, he has the power to forgive sins.

- Therefore, they reveal his identity as God's only Son, the Savior and the Messiah.

- As signs of God's Kingdom that has broken into human history, the miracles demonstrate in a remarkable way God's love and compassion for us.

- They lead people to put their faith in him, helping them recognize who he is: Emmanuel—"God-with-us."

For Review

1. What was the purpose of Jesus' miracles?

2. Name the four kinds of miracles Jesus performed.

3. Why did Jesus' opponents think he committed blasphemy?

(continued on page 100)

EXPLAINING THE FAITH

Do miracles happen today?

God continues his work through the ages. Church history is full of examples of God's miraculous intervention in the lives of people. This is true even today. For example, it is possible to view the incorrupt bodies of some saints (their bodies were not mummified at death). Science cannot explain this phenomenon. At Fatima, Portugal, where Mary appeared in 1917, more than seventy thousand people saw the sun "dance" and appear to plummet to earth. At Lourdes, France, where Mary appeared to St. Bernadette Soubirous in 1858 more than seven thousand people have reported cures in the years since to the Medical Bureau at Lourdes. An objective commission of scientists and medical personnel examined the cures and led the bureau to declare that sixty-seven cases should be officially acknowledged as miraculous.

Many miracles are attributed to saints. Holy persons like St. Pio of Pietrelcina bore the stigmata (wounds of Christ) and cured many people during his lifetime, including curing a lady of blindness. Incredibly, the woman had no pupils, and yet she was able to see. The Church conducts a very thorough procedure to determine if a candidate for canonization has worked a miracle. A doctor, whose job it is to determine if these medical wonders attributed to saints are really miracles, calls them "fantastic, incredible, and well-documented."

Modern skeptics, influenced by the belief that it is impossible for God to intervene in the natural world, claim that miracles do not happen. But this opinion does not square with the facts. For those who believe in the Good News of Jesus Christ, we know that the world is full of grace. Wonders do take place

Interpreting Jesus' Miracles

Here is a list of some key miracles of Jesus'. Write a report that summarizes the miracles listed in boldface type. Follow these directions:

1. Read all of the versions of each miracle listed in **boldface** type.

2. Note what has taken place on the surface level; for example, Jesus cures a man's blindness.

3. Decide to which of the four categories of miracle listed above this particular one belongs.

4. Then interpret the deeper meaning of the miracle. How does it show God's *power*? What *significance* does it have? For example, in the case of the blind man, you might say that God's power makes people see the true light. Or you might conclude that faith in Jesus enabled him to see God working through his Son who enables us to walk in the light.

5. Share your conclusions with your classmates.

Miracle	Mt	Mk	Lk	Jn
Changing Water into Wine				2:1–11
Healing of the Nobleman's Son				4:46–54
Disciples Catch Fish			5:1–11	
Stilling of the Storm	8:23–27	4:35–41	8:22–25	
Demoniacs of Gerasene	8:28–34	5:1–20	8:26–39	
Raising Jairus's Daughter	**9:18–26**	**5:21–43**	**8:40–56**	
Healing the Woman with a Hemorrhage	9:20–22	5:24–34	8:43–48	
Healing of the Two Blind Men	9:27–31			
Healing of Possessed Mute	9:32–34			
Healing of the Paralytic	9:1–8	2:1–12	5:17–26	
Cleansing of the Leper	8:1–4	1:40–45	5:12–16	
Healing the Centurion's Servant	8:5–13		7:1–10	
Demoniac at Capernaum		**1:23–27**	**4:33–36**	
Healing of Simon's Mother-in-Law	8:14–15	1:29–31	4:38–39	
Raising of the Widow's Son			7:11–17	
Healing at the Pool of Bethesda				5:1–15
Healing of the Blind and Deaf Mute	12:22			
Feeding of the Five Thousand	**14:15–21**	**6:34–44**	**9:12–17**	**6:5–14**
Walking on Water	14:22–23	6:45–52		6:14–21
Healing the Man Born Blind				**9:1–41**
Healing the Man with a Withered Hand	12:9–13	3:1–5	6:6–11	
Healing the Woman on the Sabbath			13:10–17	
Healing the Man with Dropsy			14:1–6	
Cleansing the Ten Lepers			17:11–19	
Healing the Syrophoenician Woman	15:21–28	7:24–30		
Healing the Deaf and Dumb Man		7:31–37		
Healing of the Suffering	15:29–31			
Feeding the Four Thousand	15:32–39	8:1–9		
Healing the Blind Man at Bethesda		8:22–26		
Healing of the Lunatic Child	17:14–21	9:14–29	9:37–42	
Finding the Coin in the Fish's Mouth	17:24–27			
Raising of Lazarus				11:1–54
Healing the Two Blind Men	20:29–34	10:46–52	18:35–43	
Cursing the Barren Fig Tree	21:18–22	11:12–24		
Healing of Malchus's Ear			22:49–51	
Second Miraculous Catch of Fish				21:1–14

4. How did Jesus show through a miracle that he had the power to forgive sin?

5. What do Jesus' miracles accomplish?

For Reflection

Jesus put to the blind man this question: "What do you want me to do for you?" Name one thing you need in your life right now. Write a note addressed to Jesus telling him what you think he can do for you. Then write another note telling Jesus what you think *you can do for him.*

Two Great Miracles of Jesus

At the end of 2002, Pope John Paul II declared that the next calendar year would be the Year of the Rosary. At the same time, the Pope introduced another set of mysteries in addition to the Joyful, Sorrowful, and Glorious mysteries that have been part of praying the Rosary since the sixteenth century.

The new set of mysteries are known as the Mysteries of Light. They are made up of these mysteries: the Baptism of the Lord, the Wedding at Cana, Jesus' Proclamation of the Kingdom of God, the Transfiguration of the Lord, and the Institution of the Eucharist.

The text has previously detailed Christ's Baptism, his first miracle at Cana, and his initiation of the Kingdom of God. The next sections focus on Christ's Transfiguration and the Eucharist.

Transfiguration of Jesus (CCC, 551-556; 568)

One of the most dramatic and important miracles in the life of Jesus is his **Transfiguration**. It was witnessed by three of his Apostles and took place

after Peter's confession of Jesus as the Messiah (Lk 9:18–21). The event unfolds this way: Jesus went off to pray by himself; the Apostles were with him. On this occasion, he asked them what the crowds of people were saying about him. The answers varied. Some, perhaps even Herod Antipas, thought Jesus was John the Baptist come back to life (see Lk 9:7); others thought he was Elijah; still others believed him to be a great prophet. Although the people thought highly of Jesus, and considered him a mouthpiece for God, none of them believed that he was the Messiah.

What Jesus really wanted was for his Apostles to answer the same question: "But who do you say that I am?" (Lk 9:19). Peter, speaking on behalf of the Apostles, acknowledged the great truth: Jesus is "The Messiah of God" (Lk 9:20). Matthew's Gospel reports Peter's confession this way: "You are the Messiah, Son of the living God" (Mt 16:16).

After witnessing Jesus' miracles and hearing him teach, the Apostles grew to know him as more than just a healer and an inspired teacher. They came to know him as the Messiah, as God himself who had come to announce the Kingdom and save humanity. Though the Apostles may have had a correct glimpse of Jesus' true identity, it was not until after the Resurrection and Ascension of Jesus, and the coming of the Holy Spirit, that they fully began to understand the impact of their words. For example, immediately after Peter's confession of faith, Jesus predicted that he would suffer and die. But Peter could not believe that the Messiah would have to endure this pain and Death, and so he took Jesus aside and began to argue with him, "God forbid, Lord! No such thing shall ever happen to you" (Mt 16:22). Jesus in turn rebuked Peter for judging not by God's standards of the Messiah as Suffering Servant but by the standards of human beings (see Mt 16:23).

Eight days after Peter's confession of faith, and Jesus' first prediction that he would suffer and be killed by the leaders, yet rise on the third day, Jesus gave Peter, James, and John a glimpse of his divine glory, of his true identity as God's beloved Son. He took them on a high mountain where his face "shone like the sun and his clothes became as white as light" (Mt 17:2). Through this manifestation, known as the Transfiguration, Jesus was giving his Apostles a foretaste of God's Kingdom.

In his book on Jesus of Nazareth, Pope Benedict XVI observed that the Transfiguration happened while Jesus was praying. At the Transfiguration, Jesus' being was suffused with the light of God. "In his oneness with the Father, Jesus is himself "light from light.""

Two Old Testament figures—Moses and Elijah—also appear at Jesus' Transfiguration. This brings to mind how the Law (given to Israel through Moses) and the Prophets (Elijah was a great prophet) had announced the sufferings of the coming Messiah. The Transfiguration also reveals all Three Persons of the Blessed Trinity: the Father (in the voice), the Son, and the Holy Spirit (in the shining cloud).

In the Transfiguration, Jesus momentarily reveals his divine glory, thus confirming the faith of Peter. But he also reveals that he must die in Jerusalem in order to enter into his glory. He instructed Peter, James, and John not to report this vision until after the Resurrection. They were to withhold news of this remarkable event "until the Son of Man has been raised from the dead" (Mt 17:9). Though he was the Son of God, Jesus came not as an earthly king. He came to preach the Good News of God's love. This preaching led him to Jerusalem and his own Death at the hands of the authorities.

Institution of the Eucharist (CCC, 611, 1337–1344)

In the Eucharist, Christ shares the gift of himself. When we open ourselves to accepting this gift, we are nourished by the **Real Presence** of God in our lives. Luke 22:1–38 is a source

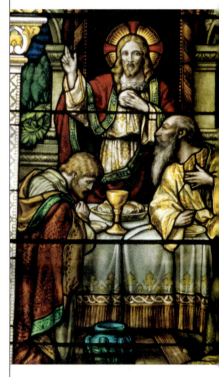

Transfiguration
The mystery from Christ's life in which God's glory shone through and transformed Jesus' physical appearance while he was in the company of the Old Testament prophets Moses and Elijah. Peter, James, and John witnessed this event.

Real Presence
The presence of Jesus Christ in the consecrated species of bread and wine.

that details the institution of the Eucharist beginning with Jesus' entrance to Jerusalem.

In reading Luke's Gospel from start to finish, it is easy to notice how the travel narrative centers on Jerusalem. This city becomes Jesus' destination "for it is impossible that a prophet should die outside of Jerusalem" (Lk 13:33). Jesus entered Jerusalem for the final time on the back of a colt to fulfill the prophecy of Zechariah who predicted the Savior would come as a humble king. As he approached the city, Jesus wept over it, foreseeing the day when the Romans would destroy the Temple in the Jewish Revolt (AD 66–70). He then entered the Temple area and drove out those who were selling things, reminding people that God's house should be a house of prayer, not a den of thieves (Lk 19:46).

During the following days, Jesus returned to the Temple to teach. He defended his authority to teach when questioned by the chief priests, scribes, and elders. In doing so, he told the parable of the tenant farmers (Lk 20:9–19) and fended off questions about the paying of taxes and the nature of the Resurrection. Jesus warned about the hypocrisy of the scribes and told how a poor widow's two small coins were more pleasing to God than the contributions of wealthy people who gave in order to be noticed by others. Jesus also taught about the destruction of the Temple, signs of the end of the world, and the coming of the Son of Man—the Resurrected Lord who will judge everyone. Jesus encouraged his disciples to watch and to pray, to always be ready for the arrival of the Son of Man.

Jesus taught these themes during the day and returned to the Mount of Olives every evening. The common people liked hearing him, but the leaders were at the same time plotting his death. Satan tempted Judas, one of the Apostles, to contact the chief priests and Temple guards to discuss a way to hand Jesus over to them. They offered him money to do so at a time when crowds of people would not be around Jesus.

The narrative turns to the preparations Jesus made with his Apostles to celebrate a Passover meal with them. Originally, the Jewish feasts of the Unleavened Bread and the Passover were celebrated separately but were soon joined to recall God's deliverance of Israel from Egypt. Passover came on the first of the seven days of Unleavened Bread. The disciples did as Jesus told them by finding a man with a jar of water who would lead them to the guest room where Jesus would celebrate the Last Supper with his Apostles.

The Synoptic Gospels report that Jesus' Last Supper was a Passover meal. In John's Gospel, the supper takes place the night before; Jesus died at the exact moment that the Passover lamb was sacrificed. John's Gospel is the only one to report that Jesus washed the feet of his disciples as a sign that they should serve one another. Jesus also gave his followers the great command to love:

This is my commandment: love one another as I love you. No one has greater love than this, to lay down one's life for one's friends. . . . This I command you: love one another. (Jn 15:12–13, 17)

Jesus understood that his hour had come and that he was to return to his Father. But he did not abandon his disciples. He left them a pledge of his love, so that he would never depart from his own, and to make them sharers in his Passover. Therefore, he instituted the Eucharist as a memorial of his Death and Resurrection. He also commanded his Apostles to celebrate the Eucharist until he returned once again. Jesus chose the Passover feast to fulfill what he proclaimed at Capernaum. He gave his disciples his Body and his Blood in the form of bread and wine.

> When the hour came, he took his place at table with the apostles. He said to them, "I have eagerly desired to eat this Passover with you before I suffer, for, I tell you, I shall not eat it [again] until there is fulfillment in the kingdom of God." Then he took a cup, gave thanks, and said, "Take this and share it among yourselves; for I tell you [that] from this time on I shall not drink of the fruit of the vine until the kingdom of God comes." Then he took the bread, said the blessing, broke it, and gave it to them, saying, "This is my body, which will be given for you; do this in memory of me." And likewise the cup after they had eaten, saying, "This cup is the new covenant in my blood, which will be shed for you." (Lk 22:14–20)

The *Catechism of the Catholic Church* explains the significance of what Jesus did at the Last Supper:

> By celebrating the Last Supper with his apostles in the course of the Passover meal, Jesus gave the Jewish Passover its definitive meaning. Jesus' passing over to his father by his death and Resurrection, the new Passover, is anticipated in the Supper and celebrated in the Eucharist, which fulfills the Jewish Passover and anticipates the final Passover of the Church in the glory of the kingdom. (*CCC*, 1340)

Jesus commanded his followers to celebrate the Eucharist in memory of him—his Life, Death, Resurrection, and his intercession for us before the Father. From her very beginnings, the Church has faithfully celebrated the Eucharist, especially by doing so on Sunday, the day of the Lord's Resurrection. Catholics recognize in the Holy Eucharist the very center of the Church's life in Christ. It both celebrates and creates the Church, allowing Jesus Christ to live in and transform us.

After the Supper was over, Jesus led his disciples to the Mount of Olives where his Passion would begin and the Paschal Mystery would unfold. The Paschal Mystery of Jesus' Death and Resurrection rescued humanity from sin and death. This is the message that the Gospels want us to hear: Jesus, the Christ, is the Son of God. He has died for your sins and risen from the dead! Everything has changed now. God's Kingdom is here. Believe the Good News of your Salvation. Repent of your sins. Be baptized. Allow the Lord Jesus and the Holy Spirit into your lives and be guided by them.

For Review

1. What were some common opinions of who Jesus was that were held by some of his contemporaries?

2. What did Peter confess about Jesus' identity?

3. What was the Transfiguration of Jesus?

4. Who appeared with Jesus at the Transfiguration?

5. How were all three Persons of the Blessed Trinity present at the Transfiguration?

6. In Luke's Gospel, why does Jerusalem play a central role for Jesus' ministry?

7. What is the significance of Jesus celebrating a Passover meal with his Apostles?

8. How did Jesus institute the Eucharist? Why did he do so?

9. Why is the Eucharist the center of the Church's life?

For Reflection

- Interview three people to see who they think Jesus is. Then write a reflection comparing and contrasting their views with your own.

- Because Jesus is present in the Blessed Sacrament, he deserves reverence. How do you show reverence to our Lord in the Blessed Sacrament? List ways "irreverence" is shown to people in your school, in your neighborhood, in our society.

Main Ideas

- The focus of our love should not be on what we have but who we are as God's beloved children. (pp. 84–85)

- Jesus announced the coming of God's Kingdom, a Kingdom of peace, justice, truth, and goodness. (pp. 85–86)

- The Kingdom of God begins small but grows on to flourish in the future. (p. 86)

- Jesus announces the Kingdom of God in a special way to the poor and lowly. (p. 87)

- God's mercy to sinners is a characteristic of the Kingdom of God. (p. 87)

- The Beatitudes instruct us on how to live in and be a part of God's Kingdom. (p. 88)

- Jesus' parables teach about God's Kingdom; they convey the heart of Jesus' message, show that he was an outstanding teacher, and give an idea of how he was able to defend himself against his opponents. (p. 90)

- The parables also teach that Salvation is here, that the Kingdom is a gift of pure love, that God loves sinners, that the Kingdom requires an urgent response and also repentance, and that it may also require suffering. (p. 93)

- The miracles of Jesus are other signs of the Kingdom; they reveal the Kingdom's presence in the life of Christ. (p. 95)

- Jesus performed different kinds of miracles, including: physical healings, exorcisms, nature miracles, and raisings from the dead. (pp. 96–98)

- Two great miracles that are part of the Mysteries of Light of the Rosary are the Transfiguration of Jesus and the Institution of the Last Supper. (pp. 100–101)

Terms, People, Places

Use a vocabulary word from the list below to help rewrite the following sentences to make them true.

allegory

Beatitudes

blasphemy

parables

prejudice

Real Presence

Transfiguration

1. At the Sermon on the Mount, Jesus appeared to Peter, James, and John, and God's glory shone through and transformed his appearance.

2. The word *racism* comes from a Latin word that we can translate as "prejudge."

3. Jesus taught that those who wish to embrace God's Kingdom must live according to the laws set out by the nation's authority.

4. Jesus is truly with us in the consecrated species of bread and wine at Mass, a mystery described as liturgy.

5. A key to understanding Jesus' parables involves realizing that they often contain metaphor.

6. The crime that Jesus was accused of and that led to his death was sorcery.

7. To teach the people in creative and interesting ways and to help them remember what he taught, Jesus addressed them with short, concise statements that took the form of dogma.

Primary Source Quotations

The Kingdom of God

Just as the life of Jesus, in his obedience and dedication to the Father, is a living parable of the "God with us," in the same way the concrete commitment of consecrated persons to God and brothers becomes an eloquent sign of the presence of the Kingdom of God for the world of today.

—Pope Benedict XVI

If there be a true way that leads to the everlasting Kingdom, it is most certainly of suffering, patiently endured.

—St. Colette

Thy Kingdom Come
It may even be . . . that the Kingdom of God means Christ himself, whom we daily desire to come, and whose coming we wish to be manifested quickly to us.

—St. Cyprian

Only a pure soul can boldly say: "Thy kingdom come." One who has heard Paul say, "Let not sin therefore reign in your mortal bodies," and has purified himself in action, thought, and word will say to God: "Thy kingdom come!"

—St. Cyril of Jerusalem

Our natural will is to have God, and the good will of God is to have us, and we may never cease willing or longing for him until we have him in the fullness of joy. [Christ] will never have full bliss in us until we have our full bliss in him.

—Bl. Julian of Norwich

In Matthew 13:44–50, Jesus offers several short parables describing what "the Kingdom of God is like." Take some time to write at least three statements beginning with "The Kingdom of God is like . . ."

Ongoing Assignments

As you cover the material in this chapter, choose and complete at least three of these assignments.

1. Read and write a summary of one of the following articles by Fr. Daniel Harrington, S.J. (both from St. Anthony Messenger Press):
   • "The Truth About Jesus and Women"
   • "Miracles: Signs of God's Presence"

2. Select several passages from your reading of the Gospel of Luke. Make a poster with the passages accompanied by your own illustrations or popular clipart. Display your poster board in the classroom.

3. The film *Jesus*, sponsored by the Campus Crusade for Christ, is based on the Gospel of Luke. Watch the film. Write a review of the acting, storyline, authenticity with the Gospel, and potential appeal to your peers.

4. Research the origins of the disputes between the Jews and Samaritans in Jesus' time. Write a report that summarizes your findings.

5. Choose a favorite parable. Then create a PowerPoint presentation or printed booklet targeted for a third-grader that includes both the words of the parable and illustrations that you find to depict the parable's scenes.

6. With several classmates, prepare and enact a mime presentation on one of the parables.

7. Choose a parable from Luke's Gospel not covered in this chapter. Research three commentaries to discover what the parable means. Write a one-page report summarizing your findings and using appropriate footnotes. Conclude the paper with your own interpretation of the parable.

8. Read the following parables. Write your answers to the questions in your journal.

   A Friend at Midnight (Lk 11:5–10)
   • What is the meaning of this parable?
   • Rewrite the parable in a modern setting. Be sure to make the same point as Jesus did.

   The Rich Man and Lazarus (Lk 16:19–31)
   • Does Jesus condemn wealth by means of this parable? Explain your response.
   • What is it that Jesus wants us to do with the "riches" we have been given?

9. Take some digital photos of some scenes in nature. Choose several as the basis of a short parable that teaches a truth about the Kingdom of God. Be sure the message is consistent with the message that Jesus

himself preached. Using your parable and digital photos, create a PowerPoint presentation to share with your classmates.

Prayer

A great way to pray with the Gospels is by using meditative prayer. Meditation is a searching form of prayer. It helps the mind to understand the "why and how of the Christian life" (*CCC*, 2705) and to respond to what Christ is asking of us. Besides the Gospels and the rest of Sacred Scripture, holy icons, liturgical texts of the day or season, writings of the Church Fathers, and other works of spirituality are among the sources of meditative prayer.

Try this simple meditation with Luke 7:36–50. Use the following steps to help you to engage in meditative prayer.

1. *Calm down.* Find a restful prayer position. Breathe slowly and deeply. Let the cares of the day drain from you.

2. *Enter into the presence of the Lord.* Feel the warmth of his love all around you. Imagine Jesus next to you assuring you of his love. Look at his features: his clothing, the length and color of his hair, his complexion, his smile, his eyes. Feel him putting his arm around you.

3. *Read the Gospel passage (Lk 7:36–50).* Put yourself and Jesus into the passage. For example, make yourself a character in the story. Use all your senses—sight, smell, touch, taste, hearing. Listen carefully to the words of the passage. Pause often and let them sink in. But let your imagination flow with the picture.

4. *Reflect.* Return to the present. Ask the Lord to show you what the passage might be saying to you in your life right now.

5. *Conclude.* Thank the Lord for the time he spent with you. Make a resolution from your prayer time and try to put it into practice.

- *Reflection*: How are you lead into sin? Are you willing to take your sins to Jesus and hear his message of love, forgiveness, and peace?

- *Resolution*: Examine your conscience this week on those actions and attitudes that are keeping you from being a more loving person. To experience the Lord's forgiveness, resolve to celebrate the Sacrament of Penance at the earliest possible time.

Chapter 4 Quick View

5

THE PASSION AND DEATH OF JESUS CHRIST

*Have among yourselves the same attitude
that is also yours in Christ Jesus,
Who, though he was in the form of God,
did not regard equality with God something to be grasped.*

—Philippians 2:5-6

So Another Might Live
St. Maximilian Kolbe gave up his own life so that another man could live. Jesus Christ, our innocent Savior, gave up his life for us so that we could be saved.

Christ's Redemptive Death
The theological and historical understandings of the events surrounding Christ's Death help to reveal its meaning.

Overview of the Passion Narratives
Each of the Evangelists shaped the events of Christ's Passion in order to emphasize certain theological points.

Tracing the Events of Our Salvation
The Paschal Mystery of Christ's Passion, Death, and Resurrection are the central part of God's eternal plan and are revealed in each of the Gospels, including Matthew 26–27.

So Another Might Live

The humility and sacrifice of Jesus Christ has inspired many people through the centuries to live and die for him. One such person was Maximilian Kolbe, a Polish Franciscan priest who was arrested and accused by the Nazis of publishing materials in opposition to them. Also, during the Nazi persecutions in World War II, his friary helped hide and shelter thousands of Jews and Poles. The Gestapo sent him to the infamous death camp at Auschwitz in 1941. There he was assigned to a special work crew that included other priests and that was supervised by vicious guards.

In July 1941, an Auschwitz prisoner tried to escape. As punishment, the camp's commander paraded all the prisoners into the blazing sun and selected ten of them to be executed. One of the men selected to die was Francis Gajowniczek who cried out, "My wife, my children, I shall never see them again!"

Fr. Maximilian stepped out of line and asked the commander to choose him to die since he did not have a family. The commander obliged since he did not care who died, just that ten men be executed to serve as a warning for any future attempts at escape. The commander did ask Fr. Maximilian why he would volunteer for execution. Maximilian replied simply, "Because I am a Catholic priest." Fr. Maximilian suffered two weeks of starvation, all the while ministering to and comforting the other men who were condemned with him. He was the last to die, on August 14, 1941, after the guards injected him with carbolic acid to bring about instant death.

In 1982, Pope John Paul II canonized Fr. Maximilian as a "martyr of charity." His feast day is August 14.

St. Maximilian Kolbe surrendered his life so that a man might live. His inspiration for doing so was his Lord and Savior, Jesus Christ. Philippians 2:5–11 (partially quoted on page 108) tells us of the humility of Jesus Christ. Jesus, God's only Son,

Fullness in Following Christ

St. Jerome said "One is rich enough who is poor with Christ." Sometimes, as in the life of St. Maximilian Kolbe, the person who aligns himself or herself with Christ is called to the gift of **martyrdom**. Take some time to brainstorm the names of people (famous or not so famous) you believe have found fullness of life by following Jesus. Don't get stuck only on "churchy-types." Think of friends, relatives, neighbors, teachers, and acquaintances who reflect a spirit of having found fullness of life in Jesus Christ. Make a list of five to ten names and then answer the questions that follow:

- What is a wise quotation about faith in Jesus or life in general you have heard someone on your list say?

- How has someone on your list incorporated sacrifice into his or her life, that is, giving up some pleasures in order to develop the self-discipline of following Jesus?

- What have you learned from anyone on your list about how you should treat others, including your enemies?

- Who on your list do you think would be willing to give up his or her life for another? Explain why you chose that person.

- Is there anyone you would be willing to die for? Describe a possible scenario when you might be willing to be a martyr.

became man and lived with us. He so loved us that he gave up his life for us. He came to save the last, the lost, and the least, dying so that our sins may be forgiven and we might have eternal life. The Letter to the Philippians continues by saying that because of Jesus' actions

> . . . God greatly exalted him
> and bestowed on him the name
> that is above every name,
> that at the name of Jesus every knee should bend,
> of those in heaven and on earth and under
>   the earth,
> and every tongue confess that Jesus Christ is Lord,
> to the glory of God the Father. (Phil 2:9–11)

Jesus Christ is Lord—our eternal friend and Savior. St. Maximilian Kolbe died so that one man might live. Jesus Christ died so that all people might have eternal life.

For Reflection

Who is someone or what is something you could be compelled to give up your life for?

Christ's Redemptive Death (*CCC*, 595-623)

Jesus Christ's redemptive Death on the cross and his Resurrection is the high point of human history. It was not the result of chance but part of the mystery of God's saving plan of Salvation, promised to humanity immediately after the Original Sin of Adam and Eve. Sacred Scripture itself had foretold God's plan of Salvation through the death of a Suffering Servant prophesied in Isaiah 53. Also, St. Paul professed that "Christ died for our sins in accordance with the scriptures" (1 Cor 15:3). After his Resurrection, when he appeared to

martyrdom
The word *martyr* means "witness." Martyrdom applies to a person who bears witness to the truth of his or her faith even unto death. Jesus died the death of a faithful martyr. St. Stephan is recognized as the first Christian martyr.

Reading the Passion

Read the Passion narrative in the Gospel of John, chapters 18-19. To summarize the reading, write one or two key Scripture passages for each of these events.

- Jesus Is Arrested
- Peter's Denials
- Trial before Pilate
- Crucifixion of Jesus
- Taking Jesus Down from the Cross
- Burial of Jesus

his disciples on the road to Emmaus, and then later to the Apostles, Jesus showed them how his Death and Resurrection were recorded in Scripture:

> He said to them, "These are my words that I spoke to you while I was still with you, that everything written about me in the law of Moses and in the prophets and psalms must be fulfilled." Then he opened their minds to understand the scriptures. And he said to them, "Thus it is written that the Messiah would suffer and rise from the dead on the third day and that repentance, for the forgiveness of sins, would be preached in his name to all the nations, beginning from Jerusalem. You are witnesses of these things." (Lk 24:44–48)

"God proves his love for us in that while we were still sinners Christ died for us" (Rom 5:8). The sins of humans, following Original Sin, result in the punishment of death. But God did not abandon humankind. He sent his own Son to redeem us from our sins. Jesus embraced his Father's plan of Salvation from the first moment of his Incarnation. Jesus said, "My food is to do the will of the one who sent me and to finish his work" (Jn 4:34). As John the Baptist testified, Jesus was the Lamb of God, the Suffering Servant who bore the sins of the people and the Paschal Lamb, the symbol of Israel's Redemption at the first Passover.

Theological Meaning of the Death of Jesus

By his Passion and Death, Jesus showed us the depth of God's love, which desires the Salvation of all people. His sacrifice redeemed us, took away our sins, and restored us to communion with God. Christ's sacrifice is unique. It is a gift from the Father who handed his Son over to sinners to reconcile us with himself. "At the same time it is the offering of the Son of God made man, who in freedom and love offered his life to his Father through the Holy Spirit in reparation for our disobedience" (*CCC*, 614).

Jesus chose to be crucified to prove beyond doubt his immense love for us. In obedience to the Father, according to God's plan, Jesus' Death on the cross won our Salvation, bestowing on us, through the Holy Spirit, God's own abundant life. In his unique and definitive sacrifice, Christ took our sins to the cross and, like a New Adam, *represented* us to the Father. By substituting for each human being, Jesus took on our guilt and died a death we deserve. His motive was simply his desire to buy our freedom with his very Person and his eternal love. In his suffering and Death, Jesus' humanity became the free and perfect instrument of divine love, a self-surrendering gift of love on our behalf. It opened eternal life to us, a supreme gift that we sinners do not deserve. Jesus shows us God with a human face. His sacrifice on the cross is the perfect example of love. He gave all that we might have eternal life.

Who Is Responsible for Jesus' Death?

With the eyes of faith, and instructed by the Magisterium, we can understand how Jesus' Death was part of God's plan of Salvation. What is more difficult to understand is why certain people living in Jesus' time conspired to put him to death. The sections below examine some of the historical reasons that led to Jesus' Death.

Crucified under Pontius Pilate

Jesus died by crucifixion, a punishment the Romans used mainly for slaves and revolutionaries. Crucifixion was one of history's most brutal forms of capital punishment. It was meant to torture and shame the condemned man and serve as a warning to those who witnessed it not to commit the same crime. The variations of crucifixion included nailing or tying the extremities to the cross, stretching the arms on the crossbeam, and impaling the genitals. The traditional image of Jesus with his feet and wrists nailed to the cross is also historically plausible. In contrast, the Jewish method of capital punishment was by stoning. This is what some tried to do to the woman caught in adultery (Jn 8:1–11). It was the way St. Stephen, the first Christian martyr, was put to death (Acts 7:54–60).

Specifically, the Roman charge against Jesus was that he was "the King of the Jews." This crime was written on the official inscription posted on the cross on which Jesus hung. Pontius Pilate, governor or prefect of Judea, in the year AD 30 condemned Jesus to death after hearing charges against him and examining him in a hearing. The Synoptic Gospels report that Pilate offered the crowd a choice of releasing Barabbas (a bandit or insurrectionist) or Jesus. The chief priests incited the crowd to ask for Barabbas, so Pilate caved in to their demands and had Jesus scourged and crucified. John 18:28–40 also tells of a hearing before Pilate. In this Gospel

as well, Pilate disregarded the truth and had Jesus executed.

Ironically, Jesus truly was the King of the Jews, the Messiah whom the Jews were awaiting. However, Jesus' rule was not one of political or military power but one of humble service. Both Pilate and the Jewish leaders who opposed Jesus viewed him as a threat to Roman authority and the relatively peaceful relations the Jewish authorities had with Roman occupation forces. So Pilate dealt with Jesus the way Romans dealt with all potential revolutionaries—by executing him. Significantly, Jesus died with two other men who were also seen as threats, men described as "bandits" or "rebels."

Ultimately, then, the one person responsible for Jesus' Death was Pontius Pilate, the Roman prefect of Judea, Samaria, and Idumea from AD 26 to 36. With the cooperation of some religious authorities in Jerusalem, Pilate sentenced Jesus of Nazareth to death, probably in April of AD 30. The Jewish writer Philo described Pilate as "corrupt, violent, abusive and cruel." The Gospels suggest that Pilate thought Jesus was probably innocent of the charge brought against him. However, he violated his conscience and did the politically expedient thing by having Jesus executed.

The Role of Jewish Officials in Jesus' Death

Jesus was a popular teacher who rubbed some of the Jewish officials of his day in the wrong way. Furthermore, though he was not a trained rabbi, he spoke with authority on points of the Law. And people listened to him.

Among the Jewish officials who were upset by Jesus were the Pharisees, a strict Jewish sect that tried to perfectly follow the requirements of the Mosaic Law. On many occasions they felt that Jesus disregarded the Mosaic Law. Jesus responded: "Do not think I have come to abolish the law of the prophets. I have not come to abolish but fulfill" (Mt 5:17). Jesus was a new lawgiver. He got to the root

of what the Law required. For example, whereas the Law forbid killing,
Jesus said that we should avoid anger
because it leads to murder. He agreed
that we should not commit adultery,
as the Law commanded, "but I say to
you whoever looks at a woman with
lust has already committed adultery
with her in his heart" (Mt 5:28). Jesus
also taught on certain ritual purity and
dietary laws, declaring that all foods
are "clean" and it is "what comes out
of a person, that is what defiles" (Mk
7:20). Moreover, Jesus criticized the
Pharisees who followed certain customs to avoid responsibility for paying lip service to what God really
requires, such as taking care of their
parents (Mk 7:8–15).

Also, Jesus associated with sinners, tax collectors, and prostitutes—
activities which scandalized the
Pharisees and scribes. Jesus defended

himself by sharing the parable of the
lost or prodigal son (Lk 15:11–32),
justifying his behavior by showing
that he and his Father are compassionate like the loving father in the
parable. To make such a claim—to do
what only God could do, to forgive
sin—was considered blasphemy and a
crime punishable by stoning to death
under Jewish Law. In John 8:31–59
Jesus even explicitly claimed to be
God when he said, "Amen, Amen, I
say to you, before Abraham came to
be, I AM." The people immediately
recognized that Jesus was claiming to
be God ("I AM" is the translation for
the Hebrew word for God, *Yahweh*),
so they picked up stones to throw at
him.

Some religious leaders thought
that Jesus was possessed by Satan.
Certain exorcisms and other miracles
Jesus performed led some of his opponents to question the source of
Jesus' power. Since they could not
accept that he was the Messiah, a
friend of sinners, and one who violated some of their customs and challenged their authority, they concluded
that his power must come from Satan.
Jesus answered:

> I am not possessed; I honor
> my Father, but you dishonor
> me. I do not seek my own glo-
> ry; there is one who seeks it
> and he is the one who judges.
> (Jn 8:49–50)

A tipping point in the judgment of
Jesus came shortly before his Passion
when he predicted that the temple
of his body would be destroyed and

rebuilt in three days (see Jn 2:14–23). Certain witnesses who heard this teaching interpreted Jesus' prediction as an attack on the Jerusalem Temple, even claiming that he was involved in revolutionary activity. Again, the actual evidence did not merit such a belief. Jesus had always honored the Temple. He was presented there forty days after his birth and taught in it at the age of twelve. In addition, Jesus traveled to the Temple in Jerusalem to celebrate the Passover feast. In his public life, he taught in the Temple precincts during certain Jewish feasts, even on one occasion removing the moneychangers stationed there. Quoting Scripture, he said, "My house shall be a house of prayer, but you have made it a den of thieves" (Mk 19:46).

The chief priest, Joseph Caiaphas, and members of the Jewish ruling body, the **Sanhedrin**, had an economic and religious interest in the Temple. They feared a rebellion. They wanted the peaceful status quo that kept them in power and did not want any excuse for the Romans to clamp down a rebellion with repressive measures. So they brought the charge of insurrection to Pilate. Coupled with it was what to many of them was outrageous and blasphemous—Jesus' claim to be the "Messiah, the son of the Blessed One" (see Mk 14:61). This led Caiaphas to say, "[I]t is better for you that one man should die instead of the people, so that the whole nation may not perish" (Jn 11:50).

In summary, there were many reasons certain Jewish officials wanted Jesus removed. His association with sinners, his exorcisms, his teachings on dietary and ritual purity laws, his teaching with unique authority, his claims to be the Messiah, his forgiving of sin, and his claim to be Lord of the Sabbath were all factors that led religious leaders like the chief priest and members of the Sanhedrin to turn Jesus over to Pilate for execution.

All People Bear Responsibility for Jesus' Death

A tragic historical reality has been to blame the Jewish people as a whole for the death of Jesus. The complex trial of Jesus shows that only a few Jewish officials were in cohort with Pilate, who ultimately put Jesus to death. The real authors and instruments of Jesus' crucifixion are sinners, that is, each of us. We believers crucify Jesus every time we betray him through our sins. It is for our sins that Jesus died.

Jesus freely offered his life to liberate us from our sins and bestow eternal life on us. He underwent the excruciating torments of the most painful form of death devised by human beings out of his immense love for us.

Today, blaming the Jews as a people for Jesus' death—a form of **anti-Semitism**—is contrary to the love of Christ. The Second Vatican Council teaches:

> [W]hat happened in His passion cannot be charged against all the Jews, without distinction, then alive, nor against the Jews of today. . . . [T]he Jews should not be presented as rejected or accursed by God, as if this followed from the Holy Scriptures. . . .
>
> Furthermore, in her rejection of every persecution against any man, the Church . . . decries hatred, persecutions, displays of anti-Semitism, directed against Jews at any time and by anyone.
>
> Besides, as the Church has always held and holds now, Christ underwent His passion and death freely, because of the sins of men and out of infinite love, in order that all may reach Salvation. . . .
>
> We cannot truly call on God, the Father of all, if we refuse to treat in a brotherly way any man, created as he is in the image of God. Man's relation to God the Father and his relation to men his brothers are so linked together that Scripture says: "He who

does not love does not know God (1 John 4:8)." (*Declaration on the Relationship of the Church to Non-Christian Religions*, No. 4–5)

For Review

1. Why did Jesus die?
2. What was the method of capital punishment used by the Romans? What was the method of capital punishment used by the Jews during Jesus' time?

3. Why did Pontius Pilate crucify Jesus?
4. Name three factors that led some Jewish opponents of Jesus to conspire against him.
5. Why is it wrong to blame the Jewish people for the death of Jesus Christ?
6. How are all people implicated in the death of Jesus?

For Reflection

Write a short reflection that discusses the following proposition: "To be anti-Semitic is to be anti-Christian."

Jesus on Trial

Develop a prosecution and defense as if you were putting Jesus on trial in a court of law. To prepare for either side of the case, read the following passages:

- Arrest of Jesus (Mk 14:43-52)
- Jesus before the Sanhedrin (Mk 14:53-62)
- Jesus before Pilate (Mk 15:1-15; Jn 18:28-38; Lk 23:1-5)

The prosecution argument must build a case against Jesus. Possible accusations might include the threat to tear down the Temple, blasphemy, claiming to be king, misleading the people on the payment of taxes (Lk 23:2), instigating riots. Draw additional "evidence" from the Gospels, such as violation of Sabbath laws and disturbing the peace.

Your defense response will examine the charges and then answer them one by one by citing appropriate Scripture passages.

You may wish to work on this exercise with a partner. Each of you will take a different side in the case. Then argue the case in front of a teacher or your classmates.

Overview of the Passion Narratives

The Paschal Mystery of Christ's Passion, Death, and Resurrection is the heart of the Gospel. These events are commemorated in a special way liturgically during Holy Week when the Church celebrates the Paschal Mystery of God's love for his people. The Sacrament of Baptism initiates us into the Paschal Mystery. The Eucharist represents (makes present) the Paschal Mystery and allows us to enter into it. In the Gospels, the **passion narratives** detail the events of Christ's Passion, Death, and Resurrection.

The Passion narratives were probably the oldest stories about Jesus proclaimed by the early Church. They were formed and added very quickly to the liturgy. They included many references to Old Testament prophecies that alluded to the death of the Messiah. For example, Mark's account of Jesus' crucifixion includes the following references to Old Testament prophecies:

- the offer of wine (Ps 69)
- the division of Jesus' garments (Ps 22)

- the presence of two robbers (Is 63)

- the reactions of the mockers (Ps 22; Wis 2)

- the darkness (Am 8)

- Jesus' final prayer (Ps 22)

- the offer of vinegar (Ps 69)

- the loud cry of Jesus (Ps 31)

- the tearing of the Temple veil (Ex 26)

Different Points of Emphasis in the Passion Narratives

The Evangelists agree on the essential details in the passion narratives but wrote from unique perspectives with different points of emphasis. Each of the Paschal narratives includes the following common elements:

- the arrest

- questioning by the high priest

- the trials before the Sanhedrin and Pontius Pilate

- the condemnation

- the crucifixion

- the death

- the burial

The Evangelists shaped the events of Christ's Passion in order to emphasize certain theological points. The Gospels of Matthew and Mark stress elements of abandonment but also vindication at the end. Some elements of abandonment include Judas betraying Jesus, the three disciples falling asleep during Jesus' agony, and Peter's denial. Also, when Jesus

is arrested, everyone flees; even the young man lurking on the outskirts runs away and loses his garment (see Mk 14:51). The Jewish and Roman authorities harshly judge Jesus, and he is sentenced to death. Even then, Jesus is mocked by the soldiers and crowds. Vindication comes immediately after Jesus breathes his last breath: the veil in the Temple is torn in two, indicating that a New Covenant is in force and that a new age has dawned. A Roman centurion—ironically a Gentile—confesses Jesus' identity: "Truly this man was the Son of God!" (Mk 15:39).

Luke's Gospel presents the disciples in a more favorable light; for example, they fall asleep only once, not three times, and only then because they are sorrowful at Jesus' impending fate. Luke emphasizes Jesus' compassion through the whole ordeal. Jesus heals the slave's ear in

passion narratives
The name for the four separate accounts of the Passion of Christ. The passion narratives of the Synoptic Gospels follow a general literary and thematic plan. The passion narrative of John's Gospel provides an independent version.

JERUSALEM AT THE TIME OF JESUS' CRUCIFIXION

After sharing the Last Supper with his Apostles in the Upper Room (lower left), Jesus walked with his disciples to the Mount of Olives. He had to pass through the Kidron Valley (1), situated to east of the old walled city of Jerusalem. At this time, the east side of the Kidron Valley was a large cemetery. Because it was Passover, there would have been a full moon lighting their way. Their destination was the Mount of Olives, a two-mile ridge that rises some two hundred feet above the level of the city. Nearby was the city of Bethany, where Jesus stayed with his friends, and Bethphage, where he began his triumphal entry into Jerusalem. Near the base of the Mount of Olives was the Garden of Gethsemane. The word *Gethsemane* means "oil press." The Garden of Gethsemane likely contained an olive grove and a press to crush the olives. It was here that Jesus prayed and the soldiers came to arrest him. Today, the Church of All Nations is located next to the Garden of Gethsemane.

After his arrest, Jesus was taken first to Annas (2) and then to the high priest Joseph Caiaphas's residence, where there was a hearing held against Jesus. Next, Jesus had a more formal hearing before the Sanhedrin, most likely at the Temple (3). From there, he was taken to Pontius Pilate, who resided at the Fortress of Anontia (4). Pilate sent him to Herod Antipas (5). Herod returned Jesus to Pilate, who finally handed Jesus over for scourging (6) and ordered his crucifixion. Jesus then carried his cross to the site of execution at Golgotha outside of one of Jerusalem's west gates (7). *Golgotha* means "place of the skull." Pilgrims entering the city would have been able to read the inscription on Jesus' cross as they passed by.

the Garden; he comforts the women while carrying his cross on the way to Calvary; he promises that the Good Thief will be with him in Paradise; and he forgives his executioners while hanging on the cross. His last words are a faith-filled cry, "Father, into your hands I commend my spirit" (Lk 24:46).

The passion narrative in John 18–19 describes Jesus in control of the events. For example, he freely enters into the Passion: "I lay down my life in order to take it up again. No one takes it from me, but I lay it down on my own. I have power to lay it down, and power to take it up again" (Jn 10:17–18). At the time of his arrest, when asked if he is Jesus of Nazareth, he answered: "I AM," the divine name, which caused the soldiers to fall to the ground. When Peter wishes to defend him, Jesus tells him to put his sword away and indicates that what is happening is part of God's plan: "Shall I not drink the cup that the Father gave me?" (Jn 18:11). In John's Gospel, during the interrogation, Pilate, not Jesus, is put on the defensive. Jesus counters Pilate's threat by saying, "You would have no power over me if it had not been given to you from above" (Jn 19:11). On the way to Calvary, Jesus carries his own cross, with no help from Simon of Cyrene. From the cross, Jesus looks to the future by entrusting his mother to the Beloved Disciple. His last words are, "It is finished" (Jn 19:30), indicating that the work he came to do, his Father's will, the prophesies made in the Old Testament, and our Salvation have now been accomplished.

For Review

1. List five Old Testament prophecies that are fulfilled in Jesus' Passion narratives.

2. Describe the different theological emphases in the passion narratives of Mark, Matthew, Luke, and John.

3. Trace the itinerary of Jesus from the Last Supper to the time of his crucifixion.

For Reflection

- Which Gospel portrait of the Passion do you most identify with? Why?

- Imagine you were with Jesus in the Garden of Gethsemane. Give an honest assessment of how you would have responded to the situation.

Tracing the Events of Our Salvation

The events of our Salvation are part of God's eternal plan. Jesus said, "the Son of Man did not come to be served but to serve and give his life as ransom for many" (Mk 10:34). He also said:

> I am the good shepherd. A good shepherd lays down his life for his sheep. . . . No one takes [my life] from me, but I lay it down on my own. I have power to lay it down, and power to take it up again. This command I received from my Father. (Jn 10:11, 18)

How did these events unfold? The account in Matthew 26–27 (drawn in good part from Mark's Gospel) provides a detailed account.

Jesus Enters Jerusalem (Mt 21:1-13)

Recall that Jesus enters Jerusalem during the week before Passover, the feast that celebrates God's deliverance of the Israelites from slavery into freedom. When Jesus and his disciples reach the small villages of Bethphage and Bethany, near the Mount of Olives, he tells two of his disciples where to find a colt and they go off to retrieve it. Jesus rides into Jerusalem on the colt, thus fulfilling a prophecy of Zechariah 9:9. The crowds greet Jesus as a prophet. They spread out their cloaks as a sign of respect for him and wave palm branches as they enthusiastically shout:

> Hosanna to the Son of David;
> blessed is he who comes
> in the name of the Lord;
> hosanna in the highest.
> (Mt 21:9)

Jesus enters the Temple area and drives out the moneychangers. He quotes to them the Scriptural passage, "My house shall be a house of prayer, but you are making it a den of thieves" (Mt 21:13). The incident is unusual because the business conducted at the Temple was religious in nature. Jesus' charge that the Temple had become a den of thieves showed that he had authority over the religious practices of Israel, a fact that enrages the religious leaders.

Conspiracy against Jesus (Mt 26:1-5)

The leaders conspire against Jesus while he teaches in the Temple. They want to do so in such a way that the crowds will not come to his defense and cause an uprising. However, the plan to not arrest Jesus "during the festival that there may not be a riot among the people" (Mt 26:5) failed. He was actually arrested on the night of Nisan 14, the Preparation Day of the Passover, and put to death the next day. Joseph Caiaphas, the **high priest**, is quoted in John 11:50 saying that it was better for Jesus to die than for the whole nation to perish. Other groups, for example, the Pharisees and Herodians (see Mk 12:13–17) also oppose Jesus. They question things like the

source of his teaching authority, his views on beliefs like the resurrection of the dead, and whether it is lawful to pay taxes to Rome or not. They are also upset by Jesus' criticism of their hypocrisy, for example, when he told them, "You pay tithes of mint and dill and cumin, and have neglected the weightier things of the law: judgment and mercy and fidelity" (Mt 23:23). Jesus also upset the Sadducees, an aristocratic class that cooperated with Roman rule. They saw Jesus as a threat to the civil order and a danger to their position of leadership: "If we leave him alone, all will believe in him, and the Romans will come and take away both our land and our nation" (Jn 11:48).

Anointing at Bethany (Mt 26:6-13)

In Mark and Matthew's Gospel, an anonymous woman anoints Jesus' head with expensive oil at Bethany. (John's Gospel identifies the woman as Mary, the sister of Lazarus.) Some people (identified as Judas in John's Gospel) complain about the waste, observing that the costly ointment could have been sold for alms for the poor. But Jesus commends the woman's generous action because it foreshadows the anointing of his body after his Death. Anointing a body for burial was considered of higher merit than giving money to the poor, a task that could always be done. Proper burial of the dead was considered an essential condition for sharing in the Resurrection. Recall also that *Christ*

high priest
In Jewish history, the priest in charge of the Temple worship. The high priest shared in the general priestly duties, however, he was the only one allowed to enter the holy of holies, and only then on the Day of Atonement. He was a descendent of Aaron.

means, "anointed one." This woman of simple faith recognizes Jesus' true identity and mission when so many others do not.

Judas's Betrayal (Mt 26:14-16)

Judas Iscariot betrays Jesus for thirty pieces of silver. His motive of avarice fits John's description of Judas as the one who kept the money purse of the Apostles and who stole from it (Jn 12:6). Judas is willing to "hand him over," the same Greek verb used to describe how Jesus is handed over to Death. The Gospels of Luke and John mention that Satan influences Judas to betray his friend (Jn 22:3–6).

The Last Supper (Mt 26:17-35)

Jesus carefully plans the Passover meal by instructing his disciples to meet a man in whose house he will celebrate with his disciples. Jesus' planning of the Passover meal shows that he is in control of the events. The sacrifice he will make on our behalf is truly free since love is only love if it is freely given.

At the meal, Jesus foretells his betrayal. The Apostles are confused and deny that they would ever betray their master. But when Judas asks, "Surely it is not I, Rabbi?" Jesus answers, "You have said so" (Mt 26:25). The emphasis in Jesus' response is on the pronoun *you* to imply that Jesus would have answered if the question had not been asked.

Jesus then celebrates a Passover meal with his Apostles where he took bread, blessed it, broke it, and gave to his disciples saying, "Take and eat; this is my body" (Mt 26:26). In a similar way he took a cup, gave thanks, and gave it to his disciples saying, "Drink from it all, of you, for this is my blood of the covenant, which will be shed on behalf of many for the forgiveness of sin" (Mt 26:27–28). With these words, Jesus instituted the Eucharist, a celebration of Jesus' Passover from death to new life and the gift of himself to all believers under the forms of bread and wine. Jesus' Passion, Death, and Resurrection is God's new covenant with us, his way of delivering his people. The Eucharist that Christ instituted at the Last Supper is the memorial of his sacrifice. The Apostles (and their successors) will serve as the priests of the New Covenant, calling to mind what Jesus has accomplished for us and commanding us to pour ourselves out in service to others in imitation of him.

After the meal, Jesus and the Apostles make their way to the Mount of Olives where Jesus prays in great sorrow, just as King David did after his trusted son Absalom had betrayed him. On the way, Jesus predicts that the disciples will flee during the coming trials. But he also reassures them that after his Resurrection, he will go before them to Galilee where he—the Good Shepherd—will re-gather his flock. Jesus then predicts that Peter will deny him three times, though Peter proclaims, "Even though I should have to die with you, I will not deny you" (Mt 26:35).

The Agony in the Garden and the Arrest of Jesus (Mt 26:36-56)

Jesus' sorrow at his impending Death reveals a natural human response. From the depths of his soul, Jesus prays that the cup of impending death, which also involves his battle with Satan and sin, be taken from him. But he also prays the perfect prayer that not his will, but his Father's be done: "My Father, if it is possible, let this cup pass from me; yet, not as I will, but as you will" (Mt 26:39).

Jesus courageously accepts his destiny and does not flee from it. The Apostles are overcome with grief and cannot stay awake to comfort Jesus during his time of trial. Three times he needs to tell them to stay awake to prepare for the coming test. He warns them, "The spirit is willing, but the flesh is weak" (Mt 26:41). Their threefold failure to heed his plea foreshadows Peter's threefold denial that is soon to come.

Sadly, one of Jesus' closest followers, Judas Iscariot, leads an armed crowd sent from the chief priest and elders of the people to arrest Jesus. Judas betrays Jesus with a kiss, and he does so under the cover of dark, the realm of Satan. A disciple of Jesus (identified as Peter in John's Gospel) draws his sword and cuts off the ear of the high priest's servant (named Malchus in John's Gospel). Jesus warns his disciple, "Put your sword back into its sheath, for all who take the sword will perish by the sword" (Mt 26:52). Jesus also reprimands the crowd that came to arrest him for using weapons. Jesus always taught openly and always taught peace. Even here in the Garden Jesus is consistent in refusing to conform to the expectation of many who believe the Messiah

would be a political, military leader who would use force against the Romans.

As he had predicted, all his disciples abandon Jesus at the time of his arrest.

Jesus before the Sanhedrin and Peter's Denial (Mt 26:57–27:10)

John 13 provides further detail that Jesus had a hearing before the former high priest Annas as well as the current high priest Joseph Caiaphas, and a session in front of the Sanhedrin. The exact sequence of events is not totally clear. However, Matthew's Gospel tells us that there was a night trial before Caiaphas at which were present scribes, elders, priests, and members of the Sanhedrin, the seventy-one-member official judicial and legislative body of the Jewish people. At this hearing, they try to obtain false evidence in order to pronounce a death penalty against him. They bring in false witnesses, two of whom claim that Jesus said he would destroy the Temple. Finally, Caiaphas asks Jesus if he is the Messiah, the Son of God. Jesus affirms he is and then says,

> From now on you will see "the Son of Man seated at the right hand of the Power" and "coming on the clouds of heaven." (Mt 26:64)

Jesus' proclamation outrages the religious leaders. The high priest tears his robes and accuses Jesus of committing the sin of blasphemy (that is, insulting God). Under Jewish law, blasphemy was punishable by death. Others (apparently the members of the Sanhedrin itself) in an act of total disrespect, spit on Jesus, strike, slap, and mock him, saying, "Prophesy for us, Messiah: who is it that struck you?" (Mt 26:68).

Meanwhile, Peter is out in the courtyard and is recognized by a maid as a friend of Jesus. Peter who had confessed Jesus to be the Messiah now betrays his friend and Master. As Jesus predicted, three times Peter denies knowing him. When the cock crows, Peter remembers Jesus' prediction. He immediately repents of his grave sin and weeps bitterly. His repentance and sorrow at his betrayal is in stark contrast to Judas who, once he realized his sin, despairs and commits suicide (Mt 27:5). Peter ends up bravely proclaiming his Lord after the Resurrection and, according to tradition, is crucified himself in an inverted position under one of Nero's persecutions. Peter's repentance and sorrow serve as a model to all sinners who have turned against Jesus through their sins. Christ will always accept us back as his friend if we repent and accept his forgiveness.

Under the Roman laws of occupation in effect in AD 30, only the Roman prefect had the right to inflict the death penalty for crimes of a nonreligious nature. Pilate would have scoffed at the Sanhedrin's religious charge of blasphemy. However, accusing Jesus of trying to usurp the emperor was seditious and a capital offense. This is the charge the Jewish authorities took to Pontius Pilate, hoping that he would pronounce the death penalty.

Jesus before Pilate (Mt 27:11-31)

The Jewish historian Josephus, writing in an independent source apart from Scripture, portrays Pontius Pilate as arrogant and cruel. He tells how Pilate once unleashed his soldiers, dressed as civilians, to beat Jewish citizens who were protesting Pilate's use of the Temple treasury to build an aqueduct. According to Josephus, toward the end of Pilate's ten-year rule (26–36), he inflicted violence on a Samaritan religious procession, an act that got him dismissed from his post and sent into exile.

Corroborating this evidence, all the Gospels portray Pilate as cynical. He knows that Jesus is innocent, yet he fails to follow his conscience. Matthew records Pilate's wife's warning to her husband not to execute Jesus. Luke's Gospel testifies that Pilate sends Jesus to Herod Antipas, the tetrarch of Galilee, who was in Jerusalem for the Passover celebration. When Jesus refuses to perform a sign, Herod mocks Jesus and his soldiers abuse him and send him back to Pilate.

Pilate then schemes to escape his responsibility by involving a Passover custom of freeing a prisoner of the citizens' choosing. Mark's and John's Gospels also mention this custom; Luke's original manuscript does not. There is no mention of this custom anywhere else apart from Scripture. Pilate thinks the crowd might call for Jesus to be released, but they choose Barabbas instead, a criminal who in fact is responsible for inciting riots. Jesus accepts Pilate's charge that he is King of the Jews, but

does not answer the inquiries of the priests and elders. Pilate caves into the crowd's cry "Let him be crucified" when they ask him what he should do

with Jesus. Pilate pronounces Jesus guilty of sedition, has Jesus scourged, and hands him over for crucifixion.

Pilate's soldiers mock Jesus, strip him, and dress him in a scarlet military cloak. They crown him with thorns and put a reed in his right hand. Kneeling before him, they mock him, calling him "King of the Jews." All the while they treat him as an object to be scorned. They spit on him in utter contempt and lead him off to the site of crucifixion.

Crucifixion and Death of Jesus Christ (Mt 27:32-56)

The beatings so weakened Jesus that a passerby, Simon of Cyrene, is pressed into carrying the horizontal crossbeam. (The vertical beam was fixed in the ground at the site of crucifixion—Golgotha—a small, elevated hill that resembled a skull.)

When Jesus arrives at Golgotha, he refuses to drink the wine mixed with gall—a slight narcotic meant to ease the pain of the condemned men. As mentioned, crucifixion was one of humanity's worst forms of torture ever invented. While it is possible that Jesus' wrists and feet were nailed to a cross in an elongated plus sign, as traditionally pictured, it

is also possible that the cross was in the form of the letter "T". Whether the cross had a support for his feet, or a little seat for his buttocks, is unknown. The purpose of the supports was to allow the person to breathe and thus prolong the agony. Whatever the mode of crucifixion, it resulted in a horrible death, usually by dehydration, loss of blood, shock, and respiratory arrest. (The emperor Constantine finally banned crucifixion as a form of capital punishment in the fourth century.)

After stripping Jesus and nailing him to the cross, the soldiers cast lots to divide his garments. Jesus is crucified between two bandits, called by Matthew "revolutionaries," thus showing the indignity that befell the innocent Jesus. Both men taunt Jesus. (Luke's Gospel, however, reports that one of these bandits rebukes his fellow criminal and asks Jesus to remember him when he enters his Kingdom. Jesus assures him that he will be in Paradise with him that very day.) An inscription written in Hebrew, Greek, and Latin ironically advertises Jesus' crime—"King of the Jews." Passersby, priests, scribes, and elders mock him and challenge him to rescue himself. We can only imagine the indignities heaped on Jesus. Yet, he resists any temptation to strike his tormenters and save himself. He is faithful to his Father to the very end.

Darkness descended on the land from noon until three in the afternoon, the time of Jesus' death. His last words are "My God, my God, why have you forsaken me?" (Jesus' address to his Father as "God" symbolizes his utter agony as a human being who cries out to his God for help.) Observers mistakenly think that Jesus is calling on the prophet Elijah for help, again displaying their continued misunderstanding of Jesus. They fail to recognize that Jesus is reciting the first lines of Psalm 22 in Arabic: *"Eli, Eli, lema sabachthani."* This heartfelt Psalm ends with joyful confidence that God will indeed rescue the petitioner out of his terrible fate. Soon thereafter Jesus lets out a loud cry and gives up his spirit. At the moment of his death, the veil in

MARY,
THE MOTHER OF GOD

Mary, a young Jewish girl living in or around Nazareth near the beginning of the first century AD, was born to play a crucial role in Salvation History. At that time, an angel appeared to her with a message that most would find unbelievable: "Behold, you will conceive in your womb and bear a son, and you shall name him Jesus" (Lk 1:30). This news was immense, for Mary was a virgin and engaged to Joseph but unmarried at the time she conceived her Son. Jesus was conceived solely by the power of the Holy Spirit, fulfilling the prophecy of Isaiah: "Behold, a virgin shall conceive and bear a son" (Is 7:14). Mary's virginity was perpetual throughout her life. The Church holds that Jesus is Mary's only son, but her spiritual motherhood extends to all.

Mary gave birth to Jesus, and she and Joseph raised him in a loving, prayer-filled home. They taught and cared for him. When Jesus came on the public scene, Mary continued to witness to and support him, even as he experienced his arrest, suffering, and Death on the cross. In addition, she was the first and foremost disciple who prayed with the Apostles in the Upper Room awaiting the descent of the Holy Spirit on Pentecost Sunday. Without a doubt, Mary was the most faithful witness to Jesus. She obeyed God's will; she fully cooperated with Jesus' work of Salvation; she generously responded to the graces of the Holy Spirit. All of these qualities make her the perfect model of Christian faith and love.

Because of her example, the Church honors Mary with many titles, all of which tell us something about what we believe about her. Mary is Our Lady, the Immaculate Conception, the Blessed Mother, the Mother of the Church, Ever Virgin, the Queen of Heaven and Earth. Mary continues to plead with us before her Son. This is why the Church prays to Mary using these titles: Advocate, Helper, Benefactress, and Mediatrix.

Of all the titles of Mary, the most significant is that she is the Mother of God. She is our Mother, too, the loving Mother who fully cooperated with the Holy Spirit to bring Christ into the world.

the Temple's sanctuary is split in two. This symbolizes that the days of the Old Covenant have ended. Jesus' death initiates the New Covenant, a new age when all people can worship God directly, in truth and justice. Jesus has removed the barrier separating us from God.

The Gospel describes certain signs in Matthew 27:51b–53 that were supposed to take place when God's Kingdom came in its fullness. Drawing on Ezekiel 37, Matthew shows how Jesus' Death launches a new stage in history, a stage that will result in the resurrection of the dead. Matthew's Gospel goes on to report how the Roman centurion and his men greatly feared the events they witnessed and immediately understood their significance. They proclaimed, "Truly, this was the Son of God!" Ironically, it is Gentiles, not Jesus' closest followers, who recognize Jesus' true identity.

Not everyone abandons Jesus at his crucifixion. Matthew's Gospel states that many women were present, looking on from a distance. Among them were Mary Magdalene; Mary, the mother of James and Joseph; and the mother of the sons of Zebedee, that is, the Apostles James and John. The Gospel of John also tells us that Mary, the Blessed Mother, stood beneath the cross with the Beloved Disciple, likely John. All these disciples were witnesses to the Death of Jesus.

Burial of Jesus (Mt 27:57-66)

Joseph of Arimathea was a wealthy disciple of Jesus. The Gospels of Mark and Luke identify him as a member of the Sanhedrin but as one who did not approve of the council's condemnation of Jesus. Pilate releases Jesus' body to Joseph of Arimathea because he is completely certain that Jesus is dead. Joseph wraps Jesus' body in a clean linen cloth and places it in a new tomb in the rock. (John's Gospel reports how Nicodemus assists Joseph in anointing Jesus' body with a hundred pounds of spices, an anointing worthy of a king). This takes place hurriedly late on Friday afternoon since the Sabbath begins

INRI

You have probably noticed some crucifixes with the letters *INRI* at the top. These letters are related to the custom of Roman authorities of posting the crime of condemned criminals on their crosses. The idea was to advertise the crime to thwart others from even thinking about committing something similar. In the Holy Land, Romans would have affixed a sign in three languages: Greek, Hebrew, and Latin. Visitors to Jerusalem during the religious festivals could understand at least one of these languages.

INRI abbreviates the Latin words that would have been posted: *Iesus Nazarenus Rex Judeorum*, which translates to "Jesus of Nazareth, King of the Jews."

at sundown. After the tomb is sealed, Mary Magdalene and the other Mary remain sitting, mourning the loss of their master.

Matthew's Gospel is the only one that mentions how certain priests and Pharisees petition Pilate to post a guard at the tomb to guard against Jesus' disciples stealing his body and claiming that he rose from the dead. Pilate refuses their request, so they post their own guard. This interesting point reveals that Jesus' opponents knew he was dead and could identify the place of his burial. This is important because after Jesus' Resurrection, nonbelievers could never produce Jesus' body, even though they knew where he was buried.

Jesus' Death on the cross was a unique sacrifice that has accomplished our Redemption and restores us to communion with God. Because Jesus is true God and true man, in the unity of his divine person, for this reason he is the "one mediator between God and man" (1 Tm 2:5). Yet because Jesus has united himself to every human being, it is possible for us to share in Christ's Paschal Mystery, in a way known to God. Jesus told his disciples, "Whoever wishes to come after me must deny himself, take up his cross, and follow me" (Mt 16:24). Jesus showed us the way, and he wants us to walk in his footsteps.

We do this by trying to discern what God wants us to do and then following the path he has in store for us. This includes offering any sufferings and disappointments that come our way, joining them to the sufferings of Jesus. Our model is the Blessed Mother who, as she stood beneath the cross, quietly endured the death of her beloved Son. As St. Rose of Lima tells us, "Apart from the cross there is no other ladder by which we may get to Heaven."

For Review

1. Why does Jesus enter Jerusalem on a colt?
2. What is the significance of the woman anointing Jesus at Bethany?
3. What motivated Judas to betray Jesus? Why did the priests and elders involve Judas in the betrayal?
4. What is the theme of Jesus' prayer in the Garden of Gethsemane?
5. What crime does the Sanhedrin accuse Jesus of committing?
6. What role did Pilate have in Jesus' Death?
7. How did the crucifixion take place?

You Are There

Imagine standing under the cross at the time of Jesus' crucifixion. You are an interested bystander who had heard Jesus teaching in the Temple. You think he is a very special person. You look at him suffering on the cross. He looks down from the cross into your eyes. You look at him. He looks at you. Write a prayer reflection to Jesus telling him what you feel and think about his sacrifice *for you* on the cross. Tell him of your love for him.

8. Who buried Jesus? Why is a guard posted
   at his tomb?

 **For Reflection**

What does it mean to pick up your cross and
follow Jesus?

EXPLAINING THE FAITH

Why would God the Father allow Jesus, his only begotten Son, to suffer and die?

Simply put, God the Father permitted the suffering and Death of Jesus Christ, his only begotten Son, because of his immense love for us humans (see *CCC*, 599-609). God's love invites us to live eternally with him in Heaven. Through his Passion and Death, we learn from Jesus about the depth of the Father's love that helps overcome evil, sin, and death.

It is because of the sin of Adam and Eve that all of us are born with a wounded human nature. Original Sin deprives us of Original Holiness and Original Justice; has wounded the natural powers proper to human nature; subjects us to ignorance, suffering, and death; and inclines us to sin (*CCC*, 405). Because of Original Sin and our fallen state, the life of Christ's grace did not live in us. As a result, we could not live with God in eternity without first being redeemed.

Jesus' suffering and Death was a supreme sacrifice that destroyed once and for all the power of sin and restored our friendship with God. Out of love for his Father and all human beings, whom his Father wants to save, Jesus freely accepted his Passion and Death. The *Catechism of the Catholic Church* puts it this way:

> By giving up his own Son for our sins, God manifests that his plan for us is one of benevolent love, prior to any merit on our part: "In this is love, not that we loved God but that he loved us and sent his Son to be the expiation for our sins" (1 Jn 4:10, 4:19). God "shows his love for us in that while we were yet sinners Christ died for us" (Rom 5:8). (*CCC*, 604)

One final point: When we reflect on the terrible sufferings and Death Jesus endured on our behalf, we begin to understand the seriousness and gravity of sin and its horrible consequences. Jesus' Paschal Mystery of his Passion, Death, and Resurrection have destroyed the worst effect of sin—death—by opening the gates of Heaven to us and promising us a participation in his Resurrection and a life of eternal joy with the Blessed Trinity. The Father allowed his Son to make this sacrifice simply out of his and his Son's immense love for each one of us—none of whom he wants lost.

Main Ideas

- St. Maximilian Kolbe modeled his sacrifice and martyrdom on the Life and Death of Jesus. (p. 110)

- Jesus' redemptive Death and Resurrection is the high point of human history. (pp. 111–112)

- Jesus' motive for accepting Death was the desire to free humans from sin and to buy our freedom with his very Person and his eternal love. (pp. 112–113)

- Ultimately, the one human most responsible for Jesus' Death was Pontius Pilate. (p. 113)

- There were many reasons certain Jewish officials wanted Jesus condemned, including his association with sinners, his exorcisms, his teachings on dietary and ritual laws, his teaching with authority, his claims to be Messiah, and his forgiveness of sins. (pp. 114–115)

- Blaming Jews for the Death of Christ is a form of anti-Semitism and is contrary to the love of Christ. (p. 115)

- In reality, all people bear responsibility for Jesus' Death. (p. 115)

- The passion narratives detail the events of Jesus' Passion, Death, and Resurrection. (pp. 116–117)

- The Evangelists agree on essential details in the passion narratives but wrote from unique perspectives and different points of emphasis. (pp. 117–119)

- A detailed account of Jesus' Passion and Death is recorded in Matthew 26–27. It includes: Jesus' entry into Jerusalem; the conspiracy against Jesus; his anointing at Bethany; Judas's betrayal; the Last Supper; the agony in the garden; the arrest of Jesus; Jesus before the Sanhedrin and Peter's denial; Jesus before Pilate; the crucifixion and Death of Jesus; and the burial of Jesus. (pp. 120–127)

Terms, People, Places

Choose the italicized term in parentheses that best completes each sentence.

1. Joseph Caiaphas, the (*Roman procurator/ high priest*) was present at a hearing concerning Jesus that also included the members of the Sanhedrin.

2. Many members of the (*priesthood/ Sanhedrin*) were Sadducees.

3. (*Martyrdom/Redemption*) was an act of St. Maximilian Kolbe, who gave up his life for another man from the motivation he found in the Passion, Death, and Resurrection of Jesus Christ.

4. The (*evangelists/passion narratives*) are the name for the separate accounts in the Gospels that trace the events leading up to and including Jesus' Death.

Primary Source Quotations

Jesus' Identity

A man who was merely a man and said the sort of things Jesus said would not be a great moral teacher. He would either be a lunatic—on a level with the man who says he is a poached egg—or else he would be the Devil of Hell. You must make your choice. Either this man was, and is, the Son of God; or else a madman or something worse. You can shut Him up for a fool, you can spit at Him and kill Him as a demon; or you can fall at His feet and call Him Lord and God. But let us not come with any patronizing nonsense about His being a great human teacher. He has not left that open to us. He did not intend to.

—C. S. Lewis

Unique and Definitive Sacrifice

This sacrifice of Christ is unique; it completes and surpasses all other sacrifices. First, it is a gift from God the Father himself, for the Father handed his Son over to sinners in order to reconcile us with himself. At the same time it is the offering of the Son of God made man, who in freedom and love offered his life to his Father through the Holy Spirit in reparation for our disobedience.

—*Catechism of the Catholic Church*, 614

Desire of the Martyrs
The martyrs desired death, not to fly labor, but to attain their goal. And why do they not fear death, from which man naturally shrinks? Because they had vanquished the natural love of their own bodies by divine and supernatural love.

—St. Catherine of Siena

Suffering for the Lord
Say always, "My beloved and despised Redeemer, how sweet it is to suffer for you." If you embrace all things in life as coming from the hands of God, and even embrace death to fulfill his holy will, assuredly you will die a saint.

—St. Alphonsus Liguori

Think again about Christ's Passion and Death. Make a list of fifteen things that you had not previously thought of that could have happened on Good Friday.

Ongoing Assignments

As you cover the material in this chapter, choose and complete at least three of these assignments.

1. Dedicate a time to pray the Stations of the Cross.

   Write a summary paper that tells when, where, how, and with whom you prayed the stations. *Optional*: Make a PowerPoint presentation of your own Stations of the Cross. Write your own reflections and download images to accompany your prayers.

2. Research and write a report on the Shroud of Turin, what many believe to be the burial cloth of Christ.

3. Create a PowerPoint presentation that describes the geography, history, and religious nature of the Mount of Olives.

4. Investigate and write a report on crucifixion as it was used as the death penalty in the ancient world.

5. Research meditations the saints have written on the Passion of Jesus. Then write your own meditation on Jesus' Passion.

6. Write a script dialogue that retells the Passion story from the point of view of Peter or the Blessed Mother.

7. In an artistic representation, design a crucifix made up of a collage of photos that depict the sufferings of the world—past and present—that Christ redeemed by his Death on the Cross. Share a short oral report that explains your work.

8. Prepare an illustrated talk on the symbolism of several different types of Christian crosses.

9. Write a three- to five-page report on the life of St. Maximilian Kolbe.

Prayer

Throughout the ages, Christians have memorized and meditated on the "Seven Last Words of Jesus," that is, the seven last things Christ said from the cross. These words reveal his values and tell us about his suffering for us.

1. *"Father, forgive them, they know not what they do"* (Lk 23:34).
   - Who has trouble understanding me? How can I help them to know and love the real me?

2. *"Amen, I say to you, today you will be with me in Paradise"* (Lk 23:43).
   - Do I comfort others when they are hurt or lonely?

3. *"Woman, behold, your son. . . . Behold, your mother"* (Jn 19:26–27).
   - What good things have I done for my mother of late? How do I make her proud of me?

4. *"My God, my God, why have you forsaken me?"* (Mt 27:46).
   - Do I have faith that God will be there for me when the going gets tough?

5. *"I thirst"* (Jn 19:28).
   - Do I thirst for what is right? Or do I pursue false values?

6. *"It is finished"* (Jn 19:30).
   - Am I dependable? Do I finish what I start?

7. *"Father, into your hands I commend my spirit"* (Lk 23:46).
   - To what have I given myself? Is Jesus Christ the top priority in my life?

- *Reflection*: Pray these words of Jesus and reflect on their meaning in your own life.

- *Resolution*: Memorize these seven last words of Jesus.

THE RESURRECTION OF JESUS CHRIST

*For I handed on to you as of first importance what I also received:
that Christ died for our sins in accordance with the scriptures;
that he was buried; that he was raised on the third day in accordance
with the scriptures; that he appeared to Cephas, then to the Twelve.
After that, he appeared to more than five hundred brothers at once,
most of whom are still living, though some have fallen asleep.
After that he appeared to James, then to all the apostles.
Last of all, as to one born abnormally, he appeared to me.*

—1 Corinthians 15:3-8

The Fog Lifted

With Christ's Resurrection, the clouds of despair were lifted and his disciples were able to understand more fully God's plan.

Redemption Accomplished and Promise Fulfilled

Christ's Resurrection, part of the Paschal Mystery, is both a historical event and a transcendent event.

The Resurrection Accounts in the Four Gospels

The Resurrection accounts in the four Gospels point to some differences, which in fact highlight their authenticity, as well as many similarities.

Our Participation in Christ's Resurrection

The Resurrection of Jesus gives new meaning to our lives. Death does not have the final word.

The Ascension and Glorification of Jesus Christ

Jesus' glorification consists of his Resurrection, his Ascension into Heaven, and Pentecost, the day when the Father and Son sent the Holy Spirit to the Church.

The Fog Lifted

Arthur Wellesley (1769–1862), the First Duke of Wellington, was a famous general and Prime Minister in England. His military prowess was displayed in the Battle of Waterloo (1815), a bitterly fought battle that, along with the support of the Prussian army, ended Napoleon Bonaparte's attempt to return to power. After the battle was over, Wellington sent word of his great victory to England. He had set up a series of stations, each within sight of the next, so that code messages could be exchanged between England and the continent. The message of his victory was worded like this: "Wellington Defeated Napoleon at Waterloo."

Shortly after the message started down the chain of stations, a fog set in and caused some confusion. Only part of the message got through: "Wellington defeated." The British, who only heard this part of the message, were deflated. Some time later, the fog lifted and the full message got through. Imagine the joy when the British heard the full truth of what happened: Napoleon had been defeated!

Something similar happened with the crucifixion of Jesus Christ. The Apostles and other disciples of Jesus must have felt abandoned and defeated by the death of their good friend. They had come to love him and had risked their lives to follow him. They believed he was the Messiah. But he was dead, executed as a common criminal, rejected by the authorities, and abandoned even by his friends. Yet, the story was not over. Three days later, on the first Easter Sunday, Christ rose from the dead. What Jesus came to do was now complete. God's work was now done. His Resurrection spelled victory for humanity—victory over Satan, victory over sin, and victory over death.

The Resurrection of Jesus is the fundamental fact of our faith. Had this simple, yet profoundly earth-shattering fact not have happened, the Gospels would not have been written. The Resurrection of Jesus forms the heart of the **kerygma**, that is, the essential message of our faith. If Jesus has not been raised from the dead, then our faith itself is dead. St. Paul put it this way:

> And if Christ has not been raised, then empty (too) is our preaching; empty, too, your faith. [I]f Christ has not been raised, your

How Much Do You Believe?

For each of the following statements, write one follow-up sentence that supports it and tells why you believe the statement. Alternatively, if you have doubts about the validity of any statement, write one sentence expressing why this is so.

- Jesus is alive.
- Someday I will be with Jesus for all eternity.
- It is a privilege to receive and meet the Risen Lord in the Eucharist.
- I look forward to my own resurrection and the resurrection of all people.
- My life is filled with joy because death is not the end of everything!

faith is vain; you are still in your sins. Then those who have fallen asleep in Christ have perished. If for this life only we have hoped in Christ, we are the most pitiable people of all. (1 Cor 15:14, 17–18)

This chapter explores the Scriptural details of the Resurrection, including the significance of Christ's Resurrection for us in the mystery of Redemption.

For Reflection

Who has best infused you with the essential message that Jesus is risen?

Redemption Accomplished and Promise Fulfilled (*CCC*, 631-650)

After Jesus' Death, his secret disciple, Joseph of Arimathea, a member of the Sanhedrin, sought permission from Pontius Pilate to take the body of Jesus down from the cross and bury him in a new grave, one owned by Joseph and near the site of Jesus' crucifixion. Other disciples of Jesus, including Nicodemus, the Blessed Mother, and Mary Magdalene witnessed Jesus' burial. Matthew 27:62–66 verifies that Pilate permitted some of Jesus' opponents to post guards at Jesus' tomb, for fear that his disciples would steal his body. All of these facts argue strongly that Jesus had really died.

While in the grave, Jesus' corpse was preserved from corruption because his human soul and body were still linked to the Divine Person of the Son. The Apostles' Creed professes that the dead Christ went to the abode of the dead (*Sheol* in Hebrew, *Hades* in Greek, "hell" in English) and there proclaimed the Good News of Salvation to the just who were awaiting the Redeemer. As the First Letter of Peter points out:

Essentials of Our Faith

The word *kerygma* comes from the Greek meaning "proclamation, announcement, preaching." The kerygma contains the basic message of Christianity about Jesus. The heart of the kerygma is the Resurrection of Jesus.

According to the New Testament, some of the essential elements of the kerygma in the early Church were the following:

1. God's promises foretold by the prophets have now been fulfilled through Jesus Christ.
2. God has exalted his Son, Jesus Christ, at his right hand.
3. The Holy Spirit is present in the Church and is the sign of Christ's present power and glory.
4. Christ will come again, at which time the Messianic Age will reach its fulfillment.
5. Because all this is true, we should repent of our sins, be baptized, and receive the Holy Spirit.

Many elements of the kerygma can be found in the sermons of St. Peter that are recorded in the Acts of the Apostles. Read one of Peter's sermons in Acts 2:14-41. Make notes of the verses in this section that correspond to the various kerygmatic statements listed above.

kerygma
The core teaching about Jesus Christ as Savior and Lord.

Paschal Lamb

In Jewish history, the Paschal Lamb was what the Israelites were commanded to eat as part of the Passover celebration. Jesus is the new Paschal Lamb because he shed his blood for the Redemption of the world.

grace

A free and unearned favor from God, infused into our souls at Baptism, that adopts us into God's family and helps us to live as his children.

soul

The innermost or spiritual part of a person. The soul is the subject of human consciousness and freedom. Body and soul together form one human nature. The soul does not die with the body. It is eternal and will be reunited with the body in the final resurrection.

Last Judgment

Jesus Christ's judgment of the living and the dead on the last day when he comes to fully establish God's Kingdom.

For this is why the gospel was preached even to the dead that, though condemned in the flesh in human estimation, they might live in the spirit in the estimation of God. (1 Pt 4:6)

Jesus' mercy and love for sinners extends to all people, opening the gates of Heaven for all the good and just people who lived before the Son of God came to earth. Then, on Easter Sunday, the most important event in Salvation History took place.

The Resurrection and the Paschal Mystery

The Paschal Mystery refers to Christ's Death *and* Resurrection. They are inseparable. It is called a *mystery* in the sense that the Salvation won by Jesus Christ is a visible sign of the invisible action that God accomplished on our behalf. *Paschal* refers to the Passover, Christ's passing through death to new life. He is the **Paschal Lamb** whose Death leads to his Resurrection and Salvation for all humanity. When we participate in Christ's Paschal Mystery, we die to sin's power over us, and the influence of Satan. We also receive **grace** in this life and eternal life with the Blessed Trinity in Heaven. Jesus' Death and Resurrection have defeated sin. What this means is that our **souls** will survive physical death and our bodies will rise again at the **Last Judgment**.

The Resurrection was a Historical Event

The disciples were not expecting Jesus' Resurrection. In fact, they were heartbroken, saddened, and afraid after his crucifixion. They were in hiding in Jerusalem, fearful that they too might be arrested and executed. Yet, verifiable evidence indicates that the Resurrection of Jesus was a real, historical event that took place in a definite place at a definite time and totally changed the frightened disciples into zealous preachers of the Gospel of Jesus Christ.

The empty tomb—reported in each Gospel—is one of the signs that Jesus rose from the dead. Neither Jesus' friends nor his enemies ever claimed to have found Jesus' body. No one ever proved that his corpse was stolen. The empty tomb does not of itself prove faith. In fact, some disciples were skeptical, simply refusing to believe when told the tomb was empty. Even seeing it empty for themselves did not cause all of them to believe that Jesus had actually risen from the dead. Nevertheless, the empty tomb is a concrete historical marker, a sign that points toward belief that the Father brought his Son back to life, as had been prophesied by Jesus himself.

More definitive are the reports that Jesus was *actually seen* by various people: Mary Magdalene, who embraced Jesus' feet; doubting Thomas, who saw Jesus' wounds and proclaimed, "My Lord and My God" (Jn 20:28); the Apostles in the Upper

No one actually saw how Jesus' earthly body transformed into a risen or glorified body. It is true that Jesus' glorified body could be seen and touched by others. Jesus could even share a meal with his disciples. (Jesus did these things to prove to his disciples that they were not seeing a ghost. Ghosts do not eat meals with their living friends.) However, Jesus' Resurrection and his glorified body go beyond his earthly body and historical events. In his Resurrection, Jesus was fully restored to life: "In his risen body he passes from the state of death to another life beyond time and space" (*CCC*, 646).

Jesus' glorified body had certain qualities that transcend ordinary life. For example, unlike Lazarus, whom Jesus raised and who did die again, Jesus' glorified body would never again die. His resurrected body is both immortal and eternal, possessing supernatural qualities. Jesus' resurrected body could appear wherever he wished, whenever he wished. For example, Jesus materialized in the Upper Room by passing through a closed door. He has a real body, but it is glorified, belonging to Heaven. The Holy Spirit transformed Jesus' body, giving it "the glorious state of Lordship" (*CCC*, 648). In sum, Jesus' human body was gloriously transfigured, filled with the Holy Spirit, into an incorrupt, glorious, immortal body "seated at the right hand of the Father."

Room; two disciples, who walked with Jesus on the road to Emmaus and recognized him in the breaking of the bread. As 1 Corinthians 15:38 states, the Risen Lord appeared to more than five hundred people at one place, many of whom were still alive when St. Paul was writing his Letter to the Corinthians in the 50s. Finally, St. Paul himself claims to have seen the Risen Jesus, now ascended to Heaven, on the road to Damascus. This encounter changed Paul from a fierce persecutor of Christians into a great missionary who preached the Gospel of Jesus Christ far and wide.

The Resurrection as a Transcendent Event

All of these facts reveal that the Resurrection was a real, verifiable historical event. Yet the Resurrection of Jesus is also a *transcendent* event, that is, one that goes beyond history and our own understanding of space and time. The Resurrection can be described as transcendent because no Gospel account reports anyone seeing how it physically happened.

For Review

1. Define *kerygma*.

2. Summarize the main points of the kerygma preached in the early Church.

3. Why did Jesus' body not decay in the tomb?

4. What does it mean to say that Jesus "descended into hell"?

5. Cite evidence that Jesus' Resurrection is a historical event.

6. What does it mean to say that the Resurrection is also a transcendent event?

🌐 For Reflection

- How is your life different because Jesus is risen?
- What is more important to you: historical or transcendent evidence of Jesus' Resurrection? Explain.

The Resurrection Accounts in the Four Gospels

The Resurrection accounts in the four Gospels can be outlined by the main events in the chart on page 139. The next sections examine Scriptural evidence on the Resurrection of Jesus from all four Gospel accounts. Prior to reading each section, make sure to first read the Gospel citation that is suggested.

The Resurrection in Matthew 28

Women at the Empty Tomb (Mt 28:1-8)

Mary Magdalene and her companion know exactly where Jesus is buried. When they get to his grave, they meet an angel who had rolled back the stone in front of the tomb. The angel tells the women not to be afraid because Jesus, the crucified one, has been raised from the dead. The angel asks the women to inspect the empty tomb and then to report to the disciples that Jesus is raised from the dead and that the disciples should go to Galilee to meet him.

Jesus Appears to the Women (Mt 28:9-1)

The women, both afraid yet filled with joy, report to the disciples what they discovered. Along the way, Jesus appears to them. They embrace Jesus' feet and pay him homage. The Risen Lord then tells the women to instruct the Apostles to leave Jerusalem, the place where he was rejected, and go to Galilee where he will meet them.

The Report of the Guards (Mt 28:11-15)

Only Matthew's Gospel tells us why the Pharisees and chief priests posted guards at Jesus' tomb; it was due to their fear that Jesus' body would be stolen. When the guards report what actually happened, they are bribed to say that Jesus' disciples stole his body from the tomb. Jesus' foes do not actually doubt that Jesus died and was buried, but they do not believe he was raised from the dead. Therefore, they circulate the story that "His disciples came by night and stole him while we were asleep" (Mt 28:13).

Jesus Appears to the Eleven before His Ascension (Mt 28:16-20)

In Matthew's Gospel, both the mountain and Galilee are important places where Jesus revealed himself

Event	Matthew	Mark	Luke	John
Some women find Jesus' tomb empty	28:1–8	16:1–8	24:1–11	20:1–2, 11–13
Peter and the Beloved Disciple run to the tomb	*	*	24:12 (only Peter)	20:2–10
Jesus appears to the women	28:9–10	16:9–11	*	20:14–18
Guards report to the authorities	28:11–15	*	*	*
Jesus and the two disciples on the road to Emmaus	*	16:12–13	24:13–35	*
Jesus appears to the disciples on Sunday evening	*	*	24:36–43	*
Jesus appears to Thomas and the disciples	*	*	*	20:24–29
Jesus appears to the Eleven at the table	*	16:14–18	*	*
Jesus appears to the Eleven before his Ascension—giving the Great Commission	28:16–20	*	*	*
Jesus' last words before the Ascension	*	16:19–20	24:44–53	*
Jesus appears to his disciples at the Sea of Tiberias	*	*	*	21:1–23

to his disciples. For example, Jesus began his public ministry in Galilee after the arrest of John the Baptist. He taught the Sermon on the Mount with authority on a mountain. At the Transfiguration, he revealed his glory to Peter, James, and John on the mountain.

After the suicide of Judas Iscariot, there are now eleven Apostles left, all of whom initially doubt that Jesus has been raised. However, like the women, they quickly worship Jesus once they see him.

The very last verses of Matthew's Gospel contain the commissioning of Jesus' disciples (Mt 28:16–20). Jesus says that his heavenly Father has given him supreme power in Heaven and on earth. All authority on earth and in Heaven is his. Therefore, Jesus is sending the Eleven out to all nations of

discipleship
The life of following Jesus Christ. The word *disciple* comes from a Latin word that means "learner."

the world, not just the Jews, to make them disciples. They are to preach the Gospel, teach Jesus' commandments, and baptize in the name of the Father, and of the Son, and of the Holy Spirit. Finally, Jesus promises that he will remain with the Church until the final coming of God's Kingdom at the end of time. The Risen Jesus Christ is truly Emmanuel, God-with-us, who will guide and protect his followers until the end of time. On this hope-filled promise of the Risen Lord himself, the Gospel of Matthew ends.

The Resurrection in Mark 16

Women at the Tomb (Mk 16:1-8)

Mary Magdalene; Mary, the mother of James; and Salome go to the tomb to anoint Jesus' body, since there had not been time to do so before the Sabbath began after Jesus' Death late Friday afternoon. (According to John's Gospel, Jesus' corpse had already been anointed, but Mark assumes that the preparations had not been completed.) The women are concerned about who will roll back the large round slab that fits into the groove at the entrance to Jesus' tomb. Apparently, the women did not consider who would do this before they set out for Jesus' tomb. However, when they get there, the task is already done. A young man (an angel) clothed in white greets them. The women are "utterly amazed." The young man tells them that Jesus of Nazareth has been raised. After inspecting the empty tomb, the women are instructed to tell Peter and the disciples to go meet

Jesus in Galilee where they will see him, as Jesus himself told them. "Then they went out and fled from the tomb seized with trembling and bewilderment. They said nothing to anyone, for they were afraid" (Mk 16:8).

The abrupt conclusion in Mark 16:8 causes some to believe that the original ending of Mark's Gospel may have been lost. However, that the women disobey Jesus' instructions and say nothing is consistent with the rest of Mark's Gospel where his disciples continually misunderstood Jesus. But consider the brilliance of the Evangelist Mark. He wants us to step into the story and to do what the women failed to do through chapter 16, verse 8. He challenges us to spread the Good News—without fear or confusion—that Jesus of Nazareth is risen from the dead. This is the task of all believers: to be bearers of the Gospel, to tell the world of the Salvation won for us by the Death and Resurrection of Jesus Christ. Mark wrote his Gospel to show us the example of Jesus who endured all so that we may have eternal life. It is now our task to carry on his work, the work of **discipleship**.

The Longer Ending of Mark's Gospel (Mk 16:9-20)

The vocabulary and style of Mark 16:9–20 indicate that Mark's Gospel was likely composed by someone other than Mark. The Church has traditionally accepted it as part of the canon and it was defined as such at the Council of Trent. It was likely added by the Church in the second century, perhaps not believing that Mark intended to end the Gospel the way he did—with astonished women who were too afraid to spread the news about Jesus' Resurrection. Notice how similar they are to the stories from some of the other Gospels, especially Luke, from which they were probably taken. The scenes that appear in the Longer Ending are:

- *Mary Magdalene (16:9–11).* Jesus appears to Mary Magdalene "out of whom he had driven seven demons." When she told the Apostles that she had seen the Risen Jesus, they did not believe her. Note the similarity between the Risen Jesus and Mary Magdalene in this passage compared to John 20:11–18.

- *Two disciples on the road (16:12–13).* Jesus appears to two disciples on a country road. The disciples report what they saw to the others, but once again they are not believed. Note the similarity in this meeting to Jesus' appearance on the road to Emmaus (Lk 24:13–35).

- *Jesus appears to the Eleven (16:14–18).* Similar to the commissioning of the disciples in Matthew 28:1–10, Jesus appears to the Apostles at a meal. Jesus rebukes them for not believing the reports of others who had seen him. He then instructs them to go to into the whole world and proclaim the Gospel. Jesus also tells them that the disciples will be able to perform exorcisms, speak in tongues, handle deadly serpents and drink poisons without harm, and heal the sick in his name.

- *The Ascension of Jesus (16:19–20).* The last two verses of Mark's longer ending parallel the report of Jesus' Ascension in Luke 24:50–53. The Gospel tells how the Apostles boldly preached the Gospel everywhere and how the Lord worked with and through them by confirming their preaching with signs.

The Shorter Ending

The so-called "shorter ending" placed in brackets after Mark 16:20 was found immediately after Mark 16:8 and before the Longer Ending in fourth- to ninth-century Greek manuscripts, as well as in one Latin manuscript. The shorter ending tells how the women did indeed report to Peter and the other Apostles. It also gives Jesus' commission to preach the Good News of Salvation from east to west. The Church may have thought the Gospel ended at Mark 16:8 because either Mark wrote a longer ending but it was lost, or something happened to Mark before he was able to complete his Gospel. This may have also been the motive for the Church to tack on the new endings. Nevertheless, there is good reason to

men who become the first evangelists by telling what they had learned at the tomb. The Apostles and others, however, did not believe them. Peter runs to the tomb to see for himself the empty shelf on which Jesus' body had rested. He found there only the burial clothes and went home amazed at what happened. However, Peter's amazement still did not translate to faith in Jesus' Resurrection. He would have to see the Risen Jesus for himself.

Appearance on the Road to Emmaus (Lk 24:13-35)

Two disciples, one named Cleopas, were going to the village of Emmaus, seven miles outside of Jerusalem. On the road, Jesus joins them, though they are prevented from recognizing him. They tell their new companion about the recent events that transpired in Jerusalem, including the strange report of the women who had been visited by angels and their account of the empty tomb. The Risen Lord then explains to the disciples the prophecies from the Scriptures about how the Messiah had to suffer before he entered into his glory. When they arrive at the village, the two men invite their companion to stay with them for the evening. While he is with them at the table he takes bread, says the blessing, breaks it, and gives it to them. The disciples recognize him as Jesus.

Jesus' words and action bring to mind his feeding of the five thousand (Lk 9:16) and the institution of the Eucharist at the Last Supper (Lk 22:19). Jesus then vanishes from

believe that the Evangelist really did intend to end the Gospel at Mark 16:8 to challenge us to spread the Gospel, to do what the women were too frightened to do.

The Resurrection in Luke 24

Appearance to the Women at the Tomb (Lk 24:1-12)

Like the Gospels of Matthew and Mark, Luke's Gospel tells of women going to the tomb on Sunday, the first day of the week. There they find the tomb empty and are met by two men in dazzling garments. These angels also help the women recall that Jesus had prophesied his Resurrection. It is also interesting to note that it is women—Mary Magdalene, Joanna, and Mary, the mother of James—not

Beloved Disciple

The Fourth Gospel refers in several places to the "disciple whom Jesus loved." Church Father St. Irenaeus attributed the Gospel of John to the Beloved Disciple. Church tradition identified this John as one of the Apostles.

their sight. The disciples are filled with love and understand what Jesus had been saying to them on the road. Their hearts were burning within them because the Lord had visited them. They immediately return to Jerusalem to tell the Eleven what they had experienced. But they also learn that Jesus had already appeared to Peter, "The Lord has truly been raised and has appeared to Simon!" (Lk 24:34). Neither Luke nor any other Gospel elaborates on this special appearance to Peter, but it is important because Peter is the one Jesus appointed to be leader of the Apostles, the one on whom he established the Church.

This Emmaus story includes rich themes that Luke developed in his Gospel, including those of journey, faith correlated to seeing, and hospitality to the stranger. Luke closes this vignette by reminding us that Jesus was made known "in the breaking of the bread." This is a reference to the Eucharist, the event in which we both hear the Word of God proclaimed in the readings and receive the Lord in Holy Communion. Even though Catholics of later generations do not "see" Jesus in visions as did the early disciples after the Resurrection, we can experience the living Lord in Sacred Scripture, his Holy Word, and in the Seven Sacraments, especially the Eucharist.

Jesus Appears to the Disciples in Jerusalem (Lk 24:36-49)

Immediately after the disciples from Emmaus report what they have experienced, Jesus appears in their midst and greets them: "Peace be with you" (24:36). The disciples are startled, thinking they are seeing a ghost. But Jesus assures them he is not a ghost, showing them his wounded hands and feet, inviting them to touch him, and eating a piece of baked fish. We learn here that there is a continuity between the body of the historical Jesus and the Resurrected Lord. He is recognizable as the same Person.

The Lord then opens his disciples' minds to understand what the Scriptures had foretold: the suffering of the Messiah and his Resurrection on the third day. He tells the Apostles that they were witnesses to all that he had done and that their task has only begun because he and the Father are going to send the Holy Spirit to empower them to go forth from Jerusalem to the ends of the world to proclaim the Gospel.

The Ascension (Lk 24:50-53)

Jesus' final appearance to his disciples is near Bethany, where the Lord raises his hands, blesses them, and is taken up to Heaven. The Acts of the Apostles, also written by Luke, describes this taking place after Jesus appears to his disciples for forty days (Acts 1:3). Overwhelmed, the disciples worship Jesus, return to Jerusalem joy-filled, and go to the Temple to praise God as they await Jesus' sending of the Holy Spirit. Luke's Gospel ends where it began—in the Temple in Jerusalem. From there, the Apostles will take the Good News of Salvation to the ends of the earth.

The Resurrection in John 20-21

The Empty Tomb (Jn 20:1-10)

All the Gospels agree that Mary Magdalene went to the tomb on the first day of the week, in the morning. Only in John's Gospel does Mary go and report the empty tomb to Peter and the "other disciple whom Jesus loved." She thinks someone has taken Jesus' body. Peter and the **Beloved Disciple** run to the tomb to see for themselves. The Beloved Disciple arrives first and sees the discarded burial garments. However, he allows Peter to enter the tomb first to see the burial clothes. The Beloved Disciple then goes in, and with only minimal proof of Jesus' Resurrection (the discarded burial clothes), he believes.

The Lord Appears to Mary Magdalene (Jn 20:11-18)

Mary stays at the tomb after Peter and the Beloved Disciple depart. She is weeping. But then she looks into the tomb and sees two angels. When questioned why she is weeping, Mary says, "They have taken my Lord, and I don't know where they have laid him" (Jn 20:13). After saying this, she turns and sees Jesus, at first thinking he is the gardener. It seems that even the friends of Jesus have some difficulty recognizing him. He is the same, but different. However, when Jesus addresses Mary by name, she recognizes Jesus and calls him "Rabbouni" (Teacher). Her recognition of Jesus' voice recalls a theme in John's Gospel where Jesus says that the sheep will recognize the voice of the Good Shepherd. Mary then tries to hold Jesus, but the Lord tells her not to cling to him because he has not yet ascended to his Father. The Lord instructs Mary to go and tell the brothers that she has seen Jesus and to deliver this message: "I am going to my Father and your Father, to my God and your God" (Jn 20:17).

Jesus Appears to the Twelve (Jn 20:19-23)

On Sunday evening, Jesus appears in the room where the Apostles are staying. He mysteriously appears in their midst even though the doors are locked. The Apostles are hiding in fear of the authorities. Jesus wishes them peace, shows them his wounds, and commissions them to continue his work. In John's Gospel, it is here on Easter Sunday that Jesus gives his disciples the gift of the Holy Spirit and the authority to forgive sins in his name through the Sacraments of Baptism and Penance and to announce God's Salvation through the forgiveness of sins in the name of his Son, the Lord Jesus Christ.

The Lord Appears to Thomas (Jn 20:24-29)

The Apostle Thomas was not present when Jesus appeared to the others, so he did not believe in the Resurrection. A week later, the Lord once again appears behind the locked doors, offers peace to his disciples, and invites Thomas to put his fingers in his wounds so that he will believe. Thomas cries out a great act of faith, "My Lord and my God!" (Jn 20:28). Jesus says to the doubting Thomas, and to all Christians, "Blessed are those who have not seen and have believed" (Jn 20:29). These verses lead to what many scholars think is the original ending of the Gospel of John (20:30–31) where the Evangelist says that Jesus performed many other signs not recorded in the Gospel. But the ones that have been recorded were done for one purpose—that we "may come to believe that Jesus is the Messiah, the Son of God, and that through this belief you may have life in his name" (Jn 20:31). Thomas proclaims what every Christian must proclaim: Jesus is Lord. Jesus is God.

Appearance by the Sea (Jn 21:1-14)

John 21 is labeled as an "epilogue" to the Gospel. There are many parts of this chapter that are similar to other writings of John, and others that suggest the Greek style present in Luke. It treats some issues that were of concern to the original community for whom the Gospel of John was written, especially the relationship between Peter and the Beloved Disciple. The first appearance recounted in this section takes place at the Sea of Tiberias in Galilee. This particular story gives us the impression that this was the Lord's first appearance to the disciples because they have gone back to their occupation as fishermen. It parallels somewhat the traditions of Mark and Matthew who say Jesus appeared to his disciples in Galilee.

In the same account, the men have been out all night, but have caught nothing. However, it is now daylight, and Jesus stands on the shore. He instructs his disciples to cast their net out the right side of the boat. They obey him, and their catch is so great (153 large fish) that they cannot pull it in to the boat.

The Beloved Disciple is the first to recognize Jesus. He tells Peter, who then impetuously jumps into the water and runs to the shore. When all the disciples arrive with the catch, Jesus cooks breakfast, providing them with fish and bread. He does so on a charcoal fire, which brings to mind the fire that was burning in the courtyard when Peter denied knowing Jesus. Once again, it is the Lord who serves his disciples. Somewhat mysteriously, they do not ask who Jesus is because they recognize that he is the Lord.

The meaning of this particular story is striking. It talks about a large catch of fish, symbolizing that the Apostles, with Peter as the rock, will be fishers of people, bringing the whole world to Christ. Further, the Apostles recognize Jesus in the course of a meal as the host who provides them with the fish and bread. This is remindful of the Eucharist where believers recognize and receive the Lord.

Dialogue between the Risen Lord and Peter (Jn 21:15-25)

After breakfast, the scene turns to an interchange between Jesus and Peter. Jesus asks, "Simon, son of John, do you love me more than these?" The most intimate Greek word for love, *agape*, is used in this passage by Jesus. When Peter responds to Jesus, "Yes, Lord, you know that I love you," the Gospel records the word for love as the Greek *phile*, meaning love for a friend. Jesus, again repeats, "Agape, Simon?" Peter responds "Phile." At the third question Jesus says, "Simon, son of John, Phile?" One meaning of this exchange is that Jesus will accept whatever level of love and commitment Peter (and we) can give.

Peter's threefold "yes" to Jesus reverses his betrayal in the courtyard. The Lord establishes Peter as the leader of the Church by telling Peter to feed his sheep. Thus, Peter is the pastor (or shepherd) who is to guide the Church, to be its leader, to serve others in love. Jesus had previously taught on the role of the Good Shepherd, one who is willing to lay

down his life for his flock. This is what Jesus himself did for the sake of our Salvation. It is also what all good pastors must be willing to do for their flock and what our Lord said would happen to Peter, who himself was crucified under one of the persecutions of the emperor Nero.

Peter then asks the Lord what would happen to the Beloved Disciple. Some in the community for which the Gospel was written might have misinterpreted Jesus, thinking that the Beloved Disciple would not die before the Lord would return again. The scene takes on a different significance, however, if the Beloved Disciple, who was the probable eyewitness source for the Gospel of John, had already died at the time chapter 21 was written. The death of the Apostles and those of their generation caused problems in the early Church because of a belief that Jesus was to have returned first. Ultimately,

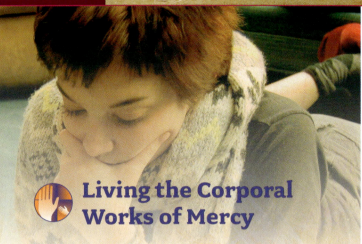

Living the Corporal Works of Mercy

When the women went to anoint Jesus' body, they were engaged in an act of mercy, showing respect to a person's human remains. All Christians are called to engage in the corporal works of mercy, traditionally listed as follows:

The Corporal Works of Mercy

1. Feed the hungry
2. Give drink to the thirsty
3. Clothe the naked
4. Shelter the homeless
5. Visit the sick
6. Visit those in prison
7. Bury the dead

Resolve to do one of the following actions in the coming week. For example:

1. Volunteer at a homeless shelter.
2. Collect canned goods for a bank.
3. Have a clothing drive at school for the St. Vincent de Paul Society.
4. Collect toiletries for homes for abused women.
5. Visit a sick relative, neighbor, or friend.
6. Send a get-well card to a sick friend.
7. Collect magazines to distribute to patients in the hospital.
8. Visit a neighbor who has recently experienced the death of a loved one.

what is important for the Church to know is that his testimony is reliable and true and that the Gospel was written to tell the Good News of Salvation that has been won for us in Jesus Christ.

Summary of the Four Gospel Accounts

Putting all of the information together from all four Resurrection accounts, it is clear that there are some differences between them. Because of this, certain questions may arise. For example, how many angels (or men) were at the empty tomb—one or two? Did Peter run to the tomb alone or did the Beloved Disciple go with him? Did Jesus appear just in Galilee or just in Jerusalem or in both places?

These differences can be explained by remembering that the stories were handed down originally through oral tradition. The Gospel writers made no attempt to mask the differences, to make a smooth seamless story line connecting them all and making them consistent. This argues very strongly that there were valid, true experiences behind the various accounts. The early witnesses knew exactly what happened—what they saw, what Jesus said, how their hearts burned with love for him. They refused to change anything in their testimony.

Also, it is important to note these similarities in the Gospel accounts:

- The Resurrection took place early in the morning on the first day of the week.

- Women were present at the tomb. Mary Magdalene is mentioned in each account.

- The empty tomb was important to the Resurrection stories. It was an essential sign of Christ's Resurrection, a first step in acknowledging God's work in bringing the Son back to life. It corroborates that something happened. The enemies of the early Christians were never able to produce Jesus' corpse, though they probably tried to do so.

- There were "messengers" at the tomb. The women were instructed to tell the disciples what they had witnessed.

- Jesus appeared to his disciples. Note the different people mentioned who encountered the Risen Jesus: Mary Magdalene, Peter and the other Apostles (with and without Thomas), two disciples on the road to Emmaus, and seven disciples by the sea of Tiberias. These appearances convinced a group of frightened men and women that the crucified Jesus was alive, that he was Lord, that he was God's Son. So life-changing were these appearances that, along with the coming of the Holy Spirit, they transformed Jesus' disciples from frightened, confused, and disappointed followers into bold, courageous witnesses who willingly lived and died proclaiming, "Jesus Christ is Lord."

Note several aspects of Jesus' appearances. Jesus appeared only to his disciples. Sometimes they were slow to recognize him. Why? First, they were not expecting the Lord to come back to life. And second, Jesus appeared in his glorified body, one recognizable to the disciples yet shining with the glory of God's life. The Gospel accounts also insist that Jesus was not a ghost. Luke, for example, reports that the resurrected Jesus ate fish, while John reports that Jesus ate breakfast with his disciples. Furthermore, Jesus asks Thomas to touch his wounds. The resurrected Jesus is not a ghost; but neither is he a corpse that is breathing again. He is alive in a transformed, glorified body that still has an aspect of "bodiliness" to it. He is the same but different.

For Review

1. What is the significance of the empty tomb?

2. Explain why Mark 16:8 may be the place where the Evangelist concluded his Gospel.

3. Who are the first evangelists of the Resurrection of Jesus in Luke's Gospel?

4. When do the disciples on the road to Emmaus recognize Jesus?

5. Where do Catholics meet the Risen Lord in the Sunday liturgy?

6. What typical greeting did the Risen Lord give to his disciples when he appeared to them?

7. Who is a model of faith in the Resurrection narratives in John's Gospel?

(continued on page 149)

 ## Who Is Jesus to Me?

While she was recovering in the hospital in Rome in 1983, Blessed Mother Teresa wrote down these thoughts and feelings about who Jesus was to her. Write your own series of statements of who Jesus is to *you*, perhaps in a similar style. Select two or three photos to help illustrate your reflections. Use these reflections as a prayer of thanksgiving to Jesus:

> Jesus is the Word Made Flesh.
> Jesus is the Victim offered for our sins on the Cross.
> Jesus is the Word—to be spoken.
> Jesus is the Truth—to be told.
> Jesus is the Way—to be walked.
> Jesus is the Light—to be lit.
> Jesus is the Life—to be lived.
> Jesus is the Love—to be loved.
> Jesus is the Hungry—to be fed.
> Jesus is the Homeless—to be taken in.
> Jesus is the Lonely—to be loved.
> Jesus is the Unwanted—to be wanted.
> Jesus is the Little One—to embrace him.
> Jesus is the Old—to be served.
> Jesus is my God.
> Jesus is my only Love.
> Jesus is my Everything.

EXPLAINING THE FAITH

How can we respond to those who deny that Jesus rose from the dead?

We live in a skeptical age where it becomes rote to deny the possibilities of grace and goodness. There have always been people who doubted that Christ rose from the dead, even among his first disciples. To counteract those who doubt, Scripture testifies to these facts about the Resurrection of Jesus.

1. *Jesus actually did die by being crucified on a cross by Pontius Pilate*. The reality of his death was reported by the Jewish historian, Josephus, and the Roman historian, Tacitus. Even the Jewish Talmud reports that Jesus was crucified. The fact of his death is as certain as any death reported in the ancient world.

2. *The Apostles and other disciples of Jesus were convinced that he rose from the dead*. In fact, after the Resurrection, the disciples changed from frightened men hiding from the authorities to brave missionaries who suffered martyrdom for spreading the Gospel. Their testimony of the Risen Jesus is supported by other early Church writers, for example, by St. Clement of Rome, the fourth pope. Clement personally knew some of the Apostles. In a letter to the church at Corinth, composed at the end of the first century, he wrote:

> Now, the Gospel was given to the Apostles for us by the Lord Jesus Christ; and Jesus the Christ was sent from God. That is to say, Christ received His commission from God, and the Apostles theirs from Christ. The order of these two events was in accordance with the will of God. So thereafter, when the Apostles had been given their instructions, and all their doubts had been set at rest by the resurrection of our Lord Jesus Christ from the dead, they set out in the full assurance of the holy Spirit to proclaim the coming of God's kingdom.

3. *St. Paul saw the Risen Lord*. Saul of Tarsus was a fierce opponent of the early Christians and played an instrumental role in persecuting them. He was even involved in the death of St. Stephen, the first martyr. On his way to Damascus to persecute Christians, Saul had a vision of the Risen Christ that totally changed his life. He went from a fierce opponent of Christians to a zealous missionary who sacrificed his life for the truth of the Gospel.

4. *Jesus' tomb was empty*. The empty tomb was substantiated by several witnesses, including Jesus' enemies.

Arguments against Christ's Resurrection

Given the bedrock facts, there are still those who do not believe in the incidents around Jesus' Death, and especially his Resurrection. Note some of the following alternative theories that have been proposed:

1. *The Gospel writers fabricated the Resurrection stories*. If this is true, then they did not do a very good job. For one thing, all of the Gospel accounts say that Mary Magdalene had a prominent role in testifying to the empty tomb. Furthermore, John's Gospel singles her out as being the first person to whom Jesus appeared. If Jesus' followers were going to make something up during the first century in either the Roman or Jewish cultures, a woman wouldn't be named because her testimony would not hold up in court. Second, the Gospel writers did not attempt to smooth out the discrepancies in the various accounts. If they were going to make something up, it would have made more sense to change various elements so that there would be total harmony in the accounts. They did not.

2. *There is nothing unique about Christianity. The Resurrection accounts simply copy other religious myths, for example, the spring fertility rites*. In stark contrast to the mythological stories associated with pagan religions, Christianity was founded by Jesus of Nazareth, a real, historical person. He was actually born, lived with a family in a historical place, and died a Death that was publicly recorded, even by his enemies.

3. *The Apostles stole Jesus' body or had it moved*. This theory begets several questions that begin with "how" or "why." For example, How were they—simple fishermen—able to overpower the Roman guards? And why would they steal or move his body? Additionally, what did they gain from it? Remember

Talmud
A collection of rabbinical teachings collected after the destruction of the Jerusalem Temple in AD 70.

they were afraid when Jesus was killed and went into hiding. Would they really have been willing to die for such a lie and cover-up? The only thing the Apostles gained was the loss of their lives.

4. *His friends so much wanted to see Jesus alive that they imagined or hallucinated that they saw him.* Hallucinations are an individual, subjective experience. There is no such thing as mass hallucination.

5. *Paul was delusional. He felt guilt for persecuting the Christians and only imagined he saw the Risen Lord.* Those who were with Paul said they heard a voice and saw a bright light, though they themselves did not see Jesus.

6. *The Resurrection stories are merely symbolic ways of saying that Jesus' spirit lives on.* If true, the Apostles could have simply said, "Our teacher's spirit lives on." They had the vocabulary to do so.

7. *Resurrection is scientifically impossible.* Science cannot explain many things, including the creation of the universe. The Resurrection of Jesus is only impossible if our human existence is impossible. But it is not. Consider the words of the famous philosopher and mathematician, Blaise Pascal:

> What reason have they [atheists] for saying that we cannot rise from the dead? What is more difficult, to be born or to rise again; that what has never been should be, or that what has been should be again? Is it more difficult to come into existence than to return to it?

For Reflection
What for you is the strongest argument for the fact that Jesus really did rise from the dead?

8. Describe two qualities of Jesus' resurrected body.

9. According to the original ending (Jn 20:30-31), why did John write his Gospel?

10. How do the discrepancies in the Resurrection narratives actually argue for their historical value?

11. List four similarities in all the Resurrection narratives.

For Reflection

Imagine you were one of the Apostles in the room when Jesus appeared in your midst. Describe the scene: your feelings, what Jesus said to you, how he looked, etc. Explain how you think your life might change as a result of this encounter.

Our Participation in Christ's Resurrection (*CCC*, 651-655)

Jesus' Resurrection is the essential fact of Salvation History, the bedrock of our faith, the heart of the Good News. As St. Paul observed, "If Christ has not been raised, then empty [too] is our preaching; empty, too, your faith" (1 Cor 15:14). The following points summarize the meaning and saving significance of Christ's Resurrection:

• *The Resurrection confirms all Christ's works and teaching.* It proves Jesus' claims to be God's Son. It fulfills the Old Testament promises and those of Jesus himself made during his earthly life. Jesus referred to himself by the Hebrew name for God—Yahweh: "When you lift up the Son of Man, then you will realize that I AM" (Jn 8:28). Therefore, the Resurrection offers proof for the divinity of Jesus.

- *The Resurrection, following Christ's sacrifice on the cross, accomplished our Salvation.* By vanquishing death, Jesus conquered the most evil effect of sin. Thus, he is victorious over sin, has opened Heaven's gates, and has won our Redemption.

- *The Resurrection gives us new life, justifies us in God's grace, and adopts us into the divine family.* We become, through the gift of God's grace and love, brothers and sisters to Jesus Christ. We share in his life. The Gospel of John states: "For God so loved the world that he gave his only Son, so that everyone who believes in him might not perish but might have eternal life" (Jn 3:16). The Resurrection allows Jesus to live in us; thus, we already share "eternal life," the life of the Lord who abides in us.

- *Through the power of the Holy Spirit, Christians participate in the Life, suffering, Death, and Resurrection of Jesus.* By accepting Jesus into our lives and allowing his love to dominate our journey on earth, the Risen Lord promises that we will rise again with him to eternal life in Heaven.

The Resurrection of Jesus gives new meaning to our lives. Death does not have the last word. Superabundant, eternal life with Jesus in community with the Father and the Holy Spirit and all others who love the Lord is our ultimate destiny.

Meeting the Risen Lord

Not limited by space and time, the Risen Lord lives and reigns forever. He lives in his Body, the Church. As members of the Body of Christ, we can find Jesus in the Church, in our brothers and sisters in Christ. Recall that Jesus said that whatever we do to each other, especially the least in our midst, we do to him (Mt 25:40).

Catholics participate in the mystery of his Redemption through the sacramental life of the Church. Christ instituted the Seven Sacraments as powerful signs of his presence and love. For example, by the power of the Holy Spirit, the Lord comes to us at Baptism, forming us into his own image and initiating us into the Church. In the Sacrament of Confirmation, the Holy Spirit strengthens us with spiritual gifts to live Christ-like lives. In the Sacrament of Penance, we experience the Lord's forgiveness, just as the countless people did who met him during his earthly life. He welcomes us back into the family the way the loving father did in the parable of the Prodigal Son. In the Sacrament of the Anointing of the Sick, we experience the healing touch of the Lord in the stressful times of illness. And in the Sacraments of Holy Orders and Matrimony, Christ comes to us to help us live loving lives of service and help build up the People of God.

In a most special way, Jesus Christ is alive in the Holy Eucharist, which is "the heart and summit of the Christian life, for in it Christ associates his Church and all her members with his sacrifice of praise and thanksgiving offered once for all on the cross to his Father" (*CCC*, 1407). The Eucharist contains our Paschal sacrifice, who is Christ himself. By his sacrifice he pours out the graces of Salvation on the Church. Additionally:

> At the heart of the Eucharistic celebration are the bread and wine that, by the words of Christ and the invocation of the Holy Spirit, become Christ's Body and Blood. (*CCC*, 1333)

When we worthily receive the Lord under the forms of bread and wine, the Risen Jesus joins us. In Holy Communion, we become united with our Lord and Savior. We receive Christ to become Christ for one another and, in a special way, the least in our midst: poor people, victims of discrimination, the powerless, the suffering, the lonely.

The word *Eucharist* means "thanksgiving." In this holy sacrament it is indeed right and just to give thanks to God for the gift of his Son, for the Salvation he has won for us, for his defeat of sin and death, and for the eternal life he bestows on us. In this sacrament, we praise the Lord and recognize his presence to us in Holy Scripture, in the assembled Church, in the priest who represents us before God, and most especially in the consecrated bread and wine that we receive as the most precious gift Christ has left us: himself. The graces or effects of receiving Holy Communion are many, including:

- a more intimate union with Jesus Christ;

- separation from sin by wiping away venial sin and strength to combat mortal sin;

- greater unity with other members of Christ's body, the Church;

- better ability to see Christ in the poor whom we must serve;

- a commitment to work for unity among all Christians. (*CCC*, 1391–1401)

In the Eucharist, the Lord comes to us and he is present in our midst, though in a hidden way. The Eucharist anticipates the Savior's Second Coming. On that day we shall see God as he is. Each Mass carries on the work of Redemption because it provides what we need for eternal life—the Lord Jesus himself who makes it possible for us to live forever with him, the Father, and the Holy Spirit in Heaven.

For Review

1. What has Christ's Resurrection accomplished for us?

2. How can we meet Christ in each of the sacraments?

3. List four benefits of receiving Christ in Holy Communion.

For Reflection

When was a time that you felt especially close to the Lord in the Sacrament of the Holy Eucharist?

The Ascension and Glorification of Jesus Christ (*CCC*, 659-667)

It is important to remember that though the focus of Chapter 6 has been on the Resurrection of Jesus Christ, the Resurrection should be considered as part of the Paschal Mystery, the saving action of Christ that includes Jesus' Death (Good Friday), his descent to the dead (Holy Saturday), and his glorification. Jesus' glorification consists of the Resurrection (Easter Sunday), his Ascension into Heaven (forty days after Easter), and Pentecost, when the Father and Son send the Holy Spirit to the Church (fifty days after Easter).

The **Ascension** of Jesus refers to the time when Jesus stopped appearing to the disciples in visible form and his glorified body took its rightful place in Heaven as equal to the Father. Jesus' body was glorified at the moment of his Resurrection, as proved by the supernatural qualities it manifested. But during his appearances to his disciples, which lasted forty days, his glory remained hidden under the appearance of ordinary humanity. His "final apparition ends with the irreversible entry of his humanity into divine glory, symbolized by the cloud and by heaven, where he is seated from that time forward at God's right hand" (*CCC*, 659).

The Ascension indicates a difference between the way the glory of the Risen Christ was revealed and that of "Christ exalted to his Father's right hand" (*CCC*, 660). "Being seated at the right hand" means that Christ now glorifies the Father as the Incarnate Son of God, that he continually intercedes for us with the Father, prays for us, and prepares a place for us with him in Heaven. This is the beginning of the Kingdom of God, one that will have no end.

The Ascension of Jesus reminds us that our rightful home is Heaven; we live in the hope that we may one day follow him there. Our model is the Blessed Mother, the one who stayed with the Apostles in the Upper Room after the Death of her son, praying constantly for the coming of the Holy Spirit. When her earthly life was over, she was taken up body and soul into heavenly glory where the Lord exalted her and made her Queen of Heaven. This is known as the **Assumption** of the Blessed Virgin. Her Assumption "is a singular participation in her Son's Resurrection and an anticipation of the resurrection of other Christians" (*CCC*, 966). She is our Blessed Mother and serves as our model because she obeyed God's will, cooperated with her Son's redemptive work, and was open to the work of the Holy Spirit in her life. She is our model both in faith and in charity—our Advocate, Helper, Benefactress, and Mediatrix.

Though Jesus Christ has entered the sanctuary of Heaven once and for all, he has not abandoned us. He constantly prays for us to the Father. Moreover, he promised to be with us forever (Mt 28:20). Further, before his Death on Good Friday, Jesus promised that he would send the Holy Spirit: "I will ask the Father, and he will give you another Advocate to be with you always, the Spirit of truth" (Jn 14:16). Jesus fulfilled his promise by sending the Holy Spirit to his Church on **Pentecost** Sunday.

On Pentecost Sunday, the Holy Spirit descended on the Apostles and gave them the power and courage to preach with conviction the Good News that

Jesus Christ rose from the dead and is Lord of the universe. Peter, the one who was so afraid of being associated with his Master and thus denied him three times, became a bold and courageous witness for Jesus Christ. Inspired by the Holy Spirit, he preached to the Jewish people who had come to Jerusalem for the Pentecost feast. He reviewed with them the history of Salvation and recounted the life of Jesus Christ, proclaiming his Death and Resurrection. The crowds were amazed at his preaching and that of the other Apostles; people understood them even though many did not speak their language. So filled with the power of the Holy Spirit were Peter and the Apostles, some thought they were drunk, yet it was still early in the morning!

Three thousand people converted to Jesus Christ on Pentecost. They were baptized and received the Holy Spirit. The Holy Spirit enabled the Apostles to understand more clearly the full significance of Jesus. They now knew that he was truly the Lord, the Savior, the Son of God who is true God. The Holy Spirit was also fully revealed. The Third Person of the Blessed Trinity, the Holy Spirit, continues to live in the Church, the Body of Christ. The Church is the Temple of the Holy Spirit, the soul of the Mystical Body, the source of the Church's life. He bestows on its members divine life, the power of love, and adoption into the divine family. By joining us to the Risen Lord Jesus Christ, he makes it possible for us to inherit eternal life and join our Lord in his heavenly Kingdom.

The Good News of Christ's Resurrection is that death is not our final chapter. We do not cease to exist. We do not come back as reincarnated beings. We do not exist as mere spirits. No, Christ's Paschal Mystery—his Passion, Death, Resurrection, and glorious Ascension—offers us the opportunity for Salvation and Redemption. While remaining aware that our choices in this life may instead merit after death a time of purification (Purgatory) or even eternal separation from God (Hell), we do look forward in confidence to our own resurrection, when God will call us to himself and reunite our souls to a glorified body and bestow on us a life of eternal happiness with our loving God, our family and friends, and all those who love God.

For Review

1. What does the Ascension of Jesus remind us of?

2. What does it mean to say that Jesus sits at the right hand of the Father?

3. What is the Assumption of Mary?

4. How were Peter and the Apostles changed on Pentecost?

For Reflection

• What do you look forward to in Heaven?

• How is Mary a model in your own life?

Ascension
Jesus' passage from humanity into divine glory in God's heavenly domain forty days after his Resurrection. It is from this domain that Jesus will come again.

Assumption
The Church dogma that teaches that the Blessed Mother, because of her unique role in her son's Resurrection, was taken directly to Heaven when her earthly life was over. The Feast of the Assumption is on August 15 and is a holy day of obligation.

Pentecost
The day when the Holy Spirit descended on the Apostles and gave them the power to preach with conviction the message that Jesus is risen and Lord of the universe.

Main Ideas

- The Resurrection of Christ forms the heart of the kerygma, the essential message of our faith. (pp. 134–135)

- Christ's Resurrection is part of the Paschal Mystery. (p. 136)

- The Resurrection was also a historical event with verifiable facts reported by Jesus' disciples and his enemies. (pp. 136–137)

- The Resurrection is a transcendent event because it goes beyond the realm of history and our own understanding of space and time; there are no reports of how it physically happened. (p. 137)

- Though the Risen Jesus was recognizable, his glorified body transcended ordinary life. (p. 137)

- The four Gospels report both differences and similarities in the Resurrection accounts. (pp. 138–139)

- Matthew's Gospel concludes with the great commissioning of the disciples to the ends of the earth. (p. 140)

- Mark's Gospel may end abruptly as a challenge for us to carry on the work of discipleship. (pp. 141–142)

- The Emmaus story is unique to Luke's Gospel; it describes how the disciples eventually recognized Jesus in the breaking of the bread. (pp. 142–143)

- One of the incidents unique to John's Gospel is the Apostle Thomas first doubting the Resurrection and then later identifying Jesus as "My Lord and God." (p. 144)

- That the Gospel writers made no attempt to mask the differences between the accounts actually argues that there were true, valid, experiences behind each of them. (pp. 146–147)

- There were also several similarities in the four Gospel accounts: the Resurrection took place on Sunday morning; there were women

present; the tomb was empty; there were "messengers" at the tomb; and there were several appearances to the disciples. (pp. 146–147)

- Several verifiable facts help us to respond to those who are skeptical about the validity of the Resurrection. (pp. 148–149)

- The Resurrection of Jesus gives new meaning to our life in several ways. (pp. 149–150)

- In the Seven Sacraments, especially the Holy Eucharist, we participate in the Passion, Death, *and* Resurrection of Jesus in a tangible way. (pp. 150–151)

- The Ascension of Jesus to Heaven and the coming of the Holy Spirit on Pentecost are continuations of the Resurrection accounts. (pp. 152–153)

Terms, People, Places

Complete each sentence by choosing the correct answer from the list of terms below.

Ascension

Assumption

Beloved Disciple

discipleship

grace

kerygma

Last Judgment

Paschal Lamb

Pentecost

soul

Talmud

1. Jesus is the _____ whose Death leads to his Resurrection and Salvation for all humanity.

2. The _____ can be considered an "independent" source that reported that Jesus was crucified.

3. The _____ is the time when God's Kingdom will be fully established.

4. Jesus fulfilled his promise to send the Holy Spirit on _____ Sunday.

5. _____ is a term that describes the essential message of our faith.

6. The _____ is the innermost part of a person.

7. The feast of the _____ is celebrated on August 15.

8. The Gospel of John is attributed to the _____.

9. Jesus' passage from humanity into divine glory occurred at the _____.

10. When we participate in Christ's Paschal mystery we receive _____ in this life and eternal life with the Blessed Trinity in Heaven.

11. A message of the short ending of Mark's Gospel is that it is now our task to carry on Jesus' work through _____.

Primary Source Quotations

Eyewitness Testimony
Do not be afraid! I know that you are seeking Jesus the crucified. He is not here, for he has been raised just as he said. Come and see the place where he lay.

—Matthew 28:6

Why do you seek the living one among the dead?

—Luke 24:5

The Lord has truly been raised and has appeared to Simon!

—Luke 24:34

From the Easter Proclamation
Rejoice, heavenly powers! Sing, choirs of angels!
   Exult, all creation around God's throne!
   Jesus Christ, our King, is risen!
   Sound the trumpet of salvation.

—The *Exsultet*

On to Eternity
My understanding was lifted up into Heaven, where I saw our Lord like a lord in his own house who has called his valued servants and friends to a solemn feast.

—Bl. Julian of Norwich

Eternity, eternity, when shall I come to You at last? . . . in eternity where we will love with a glance of the soul.

—St. Elizabeth Seton

Write fifteen words that come to mind when you think about the life to come in Heaven.

Ongoing Assignments

As you cover the material in this chapter, choose and complete at least three of these assignments.

1. Imagine that you were present at the time of the Resurrection of Jesus. Write a short essay explaining what happened as if you were writing for a contemporary who does not believe.

2. Create a PowerPoint presentation on how the Resurrection of Jesus has been depicted in art through the ages. Include at least five images. Single out the one that best illustrates one of the Gospel passages and prepare an explanation for why you believe this is so.

3. Imagine you were one of the guards at Jesus' tomb. Write a letter of explanation to the Roman governor as to what happened to the missing body you were guarding.

4. Interview five practicing Catholics about Jesus' Resurrection. Ask them how essential to their Christian faith is the fact that Jesus rose from the dead. Write a report summarizing your findings.

5. Prepare a one-page report on Mary Magdalene. Illustrate it with an image from a famous piece of art downloaded from the Internet.

6. Visit a Catholic cemetery. Find symbols on tombstones that display belief in life after death. Take photos of these symbols and create a slide presentation to share with your classmates.

7. Imagine you were one of the disciples who met the Risen Lord on the way to Emmaus. Write a dialogue between you and Jesus concerning what you discussed along the way.

8. Find graphics to illustrate several images of the Holy Spirit (examples: wind, fire, dove). Explain the imagery and select an appropriate quotation from Acts 3 to accompany the images.

9. Report on the Jewish feast of Weeks/ Pentecost.

10. After reading Peter's kerygmatic sermon in Acts 2:14–39, create an outline for a talk you might deliver to a youth group on retreat. Emphasize the person of Jesus and what the teens should do in response to him.

11. Read what Luke records in the Acts of the Apostles about Paul's conversion: Acts 9:1–19; 22:1–22; 26:9–24. Compare Luke's reporting to what Paul himself wrote in Galatians 1:11–24. Then briefly summarize what happened.

12. Use Luke 24:50–53, Acts 1:6–12, and Mark 16:19 to help you write a short essay describing the Ascension.

Prayer

God the Father and God the Son sent the Holy Spirit to be with the Church and to help Christians live Christ-like lives. Pray the following Prayer to the Holy Spirit:

> *Prayer to the Holy Spirit*
> Lord our God, you call us out of darkness
>   into light,
> out of self-deception into truth,
> out of death into life.
> Send us your Holy Spirit
> to open our ears to your call.
> Fill our hearts with courage

to be true followers of your Son.
We ask this through Christ our Lord. Amen.

- *Reflection*: Who or what is calling you to respond to the Lord in your life? Are you open to the call?

- *Resolution*: The Spirit is the source of courage and perseverance. During the coming weeks, ask the Holy Spirit to give you the courage to do what you know is right.

Chapter 6 Quick View

7

REDEMPTION THROUGH THE PASCHAL MYSTERY

For God so loved the world that he gave his only Son, so that everyone who believes in him might not perish but might have eternal life. For God did not send his Son into the world to condemn the world, but that the world might be saved through him.

—John 3:16-17

The Wonders of Our Salvation
Jesus Christ, the Wonder of all Wonders, redeems us by his Life, Death, Resurrection, and Ascension to Heaven.

The Presence of God in Creation
Human beings are the pinnacle of God's creation. Jesus Christ, God's Son, shares in the joys and sufferings of being human.

Good News: The Kingdom of God Is at Hand
The Kingdom of God, ushered in by Christ, provides the structure and goal for our life in the Lord.

Forgiveness of Sins
Jesus preached repentance of our sins—the turning from sin and the embracing of God's Kingdom.

The Paschal Mystery Wins Our Redemption
Christ's work of Redemption is principally accomplished by the Paschal Mystery.

The Last Things: Christian Death and the Resurrection of the Body
We believe that our loving God will judge us fairly and compassionately after our deaths and we look forward to eternal life in both body and soul.

More about Eternal Life
Our particular judgment will confirm whether we will merit the eternal reward of Heaven, need to be purified of our sins in Purgatory, or deserve punishment in Hell.

The Wonders of Our Salvation

Classical authors once listed the "seven wonders of the world," which represented the greatest architectural, technological, and artistic achievements of ancient civilizations. The seven wonders of the ancient world were:

1. the Great Pyramid at Giza (still standing)
2. the Hanging Gardens of Babylon (destroyed by an earthquake after the first century AD)
3. the Temple of Artemis at Ephesus (burnt down in fourth century BC, rebuilt by Alexander the Great, destroyed again by the Goths in AD 409)

4. the Statue of Zeus at Olympia (destroyed by fire or earthquake in fifth–sixth century AD)
5. the Mausoleum at Halicarnassus (damaged by an earthquake and disassembled by Crusaders in 1494)
6. the Colossus of Rhodes (toppled by earthquake in third century BC)
7. the Pharos Lighthouse of Alexandria (destroyed by earthquakes in fourteenth century AD)

Ever since this classic list of ancient wonders was constructed, people have been making lists of even more wonders, that is, natural or man-made works that evoke "awe, astonishment, or admiration." For example, the Great Wall of China appears on a list of the "Seven Wonders of the Medieval Mind" while the Grand Canyon and Victoria Falls make a list of the "Seven Natural Wonders of the World." Interestingly, in 2007, a Swiss-based nonprofit group sponsored an online and telephone poll to choose the new wonders of the world. Its organizers claim that over one hundred million votes were cast, the largest poll taken in human history.

From a Christian's point of view, one of the most interesting "wonders" to make the final list of seven is the famous statue of Jesus named "Christ the Redeemer" (*Cristo Redentor*) that stands 130 feet high on Corcovado mountain overlooking the city of Rio de Janeiro in Brazil. This massive and beautiful statue is an icon both for its city and country, of which the majority of its inhabitants are Roman Catholic. The size and location of the statue are well intentioned: to dramatically point to Jesus Christ, our Redeemer, who has made it possible for us to inherit eternal life.

This chapter reminds us of the "wonders" of Salvation History that are essential to our lives as those redeemed by the Life, Death, Resurrection, and Ascension of Jesus Christ. Among those wonders are the Seven Sacraments. This chapter highlights how the sacraments make present the Paschal Mystery

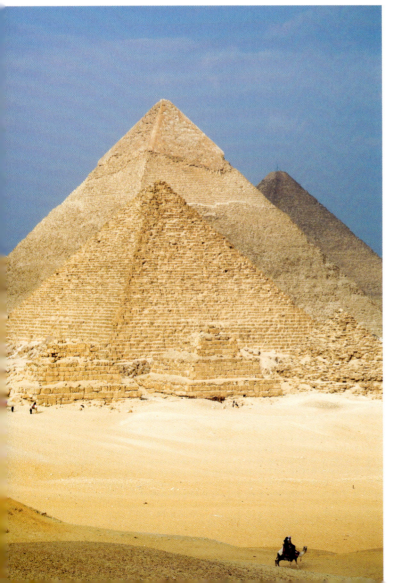

of Christ. It also offers an introduction to several other wonders given new meaning by Jesus Christ. Finally, you will be introduced to the meaning of **eschatology**, that is, the last things that await us all: death, judgment, resurrection of the body, and Purgatory, Heaven, and Hell.

For Reflection

Name a wonder of the world that has awakened a sense of God and his Kingdom for you.

The Presence of God in Creation

The first wonder of the world is creation itself. The universe, and everything that is in it, is an awe-inspiring wonder of God's love. The loving and perfect God, who exists from all eternity, did not *have* to create. But God *did* create to share the divine life and love that flows from within the Blessed Trinity. Everything God made has essential goodness. The Book of Genesis teaches that "God looked at everything he had made, and he found it very good" (Gn 1:31).

The opening verses of John's Gospel further reveal how the Word

eschatology
A study of and teaching about the "last things" (death, judgment, Heaven, Hell, Purgatory, the Second Coming of Christ, and the resurrection of the body).

My Seven Wonders

Complete each of the following exercises related to both natural wonders and wonders involving your faith in Jesus Christ.

1. Create your own list of *seven natural wonders*, the seven most beautiful, spectacular, or moving things you have personally seen in nature. (Examples: a national park you visited, an impressive waterfall, a beautiful sunset, etc.) Provide photos for at least three of the wonders you have listed. Write a short prayer of praise to God for the beauty he has created.

2. *Seven wonders of Jesus and you.* Jesus Christ is the wonder of all wonders. Everything about him is admirable. Reflect now on the qualities of Jesus that you most admire. Next, think about your own God-given qualities. Consider intellectual traits, physical appearance, emotional qualities, social graces, moral/spiritual qualities, and so on. List seven wonders for both Jesus and you. Share both lists with your classmates. Then write your response to the class discussion by answering the following questions:

    *   Which is the most popular "natural wonder" chosen by your class?
    *   What are the most outstanding qualities of Jesus recognized by most? Are these qualities we can imitate in our own lives? If so, then suggest ways to do so.

of God was involved in the creation of the world. Christ, the Son of God, participated in creation:

> In the beginning was the Word,
>   and the Word was with God,
>   and the Word was God.
> He was in the beginning with God.
>   All things came to be through him,
>   and without him nothing came to be.
> What came to be through him was life,
>   and this life was the light of the human
>   race. (Jn 1:1–4)

Creation reveals God's love in profound ways and encourages us to take notice. Consider the following:

- a glorious sunset over an ocean horizon;

- a vast, starlit sky on a cold winter night;

- majestic mountains covered with scented pines reaching to the clouds;

- a gentle rain that quenches the thirst of a parched field;

- an animal world filled with amazing creatures that enrich our diverse ecosystem: birds warbling their songs as they take flight; lions stalking their prey; porpoises dancing on waves; insects humming their songs.

The natural world asks us to take notice of God's power, intelligence, goodness, and love. And down through the ages, the vast majority of people have done just that: acknowledged a superior spiritual being—God—who has created and now keeps in existence the material world around us.

The masterpiece of God's creation is human beings. People are at the summit of God's creation. Human beings are made in God's own image and

likeness, capable of thinking, of making choices, of loving. We are a complex creature, a unity of matter and spirit, who can study the world and discover the Divine Artisan who crafted it. We know that we did not come into existence by our own efforts but that an infinitely generous and loving God gave us life and a beautiful world in which to live. Furthermore, this loving God makes it possible for us to respond to and share in God's own life and love. So marvelous and special is the human creature that the psalmist wrote:

> When I see your heavens, the work of your
> fingers,
>   the moon and stars which you set in
>   place—
> What are humans that you are mindful of
> them,
>   mere mortals that you care for them?
> Yet you have made them little less than a god,
>   crowned them with glory and honor.
> You have given them rule over the works
>   of your hands,
>   put all things at their feet. . . .
> O Lord, our Lord,
>   how awesome is your name through all
>   the earth! (Ps 8:4–7, 10)

The psalmist helps us see that each of us is a special creature of God, one he crowned with "glory and honor." Each of us is a true wonder of God's creation, a special, one-of-a-kind daughter or son, each endowed with unique gifts and talents. Our very existence is a special sign of God's love, a love that is beyond human comprehension. The prophet Isaiah tells us that God is always thinking of us. Each of us is special in his eyes:

> Can a mother forget her infant,
>   be without tenderness for the child of her
>   womb?
> Even should she forget,
>   I will never forget you.
> See, upon the palms of my hands I have
>   written your name. (Is 49:15–16)

Creation points to God's existence and tells us of his love. The Sacrament of Baptism celebrates the marvels of God's creation. It symbolizes and brings about our *re*-creation and *re*-birth into the Church. Baptism proclaims God's presence and activity in the world and brings true life, companionship, and a share in God's own life to the Church.

The Incarnation

> And the Word became flesh
> and made his dwelling among us,
> and we saw his glory,
> the glory as of the Father's only son
> full of grace and truth. (Jn 1:14)

This verse from the Gospel of John highlights the key event in God's creation and the history of the world: the Incarnation of Jesus Christ, the Second Person of the Blessed Trinity. By becoming flesh in the Person of Jesus Christ, God accomplished the work of our Salvation. We can never totally appreciate what God has done for us in becoming one of us. In an act of supreme humility, the Son of God became human in order to save us, conquer sin, and bring us into eternal life. The Incarnation of the Son of God is an essential truth of our faith: Jesus Christ is God-made-man, Emmanuel, "God-with-us."

Recall that the Incarnation was the fulfillment of a series of promises God made to human beings after the Original Sin of Adam and Eve. Though Adam and Eve lost their friendship with God through their sinful disobedience, God never abandoned them. Salvation History records the gradual unfolding of God's plan to save all people through his Son Jesus Christ. God's Revelation, or self-communication to humanity, led to his promise to a man of faith—Abraham—that he would fashion a people from his family, a people from whom would come the Messiah.

An important chapter in Salvation History was God's freeing the Israelites from slavery in Egypt during the time of the Exodus. He sustained them in the desert and, after forty years, delivered them into a land flowing with milk and honey. Using Moses as his prophet and spokesman, Yahweh entered into a covenant with the people, a solemn agreement that made them his Chosen People. For their part, the Israelites were to witness to the one true God and to live the Law, that is, a life worthy of their vocation as God's people. In return, God promised everlasting love and protection.

In the Old Testament, which is the written record of Divine Revelation, we learn how time and again the Chosen People repeatedly ignored the covenant. Though their actions led to a divided kingdom, then the destruction of the northern kingdom and the enslavement of the southern kingdom, God never abandoned his People. Through their sufferings, captivity by foreign powers, and oppression by pagan leaders, God remained with them. He sent prophets to warn them to be faithful, to comfort them in their sorrows, and to recall God's promises to be with them always.

Finally, in the fullness of time, Jesus of Nazareth was born in Bethlehem, as prophesied. As a child, he grew in wisdom, age, and grace before God and man. Around the age of thirty, he was baptized by a distant relative, John the Baptist, and after John's arrest began his own preaching and healing ministry. He gathered twelve Apostles to assist him in his work and to carry it on after his time on earth was complete.

The Incarnation of the Son of God teaches us many important truths:

- By becoming a human being, God teaches that all human beings have tremendous dignity. He shows us that we can be godlike, that we are not insignificant "nothings" in the cosmic scheme of things. Rather, each of us is valuable in God's eyes, a brother and sister to the Son of God.

- The Incarnation gives worth to *all* of creation. Everything connected to human life is valuable. The food we eat, the clothes we wear, the games we play, the jokes we enjoy, the work we do, the rest we seek are all important to God. Jesus shared our life. He was born and died. He laughed and cried. He worked. He was tempted. He was like us in everything but sin.

- God shares both our personal joy and suffering. What concerns us matters to the Lord. What is important and has meaning for us concerns Jesus, God made man, who took on our life and shares every aspect of it. We should never forget his words:

Come to me, all you who labor and are burdened, and I will give you rest. Take my yoke upon you and learn from me, for I am meek and humble of heart; and you will find rest for your selves. For my yoke is easy, and my burden light. (Mt 11:28–30)

The Seven Sacraments help us celebrate the wonder of the Incarnation. The Lord continues to come to us in the special moments of our lives. For example, God comes to us at birth (in Baptism) and in illness and death (Anointing of the Sick). The Holy Spirit strengthens us as we grow and gives us courage to live authentically (Confirmation). The Lord feeds us at the banquet table of his Eucharist. He forgives us when we sin and are guilt-ridden (Penance). He sustains us in the vocation of marriage (Matrimony) or as a special minister to God's people (Holy Orders). In the Seven Sacraments, ordinary objects and actions—bread and wine, water and oil, human touch—become instruments of God's grace.

For Review

1. How does creation reveal God's love?

2. Why is the Incarnation a wonder of God's love?

3. What does Jesus' Incarnation teach us about human dignity and worth?

4. How do the Seven Sacraments meet us in the special moments of our lives?

🌸 For Reflection

Jesus preached against being anxious. He said: "Do not worry about tomorrow; tomorrow will take care of itself" (Mt 6:34). What are your five most common worries? What might be an antidote to worrying about these concerns that you have?

Good News: The Kingdom of God Is at Hand

The Gospel or Good News itself is another wonder or truth that flows from God. The structure around which the Good News was preached is Christ's ushering in of the Kingdom of God. Jesus proclaimed with authority that God's effective rule over people was drawing near. Jesus himself is the principal agent of this rule, or Kingdom. Preaching in his own town of Nazareth, Jesus claimed that he fulfilled the prophecy from Isaiah about the coming of the Messiah; he himself is the Promised One:

> The Spirit of the Lord is upon me,
> because he has anointed me
> to bring glad tidings to the poor.
> He has sent me to proclaim liberty to captives
> and recovery of sight to the blind,
> to let the oppressed go free,
> and to proclaim a year acceptable to the
> Lord. (Lk 4:18–19)

In his parables and other teachings, Jesus revealed the true nature of God: a loving Abba, a gentle father who cares deeply for his children and will do anything to nourish, teach, welcome, and save them. Jesus' public life began the process of healing the world through peace, justice, and love. Through him, the Father is drawing all men, women, and children to him. Salvation is taking place *right now*—through Jesus.

The miracles of Jesus were signs that God's Kingdom has broken into human history. These mighty works demonstrated the power of God's presence and love through Jesus. When Jesus announced the advent of God's Kingdom, he called his listeners to both repentance and faith. Mark's Gospel sums up Jesus' preaching: "This is the time of fulfillment. The kingdom of God is at hand. Repent, and believe in the gospel" (Mk 1:15). Repentance means a change of mind, a turning from sin so one can be open to Jesus and his message. We must believe that Jesus is the way, the truth, and the life (Jn 14:6); the bread of life (Jn 6:51); and the one who brings us everlasting life: "I am the resurrection and the life; whoever believes in me, even if he dies, will live, and everyone who lives and believes in me will never die" (Jn 11:25–26).

Jesus wants all of his followers to be open to God's Kingdom in their lives. Openness to God's Kingdom requires faith, that is, a wholehearted acceptance of and commitment to Jesus, his message, and his example. Jesus calls people to *conversion*, that is, turning our hearts and minds away from sin. This means we must give up whatever is keeping us from God—fighting and complaining, senseless competition where we try to best others, making gods out of pleasure or sex or material possessions, ignoring others and their needs, and so forth. Service, peace, harmony, and loving God above everything and our neighbor as ourselves—these are the necessary virtues for God's Kingdom to reign in our hearts.

The Seven Sacraments celebrate the Good News. They are sacred signs of God's reign and they help bring it about. They increase our faith and help us continue to embrace Jesus and the Gospel. For example, at Mass, we hear the Kingdom proclaimed in the **Liturgy of the Word**. We receive Jesus in Holy Communion so that we can allow him, with the help of the Holy Spirit, to live in us and move us out to love and serve the world.

Liturgy of the Word
An essential part of the celebration of the Sacrament of the Holy Eucharist that draws on readings from the Old and New Testaments and features a reading from one of the Gospels and a homily that is an exhortation to accept these readings as the Word of God.

For Review

1. What does Jesus preach about the Kingdom of God?
2. What is the connection between the Kingdom of God and the Person of Jesus?
3. What does it mean to repent?
4. How does the Eucharist celebrate God's Kingdom?

For Reflection

What is evidence that God's Kingdom is alive in your family, school, parish, and community?

Forgiveness of Sins (*CCC*, 1691-1698)

Some of the most powerful words Jesus spoke during his public life were to a paralyzed man: "Child, your sins are forgiven" (Mk 2:5). These words summarize an essential part of Jesus' mission—the forgiveness of sins. Jesus preached repentance—turning from sin and embracing God's Kingdom. Moreover, he makes it possible

Conversion of Heart, Body, and Soul

Read the following miracle accounts. Summarize how each illustrates the theme of conversion.

- Water into wine (Jn 2:1-11)
- Canaanite woman (Mt 15:21-28)
- Woman with hemorrhage (Lk 8:43-48)
- Blind Bartimaeus (Mk 10:46-52)

for us to do what he commands—he forgives our sins.

Sin is destructive. It alienates us from God, other people, and ourselves. It riddles us with guilt. It demeans and depersonalizes. Sin is evil, all-pervasive, and its effects are all around us. Ultimately, sin leads to death. Forgiveness, then, is a true marvel of God's graciousness.

Jesus, whose name means "Yahweh saves," brings Salvation. He came to forgive sin and free all people from its powerful grip. He announced forgiveness and embodied God's loving forgiveness by welcoming the worst of sinners.

Through the forgiveness of sin, Jesus reveals the profound love of his heavenly Father. Recall that when Jesus forgave the paralytic, the scribes accused him of blasphemy because only God can forgive sin. But Jesus—God's own Son—indeed had power to both forgive sin and make a paralyzed man walk:

> "But that you may know that the Son of Man has authority to forgive sins on earth"—he said to the paralytic, "I say to you, rise, pick up your mat, and go home." He rose, picked up his mat at once, and went away in the sight of everyone. They were all astounded and glorified God, saying, "We have never seen anything like this." (Mk 2:10–12)

Jesus demonstrated by his ongoing example the astonishing truth that God loves and forgives sinners. Jesus proved this by associating with those who did not keep the Law, tax collectors, prostitutes, and other outcasts. He also taught about forgiveness, including especially the parable of the Prodigal Son, which challenged his enemies with the truth of God's immense, unfathomable love for sinners. Like the father in the parable, Jesus and his Father will welcome back anyone who repents of sin.

Forgiveness is central to Jesus' message. He wants us—his friends and followers—to imitate him. In the Lord's Prayer, Jesus instructs us to pray, "Forgive us our debts, *as* we forgive our debtors"

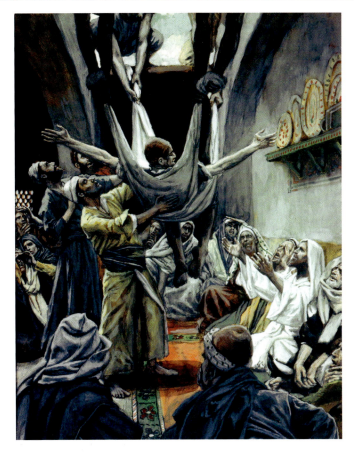

(Mt 6:12). Our forgiveness of others should have no bounds. For example, when Peter asked how many times we should forgive, Jesus said "seventy-seven times" (Mt 18:22), a symbolic number meaning an infinite number of times. We are called to be forgiving.

The most powerful example of God's forgiving love occurs at Jesus' crucifixion. In the midst of his horrific pain, Jesus said: "Father, forgive them, they know not what they do" (Lk 23:34). Even at his Death, Jesus prays to his Father to forgive us. And his Father listens!

All of the sacraments help us celebrate and make real God's compassion for us. The *Catechism of the Catholic Church* teaches:

> By the sacraments of rebirth, Christians have become "children of God," "partakers of the divine nature." Coming to see in the faith their new dignity, Christians are called to lead henceforth a life "worthy of the gospel of Christ." They are made capable of doing

so by the grace of Christ and the gifts of his Spirit, which they receive through the sacraments and through prayer. (*CCC*, 1692)

Baptism incorporates us into Christ so that we can participate in the life of the Risen Lord. With the graces of the Holy Spirit, this sacrament helps us to imitate Jesus Christ and live a life worthy of being a child of his Father. All of our sins—including Original Sin—are wiped clean at Baptism. Penance helps us convert and recover the grace of justification (*CCC*, 1446).

Friendship with Jesus

Another gift of our Redemption is that we can experience an intimate, loving friendship with Christ. The fruit of this love is membership in the Church in which we live as brothers and sisters under a loving God whom Jesus said we could address as "Our Father."

Jesus is always available to his friends. We can meet him in prayer and in our fellow believers. He also comes to us in the sacraments. In the Sacrament of Confirmation, he deepens the gift of the Holy

Spirit in us. It is the Holy Spirit who enables us to call God, *Abba*, "Father" (Gal 4:6), and the one who binds us into one Christian family. The Spirit also bestows gifts like courage and wisdom that help us serve and love all God's children.

The Sacraments at the Service of Communion—Holy Orders and Matrimony—celebrate Christian love and service. They provide special graces that are directed to the Salvation of others (*CCC*, 1534), giving ordained men—bishops, priests, and deacons—and married couples the graces needed to live joy-filled lives for others. The graces of these sacraments help increase Christ's love in us and help build up the Body of Christ.

The Holy Eucharist sends us out into the world, strengthened with the Lord whom we receive in Holy Communion. The way we love God and serve others is modeled in our efforts to love God and neighbor, especially the most vulnerable.

It is a privilege to be a friend of Jesus. But it is also a responsibility to be true to that friendship by being like Jesus. Our life becomes wonderful when we, too, imitate him and become Christ-like, thus

 ## The Challenge of Forgiveness

How difficult is it for you to forgive others? Rate the difficulty of the following situations:

- someone spreads lies about you behind your back
- someone cheats you out of money
- someone lies to your face
- someone intentionally harms you physically
- someone embarrasses you
- a friend refuses to defend you in an argument
- a friend whom you counted on to help you with a project does not follow through

Write a summary explaining how you both verbally and nonverbally show that you forgive a person who has hurt you. Also, cite a specific incident when you asked someone to forgive you. How did he or she react? How did you feel about his or her reaction?

attracting others to him. This is our vocation as his followers . . . and friends.

⚙ For Review

1. What are the effects of sin?
2. Give evidence that forgiveness is central to Jesus' mission.
3. Why must Jesus' followers forgive others?
4. Discuss how the sacraments of Baptism and Penance celebrate Christ's forgiveness.
5. Which are the sacraments in the Service of Communion?

✦ For Reflection

- What is required of a friend of Jesus?
- When was a time you called on Jesus to share either an experience of joy or suffering?

The Paschal Mystery Wins Our Redemption

Christ's work of Redemption, whereby "dying he restored our death, and rising he restored our life," is accomplished principally by the Paschal Mystery, his Passion, Death, Resurrection, and Ascension into Heaven. The Paschal Mystery is celebrated and made present in the liturgy of the Church, and its saving effects are communicated in the sacraments, especially the Eucharist. Christ's own work in the liturgy is sacramental. Now seated at the right hand of the Father, Christ pours out the blessings of the Holy Spirit through the sacraments of the Church. His Body, which is the Church, dispenses the gift of Salvation. Through the liturgy, we are able to participate, as a foretaste, in the heavenly liturgy.

Also, through the sacraments, we receive the Lord's help and strength to live the Paschal Mystery in our own lives. The sacraments also proclaim the Good News of a future resurrected life in eternity.

The Holy Eucharist in a special way commemorates the Paschal Mystery by celebrating Jesus' sacrifice and Resurrection and his exalted place at the Father's right hand. The Eucharist also helps us participate in the Paschal Mystery by giving us the Lord himself in Holy Communion. It is the Risen Lord himself, in the Holy Spirit, who enables us to love by reaching out to our brothers and sisters. Finally, the Eucharistic liturgy looks to the time when we will gather in a heavenly banquet to celebrate God's goodness and love.

Jesus calls all of us to live the Paschal Mystery in our daily lives by dying to sin and selfishness and by reaching out in love to others. The Holy Spirit is God's gift to us, helping us to better imitate the Lord in this life while preparing to live in communion with the Blessed Trinity, the angels, saints, and our faithful friends and relatives in eternity. The Spirit guides us to

- live the Beatitudes and the Christian and human virtues,
- recognize sin in our lives and turn from it, and
- put into practice Christ's command to love both God and neighbor as part of the Church community which is the Body of Christ.

The Gift of the Holy Spirit

Blessed Mother Teresa said, "The most terrible poverty is loneliness, and the feeling of being unloved." And the poet John Milton remarked, "Loneliness is the first thing which God's eye named not good." It is truly a marvel of God's love that Jesus did not leave us alone. At the Last Supper, he made this promise to his friends:

If you ask anything of me in my name, I will do it. If you love me, you will keep my commandments. And I will ask the Father, and he will give you another Advocate to be with you always, the Spirit of truth, which the world cannot accept, because it neither sees nor knows it. But you know it, because it remains with you, and will be in you. I will not leave you orphans; I will come to you. (Jn 14:14–18)

The Father and the Son kept this promise when they sent the Holy Spirit on Pentecost. God's love comes to us through the Holy Spirit who is poured into our hearts (*CCC*, 733). The mission of Christ and the Holy Spirit is brought to completion in the Church. It is Christ, as head, who pours out the Holy Spirit on the Church, building, animating, and sanctifying us, her members, to live out our baptismal calling. The Church does not have a new mission apart from the mission of Christ and the Holy Spirit. Rather, the Church spreads the mystery of the communion of the Holy Trinity.

By virtue of our Baptism, the first sacrament of the faith, the Holy Spirit in the Church communicates to us, intimately and personally, the life that originates in the Father and is offered to us in the Son. (*CCC*, 683)

The Holy Spirit is the first to awaken faith in us and to communicate to us new life. He binds us into one family and showers us with countless gifts that help us live fully with dignity and worth. Allowing the gift of the Holy Spirit to work in us brings forth much spiritual fruit, which are defined as follows:

The fruits of the Spirit are perfections that the Holy Spirit forms in us as the first fruits of eternal glory. The tradition of the Church lists twelve of them: "charity, joy, peace, patience, kindness, goodness, generosity, gentleness, faithfulness, modesty, self-control, chastity." (*CCC*, 1832, see also Gal 5:22–23)

When the fruits of the Spirit are enacted in our lives, the outcome is that we are able to be more like Christ.

The Holy Spirit is present in all the sacraments. At Baptism we are initiated into the life of the Holy Spirit. At Confirmation, the Spirit's gifts are strengthened in us. The Sacrament of the Anointing of the Sick asks the healing power of the Holy Spirit to touch those who are ill and suffering. In the Sacrament of Holy Orders, the Spirit empowers a man to serve the Church in a special way, especially in proclaiming the Gospel, celebrating the Eucharist, and extending Christ's forgiving love.

The poet Gerard Manley Hopkins wrote, "The world is charged with the grandeur of God." This faith-filled exclamation declares that God's grace, love, and presence fill up the entire universe. Hopkins looked at creation and saw God's loving touch everywhere. When we reflect on the mysteries of our faith—God's wonderful creation, Jesus and his message about God's Kingdom, forgiveness, love, the Paschal Mystery, and the gift of the Holy Spirit—we too stand in awe at the incredible grandeur and goodness of God's love. These gifts of our faith help us to reflect on the eternal life to which our loving God calls us.

For Review

1. How is the Paschal Mystery made present?

2. What is the greatest and first gift God gives to us? How do we receive it?

3. What are the "fruits" of the Holy Spirit?

4. Name two examples of how the sacraments celebrate the gift of the Holy Spirit.

For Reflection

Love is the greatest gift of the Holy Spirit (see 1 Corinthians 13:1–31). Share examples of how you have put each of the following qualities of love into practice both at school and among your family and friends: patience, kindness, unpretentiousness, good manners, amiableness.

The Last Things: Christian Death and the Resurrection of the Body (*CCC*, 1002-1003; 1005-1014; 1016-1019)

One day, all of us will face death, defined as the separation of the eternal soul from the body. The Church teaches about the last things—death, resurrection of the body, particular judgment, the Last or General Judgment, Heaven, Purgatory, and Hell. The study of these last things is called eschatology.

Consider the last words of St. Robert Francis Bellarmine (1542–1621), an Italian Jesuit cardinal, archbishop, and Doctor of the Church, whose written works responded brilliantly to the Protestant reformers. As he lay dying of a fever, he recited the Apostles' Creed. His very last words were: "I believe . . . in the resurrection of the body and the life everlasting. Amen." What a fitting end to a life dedicated to Jesus Christ and his Church. St. Robert Bellarmine believed the truth of what Jesus taught, "I am the resurrection and the life; whoever believes in me, even if he dies, will live, and everyone who lives and believes in me will never die" (Jn 11:25–26).

God did not originally intend for us to die. Scripture reveals that death is a price we pay for sin. Because of Adam's sin, humanity was infected with death: "Therefore, just as through one person sin entered the world, and through sin, death, and thus death came to all, inasmuch as all sinned" (Rom 5:12). Jesus Christ has rescued us from our natural fate. He has conquered death.

Also, Jesus showed us how to accept our inevitable deaths. In the Garden of Gethsemane, anxious about his own impending death, Jesus prayed, "Abba, Father, all things are possible to you. Take this cup away from me, but not what I will but what you will" (Mk 14:36). Jesus' words describe his final act of total self-giving to the Father. In faith we imitate him and say, "Father, into your hands I commend my spirit" (Lk 23:46).

Our fervent hope as Christians is that we will rise on the last day with Christ in all his glory. Our Baptism has already united us with the Risen Lord; in a mysterious way we already participate in his heavenly life. The Eucharist helps nourish us with Christ's heavenly life; we are already members of his body. We must always to be ready to live each day as though it were our last so that we can die in union with the Lord. As he lay dying, Pope Clement XI (1649–1721) advised his nephew, a cardinal, about what is really important in life: "See how all the honors of the world come to an end. Only that is great which is great in God's sight. Make it your endeavor to be a saint." Pause and take up the exercise yourself. Imagine that you only have one day left to live. Would you not try to live like a saint, loving God above everything and loving your neighbor as yourself? If we imitate Jesus in the way we live, then we need not fear death. If he is our friend in this life, he will not forget us in eternity.

Resurrection of the Body after Death (CCC, 988-1001; 1004; 1015-1017)

God created human beings with bodies of flesh. The term *flesh* refers to humans in our state of weakness and mortality. God's Son took on a human body (flesh) in order to redeem it. Furthermore, the "resurrection of the flesh" completes the creation and Redemption of the human body. It means that not only will our immortal souls live on after death, but our mortal bodies will also come to life. These interlocking truths of the resurrection of our bodies and the gift of everlasting life are fundamental Christian beliefs, based on our faith in the Lord's own Resurrection.

How will this occur? At death, our souls will separate from our human bodies, which we know do corrupt. We believe that immediately after death, God will judge us in a particular judgment that refers our lives to Christ. We will receive either entrance into Heaven—immediately or through a purification—or immediate damnation. At the Second Coming, by the power of his own Resurrection, the most Blessed Trinity will

raise our bodies in a way that goes beyond our imagination and understanding. Our resurrected bodies will be made incorrupt, and they will rejoin our souls. God will raise all people, both good and evil, from the dead on the last day. In talking about that day, Jesus said,

> Do not be amazed at this, because the hour is coming in which all who are in the tombs will hear his voice and will come out, those who have done good deeds to the resurrection of life, but those who have done wicked deeds to the resurrection of condemnation. (Jn 5:29)

In a miracle of God's love, he will make our bodies incorruptible when they reunite with our souls.

The most important quality of our resurrected bodies will be immortality; we will never die again. In 1 Corinthians 15, St. Paul lists certain qualities of our resurrected bodies, including immortality. Our resurrected bodies will be imperishable, glorious, powerful, and spiritual. We will never feel pain, and our bodies will shine brightly, reflecting the glory of the **Beatific Vision**, that is, "seeing God face to face" in heaven. Material creation will not hinder us; for example, we will be able to move about easily and swiftly. Finally, our spirits will control our glorified bodies.

We also believe that God will transform *all* material creation in Christ, creating a suitable environment where our resurrected, glorified bodies will thrive for eternity.

Beatific Vision
Seeing God "face to face" in Heaven; it is the source of our eternal happiness and final union with the Triune God for all eternity.

particular judgment
The individual's judgment immediately after death, when Christ will rule on one's eternal destiny to be spent in Heaven (after purification in Purgatory, if needed) or in Hell.

Purgatory
The state of purification that takes place after death for those who need to be made clean and holy before meeting the all-holy God in Heaven.

Parousia
The Second Coming of Christ when the Lord will judge the living and the dead.

EXPLAINING THE FAITH

What do we believe occurs after we die?

Immediately after death there will be a particular judgment based on how we have lived. This individual judgment will determine whether we go to Heaven immediately, need purification in Purgatory (see pages 172, 176), or suffer the punishments of Hell and eternal damnation. St. Paul writes:

> For we must all appear before the judgment seat of Christ, so that each one may receive recompense, according to what he did in the body, whether good or evil. (2 Cor 5:10)

Jesus himself referred to the particular judgment in the parable of the Rich Man and Lazarus (Lk 16:19-31). Because of his selfish lifestyle of not feeding the starving Lazarus, the rich man suffered the fires of Hades. In contrast, the good man Lazarus went to a peaceful resting place.

If we live a just and loving life, we have nothing to fear when we die. Our God is a God of justice *and* mercy. His judgment is based on whether we loved him and our neighbor as ourselves. At the particular judgment, God is not out to trick us. There will be no surprises. Christ will judge us according to our own free decision to accept or refuse the grace of his love. People know if they have lived loving and God-centered lives or not. Venerable Maria Guadalupe Garcia Zavala (1878-1963), known as Mother Lupe, was the Mexican founder of the Servants of Saint Margaret Mary and of the Poor. As she lay dying, her doctor asked her, "How are you doing, Mother Lupe?" She replied, "I'm walking toward Heaven." Our goal is that we each live our lives so that we can say the same thing near to the time of our own death.

Our Catholic belief in the resurrection of the body should encourage us to respect our bodies and those of others. Human existence includes our having both a soul and body. They come from God as gifts and will return to glorify him. When we care for and respect our own bodies and the bodies of others, we are expressing profound respect and gratitude to a loving God who made us as a composite being of body and soul.

The doctrine of the resurrection of the body contrasts sharply with other belief systems, for example ones that teach some nebulous spiritual form of existence. Catholic belief is much richer in holding that the whole person—body and soul—will survive death.

The Last or General Judgment (CCC, *1038-1050; 1059-1060*)

Christians believe that the resurrection of both the just and unjust will come immediately before the Last or General Judgment. On that last day of human history, the Risen Glorified Lord will come again. This is known as the **Parousia**, his arrival in glory at his Second Coming. Christ, who is Truth itself, will lay bare each person's relationship with God. Finally, everyone will recognize God's saving plan in Christ Jesus. On this day, the Son of Man, in the presence of all the angels, will separate the sheep (good people) from the goats (evil people) (Mt 25:31–32).

As to *when* this will take place, only the Father knows. When the day comes, however, everyone will see "that God's justice triumphs over all the injustices committed by his creatures and that God's love is stronger than death" (*CCC*, 1040). Followers of Christ look forward to this day of final judgment because the unity our hearts yearn for will be accomplished. Furthermore, on this day God will transform and restore the entire physical universe. Along with a transformed humanity, "the new heavens and new earth" will share in Christ Jesus' own glory. Since we do not know the exact hour of Christ's return and our final judgment, we should always be ready.

Today we have a glimpse of our future life because Christ has already initiated the Kingdom of God on earth. The Church "is the Reign of Christ already present in mystery" (*Lumen Gentium* 3, quoted in *CCC*, 763). Despite the sinful forces at work in the world to undermine God's saving love, his loving grace in the Church is very much alive to help attract people to the Triune God. The Holy Spirit gives Catholics the power and the mission of cooperating with Christ's work of freeing people from the bondage of sin. The Spirit strengthens us with virtues like fortitude to work tirelessly as peacemakers. We can work for justice by helping people attain their God-given rights. We also cooperate in Christ's plan when we promote human solidarity and respect the dignity of every human being. In a special way, we promote the Kingdom of God when we extend mercy to the weak, poor, and defenseless.

The Holy Spirit also gifts us with the virtue of hope. Hope helps us look forward to the glorious day of Christ's Second Coming. It helps us pray the prayer that ends the very last book of the Bible: "Amen! Come, Lord Jesus! The grace of the Lord Jesus be with you all" (Rv 22:20–21). In his encyclical *Spe Salvi* (Saved in Hope), Pope Benedict XVI described the hope we have in eternal life when we will join with Christ forever. He wrote about eternity this way:

> The term "eternal life" is intended to give a name to this known "unknown." . . . It would be like plunging into the ocean of infinite love, a moment in which time—the before and after—no longer exists. We can only attempt to grasp the idea that such a moment is life in the full sense, a plunging ever anew into the vastness of being, in which we are simply overwhelmed with joy. This is how Jesus expresses it in Saint John's Gospel:

Reflection: RIP

RIP is an abbreviation for the short Latin prayer, *Requiescat in pace*, "May he/she rest in peace."

Perhaps you have also seen a print of a medieval painting with a monk at his desk. A skull sits on his desk. The monk is contemplating the skull and what it represents. The artist may also have added the words, *Sic transit gloria mundi*, "Thus passes the glory of the world." The skull reminds us that we have only a brief time to make our mark. Time speeds quickly by. What the world holds important may not be so in God's eyes.

Let these Latin phrases help you reflect on your own life. What would you like to do with your life? Write an obituary notice for yourself that would appear in a daily newspaper. Include things like:

- Your name and age
- Cause of death
- Occupation
- Loved ones left behind
- Major accomplishments
- Unfinished tasks
- Epitaph on gravestone

In your journal, write an entry that describes five personal qualities that you could offer to Jesus at your particular judgment that show how you have lived a Christian life. Write a detailed plan explaining how you will implement practice of these qualities in the next two weeks.

"I will see you again and your hearts will rejoice, and no one will take your joy from you" (16:22). We must think along these lines if we want to understand the object of Christian hope, to understand what it is that our faith, our being with Christ, leads us to expect." (*Spe Salvi,* 12)

The joy and happiness that God has in store for us is indeed something for which to hope and pray.

For Review

1. Why is death a part of the human experience?

2. How does Jesus' example of dying help us at the time of our own deaths?

3. What do Catholics believe about the resurrection of the body?

4. Define *Beatific Vision.*

5. What is the particular judgment?

6. Define *Parousia.*

7. What will happen at the Second Coming of Christ?

For Reflection

• How do you imagine an incorruptible heavenly body?

• Describe a situation when you feel you have been judged fairly.

More about Eternal Life (*CCC,* 1023-1037; 1052-1058)

Our eternal life will begin immediately after death and the particular judgment. The particular judgment will be confirmed in the final judgment at the

end of time when Christ will come again and raise our bodies, those who have lived a life of love and merit eternal reward (in Heaven) as well as those who have died separated from God and deserve punishment (in Hell). The reward of Heaven is eternal life spent in union with God and all those who share in God's life. Hell is eternal separation from God.

The existence of Heaven and Hell show very seriously the reality of human freedom. If we use our freedom properly, then we will choose our own eternal destiny—a joyous life with our loving, Triune God. On the other hand, if we choose freely to model ourselves into heartless, unloving, selfish people, then God will respect our decision. When we choose self over God, then it is we who have chosen Hell. Our loving God respects our freedom and will give us what we want. More significantly,

God generously rewards those who use freedom to choose what is right and good.

Heaven

If we die in God's friendship and grace, and are perfectly purified, we will receive the reward of a life of perfect eternal happiness in Heaven. Living with Jesus Christ forever, we will be blessed with the Beatific Vision where we will see God face to face, as he really is, contemplating his heavenly glory. Perfect life with the Most Holy Trinity, our Blessed Mother, and all the angels and saints, including our relatives and friends who have lived a God-centered life, is called **Heaven**. In Heaven, God

> will wipe every tear from their eyes, and there shall be no more death or mourning, wailing or pain, [for] the old order has passed away. (Rv 21:4)

Jesus' Death and Resurrection have opened Heaven to us. In Heaven, we will be fully incorporated into Christ. Although we will have perfect communion with him, we will both retain and find our true individual identities as his brother or sister. We will continue to fulfill God's will in Heaven and will reign with Christ Jesus forever.

The pleasures and happiness in store for us in Heaven are beyond human imagination. Scripture uses images to help describe them: wedding feast, light, life, peace, paradise, the Father's house, heavenly Jerusalem. But as it is written, the joy is really incomprehensible to us on earth: "What eye has not seen, and ear has not heard, and what has not entered the human heart, what God has prepared for those who love him" (1 Cor 2:9).

The Hall of Fame baseball great, Yogi Berra, once observed, "You've got to be careful if you don't know where you are going, because you might not get there." Another time he cautioned, "If you don't know where you are going, you'll wind up somewhere else." His amusing remarks seem a little confused, but his main point is clear: if we do not have a well-planned, positive goal in life, wrong turns can lead us to a place we do not want to be. There is no goal more worthwhile than getting to Heaven. This is why we should take to heart the advice of St. Francis de Sales who said, "Resolve henceforth to keep Heaven before your mind, to be ready to forgo everything that can hinder you or cause you to stray on your journey there." However, if we do stray, we should never forget that we are able to turn to our merciful Lord and ask for his forgiveness in order to get back on the path that leads to eternal happiness.

Purgatory

Purgatory is the name the Church gives to the final purification of those who die in God's grace and friendship but who need purification or cleansing to achieve the holiness necessary to enter Heaven.

Catholic belief in the existence of Purgatory is based on Biblical passages like 2 Maccabees 12:41–45, which encourages those who are living

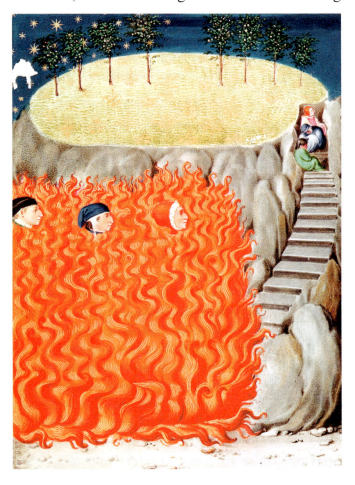

to pray for the dead so that they may be released from their sins. In addition, Church Tradition has interpreted certain New Testament passages (see 1 Corinthians 3:15; 1 Peter 1:7) as referring to a place of a "cleansing fire" after death.

Church teaching on the **Communion of Saints**, that is, the unity in Christ of all those he has redeemed, is also related to the existence of Purgatory. The Communion of Saints includes three groups of people:

- the *pilgrim Church* (those of us who are living today on earth, also known as the "Church militant");

- the *Church suffering* (those undergoing purification in Purgatory); and

- the *Church triumphant* (the blessed in heaven).

By the power of the Holy Spirit, the Risen Lord, who is the source of all holiness, makes holy and binds the Church into a communion of the faithful. We—both the living and those who have died—are one family united in the Spirit of Jesus Christ. As a family, we can continue to show our love and concern for each other, even after death. This is why, from the first centuries, the Church has honored the dead by offering the Eucharist for them and encouraging the faithful to pray for them. In addition, the Church recommends almsgiving, indulgences, and acts of penance for the "poor souls in Purgatory."

The doctrine of Purgatory, "purification," makes sense. To embrace an all-loving God, we must be free of any imperfection in our own capacity to love. Only a pure person can enter Heaven to embrace the all-holy God. Not everyone who dies has cleansed himself or herself of his or her **venial sins** or any punishment due sins that are present at death. Although with God's help we can accomplish the process of purification while we are alive, the process of dying to attachment to sin and selfishness is long and painful.

Purgatory involves "letting go" to our sins and selfishness, a process that is both joyful and painful. Those in Purgatory are happy that the Lord has promised them Heaven. At the same time, the Church suffering need to leave behind their selfish attachments before meeting the all-holy God. Giving up what we have clung to in life (for example, the desire to dominate others) can be difficult. This painful process of "letting go and letting God" may be what the expression "cleansing fire" means. The process of purgation might be one of burning with sorrow and shame over a sinful life, and a profound wish to be united to the loving, good, and saving God. To be separated from the Lord whom they love so deeply brings suffering to our brothers and sisters in Purgatory. However, when their purgation is complete, their suffering will end as they enter into the bliss of Heaven.

Because we in the pilgrim Church are members of the Communion of Saints, we should remember to pray for those in Purgatory, especially at Mass, and to ask for their prayers as well. We can honor our relatives who

Heaven
Our final communion with the Blessed Trinity, Mary, the angels, and all the saints.

Communion of Saints
The unity of Jesus Christ with all those he has redeemed—the Church on earth, in Heaven, and in Purgatory.

venial sins
Actual sins that weaken and wound our relationship with God but do not destroy divine life in our souls.

have gone before us by praying for them and offering our good works and sacrifices on their behalf. When they make it to Heaven, they will be sure to remember us before our heavenly Father.

Hell

Hell is defined as an eternal separation from God brought on by deliberate **mortal sin**. Its principal punishment is separation from our loving God who created us with the intention that we would find and seek love, life, joy, and happiness—our deepest yearnings that only God can satisfy. Sacred Tradition speaks of the "fires of Hell." These describe the loss of love, self-hatred, and the total loneliness that results from failure to love God above all others and our neighbor as ourselves for the love of God. Those in Hell grieve over their eternal punishment, suffer

spiritually and physically, and give up all hope of Salvation.

God does not predestine anyone for Hell. God made us to love him. However, for those who freely choose to commit mortal sin by refusing to love God, and die without repenting of their lack of love, their own free choice will forever separate them from God.

Sacred Scripture and Sacred Tradition both affirm the existence of Hell. For example, Jesus referred several times to *Gehenna,* a Jewish term associated with Hell. One example is the parable of the sheep and goats—a judgment scene at the end of time when those who fail to love the needy are condemned to Hell. On other occasions, Jesus talked about divine judgment (Mt 13:41–42) and separation from God because of selfishness, as in the parable of Lazarus and the rich man (Lk 18:19–31).

The doctrine of Hell is related to our belief that God is a loving God who made us truly free. God respects our freedom, even if, out of pride, we choose to reject his love, grace, and mercy. God forever showers his love on us; his mercy is always there for us to embrace. However, despite God's constant love, people can be hard-hearted and stiff-necked, adamantly selfish and unloving. Humans can and do commit mortal sin. Having created us free beings, God respects our freedom, even if it results in destructive and sinful actions.

God does not send anyone to Hell; unrepentant mortal sin does. We cannot say with certitude who is in Hell because we do not know which persons have defiantly turned their backs on God. Jesus warns us not to judge others lest we be judged ourselves (see Luke 6:37). What we can and should do is pray for all sinners, including ourselves, to repent of sin and accept God's love and forgiveness.

If we try to live with love in our hearts, and perform acts of love for God and others, the existence of Hell should not frighten us. If we turn from sin as Christ calls us to do and struggle to live lives of love, then we should trust and believe that Christ

THE BIBLE ON JUDGMENT

Read John 5:19-41 and answer the questions that follow:

- What is assigned to the Son by the Father? (v. 22)
- What is the basis of judgment? (v. 29)
- What is the downfall of Jesus' opponents? (v. 44)

Read 1 Peter 4:1-11 and complete the following:

- List three things the Gentiles like to do. (v. 3)
- List three things one should do as the end nears. (vv. 7-11)

HOLY BIBLE

Jesus will save us. He is a merciful, loving Savior who will always forgive us if we repent. His Father is our Father who loves us more tenderly than any human mother or father possibly can.

The doctrine of Hell reminds us to live a responsible life, to ask God to forgive our sins, and to try to imitate Jesus. It also reminds us to live a good and moral life because we never know when God will call us home.

For Review

1. What is Heaven?
2. What are some Scriptural images of Heaven?
3. Define *Purgatory*.
4. What is the Communion of Saints?
5. Who is the "Church suffering" and what can we do for them?
6. What is the principal punishment of Hell?

For Reflection

What do you imagine Heaven to be like? What do you think you have to do to get there?

mortal sin
A serious violation of God's law of love that results in the loss of God's life (sanctifying grace) in the soul of the sinner. To commit mortal sin there must be grave matter, full knowledge of the evil done, and deliberate consent.

Main Ideas

- The Life, Death, Resurrection, and Ascension of Jesus Christ is life's greatest "wonder." (pp. 160–162)

- The sacraments make God's work present and help us to celebrate the gift of Redemption. (p. 161)

- Creation itself is the first wonder of the world; it reveals God's love for us in profound ways. (pp. 161–162)

- The masterpiece of God's creation is human beings. (pp. 162–163)

- The Incarnation of Jesus Christ was the fulfillment of God's promises and effected our Salvation. (p. 163)

- The Incarnation teaches that humans have great dignity, that all creation has worth, and that God shares in both our personal joy and suffering. (pp. 163–164)

- The Kingdom of God was ushered in with the birth of Jesus; it brings structure to the events of our Redemption. (pp. 164–166)

- An essential part of Jesus' mission was his forgiveness of sin; he calls us to forgive others, including our enemies. (pp. 166–167)

- Another gift of our Redemption is that we can experience a deep friendship with Christ. (p. 168)

- It is through the events of the Paschal Mystery that our Redemption is ultimately won. (p. 169)

- God's gift of the Holy Spirit helps us to imitate Christ; by enacting the fruits of the Spirit we become more like him. (pp. 169–170)

- The study of the last things is called eschatology. (p. 171)

- We believe in the "resurrection of the flesh," that is, that our soul will be reunited with the body after the Final Judgment. (p. 172)

- We also believe that God will transform all material creation in Christ. (p. 172)

- Immediately after death, we will experience an individual, particular judgment to determine whether we will go to Heaven, Purgatory, or Hell. (pp. 173–174)

- At the Last or General Judgment, Christ will come again, and everyone will recognize God's saving plan in Christ Jesus. (p. 175)

- The virtue of hope helps us to look forward to the glorious day of Christ's Second Coming. (pp. 175–176)

- If we die in God's friendship and grace, and are perfectly purified, we will receive the reward of eternal life in Heaven. (pp. 175–176)

- Purgatory is the name for the place that those who die in God's grace and friendship but need purification or cleansing go before entering Heaven. (pp. 176–177)

- Our belief in the Communion of Saints, including the pilgrim Church, the Church suffering, and the Church triumphant, help to support our understanding of Purgatory. (pp. 176–177)

- Hell is the eternal separation from God brought on by deliberate mortal sin and the failure to repent. (p. 177)

Terms, People, Places

On a separate piece of paper, write the following statements. Then supply the missing term from the vocabulary list.

Beatific Vision

Communion of Saints

eschatology

Liturgy of the Word

mortal sin

Parousia

particular judgment

Purgatory

venial sins

1. _____ These weaken our relationship with God but do not destroy divine life in our souls.

2. _____ A goal for our lives; this is a gift that we desire for eternal life.

3. _____ A study of the "last things."

4. _____ This is a time when we hear the Kingdom of God proclaimed.

5. _____ A determination will be made at this time whether we go to Heaven immediately, need purification in Purgatory, or suffer the punishments of Hell.

6. _____ The Second Coming of Christ when the Lord will judge the living and the dead.

7. _____ Its principal punishment is separation from our loving God.

8. _____ Catholic belief in this is based on Biblical passages that encourage us to pray for the dead.

9. _____ It includes three groups: the pilgrim Church, the Church suffering, and the Church triumphant.

Primary Source Quotations

On Death
For we brought nothing into the world, just as we shall not be able to take anything out of it.

—1 Timothy 6:7

To the good man to die is gain. The foolish fear death as the greatest of evils, the wise desire it as a rest after the labors and the end of ills.

—St. Ambrose

On the Brink of Hell
However wicked I may be, however great a sinner, I *must* hope that I should get to Heaven. You forbid me to despair.

—Charles de Foucauld

If I saw the gates of Hell open and I stood on the brink of the abyss, I should not despair, I should not lose my hope

of mercy, because I should trust in Thee, my God.

—St. Gemma Galgani

On Heaven
God is so good and merciful that to obtain Heaven is sufficient to ask it of him in our hearts.

—St. Benedict Joseph Labré

To get to heaven, turn right and keep straight. The peace of the celestial city is the perfectly ordered and harmonious enjoyment of God, and of one another in God.

—St. Augustine, *City of God*, 426

In his novel *The Screwtape Letters*, C. S. Lewis wrote, "The safest road to Hell is the gradual one—the gentle slope, soft underfoot, without sudden turnings, without milestones, without signposts." What did Lewis mean by that statement? Is Lewis correct? Offer evidence.

Ongoing Assignments

As you cover the material in this chapter, choose and complete at least three of these assignments.

1. Research and report on any two of the so-called "wonders of the world" that you find interesting.

2. Great and impressive basilicas, churches, and abbeys belong on any list of great wonders of the Christian world. Do an illustrated slide or PowerPoint presentation on one of the following (or a similarly famous) churches or basilicas:

   • St. Peter's Basilica in Vatican City

   • Sistine Chapel in Vatican City

   • Chartres Cathedral in Chartres, France

   • St. Mark's Basilica in Venice, Italy

   • Mont Saint-Michel in Normandy, France

   • Basilica of the National Shrine of the Immaculate Conception in Washington, DC

Chapter 7 Quick View

- St. Joseph's Oratory, Montreal, Quebec, Canada

3. Read Psalm 104, which praises God for his wondrous creation. Find a picture that speaks to you of God's grandeur. Then compose your own prayer of praise to God for the wonders of creation. Create a poster of your prayer and picture.

4. Read Matthew 18:23–35. What is the point of this parable? Rewrite it in a modern-day setting. Be sure to make the same point that Jesus does in his parable.

5. Prepare a report that contrasts belief in reincarnation with the Catholic doctrine of the resurrection of the body.

6. Research and report on what one of the following religions teaches about the afterlife: Judaism, Islam, a Native American religion.

7. Read 1 Corinthians 15:35–58. Answer the following questions:

   - What analogy from agriculture does St. Paul use to describe what will happen to our bodies in the resurrection?

   - How will the resurrection take place as described in verses 50–54?

   - What is the "sting of death"?

   - Assemble Scripture quotations related to Christ's Second Coming.

8. Report on the life of a saint that Pope Benedict XVI mentions in his encyclical *Spe Salvi*: St. Josephine Bakhita. See: www.vatican.va/news_services/liturgy/saints/ns_lit_doc_20001001_giuseppina-bakhita_en.html

9. Devise a project with several other classmates to put into action two of the corporal works of mercy: visiting the sick and burying the dead. For example: (1) visit a nursing home and chat with some of the lonely patients there; (2) do chores for an elderly neighbor; (3) help serve a luncheon (through your parish's hospitality committee) for the family members and friends of a deceased parishioner after the funeral Mass and burial.

10. Read the parable of the Weeds (Mt 13:24–30, 36–43) and the parable of the Dragnet (Mt 13:47–50). Write an interpretation of each these parables. In the parable of the Weeds, identify the following symbols: the field, the sower of the wheat, the good seed, the sower of the weeds, the weeds, the harvest, the harvesters.

Prayer

Pray these prayers for the souls in Purgatory:

Prayer for the Forgotten Dead
O merciful God, take pity on those souls who have no particular friends and intercessors to recommend them to You, who either through negligence of those who are alive or through length of time, are forgotten by all. Spare them, O Lord, and remember Your own when others forget to appeal to Your mercy. Let not the souls You have created be parted from You, their Creator. Amen.

Prayer for the Faithful Departed
Eternal rest grant unto them, O Lord, and let perpetual light shine upon them. May their souls and the souls of all the faithful departed, through the mercy of God, rest in peace. Amen.

- *Reflection*: Which deceased relatives, friends, or acquaintances need your prayers?

- *Resolution*: In the upcoming weeks, offer some prayers for the souls in Purgatory.

8

LIVING THE PASCHAL MYSTERY: A CALL TO HOLINESS

As he who called you is holy, be holy yourselves in every aspect of your conduct, for it is written, "Be holy because I (am) holy."

—1 Peter 1:15-16

The Light of Christ

A mark of holiness is to let Christ's light shine through in our lives.

Living a Life of Virtue

The habitual and firm disposition to do good—the meaning of living a virtuous life—empowers us to perform good acts and give the best of ourselves.

God Helps Us Grow in Holiness

Growth in holiness is a difficult but not impossible task as long as we rely on God's help, including through his sharing of grace and the seven gifts of the Holy Spirit.

Essential Elements of Holiness

Our God-given gifts of human reason, free will, and conscience impact our moral decision-making and allow for growth in holiness.

The Light of Christ

A little boy was on vacation with his family, touring one of the great cathedrals in Europe. The child was fascinated with the great stained-glass windows that adorned the massive structure. He especially was awestruck by the sun streaming through the stained glass and the beautiful, rainbow colors that splashed on the floor of the cathedral. He looked up to his father and asked, "Who are all those people in the pretty window?" His dad replied, "They are the saints."

Later that night as the father was tucking his boy into bed, his son told him, "I know who the saints are."

The father smiled and said, "Do you? Who are they?" The boy replied, "They are the persons who let the light shine through."

The boy in the story was correct. Saints are indeed those who allow the light of Christ to shine through. The word *saint* comes from the Latin word, *sanctus*, which means "holy." The words *holy* and *holiness* originally referred to God. In the Old Testament, *holy* meant being separated from the ordinary, everyday world. God is holy in the sense that he is "wholly other," perfectly good, and totally and absolutely separated from evil and sin. When we speak of people, places (like a cathedral), or things (like a blessed water) as being "holy," it is because they are related to God. God is the source of all holiness because he alone is truly holy, that is, all-good and separate from all evil.

We are called by God to be holy people, that is, to be good and to be Christ-like. This is a call or **vocation**, one given to us by Jesus himself. With the help of God's grace, the presence of the Holy Spirit in our lives, and a life of self-denial and prayer, each of us can work at growing in holiness, that is, to separate ourselves from sin and evil. This is a worthy goal, one that not only makes us better people for this world but also helps us gain a place in God's

Growing in Everyday Holiness

Every day presents many ways we can let the light of Christ shine through our lives. Read through the list of situations where you have the opportunity to bring Christ to others. For each category, evaluate and briefly write how you are doing, as well as how you can improve in this area.

At Home
- I readily obey my parents without arguing.
- I am patient with my brothers and sisters.
- I volunteer to do some chores without being asked.
- I willingly spend time with my family.
- I make a point to be on time for family meals.

At School
- I am respectful of my teachers and other adults.
- I greet my classmates.
- I try to make new friends.
- I fully participate in the extracurricular activities of which I am a member.
- I resist temptations to cheat.

Other
- I carefully listen to others when they speak to me.
- I go to Mass every weekend.
- I pray every day.
- I'm careful with how I use the Internet, spending my time wisely and avoiding harmful and immoral sites.
- I share some of my wealth of talents, time, and money with others, including those who are less fortunate.

Assignment
Write a profile of the "holiest" person that you personally know. How does the light of Christ shine through this person? What might you have to do in your own life to become more like him or her?

eternal kingdom. In short, we are called to be saints, holy ones of God, who, with the help of the Holy Spirit, allow the life and light of Christ to shine through us to attract others to him and to his heavenly Father.

Don't think of saints as "perfect people" or without sin. They aren't. Also, don't think you can become a saint in one day. Becoming a saint is a lifelong task. Holiness requires perseverance, repenting of our sins when we fall, fighting temptations that come our way, and the constant help of God and the graces he sends to us. The key to growing in holiness, goodness, and freedom from sin requires staying close to Jesus Christ who meets us in his Church, in the sacraments, and in prayer. These are tasks addressed in this chapter.

For Reflection

What is your reaction to the thought that you are called to be a saint?

Living a Life of Virtue (*CCC*, 1803-1845)

The Paschal Mystery of Christ's saving actions has redeemed us. This means that the Passion, Death, Resurrection, and glorious Ascension of Jesus Christ gained for us eternal life and made us adopted children of the Triune God. We need God's grace in order to accept grace. His preparation of us for the reception of grace is already the work of grace. For our part, we are then to accept and live the grace of Redemption by

- repenting of our sins,
- believing in the Gospel of Jesus Christ, and
- living a life of holiness.

Living a virtuous life and cooperating with the graces God sends to us are two important ways to grow in holiness.

What is a **virtue**? In general, "a virtue is an habitual and firm disposition to do the good" (*CCC*, 1803). Virtues enable us to perform good acts and to give the best of ourselves, empowering us to become what God wants us to be. Practicing virtues helps us to be more like Jesus Christ. There are two major categories of virtues: the human virtues (especially the four cardinal virtues) and the theological virtues.

vocation

A word that means "call." For Catholics the primary call is to be disciples of Jesus Christ. This call, given at Baptism, requires Catholics to bring God's love to others and to share the Good News.

virtue

A firm attitude, stable disposition, and habitual disposition of our intellect and will that regulates our actions, directs our passions, and guides our conduct according to reason and faith.

cardinal virtues
The four hinge virtues that support moral living: prudence, justice, fortitude, and temperance.

vice
A bad habit, such as laziness, that inclines us to choose the evil rather than the good.

religion
The relationship between God and humans that results in a body of beliefs and a set of practices: creed, cult, and code. Religion expresses itself in worship and service to God and by extension to all people and all creation.

Human Virtues

Virtues that we are able to acquire by our own human efforts are known as human or moral virtues. The human virtues help us to choose the good and then to follow the right course of action. According to the *Catechism of the Catholic Church*:

> Human virtues are firm attitudes, stable dispositions, habitual perfections of intellect and will that govern our actions, order our passions, and guide our conduct according to reason and faith. They make possible ease, self-mastery, and joy in leading a morally good life. (*CCC*, 1804)

Effort on our part can help us acquire and strengthen the human virtues. They are also called *moral virtues* because when we perform morally good acts, virtues become good habits that help us draw closer to God and to relate to other people with Christ-like love. There are countless human virtues, including forgiveness, compassion, courage, courtesy, devotion, generosity, honesty, humility, kindness, loyalty, patience, purity, respect, and trustworthiness. However, four moral virtues play a central role in living a moral life. They are the **cardinal virtues** prudence, justice, fortitude, and temperance. The term *cardinal* comes from the Latin *cardo*, which means "hinge." These four virtues are the source of all other virtues.

How can we gain the cardinal virtues and make them part of our lives?

We gain cardinal virtues through understanding their meaning and by putting them into practice through frequent repetition. However, it is not as easy as it may sound. Because humans are weakened by the effects of Original Sin and are prone to laziness, moral living is a challenge. Yet, God helps us in this struggle to live a virtuous life by sending us the Holy Spirit and giving us graces that enable us to grow in holiness. A worthy goal for all is to live a virtuous life. Living the virtues is a foundation for being more like Jesus Christ. A brief description of the four cardinal virtues follows.

Prudence

Prudence is a virtue that helps us decide responsibly. It equates with common sense and wisdom. Following the ancient Greek philosopher Aristotle, St. Thomas Aquinas defined prudence as "right reason in action." When we exercise prudence, we use our memory, foresight, imagination, and openness to learning to help our intellects discover the right course of action in every situation. Prudence helps form our conscience and the right means of achieving what is good. In short, prudence is a virtue that helps us think and judge carefully before acting so that we can make wise choices and do things well. The *Catechism* teaches that:

> With the help of this virtue we apply moral principles to particular cases without error and overcome doubts about the good to achieve and the evil to avoid. (*CCC*, 1806)

Consider the example of Tara, a high school student, deciding whether or not to go to a concert on a school night. Tara has an important exam the next day, which demands several hours of study. After weighing all the options, and considering that if she went to the concert, she would likely do poorly on the exam, Tara made a prudent decision to forego the pleasure of the moment for the greater good of academic success. She stayed home, studied, and got a good grade on the exam.

The opposite of a virtue is a **vice**, or a bad habit that is acquired by repeated sin in violation of the proper norms of morality. Impetuosity, or acting on the spur of the moment without thinking, is contrary to the virtue of prudence. For example, when Tim, a college freshman, is free of parental supervision, he gives in to the temptation to party and engages in binge drinking the first days he is on campus. His impetuous behavior does not consider the consequences of his snap decision, consequences that can lead to great physical and spiritual harm.

Justice

Justice consists of a person always giving his or her due to God and neighbor. Justice toward God results in the virtue of **religion** where we worship God and thank him as the source of all that is good. God is all-loving, the One who calls us into existence; he is due our love and adoration. Justice toward our neighbor requires that we respect the rights of others and work for equity in regard to persons and the common good. Catholic teaching has distinguished among four types of justice: commutative, distributive, legal, and social.

Commutative justice regulates relationships of exchange, for example, in contracts between individuals and social groups. An example of commutative justice would be if you agree to baby-sit your neighbor's child for a given wage per hour, then your neighbor is obligated to pay you the negotiated amount. This is only fair. Respect for the dignity of

others takes place when we fulfill our obligations toward them.

Distributive justice protects and guarantees the common welfare. It seeks the fair distribution of the goods of creation. Governmental agencies are often responsible for guaranteeing distributive justice to a country's citizens, especially the most vulnerable. Laws that require citizens to pay taxes to support school systems, police forces, and health-care agencies for the poor are ways that the government and citizens support the work of distributive justice.

Legal justice governs what individuals owe society as a whole. Because we are members of a society, living with and for other people, we have the duty to contribute to the common good. Therefore, it is a work of legal justice to obey the just laws of the society in which we live—for example, paying taxes, serving on juries, and coming to the aid of our fellow citizens in times of peril.

Finally, *social justice* applies the Gospel message of Jesus Christ to the structures, systems, and laws of society in order to protect the dignity of persons and guarantee the rights of individuals. Social justice holds that each person has a right to a fair voice in the economic, political, and social institutions of the society in which he or she lives. According to one's ability, each person has a right to contribute to how society functions. Therefore, social justice is sometimes called *contributive justice*.

Justice also equates with avoiding all forms of discrimination and prejudice and justice always respects the God-given rights of other people. The person practicing this virtue looks out for the needs of the poor and powerless, those whom society tends to ignore.

Fortitude

Fortitude is another word for courage. It is a virtue that enables a person to conquer fears, even the fear of death, for a just cause. Fortitude helps us overcome fears of other people's criticisms, failure, rejection, and disappointment when we are trying to do right. The virtue of fortitude can help in resisting peer pressure, which is often the source that leads to sin.

How can you increase this virtue for your life? One way is through acts of self-denial. Being consistent in all our endeavors, especially by hard work, gives us the courage to follow through when tempted to take the easy way out. The Holy Spirit

also strengthens us with the gift of fortitude so that we can live a Christian life.

The ultimate example of fortitude is martyrdom. Recall that *martyr* means "witness." Though most of us will never be called to lay down our lives for others, we do witness to our faith each time we are courageous enough to do the right thing, especially in the face of strong peer pressure. For example, it takes fortitude to stick up for a classmate who is picked on or to not cheat on a test when everyone else is doing it. Doing the right thing often takes the courage of standing alone. St. Bruno wrote,

> What shall I say of fortitude, without which neither wisdom nor justice is of any value? Fortitude is not of the body, but is a constancy of soul; with it we are conquerors in righteousness, patiently bearing all adversities, and in prosperity are not puffed up. Fortitude is never conquered, or if conquered, is not fortitude.

Temperance

Temperance is a virtue of self-control, delayed gratification, and moderation. Humans are weak and subject to sin. We live in a world where advertisements and other media tempt us to indulge all of our appetites. A common mantra today is "If it feels good, do it." But the trouble is, the pursuit of pleasure can get out of hand. When we are intemperate, the vices of greed, gluttony, and lust control us. Temperance is the "moral virtue that moderates the attraction of pleasures and provides balance in the use of created goods" (*CCC*, 1809). As humans, we have the wherewithal to temper the pleasures of food, drink, and sex in ways that God intends for our own good.

St. Thomas Aquinas distinguished three parts to practicing the virtue of temperance. *Abstinence* tempers our desires for food and other pleasure-producing substances like tobacco and drugs. *Sobriety* moderates our desires for alcoholic beverages. And *chastity* helps us control our sex drive in a way that fits our state in life.

The virtue of temperance is freeing because it helps us become fully functioning persons in control of our own lives. The person who becomes addicted to pleasure, for example, in the case of sex or alcohol, becomes a slave and has lost self-control. Being controlled by our appetites leads us to ignore God and other people. Pleasure becomes our god, the be-all and end-all of our life, and we neglect those who need us. Instead, by controlling our desires through temperance, we gain self-mastery and grow in holiness, gentleness, compassion, and courtesy.

The cardinal virtues help us to enjoy the good things in life that God has given us. Prudence helps us determine the proper balance between the excessive pursuit of pleasure and the renunciation of all the good things God has made. Prudence and temperance help us put things in proper perspective. Fortitude gives us the courage to follow through with what we know is the right thing to do. Justice helps us treat everyone with fairness, never letting anything—including our own pursuit of pleasure —threaten the rights of others. All the cardinal virtues work hand in hand to help us grow in holiness.

Theological Virtues (CCC, *1812-1828*)

The human virtues have their roots in the **theological virtues**, virtues related directly to God. The theological

virtues—faith, hope, and charity (love)—are gifts that God gives us to lead a moral life. God infuses these virtues into our souls, making it possible for us to relate to the Blessed Trinity. The Triune God is their origin, motive, and object. By putting these virtues into practice, we can grow in holiness and learn to live a moral, ethical, upright, Christ-like life and to avoid sin. Each virtue is discussed below.

Faith

"Faith is the theological virtue by which we believe in God and believe all that he has said and revealed to us, and the Holy Church proposes for our belief, because he is truth itself" (*CCC*, 1814). Faith makes it possible for us to commit ourselves totally to God. Because faith is central to the Christian life, it must be a *living faith* that shows itself in concrete

theological virtues
Three important virtues bestowed on us at Baptism that relate us to God: faith, hope, and charity.

corporal works of mercy

Charitable actions that include feeding the hungry, clothing the naked, visiting the sick and the imprisoned, sheltering the homeless, and burying the dead.

spiritual works of mercy

Seven practices of Catholic charity directed toward the soul of our neighbor; based on the teaching of Christ and the Tradition of the Church from the time of the Apostles. They are: counsel the doubtful, instruct the ignorant, admonish the sinner, comfort the sorrowful, forgive injuries, bear wrongs patiently, and pray for the living and the dead.

acts: professing it, bearing witness to it, and spreading the Good News of Salvation in Jesus Christ to others, even if it leads to suffering. Faith is strengthened through practices like the following:

- *Pray.* We can ask the Lord to make our faith stronger, much like the father of the son suffering from epilepsy in Mark's Gospel: "I do believe, help my unbelief" (Mk 9:24).

- *Read Scripture.* Reading, studying, and praying with the Bible brings us closer to God and his word. The Scriptures are also proclaimed at Mass. The dismissal rite at Mass encourages us to take the Gospel out to the world and translate our faith into concrete deeds of love of and service to others.

- *Celebrate the sacraments.* The sacraments themselves celebrate the mysteries of our faith, especially the Paschal Mystery. Participation in the Sacrament of Penance can remind us of Christ's forgiving love. Receiving our Lord in Holy Communion nourishes and strengthens our belief.

- *Study your faith.* Studying and deepening our understanding of the lessons of faith is a lifelong experience. We can exercise our faith by learning more about it— in religion classes, on retreats and days of recollection, and in homilies. Catholic colleges and parishes offer courses and workshops to facilitate study. We can also study summaries of our faith like the Apostles' Creed and the Nicene Creed, learning what each phrase means.

- *Draw on the faith of friends.* Choose friends and companions who share your commitment to God and the Church. Their Christian values and virtues will help you in times of temptation. Join with peers who participate in youth group, retreats, pilgrimages, service projects, and faith rallies.

- *Put your faith into action.* Keep your faith alive by being Christ for others. An excellent way of doing this is to practice the **corporal works of mercy** and the **spiritual works of mercy**, thereby serving and loving others in imitation of Christ.

Hope

Hope is related to the virtue of faith. Because we believe that God is all-good, all-loving, all-just, and all-merciful, we trust that he controls the future and looks out for each of us. As the *Catechism* defines: "Hope is the theological virtue by which we desire the kingdom of heaven and eternal life as our happiness, placing our trust in Christ's promises and relying not on our own strength, but on the help of the grace of the Holy Spirit" (*CCC*, 1817).

We believe and hope that good does triumph over evil; that eternal life awaits us on the other side of death; and that every wrong will be righted. Christians who hope place great value in Jesus' comforting words:

> Therefore I tell you, do not worry about your life and what

you will eat, or about your body and what you will wear. For life is more than food and the body more than clothing. Notice the ravens: they do not sow or reap; they have neither storehouse nor barn, yet God feeds them. How much more important are you than birds! Can any of you by worrying add a moment to your lifespan? If even the smallest things are beyond your control, why are you anxious about the rest? Notice how the flowers grow. They do not toil or spin. But I tell you, not even Solomon in all his splendor was dressed like one of them. If God so clothes the grass in the field that grows today and is thrown into the oven tomorrow, will he not much more provide for you, O you of little faith? As for you, do not seek what you are to eat and what you are to drink, and do not worry anymore. All the nations of the world seek for these things, and your Father knows that you need them. Instead, seek his kingdom, and these other things will be given you besides. Do not be afraid any longer, little flock, for your Father is pleased to give you the kingdom. (Lk 12:22–32)

Christ's own life is a model of hope. For example, as he was suffering on the cross and dying for our Salvation, Jesus turned to his Abba in prayer and, in the midst of his agony and loneliness said, "Father, into your hands I commend my spirit" (Lk 23:46). In his encyclical *Spe Salvi* (Saved in Hope), Pope Benedict XVI offers wise advice on how to grow in the virtue of hope:

A first essential setting for learning hope is prayer. When no one listens to me any more, God still listens to me. When I can no longer talk to anyone or call upon anyone, I can always talk to God. When there is no longer anyone to help me deal with a need or expectation that goes beyond the human capacity for hope, he can help me. When I have been plunged into complete solitude . . . ; if I pray I am never totally alone. (*Spe Salvi*, 32)

Charity

St. Thomas Aquinas stated that charity (*agape* in the Greek, *caritas* in Latin)—also translated as love—is the "mother of all virtues." "Charity is the theological virtue by which we love God above all things for his own sake, and our neighbor as ourselves for the love of God" (*CCC*, 1822). God's very nature is love; God *is* love. As God's adopted children, we are called to a holy relationship with him in the same way as expressed in the relationship among the Three Persons of our Triune God. The First Letter of John describes this goal:

Beloved, let us love one another, because love is of God; everyone who loves is begotten by God and knows God. Whoever is without love does not know God, for God is love. In this way the love of God was revealed to us: God sent his only Son into the

world so that we might have life through him. In this is love: not that we have loved God, but that he loved us and sent his Son as expiation for our sins.

Beloved, if God so loved us, we also must love one another. No one has ever seen God. Yet, if we love one another, God remains in us, and his love is brought to perfection in us.

This is how we know that we remain in him and he in us, that he has given us of his Spirit. Moreover, we have seen and testify that the Father sent his Son as savior of the world. Whoever acknowledges that Jesus is the Son of God, God remains in him and he in God. We have come to know and to believe in the love God has for us. God is love, and whoever remains in love remains in God and God in him. (1 Jn 4:7–16)

Christ tells us that the Law is summarized in the command to love God above all things and our neighbor as ourselves (see Mt 22:34–40). The virtue of charity enables us to follow Christ's injunction to love even our enemies. It helps us practice all the other virtues and supports "and purifies our human ability to love, raising it to the supernatural perfection of divine love" (*CCC*, 1827). In today's world, many people distort the true meaning of love, for example, by claiming that unbridled sexual passion (known as lust) is love. But lust is not love. The virtue of charity—true love, which has its source in God himself—is self-giving. Jesus Christ, the perfect exemplar of love, teaches by his words and deeds that charity involves:

- *Obedience.* Jesus' will was perfectly attuned to his Father's. Love means obeying Jesus' commands.

- *Reverence.* Love involves respecting and valuing the absolute goodness of God and the goodness of other people made in his image and likeness.

- *Sacrifice.* Love requires commitment, walking the extra mile, and never giving up on God, other people, or oneself. Spiritual disciplines like fasting, prayer, sharing with the poor, and the like increase love in our hearts.

Charity results in many fruits or benefits, including joy, peace, and mercy. It is generous and reciprocal. It leads to friendship and communion with

 ## Practicing Cardinal Virtues

To build strength of character, and practice the cardinal virtues, do one of the following:

- *Prudence*: Name an important decision you are trying to make. For example, whether to begin an exclusive relationship or which college you will attend. Discuss it with a trusted adult. Write out the pros and cons of each possible course of action. Pray for the Lord's help in making your decision. After considering all your options, decide, act, and then review your decision. Write a summary of this process.

- *Justice*: Search the news for an example of an injustice that is taking place in your local community. After gathering some facts about the issue, including the teaching of the Catholic Church, write a letter to a media outlet or a government official expressing your thoughts on how to address the issue.

- *Fortitude*: Make it a practice to avoid gossip. If challenged by your peers, in a nonjudgmental way, tell them why you do not like participating in character assassination. Note in your journal how you felt when you did the right thing in this setting.

- *Temperance*: Give up dessert, snacks, or soda for two straight weeks, thus practicing the virtue of abstinence. Donate the money saved on these items to a hunger center.

God, we perceive his presence and we thus learn to recognize that presence in our daily lives. He has loved us first and he continues to do so; we too, then, can respond with love. (*Deus Caritas Est,* 17)

Finally, never forget that love is the greatest virtue, the only one that survives into eternity:

Love is patient, love is kind. It is not jealous, (love) is not pompous, it is not inflated, it is not rude, it does not seek its own interests, it is not quick-tempered, it does not brood over injury, it does not rejoice over wrongdoing but rejoices with the truth. It bears all things, believes all things, hopes all things, endures all things. . . . So faith, hope, love remain, these three; but the greatest of these is love. (1 Cor 13:4–7, 13)

For Review

1. Define *human virtue*.
2. Name the cardinal virtues. What does each do?
3. Define *vice*.
4. Distinguish among these four kinds of justice: commutative, distributive, legal, and social.
5. Give an example of a vice that is contrary to each of the cardinal virtues.
6. What does the theological virtue of faith accomplish?
7. Discuss two ways we can strengthen the virtue of faith.
8. List the corporal and spiritual works of mercy.
9. What does the theological virtue of hope enable us to do?
10. What does the theological virtue of charity enable us to do?
11. Why should Christians love?

others. In his encyclical *Deus Caritas Est* (God Is Love), Pope Benedict XVI reminds us that Christ's love is ever-present to us. By recognizing it, we are better able to respond to it.

God is visible in a number of ways. In the love-story recounted by the Bible, he comes towards us, he seeks to win our hearts, all the way to the Last Supper, to the piercing of his heart on the Cross, to his appearances after the Resurrection and to the great deeds by which, through the activity of the Apostles, he guided the nascent Church along its path. Nor has the Lord been absent from subsequent Church history: he encounters us ever anew, in the men and women who reflect his presence, in his word, in the sacraments, and especially in the Eucharist. In the Church's Liturgy, in her prayer, in the living community of believers, we experience the love of

justification
The Holy Spirit's grace that cleanses us from our sins through faith in Jesus Christ and baptism. Justification makes us right with God.

charisms
Special gifts the Holy Spirit gives to individual Christians to build up the Church.

gifts of the Holy Spirit
God-given abilities that help us live a Christian life with God's help. Jesus promised these gifts through the Holy Spirit, especially the Sacrament of Confirmation. The seven gifts are wisdom, understanding, knowledge, counsel, (right judgment), fortitude (courage), piety (reverence), and fear of the Lord (wonder and awe).

fruits of the Holy Spirit
Perfections that result from living in union with the Holy Spirit.

 For Reflection

What can you do to grow in each of the four cardinal virtues?

God Helps Us Grow in Holiness (*CCC*, 1996-2005; 1266)

God wants us to be holy, often a difficult task. But the Lord provides us with many helps along the way, including grace and the gift of the Holy Spirit who gives us many gifts that enable us to grow in holiness. **Justification** is a special gift of the Holy Spirit that not only frees us from sin but sanctifies us in the depth of our being.

Grace

Grace is God's "*favor*, the *free and undeserved help* that God gives us to respond to his call to become children of God, adoptive sons, partakers of the divine nature and of eternal life" (*CCC*, 1996). We cannot earn grace in any way because it is a total gift from God. The Holy Spirit infuses grace into our souls when we are baptized, making us different creatures from what we were when we were born. God's free gift of grace blesses us in many ways. Grace:

- enables us to address God as Abba
- adopts us into God's family
- enables us to share in the life of the Blessed Trinity
- makes us heirs of Heaven
- enables us to live as God's sons and daughters, in the way Jesus taught us
- unites us to our Lord and Savior, Jesus Christ
- allows the Holy Spirit to live in us

The Catholic Church has traditionally termed this grace of justification *sanctifying*, meaning, "to make holy." Because God's grace justifies us, God's own righteousness is given to us, and we are united to the Lord's Paschal Mystery. Therefore, sanctifying grace is a means to grow in holiness. Sanctifying grace

- enables us to believe and hope in God and to love him through the theological virtues (see pages 191–193);
- gives us the power to live under the influence of the Holy Spirit through the gifts he bestows on us; and

- allows us to grow in goodness through the moral virtues (*CCC*, 1266).

Sanctifying grace is also a *habitual* grace, a "permanent disposition to live and act in keeping with God's call" (*CCC*, 2000). We distinguish it from *actual* graces, which are God's interventions "at the beginning of conversion or in the course of sanctification" (*CCC*, 2000). Other types of grace are *sacramental* graces, which are specific gifts that come from particular sacraments; **charisms**, which are special gifts that the Holy Spirit gives to individual Christians to build up the Body of Christ, the Church; and "graces of state," which are the help God gives to particular ministries in the Church.

God never forces his grace on us. He respects our freedom. This is why we, as believers, must freely respond to the graces that God gives. He implanted in us a desire to do good and to search for truth. This inborn desire points to God himself, the only One who can satisfy the yearnings of our hearts. Thus, God has already begun the work of grace in us by preparing for and calling forth our free response. If we say yes to God's inner call, and use the gifts and helps he gives us, then our human freedom is made perfect. Our inner longing for truth and goodness is satisfied.

Gifts of the Holy Spirit

The Holy Spirit also showers on us what we need to live Christ-like lives. Another help for our growth in holiness are the **gifts of the Holy Spirit**. These gifts, given to us at Baptism and Confirmation, are qualities the Old Testament prophet Isaiah (Is 11:2–3) said would identify the Messiah. Jesus Christ himself lived each of these gifts perfectly. The traditional list of these seven gifts is given below with a brief explanation of each.

- *Wisdom* is looking at reality from God's point of view. Wisdom encourages us to pray before making decisions and to seek guidance from saints, the Church's teaching, priests, and other trusted adults. This gift helps us discover truth.

- *Understanding* involves taking the time to uncover the deeper meaning of faith and the mysteries of God's magnificent creation. We will use this gift throughout our lives to better appreciate the depth of God's love for us.

- *Knowledge* is the grace to see how God is working in our lives, especially when we are trying to judge what is right and wrong.

- *Counsel (right judgment)* helps us form our conscience in light of Church teaching. We do this by praying and by consulting others before deciding moral issues. This gift helps us act prudently.

- *Fortitude (courage)* is the strength to follow our own convictions in the face of peer pressure. It also involves the willingness to suffer for the Lord.

- *Piety (reverence)* is respect we show to the Lord through praise and worship. Respecting the dignity and worth of others is another way we express this gift.

- *Fear of the Lord (wonder and awe)* enables us to show concern about the reality of sin in our life and to avoid anything that might alienate us from God and others.

 Fruits of the Holy Spirit in Your Life

The *Catechism of the Catholic Church* defines the **fruits of the Holy Spirit** as "perfections that the Holy Spirit forms in us as the first fruits of eternal glory" (*CCC*, 1832). Write a prayer with twelve petitions that focus on each fruit of the Holy Spirit. For example: "Lord, increase the fruit of generosity in my life. When a classmate asks for my help in preparing for an exam, help me to oblige."

SIX "EASY" STEPS TO HOLINESS

As this chapter points out, there really are *not* easy steps to becoming holy. Or are there? At least one way to make good and moral choices and achieve holiness is by remaining close to Jesus. Holiness is a worthy goal because it draws us closer to our heavenly Father. Whether you think of it as an easy task or not, it is one that will take us into eternity—growing to be more like God so that we can be with God. Chapter 9 examines more fully the meaning of Christian discipleship. In the meantime, briefly review these six steps—ease dependent on your commitment—to growth in holiness.

1. *Follow Jesus, our model (CCC, 520).* You can learn what it means to be fully human by examining the life of Jesus and imitating his humble acceptance of his Father's will.

2. *Accept sacrifice (CCC, 618).* Jesus calls on his disciples to "take up [their] crosses and follow [him]." We take up our crosses whenever we strive to do the right thing, especially in the face of ridicule and criticism. We take up our crosses when we patiently endure the disappointments that inevitably come our way, offering them up to Jesus.

3. *Allow the Holy Spirit to guide you (CCC, 767).* The Spirit showers on us the gifts that help us grow in holiness. We become more Christ-like when we use these gifts and cooperate with all the other graces that come from the Holy Spirit.

4. *Remain aware of the Father's presence (CCC, 1693).* We are constantly in the presence of God, whether we consciously think of it or not. Jesus always lived in the sight of his Father and always did what was pleasing to him. He invites us to do the same. Imagine how you will strive to do your best if you can keep the awareness that you are always in the presence of God the Father in your mind.

5. *Love God and love neighbor.* Observe the Ten Commandments, live the Beatitudes, and put into practice Jesus' Golden Rule of love. These elements of our faith are covered in more detail in Chapter 9.

6. *Pray and participate in the sacraments.* Spending time with Jesus in prayer can nourish your relationship with him. Christ instituted the sacraments to extend his love and grace to us. The "sacrament of sacraments" is the Eucharist, which holds center stage in the life of Jesus' followers (CCC, 1210-1211). Receiving Jesus in Holy Communion intimately unites us with him. It also gives us life through the Holy Spirit, separates us from sin, brings us into union with other members of Christ's body, and commits us to look at the needs of the poor. Frequent reception of our Lord in the Eucharist is a prime way for Catholics to grow in holiness.

St. Paul on Charisms and Living a Holy Life

Complete each of the following assignments:

- Read 1 Corinthians 12 to find some of the special gifts that the Holy Spirit gave to certain members of the Church. List five of them.

- Read Ephesians 4:1–5:20, to see instructions on how to live a holy and moral life. List five positive actions that help us live holy lives and five practices that lead us away from God.

- Research the origins, main themes, year composed, and background of the First Letter to the Corinthians or the Letter to the Ephesians. Write a one-page report on your findings.

For Review

1. Define *grace*.

2. List five effects of sanctifying grace.

3. Distinguish between and among these terms: sanctifying grace, actual grace, sacramental grace, and charisms.

4. Name the gifts of the Holy Spirit.

For Reflection

- Reread the quotation of Pope Benedict XVI from his encyclical *Deus Caritas Est* (page 195). Then write and discuss how you have personally experienced the love of God in your life.

- Name a quality of love that you have experienced in your own life.

- Which gift of the Holy Spirit is most evident in your life right now? Which gift needs more work in your life?

Essential Elements of Holiness (*CCC*, 826, 1248, 2012-2014, 2028, 2045, 2813)

God the Father calls us to holiness in every aspect of our lives. He is the source of our life in Jesus Christ. In the Lord's Prayer, we petition that God's name be made holy. The way we do so is by growing in holiness ourselves. When each member of Christ's Body stays true to his or her Christian beliefs and convictions, and lives moral and holy lives, then Christ's presence in the world becomes more visible and the Father's glory and name are honored. In addition, the Body of Christ, the Church, of which Christ is the head, increases, grows, and develops, attracting others to Jesus Christ, the source of our Salvation.

As Catholics, we are able to grow in holiness as members of Christ's Body, the Church, in three general ways:

- *First*, we must practice the virtue of charity because it is the essential means to holiness. Charity is the "soul" of holiness because it "governs, shapes, and perfects all the means of sanctification" (*Lumen Gentium*, 42).

- *Second*, we must celebrate the sacraments because they help bring us into union with Jesus Christ by the power of the Holy Spirit.

- *Third*, Christ calls us to pick up a cross to follow him. Holiness requires effort and self-denial. It involves conversion of the heart, a turning from sin and embracing Christ's values while we reject anything that keeps us from the Lord.

These general practices do not come automatically to Catholics. The vocation to holiness, to become perfect like our heavenly Father, is a great call from God. But it is not an impossible call, because God created us with great dignity, in his image and likeness. We have been created in the divine image in and through Christ, "the image of the invisible God" (Col 1:15). Our God-given gifts of human reason, free will, conscience (and its related moral decision-making) are all essential elements of our growth in holiness. They are discussed in the following sections.

Humans Are Capable of Holiness (CCC, 1703-1706)

Humans are unique because God made us to share in his own life. We are the only creatures on earth that God willed for their own sake. God is pure Spirit, a being without physical or material qualities. He, the Supreme Being, is all-good and possesses infinite knowledge and truth. God is a Trinitarian community of perfect love: Father, Son, and Holy Spirit. By creating us in his image, God endowed humans with godlike qualities: the abilities to think, to choose, to love, and to relate to others in community. These endowments make it possible for us to share, through knowledge and love, in God's own life.

Because God made us in his image, we are spiritual beings and possess incomparable dignity, value, and worth. We are not mere *somethings*. We are *someones*—persons who can know and relate to God and to other people. From the moment of conception in our mother's womb, God destined each of us for eternal happiness.

Made in God's image and likeness, humans are created out of love, for love, and to love. This is why we can grow in holiness and enter more deeply into a relationship with our Creator.

The Gift of Human Reason

Humans participate in the light and power of the divine Spirit. Endowed with the ability to think, that is, to reason, we can understand the laws God put into his creation. We can, aided by the Holy Spirit, discover truth, goodness, and beauty. Being able to discover the truth with our intellects leads us to the highest norm of human life—the divine law. By means of this eternal objective, and universal law, "God orders, directs and governs the entire universe and all the ways of the human community according to a plan conceived in wisdom and love" (*Declaration on Religious Freedom*, 3). God has made us to participate in this law; humans must seek this truth.

Human reason enables us to recognize God's voice, which urges us to do good and avoid what is evil. We must follow this law, which we hear in our conscience (see below), by loving God and neighbor.

The Gift of Free Will

Free will is the capacity to choose among alternatives. Free choice helps humans make ourselves the kind of persons God calls us to be. God calls us to be holy. We can grow in holiness by making good choices and avoiding evil choices. We can also learn from our mistakes.

Free choices help us determine how our lives can be uniquely our own. Free will enables us to rise above heredity and environment. For example, free will makes it possible for a person raised by parents who exhibit racial prejudice to rise above that example and to not personally be prejudiced any longer. It gives us some control over our lives by allowing us to use our God-given talents and to cooperate freely with the many graces the Holy Spirit sends to us. Moreover, free will allows us to choose the good for other people, even at the cost of personal sacrifice.

This is what love is—choosing for God above everything and for our neighbor as ourselves.

Forming a Good Conscience (CCC, 1776-1802)

Basic to living any Christian life of holiness is making moral choices. To do this we must form and then follow a good **conscience**. The Second Vatican Council described conscience as "the most secret core and sanctuary" of a person. Our conscience helps us to determine what is the Christ-like, moral, and holy thing to do. It helps us distinguish between good and evil, whether something is in accord with God's plan or not. The *Catechism of the Catholic Church* defines conscience this way:

> Conscience is a judgment of reason whereby the human person recognizes the moral quality of a concrete act that he is going to perform, is in the process of performing, or has already completed. (*CCC*, 1778)

Our conscience helps us grasp what is the moral thing to do both before we perform an action as well as while we are doing it. But it also helps us judge whether we did the right thing after we act. Therefore, our conscience calls us to be responsible, telling us to repent if we have sinned by violating it and turning from the Lord's law of love.

In the depths of our conscience, we are alone with God. He calls us

free will
The "power, rooted in reason and will . . . to perform deliberate actions on one's own responsibility" (*CCC*, 1731).

conscience
A person's most secret core and sanctuary that helps the person determine between good and evil. It moves a person at the appropriate times to make specific choices, approving those that are good and rejecting those that are evil.

EXPLAINING THE FAITH

Why can't a good outcome justify any means that accomplish it?

There are those who say the decisive factor in any moral decision is the outcome. If the effect or consequence is good, then that is all that matters. However, this kind of thinking can ultimately justify any behavior as long as some good results. For example, it would justify medical experiments on unwilling subjects, or the destruction of embryos (unborn human beings) in doing stem cell research—in the pursuit of finding a cure for certain diseases.

St. Thomas Aquinas clearly taught that "an evil action cannot be justified by reference to a good intention." In other words, the end does not justify the means.

Outcomes or consequences of moral acts are circumstances. They are *not* the central factor in morality. The object of the act is. And the object (what we do) must always be good. "A *morally good* act requires the goodness of the object, of the end, and of the circumstances together" (*CCC*, 1755).

to love the good and avoid evil. Every human being has a fundamental right to follow his or her conscience and to act with freedom on it by making sound, moral, responsible judgments. No one should be forced to act contrary to the true dictates of conscience. This is especially true in decisions involving one's religious beliefs.

Forming a true and upright conscience requires sincerity on our part and an examination of our lives before God. It is a lifelong task that never ends. It requires us to be present to ourselves, that is, sufficiently reflective so that we can continually learn from our conscience so that we can follow it responsibly. Several steps for conscience formation apply:

- Use your human intellect to discover God's goodness and truth. Moral laws like the Ten Commandments guide us on the right path to making good decisions.

- Grow close to Jesus through prayer and the sacraments.

- Look to Jesus' Death on the cross as the perfect example of how to love and how to obey God the Father.

- Look to the example of holy people like the Blessed Mother and the saints and learn from wise Catholics who are trying to live a holy life in our own time.

- Use the gifts and graces that the Holy Spirit has given us. Their purpose is to help us live good and virtuous lives.

We must also look to the Magisterium of the Church in forming our conscience (*CCC*, 2030–2040, 2044–2047, 2049–2051). The pope and bishops apply Christ's message to matters that affect our Salvation and to issues involving our fundamental rights as human beings made in God's image. The Church is a loving mother who helps guide us in right living and points out the path to holiness. Therefore, we are obliged to learn from, form our consciences in light of, and put into practice the teachings of the Church.

Sources for Making Moral Choices

An upright conscience properly formed will recognize that there are three sources of morality: the object chosen, the end or the intention, and the circumstances surrounding an action. The *moral object* is the matter of our actions, that is, what we do. It is the most important source of morality. There are some actions that are always seriously wrong. They involve a disorder of the will and are not ordered to the good and our ultimate end, which is God. Examples of actions that are always seriously wrong are murder, adultery, child abuse, blasphemy, and perjury. Nothing can ever justify them—including a good intention or circumstances.

The *intention* of an action involves our motivation, our purpose for doing something. We must always intend good when we act, or what we propose to do is wrong. However, a good intention can never justify an intrinsically evil act. Abortion is always wrong, even if the persons involved in the procedure are doing it for what they think is a good reason like allowing a teenage girl to finish high school.

The *circumstances* are the secondary factors that surround an action, like the time, place, and method of performing the act. They can increase or reduce the evil or goodness of an act. For example, driving while under the influence of alcohol is immoral because it threatens the lives of others. It doesn't matter when or where the incident of drunk driving occurred. It doesn't matter if the person who drove under the influence was a man or woman, a twenty-year-old or a fifty-year-old. None of these circumstances can make an immoral action moral.

In short, a good conscience will recognize the necessity of all three elements of our actions to be morally good: the object (what you do) must be good, your intention must be good, and the circumstances must be good. Jesus is our best guide to forming a sensitive, loving conscience. By praying to him and the Holy Spirit, we can learn how to live a Christ-centered life. It is always good to ask, "What would Jesus do?" to help us distinguish between good and evil. And we should always measure our acts against his Golden Rule: "Do to others whatever you would have them do to you" (Mt 7:12).

Following Your Conscience (CCC, 1790-1794; 1801)

Having made a sincere effort to constantly form our conscience, we are then obliged to follow it. Guided by the Holy Spirit, we must eventually act on what our conscience tells us is the right course of action. "A human being must always obey the certain judgment of his conscience" (*CCC*, 1800).

After we have performed an action, our conscience can help us evaluate whether or not we did the right and good thing. If we were sincere, tried to learn the truth, prayed, and followed the teaching of Jesus and the Church, then we will have a clear conscience. St. Augustine said, "A good conscience is the palace of Christ; the temple of the Holy Ghost; the paradise of delight." Making good conscientious decisions helps us grow in virtue. We form good habits that assist our growth in holiness.

On the other hand, if we violate what our conscience tells us is the good to do, or the evil to avoid, then we have sinned. The Letter of James verifies this: "So for one who knows the right thing to do and does not do it, it is a sin" (Jas 4:17). Pangs of conscience that cause guilt can alert us to a bad decision. A person of integrity will heed their conscience, ask for God's forgiveness, and then reform his or her life so as not to sin again.

It is also possible for a conscience to be wrong. For example, ignorance—lacking proper information about what should be the right and good course of action—can contribute to an erroneous conscience. Emotions also can affect our conscience

decisions. For example, anger or the strong craving for pleasure might cloud our thinking and judgment. At times, we are not fully at fault for not knowing the right course of action. But at other times we are fully blameworthy because we made little or no effort to find out the truth.

We must always strengthen our conscience by sincerely trying to correct it when it is wrong, by consulting with competent and wise people when we are in doubt, by learning from our mistakes and not repeating them, and by avoiding those situations that have led us to make wrong and sinful decisions in the past.

Because we are God's adopted children, he has called us to holiness. Jesus instructs us to "Be perfect, as our heavenly Father is perfect" (Mt 5:48). His call to holiness, to perfection, is meant for all of his followers, no matter who we are or what our walk in life might be. A way of being holy is to form a good conscience, put Jesus' example of love into practice, and ask for the help of the Holy Spirit. Doing these things allows us to make good and moral choices, an essential element of holiness.

For Review

1. Discuss three ways a person can grow in holiness.

2. Why are human beings capable of holiness?

(continued on page 206)

SUFFERING FOR CHRIST

You cannot watch television without being bombarded with advertisements for various drugs that are meant to relieve suffering. We live in a world that preaches a message of ease and convenience. Some nonbelievers simply do not understand why followers of Jesus Christ are willing to make sacrifices and endure suffering, especially in witnessing to Christ and their faith.

Christians sacrifice and endure pain for many reasons. First, they are imitating Jesus Christ whose suffering and death won Salvation for us. Jesus also told his followers that they would suffer for their faith, but he promised that he would be with them in their suffering. Therefore, Christians believe Jesus is present to them when they suffer. In faith, they patiently accept suffering while always trusting that God will send them grace and the strength of the Holy Spirit's gift of fortitude to see them through the tough times.

As Jesus' disciples, we know that suffering can guide us to Heaven because it can help make up, to a certain degree, for some of the harm caused by our sins. In the midst of our suffering, we can look to the suffering, Death, Resurrection, and Ascension of Jesus Christ and know that the sufferings of this world are not absolute and final. Eternal life with God in Heaven is the reward and the result.

When suffering comes our way, we should pray to Jesus. He will strengthen us to endure the suffering and help us become more like him. If we unite our suffering to his, it can become part of the mystery of Christ's own redemptive activity, a means of purification and of Salvation for us and for others (*CCC*, 618, 1505).

BL. PIER GIORGIO FRASSATI

Termed "the man of the eight Beatitudes" by Pope John Paul II at his beatification ceremony in Rome in 1990, Bl. Pier Giorgio Frassati was a joy-filled man who lived only to age twenty-four but who remains a model for bountiful love and service today. His sister said of him: "He represented the finest in Christian youth: pure, happy, enthusiastic about everything that is good and beautiful."

Pier was born to a wealthy and politically connected family in Turin, Italy. He was an average student but a great athlete and mountain climber. His peers adored him and called him "Terror" because of the practical jokes he played. After high school, he studied mineralogy in an engineering program. He participated in Catholic groups like Apostleship of Prayer and the Company of the Most Blessed Sacrament. Both of these groups were known for helping poor people and promoting Eucharistic adoration, Marian devotion, and personal chastity.

Pier also became active in political groups—like the Young Catholic Workers, Catholic Action, and *Milites Mariae*—that ministered to poor people, fought fascism, and put into practice the Church's social teachings. He gave his money to needy people and visited the sick. It was while ministering to the sick that he contracted an acute case of polio that took his life. Bl. Pier Giorgio offers these words of advice on how to grow in holiness:

> With all the strength of my soul I urge you young people to approach the Communion table as often as you can. Feed on this bread of angels whence you will draw all the energy you need to fight inner battles. Because true happiness, dear friends, does not consist in the pleasures of the world or in earthly things, but in peace of conscience, which we have only if we are pure in heart and mind.

Faithful Disciple

3. What is free will?

4. Define *conscience*.

5. Name at least four steps that are necessary to form a good conscience.

6. Why must we always follow our conscience?

7. What is the role of the Magisterium in helping people do the right thing?

8. What are the three sources of every moral action?

9. Explain how conscience can sometimes be in error. What must we do to correct it?

10. What role does suffering have in the life of Christians?

For Reflection

- Think about a decision dealing with right and wrong that you made this past week. What were the steps you took to make your decision to act? Did you have a clear conscience after making the decision? Why or why not?

- Quaker founder William Penn contemplated the Paschal Mystery and the meaning of suffering and said: "No pain, no palm; no thorns, no throne; no gall, no glory; no cross, no crown." What does this quotation mean to you?

Main Ideas

- Our call to holiness is a vocation given to us by Jesus himself. (p. 186)

- Living a virtuous life and cooperating with God's grace are two ways to grow in holiness. (p. 187)

- Human virtues are virtues we can acquire by human effort. (p. 188)

- The cardinal virtues—prudence, justice, fortitude, and temperance, are the source of the other human virtues. (pp. 188–190)

- Prudence is equated with common sense and wisdom. (p. 188)

- Justice—giving due to God and neighbor—is distinguished by four types of justice: commutative, distributive, legal, and social. (p. 189)

- Fortitude is a virtue that allows for the courage to conquer fears, even the fear of death, for a worthy cause. (p. 190)

- Temperance is distinguished by three parts: abstinence, sobriety, and chastity. (pp. 190–191)

- Sanctifying grace is the free and undeserved gift that God gives to us that blesses us in many ways and helps us to grow in holiness. (p. 196)

- Sanctifying grace is distinguished from actual graces, sacramental graces, and graces of state. (pp. 196–197)

- The seven gifts of the Holy Spirit—wisdom, understanding, knowledge, counsel (right judgment), fortitude (courage), piety (reverence), and fear of the Lord (wonder and awe) also help us to live Christ-like lives. (p. 197)

- The theological virtues—faith, hope, and charity (love)—are related directly to God. (p. 191)

- Faith makes it possible for us to commit totally to God. (pp. 191–192)

- Hope is the virtue that allows us to desire the Kingdom of Heaven and happiness in eternal life. (pp. 192–193)

- Charity, the "mother of virtues," is the only virtue that lasts into eternity; it allows us to love God for his own sake and our neighbor as ourselves for the love of God. (pp. 193–194)

- Humans are capable of holiness because God has made us to share in his own life. (pp. 199–200)

- Through the gift of human reason and aided by the Holy Spirit, we are able to uncover truth, goodness, and beauty. (p. 200)

- The gift of free will allows us the opportunity to make use of our God-given talents and to cooperate with the graces of the Holy Spirit. It allows us to make moral choices. (p. 201)

- Essential to making good moral choices is the formation of a good conscience. (p. 201)

- An upright conscience recognizes three sources for morality: the object chosen, the end or intention, and the circumstances surrounding the action. (pp. 202–203)

- Following a well-informed conscience and making a moral choice based on it is an opportunity for growth in holiness. (pp. 203–204)

Terms, People, Places

On a separate sheet of paper, write the answers to the following:

1. *Vocation*: Write a word that is synonymous with vocation.

2. *Virtue*: Name a human virtue that has helped you to lead a moral life.

3. *Cardinal Virtues*: Why are the cardinal virtues called "hinge virtues"?

4. *Vice*: Name an example of a vice.

5. *Religion*: How does religion express itself?

6. *Justification*: What is the grace of justification traditionally called?

7. *Charisms*: Share a special charism you possess.

8. *Gifts of the Holy Spirit*: Name the seven gifts of the Holy Spirit.

9. *Theological Virtues*: How are the theological virtues different from the human virtues?

10. *Corporal Works of Mercy*: Name two corporal works of mercy.

11. *Spiritual Works of Mercy*: Where are the spiritual works of mercy directed?

12. *Free Will*: Complete the sentence: "Free will is the capacity to choose among _____."

13. *Fruits of the Holy Spirit*: How many traditional fruits of the Holy Spirit are there?

14. *Conscience*: What is something you should do before you make a decision based on your conscience?

Primary Source Quotations

Way of Perfection
Make up your mind to become a saint.
—St. Mary Mazzarello

He who climbs never stops going from beginning to beginning, through beginnings that have no end. He never stops desiring what he already knows.
—St. Gregory of Nyssa

Cooperating with God's Grace
Indeed we also work, but we are only collaborating with God who works, for his mercy has gone before us.
—St. Augustine

Sharing Holiness
Sanctify yourself and you will sanctify society.
—St. Francis of Assisi

Remember a time when someone asked you to be perfect. Write one or two paragraphs explaining what happened next.

Ongoing Assignments

As you cover the material in this chapter, choose and complete at least three of these assignments.

1. Write a report on how consumerism corrodes virtue.

2. Prepare a written or oral report on one of the cardinal virtues.
   • prudence
   • justice
   • fortitude
   • temperance

3. Prepare a one-person skit that illustrates one of the cardinal virtues put into practice in the life of a teen. Act out your skit for your classmates.

4. Read about the gifts of the Holy Spirit in this book and online. Use any form of art to depict a representation of each gift.

5. Consult the Mass readings for next Sunday's liturgy. Outline some important points that you would include in a homily to apply the Word of God to the life of teens today.

6. Research a religious community and report on how the particular order is practicing the corporal and spiritual works of mercy.

7. Write a report on the life of Bl. Pier Giorgio Frassati.

8. Read one of the Christophers' newsletters that deal with living a Christ-like life. Prepare a report summarizing your findings.

Prayer

St. Augustine, considered one of the greatest Church Fathers, wrote extensively on the Blessed Trinity. His famous conversion to Catholicism is well-documented. He accepted Baptism in 387 after many years of prayer by his mother, St. Monica, for his soul. Pray for your ongoing conversion by reciting Augustine's prayer to the Holy Spirit.

St. Augustine's Prayer to the Holy Spirit
Breathe in me, O Holy Spirit,
That my thoughts may be all holy.
Act in me, O Holy Spirit,
That my work may all be holy.
Draw my heart, O Holy Spirit,
That I love but what is holy.

Strengthen me, O Holy Spirit,
To defend all that is holy.
Guard me, then, O Holy Spirit,
That I always may be holy. Amen.

- *Reflection*: Who is a saint you admire for their holiness? How can you be like this person?

- *Resolution*: For the next month, recite this prayer each morning upon rising.

9

DISCIPLESHIP: FOLLOWING IN THE FOOTSTEPS OF JESUS

Thanks be to Thee, my Lord Jesus Christ
For all the benefits Thou has given me,
For all the pains and insults
Which thou has borne for me.
O Most merciful Redeemer, Friend, and Brother,
May I know Thee more clearly,
Love Thee more dearly,
Follow Thee more nearly,
Day by day. Amen.

—St. Richard Chichester

- ### The Fellowship of the Unashamed
  It takes bold action and sometimes dramatic response to be a disciple of Jesus Christ.

- ### Discipleship Means Following Jesus and His Teachings
  Being a follower of Jesus involves learning from him, entering into a personal relationship with him, and imitating his example of sharing the Good News with all.

- ### Following Jesus' Commands
  We are called to both keep the Ten Commandments and to incorporate the Beatitudes into our lives as disciples of Christ.

- ### More Requirements of Discipleship
  Disciples of Christ are both evangelists of God's Word and stewards of his gifts.

- ### Putting Discipleship into Practice
  Love is the main "job" of Christian discipleship.

The Fellowship of the Unashamed

The following note was found on the desk of a pastor who was martyred in Zimbabwe, where it had been said: "You'd better watch out. One dead missionary is as good as a hundred dead terrorists to us." The author is unknown, but the message is strong. He has taken to heart Jesus' core message of what it means to be his disciple: "Whoever wishes to come after me must deny himself, take up his cross and follow me" (Mk 8:3–4). The letter defines discipleship:

> I'm part of the fellowship of the unashamed. I have the Holy Spirit's power. The die has been cast. I have stepped over the line. The decision has been made—I am a disciple of his. I won't look back, let up, slow down, back away, or be still. My past is redeemed, my present makes sense, my future is secure. I'm finished and done with low living, sight walking, smooth knees, colorless dreams, tamed visions, worldly taking, cheap giving, and dwarfed goals.
>
> I no longer need preeminence, prosperity, position, promotions, plaudits, or popularity. I don't have to be right, first, tops, recognized, praised, regarded, or rewarded. I now live by faith, lean in his presence, walk with patience, am uplifted by prayer, and I labor with power.
>
> My face is set, my gait is fast, my goal is Heaven, my road is narrow, my way rough, my companions are few, my Guide reliable, my mission clear. I cannot be bought, compromised, detoured, lured away, turned back, deluded, or delayed. I will not flinch in the face of sacrifice, hesitate in the presence of the enemy, pander at the pool of popularity, or meander in the maze of mediocrity.
>
> I won't give up, shut up, let up, until I have stayed up, stored up, prayed up, paid up, preached up, for the cause of Christ. I am a disciple of Jesus. I must go till he comes, give till I drop, preach till all know, and work till he stops me. And, when he comes for his own, he will have no problem recognizing me . . . my banner will be clear!

This brave priest knew exactly what it meant to be a disciple of Jesus Christ. Each of us can only hope to attain the level of freedom and commitment he had in following his Lord and witnessing to his faith in him.

During his ministry and on his journey to Jerusalem and the saving events of the Paschal Mystery, Jesus taught what it means to be a disciple:

- A disciple must put personal desires aside to follow his Father's will.
- A disciple must accept suffering, even to the point of death.
- A disciple must serve others.
- A disciple must love others, even those who are enemies.

This chapter explores some of the practical and dramatic tasks that make up Christian discipleship.

For Reflection

"The decision has been made—I am a disciple of his." How strongly do you agree with this statement for your own life?

Discipleship Means Following Jesus and His Teachings

You may recall from an earlier course of study the following aspects of Christian discipleship. A disciple is a:

- *pupil* of Jesus, that is, one who learns from him, demonstrating an ability to grasp

Core Gospel Values

The Sermon on the Mount (Mt 5:3–12) contains several challenges of discipleship. For example, the Beatitudes reveal what we have to do to form the kind of attitudes that lead to true happiness. They tell us what attitudes and actions we need to be really happy. Later in the Sermon, Jesus calls us to be salt of the earth and light of the world.

Read this list of Beatitude qualities that form the heart of discipleship. Rate yourself on how well you are doing and how much improvement you need in each of these areas. Write a journal reflection that addresses how you are currently living or wish to live in one of these areas.

* *Poor in Spirit*: I realize that without God's gifts to me, I am nothing. He is my all.
* *Mournful*: I mourn for those who are suffering and try to do something to help.
* *Meek*: I am not the center of attention. I am gentle with others.
* *Righteous*: I strive mightily to discover God's will for me and then work to achieve it.
* *Merciful*: I am able and willing to forgive those who have hurt me.
* *Clean of Heart*: I am totally open and honest with God and others, single-hearted in my loyalty to the Lord.
* *Peacemaker*: I build up, rather than tear down. I work to bring Jesus' peace in all situations of conflict.
* *Persecuted*: I stand up for what is right and good, even if I am ridiculed in the process.

Jesus said,

You are the light of the world. A city set on a mountain cannot be hidden. Nor do they light a lamp and then put it under a basket; it is set on a lampstand, where it gives light to all in the house. Just so, your light must shine before others, that they may see your good deeds and glorify your heavenly Father. (Mt 5:14–16)

Write your response to the following:

* What do you do on a daily basis to allow the light of Christ to shine through you?
* How do your actions and attitudes reveal his teachings? What concrete action can you do *tomorrow* to be light of Christ?

intellectually and analyze thoroughly his teachings

- a *friend* of Jesus, one who enters into a personal relationship with him. It is a relationship marked by intimacy, generosity, availability, sacrifice, concern, and, above all else, mutual love

- *follower* of Jesus, one who imitates his example and works to spread his message and work. This is what it means to *evangelize*, a word that means, "to preach the Gospel." A disciple, therefore, is an *evangelist*, one who preaches Jesus to others in word and deed.

In all three senses, a disciple of Jesus must be concerned about putting into practice specific commands that the Lord gave to us. For example, at the end of the Sermon on the Mount, Jesus said,

> Not everyone who says to me, "Lord, Lord," will enter the kingdom of heaven, but only the one who does the will of my Father in heaven. Many will say to me on that day, "Lord, Lord, did we not prophesy in your name? Did we not drive out demons in your name? Did we not do mighty deeds in your name?" Then I will declare to them solemnly, "I never knew you. Depart from me, you evildoers." Everyone who listens to these words of mine and acts on them will be like a wise man who built his house on rock. The rain fell, the floods came, and the winds blew and buffeted the house. But it did not collapse; it had been set solidly on rock. And everyone who listens to these words of mine but does not act on them will be like a fool who built his house on sand. The rain fell, the floods came, and the winds blew and buffeted the house. And it collapsed and was completely ruined. (Mt 7:21–27)

Lip service is not enough for discipleship. Our faith must be backed up with concrete deeds—doing the Father's will as revealed by his Son, Jesus Christ.

Similarly, note that Jesus calls us to be his friends. Discipleship is about relationship. We are not out on an island enduring the difficulties of being Christian by ourselves. You may be teased or mocked for living out Jesus' teachings and for professing your belief in him. But you can count on Jesus sharing this experience with you as a *friend*:

> As the Father loves me, so I also love you. Remain in my love. If you keep my commandments, you will remain in my love, just as I have kept my Father's commandments and remain in his love. I have told you this so that my joy may be in you and your joy may be complete. This is my commandment: love one another as I love you. No one has greater love than this, to lay down one's life for one's friends. You are my friends if you do what I command you. I no longer call

WHO WERE THE APOSTLES?

The word *disciple* means "apprentice, student, learner, and follower." As you know, from among the disciples Jesus selected his Twelve Apostles to help him in his work. The term *apostle* comes from a Greek word that means "to send." The number of Apostles was the same as the number of tribes of Israel, a symbolic number that suggests Jesus came to preach his message to Israel first.

Jesus selected the Twelve after a night of prayer on the mountain. Most of the Apostles were humble, lower-class people, but they were skilled at various crafts or trades. To them, Jesus was like a rabbi or teacher of his time. He expected them to learn carefully from his words and actions so that they could pass his message on to others.

Here is some background information on the Twelve Apostles:

- *Peter*, Simon, was a fisherman. Jesus named him Peter, which means "rock." He was the leader of the Apostles. He is mentioned in the New Testament more than any other person other than Jesus. Peter was the first to declare Jesus' identity.

- *Andrew*, also a fisherman, was Peter's brother. John's Gospel reports that Andrew was Jesus' first disciple and that he encouraged Peter to come to Jesus.

- *James, son of Zebedee*, was a fisherman who came to Jesus with his brother John. James became the leader of the local church in Jerusalem after the Resurrection. Herod Agrippa beheaded him in AD 44.

- *John, son of Zebedee*, may be the so-called "beloved disciple" of John's Gospel. He was the source of the Fourth Gospel and the letters named after him.

- *Philip*, from Bethsaida, asks Jesus at the Last Supper to show the Apostles the Father, to which Jesus replies: "Whoever who has seen me has seen the Father" (Jn 14:9).

- *Bartholomew* is probably the same person as the Nathanael mentioned in John's Gospel. Bartholomew means "son of Thalmai" and may have been Nathanael's surname.

- *Matthew* is probably the same person as Levi. He was a tax collector by profession.

- *Thomas* is called "the Twin" in John's Gospel. He would not believe that Jesus had risen from the dead until he saw him. Tradition holds that he preached in India, where he was martyred.

- *James, son of Alphaeus*, is called James the younger in Mark's Gospel, perhaps to distinguish himself from James, Zebedee's son.

- *Simon the Zealot* is identified for the group of revolutionaries who worked to overthrow Roman rule in Palestine through violent means. By following Jesus, Simon had to give up these notions since Jesus is the "Prince of Peace."

- *Judas, son of James*, is also known as Jude. Matthew and Mark call him Thaddeus, probably a surname, so as not to confuse him with Judas Iscariot, the traitor.

- *Judas Iscariot* is called a traitor by each of the Gospels. He betrayed Jesus for thirty pieces of silver, and when he realized the magnitude of what he did, he hung himself.

you slaves, because a slave does not know what his master is doing. I have called you friends, because I have told you everything I have heard from my Father. It was not you who chose me, but I who chose you and appointed you to go and bear fruit that will remain, so that whatever you ask the Father in my name he may give you. This I command you: love one another. (Jn 15:9–17)

To be a friend of Jesus is a wonderful privilege beyond any other human relationship. But as in all friendships, give-and-take is required. Jesus has given us everything: our lives, our talents, our friendships, our families, our material blessings, and eternal Salvation. In return, he wants us to love and to do what he commands. He also tells us we will remain in his love if we keep his commandments and that we are his friends if we do what he commands.

This theme of obeying Jesus' commands is repeated yet again in the element of evangelization, crucial to being a disciple. In the final verses of the Gospel of Matthew, Jesus commissions the Apostles to be evangelists:

All power in heaven and on earth has been given to me. Go, therefore, and make disciples of all nations, baptizing them in the name of the Father, and of the Son, and of the holy Spirit, teaching them to observe all that I have commanded you. And behold, I am with you always, until the end of the age. (Mt 28:18–20)

An evangelist must preach Christ's message and invite others to become his disciples *and* also to teach them to observe all his commandments.

What Does Jesus Ask of Us?

What does Jesus command? What are his teachings that we must put into practice? Love certainly is at the heart of his teaching. In his invitation to be his friends in John's Gospel, he calls us to love others as he loved us. Also, when questioned by a lawyer about what is the greatest of all commandments,

Jesus repeated the teaching that appears in the Old Testament.

[Jesus] said to him, "You shall love the Lord, your God, with all your heart, with all your soul, and with all your mind. This is the greatest and the first commandment. The second is like it: You shall love your neighbor as yourself. The whole law and the prophets depend on these two commandments." (Mt 22:36–40)

In effect, this teaching summarized the Ten Commandments (Ex 20:1–17). The first three commandments concern love of God; the last seven deal with love of neighbor. Disciples of Jesus live the Ten Commandments and observe the other teachings Jesus gives to us, including the Beatitudes and his command to look out for the needs of the poor. Details about following Jesus in these ways are outlined in the next sections.

For Review

1. What are the three senses of what it means to be a disciple of Jesus?

2. Cite at least two Gospel passages that indicate that discipleship involves obedience to Jesus' commands.

For Reflection

What does it mean for *you* to love others as Jesus loved you?

Following Jesus' Commands

In the Sermon on the Mount Jesus reminded his listeners that he did not come to abolish the Mosaic Law: "Amen I say to you, until heaven and earth

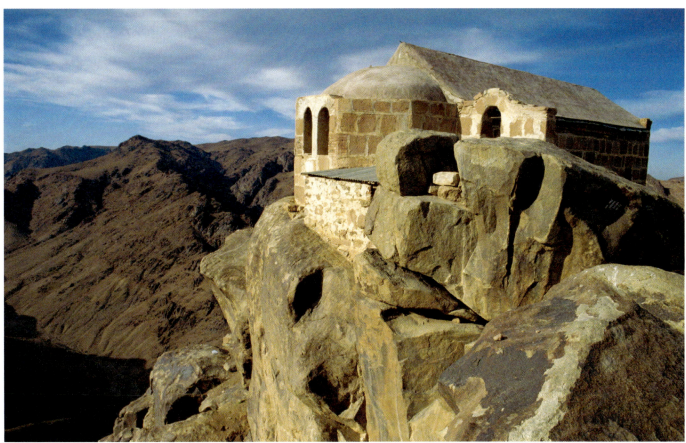

Holy Trinity Chapel, rebuilt in 1934 on the summit of Mount Sinai, where Moses received the Ten Commandments, Egypt.

pass away, not the smallest letter or the smallest part of a letter will pass from the law" (Mt 5:18). Jesus later said to the rich young man, "If you wish to enter into life, keep the commandments" (Mt 19:17).

However, Jesus was the only one who could fulfill the Law perfectly. He gave God's interpretation of the Law, summarized in the Beatitudes. We are called to both keep the Ten Commandments and to incorporate the Beatitudes into our lives as disciples of Christ.

Ten Commandments (CCC, 2052-2557)

The first three commandments show us how to love the Lord our God with our whole heart, soul, strength, and mind (Lk 10:27). The last seven commandments show us how to love our neighbor as we love ourselves. St. Paul teaches this important truth:

The commandments, "You shall not commit adultery; you shall not kill; you shall not steal; you shall not covet," and whatever other commandment there may be, are summed up in this saying, (namely) "You shall love your neighbor as yourself." (Rom 13:9)

Explanation of the individual commandments and the message of Paul's teaching follows.

I. I am the Lord your God: you shall not have strange Gods before me.

The first commandment teaches us to make God central in our lives. We do so when we exercise the theological virtues of faith, hope, and charity. We practice faith and hope by believing and trusting in God's Divine Revelation, mercy, and promises of eternal Salvation. We also show our faith when we worship God and share our Christian beliefs with others. We practice charity when we give heartfelt love to God and other people.

evangelical counsels
Vows of personal poverty, chastity understood as life-long celibacy, and obedience to the demands of the community being joined that those entering the consecrated life profess.

patron saint
Saints that are chosen as special intercessors or protectors for our lives.

domestic Church
A name for the Christian family. In the family, parents and children exercise their priesthood of the baptized by worshipping God, receiving the sacraments, and witnessing to Christ and the Church by living as faithful disciples.

The first commandment requires us to practice the *virtue of religion*, which gives God what is his just due simply because he is God. We practice this virtue through adoration, prayer, works of sacrifice, and keeping our promises and vows. When we adore God, we humbly thank him for his generosity to us. When we pray to God, we lift our minds and hearts in praise, thanksgiving, sorrow, petition, and intercession. When we join our works of self-denial to Jesus' sacrifice on the cross, we make our lives pleasing to God. Finally, by practicing the virtue of religion, we are able to keep the promises we make in the Sacraments of Baptism, Confirmation, Holy Orders, and Matrimony and any special vows we make to God like the **evangelical counsels** of poverty, chastity, and obedience.

The first commandment turns us away from sins against faith like *heresy* (false teaching against the faith), *apostasy* (denial of Christ), and *schism* (a break in union with the pope by refusing to accept his Christ-given authority). It also teaches us to avoid sins against hope like *presumption* (holding that a person can save himself without God's help or personal conversion) and *despair*, which says that God will not or cannot forgive a person of his or her sins. Also, the first commandment condemns sins against charity—like the refusal to accept God's love—ingratitude, and spiritual laziness. The worst sin of all is hatred of God; its cause is pride.

Also, the plain words of the commandment condemn the many forms of atheism that deny God's existence. They also condemn the worship of false gods, that is, idolatry, which also includes the worship of Satan and making gods out of things like money, prestige, power, sex, and so forth. *Superstition*, *divination* (seeking to discover the occult—what is hidden), *sorcery* (attempts to tame occult powers), *irreligion* (disrespect for God's loving care by tempting God), *sacrilege* (disrespecting the sacraments and sacred things, places, or persons specially consecrated to God), and *simony* (the buying or selling of spiritual things) are all violations of the first commandment and against the respect and adoration due our loving God alone.

II. You shall not take the name of the Lord your God in vain.

God's name is holy. When we honor God's holy name through praise, reverence, and adoration, we are honoring the One behind the name. This is true also when we reverence the name of Jesus Christ, the Blessed Mother, and the saints.

When we are baptized "in the name of the Father and of the Son and of the Holy Spirit," our own names are also sanctified. We become the Lord's disciples with tremendous dignity. Catholics are often named for a **patron saint** whose life can inspire them and who prays for them in Heaven. Praying the Sign of the Cross helps remind us of our dignity and that we belong to a loving God who enables us to be called a *Christian*, a disciple of Jesus Christ.

The second commandment forbids any wrong use of God's name or the names of Jesus, Mary, or any saint. It teaches us to keep our promises, for example, when we take an oath, and always to be true to our word. *Perjury* is seriously wrong because it dishonors God's holy name by calling on God to witness to a lie. Blasphemy is also seriously wrong—a sin that can never be justified. *Blasphemy*—any thought, word, or act that expresses contempt for God, Christ, the Church, saints, or holy things—also greatly dishonors God.

III. Remember to keep holy the Lord's day.

The third commandment recalls two Old Testament truths: God rested after the work of creation and God gave the Chosen People the Sabbath day as a sign of the covenant that he made with them after the Exodus. The Israelites understood that this commandment was intended for them to praise God for his works of creation and to thank him for his saving works on their behalf.

Catholics honor this commandment by celebrating the Eucharistic liturgy on Sunday, the day of our Lord's Resurrection. Christ's Paschal Mystery brought a new creation for all humanity. This is why we obey Jesus' command to break bread in his name by worshipping, praising, and thanking God for the gift of his Son and the gift of eternal Salvation. Catholics are required to attend Mass on Sundays and holy days of obligation to express, celebrate, and deepen their unity in Christ. The Eucharist is the heart of our life; it both celebrates and creates our unity in Christ Jesus. It proclaims to others that we belong to Christ and are members of his Body, the Church.

We also sanctify this day by avoiding unnecessary work and business activities. Sunday is a day to spend time with our families, reading, enjoying God's creation, serving others, and refreshing our minds, hearts, and spirits.

IV. Honor your father and your mother.

You have probably heard the expression, "Charity begins at home." There is truth to this statement because if we cannot learn to love our family members, how can we learn to love others? The family is the basic unit of society. In it a husband and wife marry freely as equals to show love to each other and to participate with God in the procreation and education of children. The family is also the **domestic Church**, a community of faith, hope, and charity that teaches virtue, love, and respect. The family mirrors the love and unity of the Blessed Trinity.

The fourth commandment calls on parents to respect their children as persons of dignity and value. Parents are to provide a loving home, see to their children's education, and raise them to be responsible adults who look out for the needs of others. Parents must always show unconditional love and affection to their children. In doing so, they model God's love.

Children, for their part, show their appreciation for the gift of life by respecting and honoring their parents throughout their lives. Children must obey their parents as long as they live in their home and honor and care for their aged parents. Brothers and

sisters must also treat each other with respect and love.

The fourth commandment also requires that we respect and obey proper Church and other authority figures like teachers, police, employers, and leaders. However, obedience is not absolute. If, for example, civil laws contradict God's teaching, we must choose God's law over it, even if our actions lead to personal suffering.

V. You shall not kill.

God is the source of life and the final goal of all human life. The fifth commandment demands that we respect life from the first moment of conception until natural death. All persons have great dignity because everyone is created in God's image and likeness. Because of these truths, direct abortion, either willed as a means or an end, gravely violates the fifth commandment. Everyone has the right to life, a right that does not have to be earned. At the other end of the life spectrum, intentional euthanasia and assisted suicide are serious crimes against life and attacks on humanity. They can never be justified.

The fifth commandment outlaws murder, that is, the deliberate killing of human beings. Murder often results from anger and hate and leads to serious wrongdoings like kidnapping, hostage taking, torture, and horrific acts of terrorism. Suicide gravely contradicts love of self, rejects God's dominion over life and death, and violates the virtues of justice, hope, and charity.

The Church teaches that society *must* always use bloodless means to defend against unjust aggressors, if possible. In the case of capital punishment, the Church teaches that today public safety and order can be achieved in many ways without recourse to the death penalty. "The cases in which the execution of the offender is an absolute necessity are very rare, if not practically non-existent" (*CCC*, 2267).

Although legitimate governments have the right to participate in just wars, once engaged in a war, the combatants must follow the moral law by protecting noncombatants and by using the minimum force necessary. The use of nuclear weapons can *never* be justified. And the arms race and the selling of arms is sinful; their cost seriously harms poor people by diverting valuable resources from assisting those in need.

Cloning, nontherapeutic genetic manipulation, medical experimentation on embryos, and other immoral medical procedures that do not conform to the natural law also violate the fifth commandment. So does scandal, which is an attitude or act that helps lead others to commit evil, for example, encouraging someone to take illegal and harmful drugs. Scandal is a grave offense when it leads others to sin mortally.

We show respect for our own lives by eating healthy food, getting proper exercise and rest, using our minds to grow, and avoiding harmful substances like drugs and practices like reckless driving. We also show respect for

chastity
The moral virtue that enables people to integrate their sexuality into their stations in life.

life when we defend the rights of others, especially the weak and defenseless in our midst, so they can live with dignity.

VI. You shall not commit adultery. IX. You shall not covet your neighbor's wife.

In his Apostolic Letter *On the Christian Family in the Modern World*, Pope John Paul II wrote about the vocation of men and women:

> God created man in his own image and likeness: calling him to existence through love, he called him at the same time for love. God is love and in himself he lives a mystery of personal loving communion. Creating the human race in His own image and continually keeping it in being, God inscribed in the humanity of man and woman the vocation, and thus the capacity and responsibility, of love and communion. Love is therefore the fundamental and innate vocation of every human being.

The sixth and ninth commandments both teach us how to use our sexuality in accord with God's plan. God gave this gift to married couples so that they can share their love and cooperate with God in bringing forth new life. These commandments direct us to do so responsibly by exercising the virtues of chastity, purity, and modesty.

Chastity helps us integrate our sexuality with all aspects of who we are. It helps us live with self-control according to our station in life. The virtues of *purity* and *modesty* help us to combat lust, the vice of a disordered craving for or enjoyment of sexual pleasures. Purity attunes our minds and hearts to God's holiness. Modesty refuses to unveil what should remain covered. It helps us be decent in the clothes we wear and to display respectful attitudes when talking about sex. All three of these virtues strengthen us to work for wholesomeness in society and combat a sex-saturated culture that demeans humans, turning them into objects for enjoyment.

Acts contrary to God's intention for marriage include *adultery* (a married person having sexual relations with a nonspouse), *divorce* (against Christ's command that marriage should last until death separates the couple), *polygamy* (having several spouses), *incest* (engaging in sexual relations with close relatives), the *sexual abuse* of children and adolescents, and *free unions* (living together without exchanging marriage vows).

Birth control is also contrary to God's intent for the true meaning of sexual intercourse: that each act of sexual love-making should be open to the two ends of marriage—the *unitive,* that is, the bonding of husband and wife as lifelong partners, and the *procreative,* that is, the cooperating with God in bringing new life into the world. Therefore, each act of sexual intercourse should be open to both purposes of marriage: the sharing of life and mutual love. In planning their families, couples must use moral and natural methods that are open to both life and love.

The respectful and moral use of our sexual faculties forbid the following actions that are often the result of lust:

- *Masturbation*, which is the deliberate stimulation of the sexual organs to gain sexual pleasure.

- *Fornication*, which is sexual intercourse engaged in by unmarried people. It seeks pleasure without responsibility and the unconditional love found only in the bond of marriage.

- *Pornography*, which depersonalizes sex.

- *Prostitution*, which debases those who sell their bodies. It is also seriously sinful for those who pay prostitutes for sex.

- *Rape*, which is always a seriously evil and violent act.

- *Homosexual acts*, which contradict God's intention of male-female bonding in a stable, permanent relationship of marriage.

VII. You shall not steal.
X. You shall not covet anything that belongs to your neighbor.

Jesus said: "Take care against all greed, for though one may be rich, one's life does not consist of possessions" (Lk 12:15). These two commandments teach us to be good stewards of our material possessions (see also pages 227–229). God created the goods of creation for everyone's benefit. We have the right to private possessions, but we must use them responsibly. The virtue of temperance teaches us that we should not let our belongings become our god or become slaves to them. The virtue of justice teaches us to respect the property rights of others and to share our wealth, especially with those who are needy.

The first Beatitude highlights how we should be poor in spirit. Poverty of spirit centers our hearts on God who is the true source of all happiness; it is the key to overcoming greed, avarice, and envy. With the help of the Holy Spirit, we can resist the temptation to acquire and consume—the message sold to us by our contemporary society as the path to happiness and contentment.

The seventh and tenth commandments forbid theft, which is the taking of someone's property against his or her reasonable will; business fraud; the paying of unjust wages; price fixing; corruption; shoddy work; tax evasion; forgery; vandalism; broken promises and contracts; and similar sins. In all cases, if one is guilty of any of these sins, he or she must make restitution.

The tenth commandment warns us that we should not covet, that is, crave unjustly the belongings of others. Covetousness leads to immoral attitudes like *greed* (the desire to amass great wealth), *avarice* (the seeking of wealth and the power that comes from it), and *envy* over another's possessions. These sinful attitudes can lead to immoral actions like theft, robbery, and fraud.

These commandments also require that we be just in our dealings with others, both individuals and with the communities in which we live. We must especially look out for the needs of the poor. This is true for individuals and for nations that have been blessed with many resources and benefits. The virtue of solidarity recognizes that we all are members of the same human family and that out of friendship and charity we must share our resources and wealth.

VIII. You shall not bear false witness against your neighbor.

Truth-telling is the focus of the eighth commandment. Truth is a matter of justice. Being truthful for Christians is a superb way to witness to Jesus Christ who is the Way, the Truth, and the Life. Jesus himself said, "Let your 'Yes' mean 'Yes,' and your 'No' mean 'No.' Anything more is from the evil one" (Mt 5:37).

Being truthful leads to respect for others, their reputations, and their right to privacy. Giving false praise, gossiping, bragging, and outright lying destroy the integrity and honesty of a person. Lying is contrary to God's gift of speech, the purpose of which is telling the truth. Lies can be mortally sinful and cause great harm to others.

The eighth commandment also forbids giving false witness in a trial and perjury (lying under oath). These are serious sins because they lead to the suffering of innocent people or to their unfair punishment. Rash or snap judgments are also wrong because they misjudge a person's blameworthiness for some action. A follower of Christ is called to counteract the tendency to misjudge by always putting a positive interpretation on another's thoughts, words, and deeds. Two other sins against the eighth commandment are *detraction*, which reveals the faults of someone without a good reason, and *calumny*, that is, spreading lies about another. These two sins do great damage to a person's reputation, thereby offending both justice and charity.

Cheating, a violation of honesty, is also a sin against this commandment. Cheating is often commonly practiced in school settings today, often with the response by those who cheat that "everyone is doing it." Even if this were true, cheating would remain a sin against the eighth commandment.

Societal institutions are also bound to be truthful. Governmental agencies and the entertainment industries must be responsible, resisting efforts at propaganda or promoting immoral behavior. Citizens and consumers of information have the right to the truth that comes from freedom, justice, and solidarity.

Live the Beatitudes (CCC, 1718-1724; 1728-1729)

The Beatitudes, summarized below, teach us how to love God and neighbor in a Christ-like way. The Beatitudes are recorded in the Sermon on the Plain (Luke 6:20–26) and Matthew 5:3–12. They complete the promises that God made to Abraham, reveal a path to true happiness, and teach the attitudes disciples of Jesus should possess in order to reach their eternal destiny of union with Christ.

Blessed are the poor in spirit, for theirs is the Kingdom of Heaven.

When we are poor in spirit, we recognize that all we have and all we are is a pure gift from God. We depend on him, the Source of all. We show our appreciation by using our gifts for others.

Blessed are they who mourn, for they shall be comforted.

We are to mourn over the injustices and evils committed against God and people who are in need. Our sorrow over their fate should lead us to help those who suffer and be Jesus' consoling presence to comfort them. We should also mourn for our own sins and the harm they cause others.

Blessed are the meek, for they will inherit the land.

A meek person is humble, gentle, patient, and compassionate, just like Jesus. The gift of meekness helps us to know the most appropriate time to feel and express anger.

Blessed are they who hunger and thirst for righteousness, for they shall be satisfied.

Jesus' disciples desire to put God's righteous will into action by working tirelessly with the help of the Holy Spirit to grow in holiness, justice, and truth. Hungering for righteousness also means acting on behalf of others, especially those who are suffering.

Blessed are the merciful, for they will be shown mercy.

God showed mercy by sending his Son to forgive our sins and win for us eternal life. He asks us to imitate him by forgiving others, even our enemies. Disciples of Jesus do not hold grudges. By showing compassion, they reveal the merciful God who loves everyone.

Blessed are the clean of heart, for they shall see God.

Those who are clean of heart are single-minded and undivided in their commitment to God. As other Christs, they look on other people with love and acceptance and recognize their unique value. Jesus' disciples have

evangelization
Sharing the Good News. Evangelization involves proclaiming the Gospel in such a way that people's hearts and lives are changed.

Delving Deeper into the Commandments

Choose and complete two of the following assignments.

1. Write a list of ten commandments applicable for parents. Write another list of ten commandments applicable for teens. Show both lists to your parents and ask them to write their comments in the margins for each list.

2. Read the United States Catholic Bishops' *Pastoral Plan for Pro-Life Activities.* Report on five public policy positions the bishops recommend for us to build a culture of life. See: www.usccb.org/prolife/pastoralplan.shtml#rededication.

3. Air Force Code: "I will not lie, cheat, or steal, nor will I tolerate anyone who does." How would this code work at your school? Write your response.

4. Examine some popular, general-interest magazines like *People*. Note some of the feature articles to discover how they might be promoting sexual sins that are contrary to the sixth commandment. Examine the ads to find symbols that are selling sex or appealing to the vice of lust. Report your findings.

their priorities in the right order: union with the Lord is the prime goal in life.

Blessed are the peacemakers, for they will be called children of God.

We are members of the same family, brothers and sisters in Christ. Fighting and arguing leads to dissension and disunity. Jesus' followers must work to settle disputes, root out violence, and show compassion through forgiveness, always in imitation of the Prince of Peace.

Blessed are they who are persecuted for the sake of righteousness, for theirs is the Kingdom of Heaven.

Ultimately to be a follower of Jesus means to pick up the cross. In doing so, disciples of Christ are often misunderstood, mocked, and abused. Some may even have to witness by offering their lives as martyrs. Though the world may reject us for preaching and living the Gospel, our Lord will never abandon us. He promises eternal happiness:

> Blessed are you when they insult you and persecute you and utter every kind of evil against you (falsely) because of me. Rejoice and be glad, for your reward will be great in heaven. Thus they persecuted the prophets who were before you. (Mt 5:11–12)

For Review

1. How do the first three commandments show love for God?

2. Name five sins that are contrary to the first commandment.

3. How should a Catholic keep the Lord's Day holy?

4. Discuss three major violations of the fifth commandment that are common in today's world.

5. How do the virtues of chastity, purity, and modesty combat the vice of lust?

6. What are the two purposes of marriage?

7. List three sins that the seventh and tenth commandments forbid.

8. Why is false witness contrary to being a disciple of Christ?

9. Define *calumny* and *detraction*.

10. Name and briefly explain each of the Beatitudes.

For Reflection

What values form your character? If someone said you were a person of high ethical character, what qualities would they be talking about?

More Requirements of Discipleship

When Christ had accomplished his work of our Salvation, the Holy Spirit was sent to his disciples in the Church that they might continue to work for the Salvation of all. It is our mission as called for by Jesus in Matthew 28:19–20 to go out to all the nations and make them disciples of all. This is another essential element of discipleship—**evangelization**. We can effectively share the Good News only when we are good stewards of our own God-given talents and gifts. These essential elements of discipleship are explored in the next sections.

A Disciple of Jesus Is an Evangelist

Before ascending to Heaven, Jesus called on his disciples to be evangelists, to go forth and make disciples of all the nations. The word *evangelist* comes from the Greek for "good news." An evangelist, therefore, is one who shares with other people the Good News, that is, the Gospel of Jesus Christ, "baptizing them in the name of the Father, and of the Son, and of the holy Spirit, teaching them to observe all that I have commanded you" (Mt 28:20).

How can you best evangelize, that is, spread the gospel to others? Consider a way St. Francis of Assisi approached evangelization on one occasion. Francis asked one of his young monks to join him to go into the town to preach. The young monk was thrilled to be chosen to accompany Francis, and joined him enthusiastically. They walked through the main streets, turned into alleys, made their way into the outlying huts, eventually working their way back to the monastery. As they approached the gate, the young monk reminded the great saint, "But, Father, you have forgotten. We went to town to preach."

Francis replied, "We have preached. We were preaching while we were walking. Many people saw us and observed our behavior. It was thus that we have preached our morning sermon. It is of no use to walk anywhere to preach unless we preach everywhere we walk."

This story reminds us of another saying of St. Francis, "Preach the Gospel always and, if necessary, use words."

Similarly, in his address to the youth of Brazil, Pope Benedict XVI challenged Catholic youth with these words:

> I send you out . . . on the great mission of evangelizing young men and women who have gone astray in the world like sheep without a shepherd. Be apostles of youth. Invite them to walk with you, to have the same experience of faith, hope, and love; to encounter Jesus so that they may feel truly loved, accepted, able to realize their full potential. May they too discover the sure ways of the commandments, and, by following them, come to God.

Pope Benedict's point is that living the commandments is an excellent way to evangelize. He encouraged young people to be free and responsible people; to make the family a center of peace and joy; to promote life; and to protect the elderly. He also encouraged youth to make their work holy by carrying it out with skill and diligence. For students, of course, this means working hard at studies to develop one's talents and to prepare for a life of service to family and community.

In addition, the Pope's words call teens and young adults to build a more just and fraternal society by respecting laws, avoiding hatred and violence, being honest, and giving Christian example in every relationship. Yet another way to bring Christ's Gospel to others is to respect the institution of marriage. The Holy Father reminds us that when a couple falls in love, they should practice the virtue of chastity by refraining from sexual relations until marriage. Imagine what a powerful witness to Jesus Christ the sacrifice, self-control, and patience involved in living a chaste life would be if practiced by teens. It would provide a great Christian witness to your peers who are bombarded with messages of sexual indulgence that are contrary to God's will

EXPLAINING THE FAITH

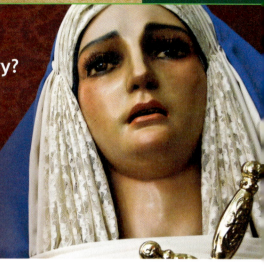

Why do non-Catholics ask me if Catholics worship Mary?

Sometimes when teens are called to evangelize, they face this question about what Catholics believe about the Blessed Mother. Here's one way to answer: you can tell them they are wrong. Catholics worship and adore God alone, as required by the First Commandment. Worship of any other person or thing would be idolatry. Catholics do venerate or respect Mary and all the saints because of their holiness as disciples of Christ. We revere Mary more than the other saints because she is the Mother of God, the Queen of All Saints.

for sexual sharing in a committed marriage open to both life and love.

This short summary of Pope Benedict XVI's address emphasizes the need for young people to live upright, moral lives as a mark of discipleship and evangelization. Like St. Francis of Assisi, the pope emphasizes that actions speak louder than words. You do not have to stand on street corners to preach the Gospel. Your life preaches the Gospel. You should always be prepared to share your faith. For example:

- When asked why you act the way you do, you can respond simply that your Catholic faith inspires you to live a Christ-like life.

- Study your Catholic faith so that you are able to explain it. Strive to pay attention in religion classes. Seek answers to questions you do not know. Learn where to find answers to tough questions. Familiarize yourself with the *Catechism of the Catholic Church*. Read the Bible on a regular basis.

- Invite a friend who does not attend Mass regularly to come to Mass with you. Evangelizing involves not only reaching out to non-Catholics but also to lukewarm or nonpracticing Catholics.

- In talking with others about hot-button issues, for example, abortion, do not be afraid to share Church teaching on the subject. Sometimes people have never heard the truth about the great moral issues of the day. You can be a witness to the truth.

- It is acceptable and good to pray in public. A simple bowing of your head and thanking God for the food you are about to eat in a restaurant can be a powerful but quiet and effective witness to your faith.

A Disciple of Jesus Is a Good Steward

A steward is a person who carefully and responsibly manages something that is entrusted to his or her care. Disciples of Jesus are called to stewardship because everything we have is a gift from God, and God wants us to share what we have been given. To be a good steward as Jesus' disciple means that we must share our time, talents, and treasures with others.

Sharing our gifts is also an act of love, following the example of God the Father who gave us the gift of his Son who won for us eternal life. Jesus gives us the gift of the Holy Spirit who is always present to us to show us God's love and goodness. In Baptism, Christ calls us to share in his **common priesthood**, that is, to show his presence in the world. Our Baptism also gives us the vocation of being a prophet so that we can speak the truth with courage and calls us to Christ's kingly role of serving others with love. The Sacrament of Confirmation increases

common priesthood
The priesthood of the faithful. Christ has made the Church a "kingdom of priests" who share in his priesthood through the Sacraments of Baptism and Confirmation.

ministerial priesthood
The priesthood of Christ received in the Sacrament of Holy Orders. Its purpose is to serve the common priesthood by building up and guiding the Church in the name of Christ.

in us the gifts of the Holy Spirit so that we can live our priestly, prophetic, and kingly vocation. And the Eucharist gives us the strength to live as Christ's disciples amidst the struggles of daily life. Based on the common priesthood, the **ministerial priesthood** is another way of participation in the mission of Christ. This ministry is conferred in the Sacrament of Holy Orders. It is directed at unfolding the baptismal grace of all Christians.

Jesus is our guide, model, and friend in the life of discipleship. Praying to and developing our friendship

with him help us to live our vocation to be good stewards. Meeting him in the Sacrament of Penance gives us the graces to start anew when we have fallen short of being the good stewards of the gifts we have been given. In addition, reading the Bible, learning the Church's social teaching and her powerful message of respect for all of life, and talking to adults whom we trust and admire are three other ways to find inspiration and support for living as faithful stewards and disciples of Jesus Christ.

In the 2007 pastoral letter "Stewardship and Teenagers: The Challenge of Being a Disciple," the United States Catholic bishops list four practical ways teens can love others through responsible stewardship. They are:

• *Share your time.* Visit people who are alone, especially those who are isolated due to age or sickness. Teach what you know to a neighbor or younger sibling. Be present with the people in your life, especially your family. Offer to help. Practice saying yes.

• *Share your talents.* No one else can do exactly what you do. Whether it be singing, cooking, drawing, or playing sports, your talents are for sharing with others. When used generously, the good they provide is immeasurable. Seek opportunities to participate in your parish or faith community as a greeter, altar server, lector, extraordinary minister of Holy Communion, or assistant in the religious education program.

- *Share your treasure.* The cost of a movie ticket or a pizza can contribute maybe more than you know to help prevent a childhood disease or build a house for someone with nowhere to live. Part of your allowance or paycheck can help your parish provide more services for its community. Decide to give a certain percentage of money at your parish each week. As you live with this decision, you will grow into a lifelong habit of generosity.

- *Share your tradition.* Embrace the rites and sacraments of the Church as beautiful gifts of God, to be appreciated, loved, and shared. Invite a friend to come to Mass with you. Pray for others, both people in your life and those in need throughout the world. Consider what plans God has for you. Whatever his call, it will require the ultimate gift of yourself—through marriage and family, or through the priesthood or consecrated life.

This pastoral letter reminds us that it *is* possible to imitate Christ and to be his disciple by being a good steward. Participation in the sacraments, especially the Eucharist, is crucial as is daily prayer.

For Review

1. What is an evangelist?
2. What are three ways a Catholic teenager can be an evangelist?
3. Define *stewardship*.
4. List three ways a Catholic teenager can be a good steward.

For Reflection

What are your three strongest talents? Write how you can use each of them to be a good steward. Resolve to put one of your gifts into good use in the coming week.

Putting Discipleship into Practice

Love is a central theme in Jesus' teaching to his disciples. Love is the main "job" of Christian discipleship. Time and again, Jesus challenges us to love others. For example:

- "Do to others as you would have them do to you" (Lk 6:31).

- "I give you a new commandment: love one another. As I have loved you, so you also should love one another" (Jn 13:34).

- "But to you who hear I say, love your enemies, do good to those who hate you, bless those who curse you, pray for those who mistreat you" (Lk 6:27–28).

Most challenging is Jesus' command for us to forgive even our *enemies*. Forgiveness can be tough at times, but it is an essential quality of love. Jesus taught us to ask for God's forgiveness in the Lord's Prayer, but he also told us that we must forgive others, too. Jesus said,

> If you forgive others their transgressions, your heavenly Father will forgive you. But if you do not forgive others, neither will your Father forgive your transgressions. (Mt 6:14–15)

Furthermore, our forgiveness should have no limits. Just as God forgives us when we ask for forgiveness, so we should forgive those who have hurt us.

> If your brother sins, rebuke him; and if he repents, forgive him. And if he wrongs you seven times in one day and returns to you seven times saying, "I am sorry," you should forgive him. (Lk 17:3–4)

Love Requires Self-Denial

To love others requires that we put the needs of others before our own needs. It often means saying no to our own wishes and desires for ourselves, a form of death to self-centeredness or self-denial. This means, in Jesus' words, to "take up our crosses," probably the most challenging task of Christian discipleship:

> Then Jesus said to his disciples, "Whoever wishes to come after me must deny himself, take up his cross, and follow me. For whoever wishes to save his life will lose it, but whoever loses his life for my sake will find it. What profit would there be for one to gain the whole world and forfeit his life? Or what can one give in exchange for his life? For the Son of Man will come with his angels in his Father's glory, and then he will repay everyone according to his conduct. (Mt 16:24–27)

Dying to self by picking up a cross is, paradoxically, the way to full and complete life. By loving, we find true life. We discover eternal life by giving up a life of self-centeredness. If we are generous to Jesus by being generous to others, then we will be rewarded. Jesus promises this:

> Give and gifts will be given to you; a good measure, packed together, shaken down, and overflowing, will be poured into your lap. For the measure with which you measure will in return be measured out to you. (Lk 6:38)

Christ insists on love, forgiveness, and generosity, and he tells us we are capable of doing all these things because God first loved us, forgives our sins, and has displayed incredible generosity by giving us the gift of life, health, talents, friends, and countless other gifts. The way we show our love for God is by loving others. The link between the two is ironclad:

> We love because he first loved us. If anyone says, "I love God," but hates his brother, he is a liar; for whoever does not love a brother whom he has seen cannot love God whom he has not seen. This is the commandment we have from him: whoever loves God must also love his brother. (1 Jn 4:19–21)

Love Requires Care for the Poor

Jesus identified with the poor and ministered to them. For example, he reminded his dinner host that he should take care to invite the poor, the crippled, the lame, and the blind to his banquet. Jesus promised: "Blessed indeed will you be because of their inability to repay you. For you will be repaid at the resurrection of the righteous" (Lk 14:14). He also told the parable of Lazarus and the Rich Man (Lk 16:19–31) to emphasize that how we treat the hungry, the poor, and the outcast will determine our eternal destiny.

Furthermore, he told his disciples that we will be judged based on how we have loved others, especially the poor. At the Last Judgment, the question our Lord will put to us is not "How popular were you?" nor "How much money did you make?" nor "What were your grades?" nor "How good an athlete were you?" but "How did you take care of those in need—your brothers and sisters?" This is one true way of judging what kind of disciple you are. Consider how Jesus describes how we are to be judged from Matthew 25:

> When the Son of Man comes in his glory, and all the angels with him, he will sit upon his glorious throne, and all the nations will be assembled before him. And he will separate them one from another, as a shepherd separates the sheep from the goats. He will place the sheep on his right and the goats on his left. Then the king will say to those on his right, "Come, you who are blessed by my Father. Inherit the kingdom prepared for you from the foundation of the world. For I was hungry and you gave me food, I was thirsty and you gave me drink, a stranger and you welcomed me, naked and you clothed me, ill and you cared for me, in prison and you visited me." Then the righteous will answer him and say, "Lord, when did we see you hungry and feed you, or thirsty and give you drink? When did we see you a stranger and welcome you, or naked and clothe you? When did we see you ill or in prison, and visit you?" And the king will say to them in reply, "Amen, I say to you, whatever you did for one of these least brothers of mine, you did for me." Then he will say to those on his left, "Depart from me, you accursed, into the eternal fire prepared for the devil and his angels. For I was hungry and you gave me no food, I was thirsty and you gave me no drink, a stranger and you gave me no welcome, naked and you gave me no clothing, ill and in prison, and you did not care for me." Then they will answer and say, "Lord, when did we see you hungry or thirsty or a stranger or naked or ill or in prison, and not minister to your needs?" He will answer them, "Amen, I say to you, what you did not do for one of these least ones, you did not do for me." And these will go off to eternal punishment, but the righteous to eternal life. (Mt 25:31–46)

In his "Letter to the Rulers of People," St. Francis of Assisi wrote these wise words, words that can speak to each of Jesus' followers:

> Keep a clear eye toward life's end. Do not forget your purpose and destiny as God's creature. What you are in his sight is what you are and nothing more. Remember that when you leave this earth, you can take with you nothing that you have received—fading symbols of honor, trappings of power—but only what you have given: a full heart enriched by honest service, love, sacrifice, and courage.

God the Father sees all of us as his precious children. For this reason, we are to treat all people—especially the poor and outcasts who need our care the most—as brothers and sisters in Christ. The one sure way we can determine what kind of disciple we are is by how we fulfill this command of Jesus: respond to the least of these in your midst.

Love Requires that We Avoid Greed

One of the reasons it is so difficult to follow Jesus' command to love is that humans can be trapped by greed. Consider these three sayings of Jesus:

- "No servant can serve two masters. He will either hate one and love the other, or be devoted to one and despise the other. You cannot serve God and mammon" (Lk 16:13).

- "Amen, I say to you, it will be hard for one who is rich to enter the kingdom of heaven. Again I say to you, it is easier for a camel to pass through the eye of a needle than for one who is rich to enter the kingdom of God" (Mt 19:23–24).

- "For where your treasure is, there also will your heart be" (Lk 12:34).

Mammon is the false god of riches and money. If money, possessions, power, and prestige become our top priorities in life, we lose sight of God. Because wealth has the tendency to blind us to God and his will, Jesus said it is hard for the rich to get to Heaven. When the Apostles heard this teaching, they were astonished. They asked Jesus if anyone, then, could be saved. Jesus replied, "For human beings this is impossible, but for God all things are possible" (Mt 19:26). We must be good stewards of all the wealth and graces we are given by God. And when we do share with others, we must do so sincerely and without calling attention to ourselves. In the Sermon on the Mount, Jesus said to his disciples:

> When you give alms, do not blow a trumpet before you, as the hypocrites do in the synagogues and in the streets to win the praise of others. Amen, I say to you, they have received their reward. But when you give alms, do not let your left hand know what your right is doing, so that your almsgiving may be secret. And your Father who sees in secret will repay you. (Mt 6:2–4)

Performing acts of kindness without fanfare, and especially for needy people, is a sure sign that wealth does not control us but that we control it and use if for the good of others.

In summary, the key element of discipleship is to love. We are able to love because God loves us first and the Holy Spirit empowers us to love. Love demands sacrifice and carrying a cross. Love means forgiving others. Love means concrete deeds

Kindness Ideas

Check out the HelpOthers.org website. Click on the "Kindness Ideas" link and read about different ways you can perform some charitable act. Good starting places to consider are these subtopics:

- Help the Homeless
- Reach Out to the Homebound
- Crafts of Kindness
- Healing Kindness
- Connect with Seniors

Pick a kindness practice, or one similar to it, that appeals to you and resolve to put it into action within the next week. In your journal, write a short summary of the project and how you felt doing it.

performed for others. Love means being wary of greed. Love means responding to the needs of the poor and outcast. When we love in the name of Christian discipleship, we can make the words of the Zimbabwe pastor our own:

> I won't give up, shut up, let up, until I have stayed up, stored up, prayed up, paid up, preached up, for the cause of Christ. I am a disciple of Jesus. I must go till he comes, give till I drop, preach till all know, and work till he stops me. And, when he comes for his own, he will have no problem recognizing me.

For Review

1. What is the connection between love and forgiveness?

2. What is a major criterion of how we will be judged?

3. What is the spiritual danger of having too much wealth?

For Reflection

"I am what I am in God's sight and nothing more." What does this statement mean to you? What does God see in you?

Act of Love

Pray this traditional prayer. As an additional assignment, use the prayer as a centerpiece for an art project. You may wish to depict in symbols or collage form people who are your neighbors, the injured, and all who are in need of your prayer.

> O my God, I love you above all things, with my whole heart and soul, because you are all good and worthy of all my love. I love my neighbor as myself for the love of you. I forgive all who have injured me, and I ask pardon of all whom I have injured. Amen.

WHAT DOES JESUS SAY ABOUT GREED?

Read the Parable of the Rich Fool, Luke 12:13-21. Answer the following questions:

- What is greed? List other areas of life besides the accumulation of material wealth that greed can affect.
- Is it more likely for a rich person or a poor person to be greedy? Explain your answer.
- How do we become rich before God?

Read the parable of the Rich Man and Lazarus, Luke 16:19-31.

- What images does Jesus use to suggest that the rich man is rich and Lazarus is poor?
- Specifically, why is the rich man punished?
- Is it difficult or easy to give to the poor? Explain.

Main Ideas

- Being a disciple of Jesus takes dramatic commitment, even to the possibility of giving up one's life. (p. 214)

- A disciple is a pupil, friend, and follower of Jesus. (pp. 212–214)

- Jesus tells us that we will remain in his love if we keep his commands. (pp. 216–217)

- Jesus did not abolish the Law of the Old Testament; he fulfilled it. We are called to keep the Ten Commandments. (pp. 216–217)

- The first three commandments concern how we can love God with our whole heart, soul, strength, and mind. (pp. 217–219)

- The first commandment requires us to practice the virtue of religion. (p. 217)

- The second commandment forbids any wrong use of God's name or the names of Jesus and the saints. (p. 218)

- The third commandment requires us to keep Sunday holy, especially by celebrating the Eucharist. (p. 219)

- The last seven commandments show us how to love our neighbor as we love ourselves. (pp. 219–223)

- The fourth commandment calls parents and children to respect one another. (p. 219)

- The fifth commandment outlaws killing; we show our respect for life by eating healthy food, exercising, getting proper rest, and avoiding harmful substances. (p. 220)

- The sixth and ninth commandments both teach how to use sexuality in accord with God's plan. (pp. 220–221)

- The seventh and tenth commandments require justice in our dealings with others, both individuals and communities. (p. 222)

- The eighth commandment demands that both individuals and societies are truthful in their relationships with others. (p. 223)

- Incorporating the Beatitudes into our lives is also a key part of being a disciple of Christ. They teach attitudes we should make a part of our lives. (pp. 223–225)

- Another essential element of discipleship is to evangelize, that is, to share the Good News with others through our words and actions. (pp. 225–226)

- To be a good evangelist we must also practice stewardship. (pp. 227–228)

- Putting discipleship into practice means that we first, last, and always are loving of God and neighbor. (pp. 229–230)

- The greatest challenge of loving is often forgiving even our enemies. (p. 230)

- Love requires self-denial, that we care for the poor, and that we avoid greed. (pp. 230–231)

Terms, People, Places

Match the following terms with the definitions below.

A. domestic Church
B. evangelization
C. common priesthood
D. patron saints
E. evangelical counsels
F. chastity

1. Special vows we make to God.
2. People Catholics are often named for; they often inspire us and pray for us.
3. A community of faith that mirrors the love of the Blessed Trinity.
4. A virtue that helps us live with self-control according to our station in life.
5. A call given at Baptism that asks us to demonstrate Christ's presence in the world.
6. Proclaiming the Gospel so that people's hearts are changed.

Primary Source Quotations

Discipleship

The Lord wills that his disciples possess a tremendous power: that his lowly servants accomplish in his name all that he did when he was on earth.

—St. Ambrose

For Jesus Christ, I am prepared to suffer still more.

—St. Maximilian Kolbe

I heard the call to give up all and to follow him into the slums and to serve among the poorest of the poor.

—Bl. Mother Teresa of Calcutta

Evangelization

All men are called to belong to the new People of God. This People, therefore, while remaining one and only one, is to be spread throughout the whole world and to all ages in order that the design of God's will may be fulfilled: he made human nature one in the beginning and has decreed that all his children who were scattered should be finally gathered as one.

—*Lumen Gentium*, 13

Love for the Poor

We must give alms. Charity wins souls and draws them to virtue.

—St. Angela Merici

The heart of a Christian, who believes and feels, cannot pass by the hardships and deprivations of the poor without helping them.

—Bl. Luis Guanella

Who are some people who are poor or outcast in your community who can use your love? Write down three practical things you can do for them to show that you care.

Ongoing Assignments

As you cover the material in this chapter, choose and complete at least three of these assignments.

1. Prepare a report on spiritism, blasphemy, idolatry, superstition, sacrilege, or some other violations of the first three commandments. Define the term and explain how the practice contradicts God's law. Consult the *Catholic Encyclopedia*.

2. Report on the life of your patron saint or a saint you admire by writing about how he or she modeled in a heroic way one of the theological virtues of faith, hope, and charity.

3. Write a pro-life letter to a legislator, newspaper, or some other media outlet. After researching the Catholic teaching on a particular issue, for example, abortion, express your concern about this issue.

4. Research the following topic: "Vatican Issues Ten Commandments for Driving." Rewrite the fifth and sixth commandments in this list in your own words.

5. Read the United States Catholic Bishops' statement "Married Love and the Gift of Life." Report on what the bishops have to say about Church teaching on married love and the difference between natural family planning and contraception. You can find this online at: http://www.usccb.org/laity/marriage/MarriedLove.pdf.

6. With a classmate, write an advertisement for a pro-life campaign. Present your ad by way of a poster, a short video, or as a radio spot. Your theme: "Choose Life!"

7. Debate the morality of the war on terrorism that began in 2003 using the Church's criteria for a just war.

8. Create a PowerPoint presentation on the perils of alcohol abuse. Present some moral arguments for the virtue of sobriety. Check out information provided by Mothers Against Drunk Driving (MADD).

Chapter 9 Quick View

9. Read the United States Catholic Bishops' statement titled "Stewardship and Teenagers: The Challenge of Being a Disciple." You can find it on the United States Conference of Catholic Bishops' website: www.usccb.org/bishops/StewardshipTeens.pdf.

Prayer

St. Ignatius of Loyola (1491–1556), the founder of the Society of Jesus—popularly known as the Jesuits—spent a year in prayer and meditation after being wounded from a battle while serving as a Basque knight. He read about the lives of Jesus and the saints and decided to serve the Kingdom of God. He wrote the following prayer that has served as inspiration for Jesuits and others in the years since.

> *Prayer for Generosity*
> Lord, teach me to be generous.
> Teach me to serve you as you deserve;
> to give and not to count the cost;
> to fight and not to heed the wounds;
> to toil and not to seek for rest;
> to labor and not to ask for any reward,
> save that of knowing that I do your will.
> Amen.

- *Reflection*: What is God's will for you?
- *Resolution*: Serve Jesus in the coming week by serving a particular person at home and at school.

10

PRAYER IN THE LIFE OF A DISCIPLE OF JESUS CHRIST

*Rejoice always. Pray without ceasing.
In all circumstances give thanks, for this is the will
of God for you in Christ Jesus.*

—1 Thessalonians 5:16-18

An Invitation to Prayer

Jesus instructs us to pray constantly: "Ask and it will be given to you; seek and you will find; knock and the door will be opened to you" (Mt 7:7).

Defining Prayer

Prayer is our response to God who seeks us. We must pray without ceasing.

How to Pray

We can pray in several ways, including vocally, through meditation, or mental prayer. Any effort at prayer is prayer itself.

Praying with Sacred Scripture

Many Catholic prayers come directly from the Bible or are partially based on Sacred Scripture.

Two Special Prayers for Jesus' Disciples

The Our Father is the preeminent Christian prayer. The Hail Mary is another favorite Catholic prayer that calls on the intercession of Mary for our needs.

An Invitation to Prayer

Prayer is essential to the life of a disciple of Jesus Christ. In the Sermon on the Mount, Jesus instructs us:

> Ask and it will be given to you; seek and you will find; knock and the door will be opened to you. For everyone who asks, receives; and the one who seeks, finds; and to the one who knocks, the door will be opened. Which one of you would hand his son a stone when he asks for a loaf of bread, or a snake when he asks for a fish? If you then, who are wicked, know how to give good gifts to your children, how much more will your heavenly Father give good things to those who ask him. (Mt 7:7–11)

Prayer is powerful. A famous story told about Bl. Mother Teresa of Calcutta points this out. One day, a novice who was in charge of the kitchen came to Mother Teresa and told her that they had no flour to make the food necessary to feed three hundred other novices who were returning for lunch. Mother Teresa instructed the young nun to go to the chapel where she was to pray to Jesus, telling him they had no food. The novice did as she was instructed. Ten minutes later, a man came to the door of the convent and told Mother Teresa that the teachers in the city schools were going on strike and that he had seven thousand lunches that he did not know what to do with. He asked her, "Can you use them?"

Mother Teresa had profound faith and trust that the Lord would provide—and he did. The heavenly Father provides for the needs of his children.

⬤ Self-Evaluation on Prayer

Evaluate how frequently you do each of the following prayer experiences. Then write your response to the questions that follow.

- celebrate the Eucharistic liturgy
- read the Bible
- ask God to heal sick relatives and friends
- talk to Jesus as with a friend
- ask God for help in studies or other activities
- recite formal prayers like the Lord's Prayer and the Hail Mary
- ask for God's help when tempted to sin
- think about Jesus and how he would act in certain situations
- say prayers before and after meals
- examine my conscience before going to sleep
- pray the Rosary
- try to figure out questions by asking the Holy Spirit for insight
- praise God for the beauty in creation
- read spiritual books
- thank God for all the gifts he has given, including my friends
- ask Jesus to help see his presence in others
- ask God for forgiveness after sinning
- think about God
- adore Jesus while visiting him in the Blessed Sacrament
- listen to music that helps me think of God's beauty or greatness

Questions

1. How do you define prayer?
2. Which of these prayer experiences do you do the most? the least?
3. Which of these experiences has brought you the greatest peace and satisfaction? Why do you think that is so?

Another story about prayer has a different result. It involves a grandmother who was helping her granddaughter with a homework assignment. However, the child was upset because she had misplaced her favorite doll. Finally, she asked her grandmother if they could kneel down together to ask God to help find the doll. Of course, the grandmother said yes. They both knelt down, closed their eyes, and offered a silent prayer. Then the girl sat down and completed the homework assignment.

The next day, the grandmother asked her granddaughter if she found her doll. "No," she replied, "but I am not thinking about my doll today."

We have Jesus' Word that our heavenly Father will give good things to us. Sometimes God answers our prayers exactly the way we hope that he would, like in the case of Bl. Mother Teresa. At other times, God tells us to be patient and to look for other answers. Perhaps God was trying to teach the little girl patience but also the value of detachment—that possessions are not all that important. Still other times God might say no to our requests because he is answering a much deeper need in our hearts, giving us a more valuable gift that will make us a better person and a better disciple of his Son.

 For Reflection

When was a time that prayer helped you the most?

Defining Prayer (*CCC*, 2558–2567; 2590; 2623–2649)

God the Father calls each of us into a vital relationship with him through Jesus Christ in the Holy Spirit. Prayer is a powerful means to grow in union with Jesus. He told us to pray always without becoming weary (Lk 18:1). St. Paul repeated Jesus' advice when he wrote, "Pray without ceasing" (1 Thes 5:17). Along the same lines, St. Frances Cabrini (1850–1917), the first American citizen to be canonized, wrote:

> We must pray without tiring, for the salvation of mankind does not depend on material success; nor on sciences that cloud the intellect. Neither does it depend on arms and human industries, but on Jesus alone.

Prayer is our response to the God who seeks us. As the *Catechism of the Catholic Church* puts it, prayer is a "vital and personal relationship with the living and true God" (*CCC*, 2558). The Holy Spirit enables us to pray. In humility, we approach our loving Father who desires only good things for us, which he grants to us through his Son, Jesus Christ.

The *Catechism* further defines prayer as "the living relationship of the children of God with their Father who is good beyond measure, with his Son Jesus Christ, and with the Holy Spirit" (*CCC*, 2565). Think of prayer, then, as a *relationship*, a coming together with God the Father who is our Abba; with Jesus Christ, our Savior, brother, and friend; and with the Holy Spirit, our Comforter and Helper, who dwells in our hearts. When we pray, we become more aware of who we are as adopted children of our loving God. Prayer brings us into unity with our loving Triune God.

Great saints have also given us excellent definitions of prayer. For example, St. John Damascene said prayer is "the raising of one's mind and heart to God." St. Augustine remarked, "True prayer is nothing but love." St. Thérèse of Lisieux observed, "For me, prayer is a surge of the heart; it is a simple look turned toward heaven, it is a cry of recognition and of love, embracing both trial and joy."

St. Clement defined prayer as "conversation with God." St. Teresa of Avila also pictured prayer this way when she recommended that we think of prayer as a journey with our invisible God, a

EXPLAINING THE FAITH

Do my prayers affect God? For example, can they get God to change his mind?

Prayer brings together two great mysteries. The first is of an eternally loving God who knows all that was, all that is, and all that ever will be. The second involves the mystery of our own free will, which enables us to accept or reject God's invitation to love.

When we pray, we are praying to a loving God who has known our prayers for all eternity. Thus, when we pray, we are not telling God anything new. Nor do we exercise any power over him, for example, the power to persuade him to change his mind about something. In fact, it is the Holy Spirit who first inspired us to pray. As a result of knowing and inspiring our prayers from all eternity, God had included them in his plan for the world. Furthermore, the very prayers that God knew we would ask have been answered! Therefore, prayer does not change God. Prayer changes us.

companion who walks next to us along the path of life. Prayer is turning to the Father and talking and listening to him as in a friendly conversation. Just as friendships thrive on conversation, so will regular conversations with our loving God give us the strength to live according to his will.

Benefits of Prayer

Certainly, though, we can say that prayer has many benefits:

- *Prayer contributes to our sense of self-worth.* In prayer we get in touch with who we are as God's child, discovering God's infinite love for us.

- *Prayer leads to happiness,* helping us discover that our restless hearts can find true happiness, not in possessions or fame, but in our relationship with Jesus Christ.

- *Prayer changes us* by making us more loving, by showing us God's will for us and what we must do to follow Christ more closely.

- Just like water helps plants grow, *prayer helps nourish in us virtues* like faith, hope, charity, humility, sensitivity to other people, compassion, and a desire to work for God's kingdom.

- *Prayer energizes, calms, and renews.*

- *Prayer heals* because we meet the Divine Physician who touches our hurting hearts and forgives our sins.

- *Prayer helps relieve anxiety* by helping us heed Jesus' teaching not to worry about everyday cares because our heavenly Father is looking out for us.

Prayer has many benefits, but the greatest is that *prayer deepens our relationship with the Triune God* who loves us beyond what we can imagine. This chapter examines prayer as a central component for the life of a disciple of Jesus Christ.

For Review

1. Give a definition of prayer. Explain its meaning.

2. What is the greatest benefit of prayer?

For Reflection

Write your own personal definition of prayer.

How to Pray

Prayer is an act of love, a personal response to God's love for us. We show this love when we pray to God the Father, our loving Abba who is the source of our life. We show our love when we pray to Jesus Christ, our Lord and Savior, asking for his friendship and help. We show our love when we pray to the Holy Spirit, the interior teacher of Christian prayer, asking for his guidance and strength to live a Christ-like life.

We also show our love when we pray in union with our Blessed Mother. She is the greatest saint. Her openness and example serve as a model of how to cooperate with the graces the Holy Spirit showers on us.

Most Catholics learn how to pray from parents, teachers, parish priests, and other believers whose example inspires them. Common to the lessons are some teachings of saints who have made prayer part of their daily lives. The following "6 Ps" make up good preliminary steps for a rich prayer life:

1. *Place.* One good rule: find a special place to pray where you can calm yourself, put yourself in God's presence, and focus your attention. Consider the following: your bedroom, a special corner in your house where you may light a **votive candle**, the school chapel or parish church, in your car with the radio off, or on a regular walking route outside where you can focus some time on prayer.

2. *Period of Time.* Prayer can take place any time, but it is good to carve out a scheduled part of the day for prayer. For example:

    *   first thing in the morning or last thing at night
    *   before or after a meal

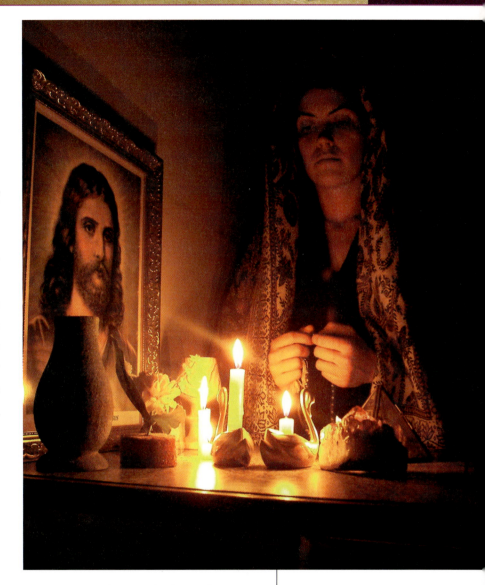

    *   ten minutes during a free period at school
    *   between homework assignments

    Catholics set aside one hour a week to worship at the Sunday Eucharist and on holy days of obligation.

3. *Posture.* You can be more alert and relaxed while praying with a suitable posture. Some people pray best when standing or walking, some while sitting upright in a chair, others by

votive candle
A prayer candle typically placed before a statue of Jesus or the Virgin Mary that is lit for a prayer intention.

lectio divina
Literally, "divine reading." This is a prayerful way to read the Bible or any other sacred writings.

beyond what we can imagine. He has showered us with the gift of life and so many other gifts. Reminding yourself of these truths will help you approach God with humility and with grateful hearts. You can enter your prayer realizing that the Holy Spirit himself has led us to spend time with our loving God, a special time of trust and companionship with the one who holds us in the palm of his hand. Being present to God in prayer is itself a prayer.

5. *Passage.* There are many ways to pray, as this chapter will point out. One time-honored and sure way to pray is to select a passage from Scripture and then meditate on it. Known as **lectio divina** (see page 245), this is a wonderful way to allow the Lord to speak to your heart.

6. *Persistence.* Amid the distractions of daily life, regular prayer can be tough. It is sometimes described as a battle because when we pray, we are fighting against ourselves, our surroundings, and Satan who tries to turn us away from our prayer. But you should remember the words of St. Padre Pio: "Prayer is the best weapon we have. It is a key to opening God's heart."

kneeling, still others (like St. Ignatius of Loyola) by lying on their backs. As you begin your prayer in whatever posture you choose, it helps to inhale and exhale slowly, letting the cares of the day drain away.

4. *Presence.* You can begin your prayer time by recalling basic truths like these: God is always present to us. He loves us

Distractions in prayer caused by a wandering mind, an overactive imagination, or external noises are normal. You can counteract them by gazing at a crucifix, holy picture or icon, or by lighting a candle to help keep your attention on God. You can call on the Holy Spirit to focus your attention. Repeatedly reciting a prayer-word or -phrase like "Abba," "Lord Jesus," "Come, Holy Spirit," or "Jesus help me" can help drive away distractions.

Jesus is pleased that we want to pray, even if we are distracted or do not think much is going on. In prayer, we are present to the Lord, and he appreciates the time we spend with him. If our prayer is united to Jesus, he will give us much more than we are asking for. His love will touch us, despite our restless minds. He will give us the Holy Spirit who strengthens us and changes us into other Christs. In the battle to pray, we should always remember that any effort we make to try to pray is itself a prayer. The next sections focus on several forms, expressions, and practices of prayer.

Prayer Expressions (CCC, 2700-2719; 2721-2724)

Recall an earlier definition of prayer as conversation with God. Conversation involves talking, where we take our concerns and requests to God. As a wise person once said, "If we want to walk with God, we must talk to God." Vocal prayer—using spoken words—is one way to pray. But we must listen to God as well, cherishing moments of silence when we can hear God speak to us. This can take place in meditation or in mental prayer leading to contemplation.

When we slow down and put ourselves in God's presence, we hear our Lord speak to us through our intellects, feelings, imaginations, wills, and memories. For example, he can put new ideas into our minds, ideas that teach us how to be more loving persons. He can calm our troubled emotions by strengthening our faith and trust that he will take care of us. He can inspire our imaginations by helping us visualize how we solve in a new way a troubled relationship. He can strengthen our wills to do the right thing when we face temptation. And he can heal our bad memories that might be troubling us or remind us of all the good things he has done for us.

Christian prayer is heartfelt, expressing itself as vocal prayer, meditation, and mental prayer.

Vocal Prayer

When we express our prayer vocally in words we are doing what Jesus himself did when he taught the Our Father. When we say our prayers aloud with others, we can strengthen our spiritual relationships with them. The Church has a rich tradition of vocal prayer. For example, this prayer of St. Francis de Sales (1562–1627) is intended for daily recitation:

My God, I give you this day.
I offer You, now, all of the good
that I shall do and I promise to accept,
for love of You,
all of the difficulty that I shall meet.
Help me to conduct myself during this day
in a manner pleasing to You.
Amen.

Meditation

Meditation is prayerful reflection, especially on the Word of God found in Sacred Scripture. When we meditate, we "tune into God." We actively use our thoughts, emotions, imaginations, and desires to think about God's presence in the world and in our lives. We meditate to gain a greater knowledge and love of the Lord so that we may better serve him.

Throughout the history of the Church, there have developed different types of *spiritualities* that teach us how to pray and to live like Christ in our daily lives. St. Teresa of Avila, St. Ignatius of Loyola, and St. Francis de Sales are examples of great Catholic saints who teach us how to use the Bible, especially the Gospels, when we meditate. In addition, we can also meditate on the writings of the saints, the events in our world, and the action of God in our own lives. Lectio divina is an example of a meditation on Scripture.

Mental Prayer

Mental prayer usually centers on Jesus. We might converse with him or reflect on one of the mysteries of his life, for example, his Passion and Crucifixion. Sometimes mental prayer can lead to **contemplation**, a form of silent, wordless prayer where we simply rest in the presence of our all-loving God. St. John Vianney told of a simple peasant who described contemplative prayer. The peasant sat daily in front of our Blessed Lord present in the tabernacle. He explained, "I look at him and he looks at me." Contemplative prayer is silently being in God's presence, gazing on him with hearts full of love. In this type of prayer, we seek Christ, give ourselves to the will of the Father, and place ourselves under the guidance of the Holy Spirit. When praying this way, we empty our minds of thoughts and images and simply allow the divine presence to penetrate our being. We do not have to do anything at all. If you are able to pray this way, you have been given a great gift from God.

Prayer Forms (CCC, 2623–2643)

The way we express our prayer may be in several forms. These have been revealed in both Sacred Tradition and Sacred Scripture and are normative for Christian people. They are as follows:

- *Blessing.* We bless God because he first blesses us, that is, he showers his graces on us. Blessing is a response to God's gifts.

- *Adoration.* When we adore God, we humbly acknowledge that he is the loving Creator of everything. Adoration glorifies the God who made us. All blessings flow from him.

- *Petition.* Petition or supplication is asking God to provide what we need—materially or spiritually. Jesus told us to petition God for the coming of the Kingdom and to ask for the gift of the Holy Spirit, the source of all gifts (see Luke 11:9–13). The Holy Spirit enables us to live Christ-like lives. **Contrition** is a special type of petition in which we ask our merciful Father to forgive our sins. A model of contrition is the tax collector who began his prayer with, "Oh God, be merciful to me a sinner" (Lk 18:13).

  Like we so often do in our own prayer, Jesus asked his Father for many things. For example, he prayed that Simon not be tempted. And at the Last Supper, Jesus prayed to his Father that we, his disciples, would always remain in the truth and stay united to him.

- *Intercession.* Intercessory prayer is a special form of petition; it is prayer that we make to God on behalf of others. Jesus Christ is our High Priest who is always offering prayer on our behalf. Our Lord calls on us to pray for each other. He also asks us to pray for our enemies. We can do this because, as Christ's disciples, we can join our prayers to Jesus. It is an honor when friends and relatives ask us to pray for them. It is a special privilege to be able to petition Christ on their behalf.

---

contemplation

Wordless prayer whereby a person's mind and heart rest in God's goodness and majesty.

contrition

Heartfelt sorrow and aversion for sins committed along with the intention of sinning no more. Contrition is the most important act of penitents, necessary for receiving the Sacrament of Penance.

Eucharist

The source and summit of Christian life, the Eucharist is one of the Sacraments of Initiation. The word *eucharist* comes from a Greek word that means "thankful." The Eucharist commemorates the Last Supper, at which Jesus gave his Body and Blood in the form of bread and wine, and the Lord's sacrificial Death on the cross.

Intercessory prayer is a wonderful example of Christian mercy and love-in-action. Praying for others at Mass or reciting a Rosary on their behalf are two examples of intercessory prayer and ways to show Christian compassion and love.

- *Thanksgiving.* Everything we have and everything we are is a pure gift from God. Think of the gift of your life, friends, health, the friendship of Jesus who has saved you, and the Holy Spirit who dwells within and showers his gifts on you. God deserves our constant thanks. The Psalmist tells us, "Give thanks to the LORD who is good, whose love endures forever!" (Ps 107:1). In truth, every breath we take is an opportunity to thank God. The Gospels record an example of Jesus expressing his gratitude to the Father when he raised Lazarus from the dead:

> Father, I thank you for hearing me. I know that you always hear me; but because of the crowd here I have said this, that they may believe that you sent me. (Jn 11:41–42)

The **Eucharist** (a word which means "to give thanks") is a very special prayer of thanksgiving. At Mass, we bless, adore, praise, and thank God for all the blessings he has given to us. We express our sorrow, ask for forgiveness, and petition God for all the good things we and others need to live our lives fully. When we receive Holy Communion, Christ lives in us and unites us to God and all our Christian brothers and sisters by the power of the Holy Spirit. At Eucharist, Christ allows us to participate in his own thanksgiving to the Father.

- *Praise.* Praise is the form of prayer that acknowledges that God is God. We praise God and give him glory because he is so good, gracious, loving, and saving. He deserves our love, blessing, adoration, and praise for his own sake. The Holy Spirit helps us praise God, enabling us to have faith in Jesus Christ and to call God Abba. True praise of God includes no selfish motive because we take joy in our loving God alone. Many of the Psalms praise, adore, and bless God. Jesus himself praised the Father for revealing his will to the humble and lowly:

> At that very moment he rejoiced (in) the holy Spirit and said, "I give you praise, Father, Lord of heaven and earth, for although you have hidden these things from the wise and the learned you have revealed them to the childlike. Yes, Father, such has been your gracious will." (Lk 10:21)

Defining Prayer in the Book of Psalms

Read any three Psalms and identify the kind of prayer taking place in the Psalm. Quote the verses and explain how they fit the definition of one of the prayer forms listed above.

Traditional Catholic Prayer Practices

Church history and Tradition offer several other ways for Catholics to pray. Some examples are listed below.

Icons

Icons are often described as "windows to heaven," where God can touch us here on earth. They are religious images painted by artists who seek to be God's channel, allowing God's spirit to guide the brush.

In Greek, the term *icon* means "image." When we pray before icons, we put ourselves in the presence of the holy person or enter into the religious mystery that is portrayed.

One example of an icon is the Enthroned Madonna (994), located in the Hagia Sophia Museum, in Istanbul, Turkey. Hagia Sophia was first built as a great Byzantine basilica by the Emperor Justinian between 532 and 537. It was the largest cathedral in the world for more than one thousand years.

When you pray with an icon, you gaze at the image coming into the presence of, for example, the Blessed Mother. Gaze at the icon. Thank the Blessed Mother for giving her child to the world. Pray to Jesus and ask him to bless you.

Prayer before the Blessed Sacrament

Keeping a holy hour or spending some time visiting our Lord in the **Blessed Sacrament** is another way to pray. A holy hour is a devotion that commemorates our Lord's vigil in the Garden of Gethsemane when he asked his disciples to stay awake and pray (Mk 14:32–39). Many parishes celebrate the **Forty Hours' Devotion**, where the Holy Sacrament is exposed continuously and the faithful are invited to come spend some time with Jesus. The Blessed Sacrament is contained in a tabernacle in a church or chapel. A sanctuary lamp is a sign of his presence.

MORE WAYS TO PRAY

Variety is the spice of life, even in our prayer life. Use your imagination in praying to God. One idea is to compose short prayers by choosing a word (or several words) that is somehow related to all the letters of the alphabet. Here are some examples:

- **A** Almighty Father, I adore you. Make me an ambassador of your love.
- **C** Christ, my friend. Help me be a worthy child of your Father. Give me courage and conviction to carry my cross.
- **G** Glory to God the Father. Glory to God the Son. Glory to God the Holy Spirit. Gracious God grant us your good gifts.
- **L** Lord, Jesus Christ, Lamb of God, I love you. You light up my life. Help me listen to you, my leader.
- **S** Spirit of God, give me, a sinner, strength to live a Christian life.

Another idea is to write a letter to God the Father or to Jesus. Write the letter as you would to a person you love very much, a person who loves you immeasurably in return. Be honest and direct. Speak of your love, your concerns, what is bothering you, what brings you joy.

You might also try writing a letter to *you* from God's perspective. Ask the Holy Spirit for guidance. Imagine God telling you of his love for you, his mercy, his compassion, his understanding. Allow him to address your hurts and concerns.

Keep your letters. Refer to them from time to time to see how your relationship with God has grown. Reflect on how he has been a part of your life.

When we are before the Blessed Sacrament we can recite short prayers, read a Gospel passage, enter into a conversation with our Lord, or simply sit in his presence, adoring him and thanking him for his many gifts. Make a point to visit Jesus in the Blessed Sacrament in your school chapel or parish church. You might also wish to come to the Sunday Mass fifteen minutes early (or stay a few minutes after Mass) to pray before the Lord.

Litanies

Jesus taught us to pray fervently, continually, and with perseverance. A **litany** is a popular way to pray because it can help us to remain persistent and focused in prayer. The Greek root of the word *litany* is "to ask in earnest."

Litanies contain a series of prayers both invocations (asking) and responses: for example, "Holy Mother of God . . . pray for us." Litanies can be either communal or private. Popular litanies are the Litany of the Blessed Virgin Mary, the Litany of the Sacred Heart, the Litany of St. Joseph, and the Litany of the Saints.

Novenas

Novena comes from the Latin word for nine. It refers to the time Mary and the Apostles spent in prayer between the Ascension of Jesus and the descent of the Holy Spirit on Pentecost Sunday. Novenas are prayed over nine days, either privately or publicly, to obtain special graces or to petition for particular intentions.

Jesus Prayer

Prayers can be short, as brief as one sentence. A famous one-line prayer is the famous **Jesus Prayer**: "Lord Jesus Christ, Son of God, have mercy on me, a sinner." This faith-filled prayer acknowledges the divinity of Jesus as both Lord and Son of God. He is the Christ, the anointed one of God, who has brought us Salvation. The prayer acknowledges that we are sinners and in need of Christ's forgiveness. You can recite the Jesus Prayer repeatedly for a period of time, concentrating on each word as you slowly inhale and exhale. It is a marvelous prayer of faith and petition to Jesus Christ, our Savior.

You can pray other one-line prayers on many different occasions. For example, when you offer a prayer at the beginning of a task, that task itself can become a prayer. If you say, "Lord, I offer you the work I am about to do preparing this PowerPoint presentation," your effort becomes a prayer. Here are some other examples of one-line prayers:

- Jesus, my friend and Savior, I love you.

Blessed Sacrament
"A name given to the Holy Eucharist, especially the consecrated elements reserved in the tabernacle for adoration, or for the sick" (*CCC*, 1330).

Forty Hours' Devotion
A prayer devotion made for forty continuous hours in which the Blessed Sacrament is exposed. It begins with a Solemn Mass of Exposition, which concludes with the exposition of the Blessed Sacrament and a procession. The forty hours models the time that Jesus spent in the tomb from Death to his Resurrection.

litany
From the Latin word *letania*, meaning "prayer or supplication," a litany is a form of prayer used in liturgies that includes prayers with responses.

Jesus Prayer
A prayer that may have originated with the Desert Fathers in the fifth century, it is a short, formulaic prayer that is said repeatedly.

 ## Trying Out Ways to Pray

During the next week, try praying using a litany or novena. And the end of your prayer time, write your reaction and reflections to praying using the form you chose.

- Help me, Lord Jesus.
- Jesus, protect me from sin.
- Praise God!
- Mary, Mother of God, pray for me.
- Come, Holy Spirit.
- Holy Spirit, enlighten me.
- Thank you heavenly Father for all the gifts you have given me.
- Thank you, Father, for creating this day.

For Review

1. Discuss three good rules for getting started in prayer.
2. Suggest two ways to handle distractions in prayer.
3. Give an example of a vocal prayer.
4. What is meditation?
5. How might a person enter into mental or contemplative prayer?
6. How does God speak to us in the listening part of prayer?

For Reflection

- Write or share some answers to questions Pope Benedict XVI posed to seminarians and youth in his visit to America in 2008: "Have we perhaps lost something of the art of listening? Do you leave space to hear God's whisper, calling you forth into goodness? Friends, do not be afraid of silence or stillness. Listen to God, adore him in the Eucharist. Let his word shape your journey as an unfolding of holiness."

- After listing several special gifts you have been given, compose your own prayer of thanksgiving.

- After reflecting on your sins, compose your own Act of Contrition.

- Note the following in your journal:

  > An ideal time for you to pray on a regular basis
  > A good place for you to pray
  > A comfortable prayer position for you
  > A good way for you to remind yourself of God's presence
  > A prayer-word or phrase that helps you refocus and handle distractions in prayer

Praying with Sacred Scripture (CCC, 2567–2589, 2653–2654)

Sacred Scripture is a rich source for prayer. Many prayers Catholics hold dear to their hearts come directly from the Bible or are partly based on Scriptural passages or events. These include prayers said at Mass, Psalms and canticles, and familiar popular prayers like the Our Father, Hail Mary, and the Angelus. Scripture tells of many people who prayed faithfully, both from the Old and New Testaments. The greatest model of prayer is Jesus himself. Finally, Scripture offers instructions on how to pray. Again, Jesus' lessons on how to pray are timeless.

A constant theme in Scripture is that God's relationship with his people is one of prayer. On the one hand, God constantly seeks us. On the other hand, our hearts, although weakened by sin, seek him. Sacred Scripture reveals that God always initiates the process. When humans respond to his invitation, prayer takes place. Prayer is God's gift to us.

Prayer in the Old Testament

There are many models of prayer in the Old Testament. For example, the patriarch Abraham heard

God's voice, responded to his invitation, and obeyed him. He did so even during the difficult times that came his way. Moses was on intimate terms with God, conversing with him "face to face, like a man with his friend" (Ex 33:11). Because of this close relationship, Moses was bold enough to intercede for his people, asking God to be merciful and guide them to the Promised Land. Moses' intercession for the Chosen People prefigured the intercession of Jesus Christ, the High Priest, who came to save us.

Led by kings, priests, and prophets, the Chosen People prayed in the Temple before the Ark of the Covenant. King David, along with other authors, composed the Psalms. Inspired by the Holy Spirit, these marvelous prayers comforted individuals and the community. These prayer-poems, quoted and prayed by Jesus himself, have appeal for all ages. Originally sung in the Temple and later in local synagogues, on pilgrimages, and in family and personal settings, the Psalms capture human emotions like joy and awe before God's creation. They express confidence and trust in a loving God, complaints at the sorrows that befall us, and thanksgiving and praise for a generous, creative God. The Church embraces the Psalms, using them in every Mass and in the **Liturgy of the Hours** (see page 254). She recommends them to us as a time-honored way to learn prayer.

The Old Testament prophets also derived great strength from prayer. They talked to God, interceded for the people, and proclaimed God's Word

to their brothers and sisters. Elijah, the father of the prophets and the one who appeared with Moses at the time of Jesus' Transfiguration, is an example of a man of faith whose prayers God answered. For example, the Lord God enabled Elijah to bring a child back to life (1 Kgs 17:7–24). After he so fervently prayed, "Answer me, O Lord, answer me" (1 Kgs 18:37), Elijah helped the people return to faith on Mount Carmel.

Liturgy of the Hours
The official daily prayer of the Church; also known as the Divine Office. The prayer offers prayers, Scripture, and reflections at regular intervals throughout the day.

Prayer in the New Testament

We learn best about prayer by contemplating Jesus himself in prayer and then by following his instructions on how to pray. Jesus learned prayer from his Mother and from the Jewish tradition. However, as the eternal Son of God, Jesus' prayer also came from who he was. This is why, at the age of twelve, he said to his parents in the Temple, "I must be in my Father's house" (Lk 2:49).

The Gospels give many examples of Jesus at prayer. For example, after his baptism in the Jordan River, Jesus went to the desert for a forty-day retreat to pray in preparation for his ministry. Jesus also prayed before making important decisions like selecting the Apostles. After performing his first miracles of healing, Jesus withdrew to pray. Likewise, after performing the miracle of the loaves and fishes, Jesus dismissed the crowd and his followers and withdrew to a hill to pray. Also, the night before Peter confessed Jesus to be the Messiah, Jesus prayed.

LEARN FROM THE MASTER

We can learn much about prayer from Jesus' own example at prayer as well as from his specific teachings on how to pray. Read the following passages that contain Jesus' teaching about prayer. For each, briefly summarize the point he is making.

- Matthew 5:44
- Matthew 6:5-8
- Matthew 18:19-20
- Matthew 21:21-22
- Mark 11:23-25
- Luke 11:5-13
- Luke 18:1
- Luke 18:10-14
- John 14:13
- John 15:7

Jesus went to a mountain to pray at the time of the Transfiguration when Peter, James, and John were privileged to see the glory of the Risen Lord. At the Last Supper, Jesus offered the great Priestly Prayer, interceding on our behalf as he asked for us to be one with him so that we can witness to God's love and Salvation. After the Last Supper, Jesus took the Apostles to the Garden of Gethsemane where he prayed over his impending Death on the cross. The content of this prayer reveals that Jesus, like us, was fearful at the thought of death. Yet he prayed, "Father, if you are willing, take this cup away from me; still, not my will but yours be done" (Lk 22:42). Jesus' prayer of *petition* to be spared suffering and death led to a prayer of *submission*, of following the will of his Father. Finally, Jesus prayed on the cross: asking God to forgive those who put him to death; reciting Psalm 22 ("My God, my God why have you forsaken me?"), and committing his spirit to God at the moment of death.

Jesus also taught his disciples how to pray. For example, in the Sermon on the Mount, he told them to pray simply, confidently, and with forgiveness in their hearts. He gave them the words of the Lord's Prayer (see pages 255–259). In Luke's Gospel he told them to pray constantly and with faith that their prayers will be answered.

The New Testament tells of other great models for prayer. The Blessed Mother (see pages 259–261) is referenced in Acts 1:14 praying with the Apostles in the Upper Room, awaiting the coming of the Holy Spirit on Pentecost Sunday. When the Holy Spirit descended on Jesus' disciples, Mary was with them as they "devoted themselves to the teaching of the Apostles and to the communal life, to the breaking of the bread and to the prayers" (Acts 2:42). Prayer was essential to the life of the new Christians.

The New Testament letters attributed to St. Paul reveal him as a man of prayer. Paul praised God for blessings bestowed and for people who joined him in his ministry. Time and again, Paul petitioned God on behalf of the people to whom he preached

ST. BENEDICT

St. Benedict founded the famous monastery of Monte Cassino around the year 520. From this community, Benedict wrote a famous *rule* for monks that was to become the monastic rule for the Western Church.

What can St. Benedict's ancient rule teach us about prayer? After Christianity was legalized and Christians were no longer regularly martyred for their faith, **monasticism** was the most extreme form of Christian witness. From every age, there have been Christians who have felt drawn to a single-minded devotion to God in prayer, solitude, and communal living. In the early centuries, some men and women withdrew from everyday life to go to the desert to be alone with God. There they prayed, fasted, read and meditated on the Scriptures, and performed other various works of penance and sacrifice. They were known as hermits.

Before long, hermits saw an advantage of gathering with others to live the same type of lifestyle in community. Monasteries were formed so that these men and women could share the burden of providing for food, shelter, and protection and could then devote more time to prayer. Benedict was a monk who founded an early monastic community and drew up a rule of life for the monks to live by.

Benedict attempted to seek a balance among three things: public prayer at set times throughout the day (called the "work of God"), the regular reading and meditation on the Bible (called "divine reading"), and manual work for the physical support of the whole monastery.

monasticism
A style of Christian life that stresses communal living and communal worship along with private prayer, silence, poverty, chastity, and obedience.

Benedict's motto was *ora et labora*, "pray and work." By doing this faithfully, those who live a monastic life grow in deeper union with God. Monastic life also provides a strong statement about God's Kingdom. The witness of the monk says, "We are dedicated to the coming of God's Kingdom without being attached to the passing things of this world." The monk's witness—codified by St. Benedict—calls us to question what we are doing and helps us to look more seriously at our own levels of commitment to God.

Faithful Disciple

the Gospel. He also wrote of his own personal relationship with God and how the Lord helped him in tough times.

In the history of the early Church up to our present day, the Holy Spirit taught and continues to teach us how to pray. There are various ways to pray with Scripture, including those described in the next section.

The Church Prays with Sacred Scripture (CCC, 2708)

Sacred Scripture is God's Word that reveals his great love for us in Jesus Christ. Therefore, the Church encourages us to read Sacred Scripture so that we may hear God's Word spoken to us today.

However, we should not only *read* and *study* God's Word but also *pray* it so that it will transform our lives. We pray it at Mass and the other liturgies of the Church. We pray it when we read the Psalms and recite prayers like the Our Father. The Church also prays Scripture by reciting the Liturgy of the Hours (or Divine Office), which is part of the official public worship of the Church. The Liturgy of the Hours extends the praise given to God in the Eucharistic celebration. Scriptural prayer, especially the Psalms, is at the heart of the Liturgy of the Hours, which is traditionally recited by priests and professed members of religious orders on behalf of the whole Church. It consists of five main divisions:

1. an hour of readings
2. morning praises
3. midday prayers
4. vespers (evening prayers)
5. compline (a short night prayer)

Each day follows a separate pattern of prayer with themes closely related to the liturgical year and feasts of the saints. In recent years, lay people have taken to praying the Liturgy of the Hours.

Another way to pray and meet the living God in Sacred Scriptures is the devotional reading of the Bible. For centuries, Catholics have practiced a method of prayer known as *lectio divina*, that is, "sacred reading." The purpose of the sacred reading of God's Word is to *meet* God through his written word and allow the Holy Spirit to lead us into an even deeper union with him. Praying this way, it is best to take a short passage, read it slowly and attentively, and let your imagination, emotions, memory, desires, and thoughts engage the written text.

The following method describes lectio divina from the Benedictine tradition:

1. *Reading (lectio).* Select a short Bible passage. Read it slowly. Pay attention to each word. If a word or phrase catches your attention, read it to yourself several times.
2. *Thinking (meditatio).* Savor the passage. Read it again. Reflect on it. This time feel any emotions that may surface. Picture the images that

Praying with the Daily Readings

Find the Scripture readings from today's Mass readings: www.usccb.org/nab/index.shtml. Read the Gospel for today and pray over it using the method outlined above. Try this each day for the next two weeks.

arise from your imagination. Pay attention to any thoughts or memories the passage might call forth from you.

3. *Prayer (oratio).* Reflect on what the Lord might be saying to you in this passage. Talk to him as you would to a friend. Ask him to show you how to respond to his word. How can you connect this passage to your daily life? How does it relate to the people you encounter every day? Might there be a special message in this Scripture selection just for you? Pay attention to any insights the Holy Spirit might send you.

4. *Contemplation (contemplatio).* Sit in the presence of the Lord. Imagine him looking on you with great love in his heart. Rest quietly in his presence. There is no need to think here, just enjoy your time with him as two friends would who quietly sit on a park bench gazing together at a sunset.

5. *Resolution.* Take an insight that you gained from your "sacred reading" and resolve to apply it to your life. Perhaps it is simply a matter of saying a simple prayer of thanks. Perhaps it is to be more patient with someone in your life. Let the Word the Holy Spirit spoke to you come alive in your life.

Through the power of the Holy Spirit, Christ prays alongside of us. We can be confident that our prayers are heard because Jesus constantly intercedes for us.

For Review

1. Name two examples of prayer from the Old Testament.
2. How is Jesus a model for prayer?
3. What is the Liturgy of the Hours?
4. Name the five steps for praying lectio divina.

For Reflection

- What is a passage from the Old Testament that inspires you to prayer?
- List four adjectives that describe Jesus as the model pray-er.

Two Special Prayers for Jesus' Disciples

The Lord's Prayer, the Our Father, holds the preeminent position among all Christian prayers. From the earliest centuries until today, the Lord's Prayer has been used in the liturgy of the church—in all the sacraments, especially the Eucharist. The early Church prayed the Lord's Prayer three times a day. It remains a part of our daily prayer. No one had dared to address the almighty Creator with the intimate term of address—Father, or more properly "Daddy"—until Jesus invited his followers to do so.

Next to the Lord's Prayer, the Hail Mary is a favorite Catholic prayer. The first part of the prayer comes from Luke's Gospel where he records the greeting of the angel Gabriel (Lk 1:28) and that of Mary's cousin, Elizabeth (Lk 1:42). The second part of the prayer asks Mary to intercede for us.

More information about the Lord's Prayer and the Hail Mary follows.

The Lord's Prayer (CCC, 2759-2865)

Jesus taught his disciples the Lord's Prayer, the perfect Christian prayer and, in the words of Church Father Tertullian, "a summary of the whole Gospel." It is recorded in Matthew 6:9–15 and Luke 11:1–4. The context in Matthew's Gospel is the Sermon on the Mount where Jesus teaches his disciples how to pray. He tells them that they are to be authentic when they pray. They should not be insincere like the hypocrites who like to show off when they pray so that others will think they are holy and devout. Jesus further instructs his disciples to pray privately and that it is not necessary to use a lot of words like pagans who babble magical incantations trying to get God to do their will. Rather, Jesus' disciples must keep their prayers simple and pray with faith-filled and forgiving hearts. Jesus then teaches them the words of this perfect prayer:

> Our Father in heaven,
>   hallowed be your name,
>   your kingdom come,
>   your will be done,
>   on earth as in heaven.
> Give us today our daily bread;
>   and forgive us our debts,
>   as we forgive our debtors;
> and do not subject us to the final test,
>   but deliver us from the evil one.
>   (Mt 6:9–13)

Luke intended his Gospel for Gentile-Christians. Unlike the Chosen People, Gentiles lacked a strong tradition of prayer. The context of Jesus' teaching the Lord's Prayer in Luke's Gospel stresses Jesus' own example of praying. Recall again that Jesus prayed all the time: for example, after his baptism, before choosing the Apostles, in the Temple and synagogues, on a mountain during the Transfiguration, in Gethsemane, and on the cross. There simply can be no better teacher of prayer than Jesus, so the disciples asked him how they should pray. Luke records Jesus' words as:

> Father, hallowed be your name,
>   your kingdom come.
>   Give us each day our daily bread
>   and forgive us our sins
>   for we ourselves forgive everyone in
>   debt to us,
>   and do not subject us to the final test.
>   (Lk 11:2–4)

Luke adds two parables of Jesus that stress important attitudes we should have when we pray

(Lk 11:5–13). The first parable tells of a friend who comes knocking at the door at midnight for some bread. Jesus says that despite the late hour, the friend will respond to the request—if not out of friendship—then certainly out of repeated and relentless requests. The point Jesus makes is clear: be persistent in prayer. Never stop praying. Why? Jesus assures us, "And I tell you, ask and you will receive; seek and you will find; knock and the door will be opened to you" (Lk 11:9–10). A second parable explains that just as a human father will give his children what is good for them (in the parable, wholesome food), how much more will our heavenly Father give us what is good for us: that is, the Holy Spirit, spiritual food that gives us eternal life.

The following sections review each part of the Lord's Prayer: the address to our heavenly Father and seven petitions.

Our Father

Jesus is God's only Son who reveals his Father to us. He invites us to address God as Father, that is, Abba in the Aramaic language Jesus spoke. *Abba* is the word children use of their fathers, stressing an intimate, close, personal, dependent relationship. This address tells us that God is a gracious, all-good, and all-loving Father whom we can approach

and address with confidence. Moreover, because we can call God Father, Abba, we begin to comprehend the awesome truth that God has adopted us into the divine family. We belong to him.

Knowing God as our Father means that we human beings are brothers and sisters with one another. The New Covenant that God made with each of us through his Son in the Holy Spirit has united us into a faith community, the Church. As members of the Church, we pray and approach God together remembering to do what Jesus commanded us to do: treat each other with understanding, compassion, and love.

Who Art in Heaven

"In Heaven" refers to God's **transcendence**, his way of being, and his majesty above all his creatures. Through Jesus, God lives in the hearts of the just. We profess that we are God's people who are united to Christ in Heaven. We wait for the day when our heavenly reward will be fully ours.

Hallowed Be Thy Name

God is the source of all holiness. This petition recognizes God's holiness. We hallow (make holy) God's name when we accept God's love and act like his Son, Jesus Christ. We make God's name holy when we do God's will, when we pray, and when we witness to his Son, Jesus Christ. When we live up to our name as Christians, we lead others to come to know and praise God because they can see God's image reflected in us.

In the Old Testament, God revealed his name to be Yahweh, "I AM," a name that reveals God who comes to us yet remains a mystery. Jesus, God's only Son, reveals that Yahweh is our heavenly Father. Christ's Paschal Mystery and our reception of the Sacrament of Baptism adopt us into God's family, permitting us to call God Father. When we imitate the Son, we witness to the Father's holiness.

Thy Kingdom Come

Jesus inaugurated God's Kingdom from the beginning of his earthly ministry and through his Passion, Death, and Resurrection. The seeds

transcendence
A term that means "lying behind the ordinary range of perception." Because of God's transcendence, he cannot be seen as he is unless he reveals his mystery to our immediate contemplation.

of the Kingdom are present now in the Church because Jesus has saved and redeemed us. The Lord has set a structure in place in the Church that will remain until the Kingdom is fully achieved. It is God's will that a reign of peace and justice, of truth and service, be advanced in the world. However, God's Kingdom is "not yet" fully established until the Lord comes again at the end of the world—a day when our Savior will transform all of creation into its fullness. Until that day, under the guidance of the Holy Spirit, we should live, experience, and work for the Kingdom right now through our participation in the Church.

We pray for Christ's return and the final coming of God's Kingdom when there will perfect righteousness, peace, and joy. To pray for the coming of God's Kingdom means to join Jesus in his work: to feed the hungry and give drink to the thirsty, to welcome the stranger, to clothe the naked, to visit the sick and imprisoned, and to respond to the needs of all who come into our lives, especially those Jesus called the "least of these."

Thy Will Be Done on Earth as It Is in Heaven

To do the Father's will is to join our will to his Son's and to his ongoing work of Salvation by loving others and responding to the least in our midst. For this to happen, we need the assistance of the Holy Spirit to help us overcome our own selfishness and strengthen us to live as faithful disciples of Jesus Christ—disciples who proclaim and witness in their lives the teachings of our Lord.

Give Us This Day Our Daily Bread

When we ask for bread, we are requesting what bread represents—both material and spiritual goods and blessings that are necessary for life: food, shelter, clothing; friendship, love, and companionship. We pray for Jesus' Real Presence in the Eucharist. He is the Bread of Life, "the Word of God and the Body of Christ" (*CCC*, 2861), whom we receive in Holy Communion.

Praying for *our* daily bread also challenges us to remember the needs of others, especially those of hungry and poor people. This petition also reminds Christ's followers of their duty to share the Bread of Life by preaching the Gospel to others in both word and deed. In this petition, we are also praying for the fullness of God's material and spiritual blessings that will be ours in Heaven.

And Forgive Us Our Trespasses as We Forgive Those Who Trespass against Us

It is difficult to ask for and extend forgiveness. To do so we must humbly acknowledge that we are sinners and that we need the Holy Spirit to help us repent of our selfishness and turn to a life of love and service. We need Jesus' help to turn our selfish ways to a more loving life of service. We confess that we need help on our journey to the Father.

Jesus teaches that for God's forgiveness to penetrate our hearts we must in turn forgive others, even our enemies. In the Sermon on the Mount Jesus teaches, "Blessed are the merciful, for they will be shown mercy" (Mt 5:7). The gift of God's forgiveness must be shared with others. Extending forgiveness is an invitation to love. It is also a superlative way to imitate Jesus who, on the cross, forgave his executioners. We cannot call ourselves Christians and children of the Father without sharing the forgiveness that we ourselves have been so graciously given.

And Lead Us Not into Temptation

Trials inevitably come our way. What we pray for in this petition is that we have the strength to overcome any difficulties that might steer us away from a Christian life of service.

We also pray to God that he not allow us to take the path that leads to sin. We pray to remain in his grace until the very end of our lives. Prayer helps us to resist what leads us to sin and gives us strength to overcome difficulties in living a Christian life. We ask the Holy Spirit to shower us with gifts like fortitude, watchfulness, perseverance, and hearts that can tell the difference between trials that strengthen us spiritually and temptations that lead to sin and death.

But Deliver Us from Evil

In union with the saints, we ask God to show forth the victory that Christ has already won over Satan. We pray that the Father will deliver us from Satan's snares, including the temptations that a godless society presents to us. We petition God to keep us from the evil of accidents, illness, violence, and natural disasters. We pray that God will help us reject any cooperation in unjust, prejudicial, and selfish actions. We pray that we never be put in a situation where we might be tempted to deny our loving Father.

Finally, we pray with the Holy Spirit and all God's people—the Communion of Saints—for the Lord's Second Coming when we will be free forever from the snares of the Evil One.

The Hail Mary (CCC, 2673-2679; 2682)

The Blessed Mother has a unique role in Salvation History. Her faith-filled cooperation with the Holy Spirit serves as a model for all Christians. Throughout history, the Church has prayed in communion with the Virgin Mary "to magnify with her the great things the Lord has done for her, and to entrust supplications and praises to her" (CCC, 2682). The Hail Mary, one of the most popular prayers for Catholics, expresses both of these aims. The meaning of the various phrases of this beloved prayer follows.

Hail Mary, Full of Grace

The Angel Gabriel greeted Mary this way, signifying that she was full of grace, without sin, and in blessed union with God who dwelled within her. The *Catechism of the Catholic Church* teaches: "She was, by sheer grace, conceived without sin as the most humble of creatures, the most capable of welcoming the inexpressible gift of the almighty" (*CCC*, 722).

The Lord Is with Thee

Out of his infinite goodness, God chose Mary, preserved her from all sin, and filled her with grace. In freedom, Mary responded to God's blessings by always loving and serving him with total devotion.

Blessed Art Thou among Women

Mary's cousin, Elizabeth, greeted Mary this way when she went to visit Elizabeth to help her before

giving birth to John the Baptist (Lk 1:42). Elizabeth rightly acknowledged that Mary has a unique role in Salvation History. She is the Mother of God whom we honor above all others. Mary is "blessed among women" because she believed that God's Word would be fulfilled in her.

Blessed Is the Fruit of Thy Womb, Jesus

Elizabeth proclaimed this blessing after her son, John the Baptist, leaped in her womb in the presence of the Son of God whom Mary was carrying in her own womb. The Holy Spirit inspired Elizabeth

to bless Mary for her faith in accepting God's Word that she was to be the Mother of God. Elizabeth is greatly honored and humbled that the Mother of God should come to visit her (Lk 1:43).

Holy Mary, Mother of God

This phrase acknowledges that Mary is the Mother of God because she gave birth to Jesus who is both true God and true man. The Council of Ephesus (431) defined the dogma that Mary is indeed *The-otokos* ("Birth-giver of God"). We can entrust all of our causes and petitions to Mary. She prays for us as she once prayed for herself: "May it be done to me according to your word" (Lk 1:38).

Pray for Us Sinners

We acknowledge ourselves as sinners and ask our Blessed Mother to intercede for us. Mary is the Mother of God and the Mother of the Church, so she cares deeply about all of her children. Just as she interceded for the couple who ran out of wine at the wedding feast of Cana, our Blessed Mother will intercede for us by taking our concerns and us to her Son. The love of our Blessed Mother knows no bounds, far exceeding the love of even our own earthly mothers. Another Marian prayer, the Memorare reminds us that "never was it known that anyone who fled to your protection, implored your help, or sought your intercession was left unaided." This is why we can confidently pray to Mary and be assured that our prayers will be heard and that in her mercy she will answer them by taking them to her Son.

Now and at the Hour of Our Death

Mary lived a faith-filled life. She witnessed the crucifixion of her Son. She knew firsthand the agonies of death and abandonment. She remained with Jesus through his Death and rejoiced in his Resurrection. In this petition, we ask her to remain with us to the very end and help us on our journey to her Beloved Son and our heavenly Father, especially at the loneliest time of our lives: the moment of our death.

It is reported that St. Francis Xavier (1506–1552) called to Jesus for mercy on his deathbed and then whispered, "O Virgin Mother of God, remember me." Similarly, Bl. Kateri Tekakwitha (ca. 1656–1680), an Algonquin Indian, died with these words on her lips: "Jesus, I love you! Jesus! Mary!" We, too, are encouraged to surrender to Mary's care at the "hour of our death" that she might lead us to her Son, Jesus, in paradise.

Prayer, especially in union with the Blessed Mother, helps us to grow closer to Jesus, our Savior, and to live lives of Christian discipleship. This message serves as a good summary for this chapter and this course. As you continue your studies, may you grow ever closer to your Lord both in knowledge and in love. Concerning your future, remember the words of St. Pio of Pietrelcina (1887–1968): "Pray, hope, and don't worry." And take to heart the words of an old Irish blessing:

> May the road rise up to meet you.
> May the wind always be at your back.
> May the sun shine warm upon your face,
> and rains fall soft upon your fields.
> And until we meet again,
> May God hold you in the palm of his hand.

For Review

1. Discuss two points Jesus makes in Matthew's Gospel about how his disciples should pray.

2. What is the point of the two parables in Luke's Gospel following Jesus' teaching of the Lord's Prayer?

3. Briefly discuss the meaning of each phrase of the Lord's Prayer.

4. Briefly explain the meaning of the Hail Mary.

For Reflection

- Recite five decades of the Rosary. Offer the Rosary for a special intention for someone who has asked you for your prayers.

- How can you be "daily" bread for someone close to you? For a classmate?

Main Ideas

- Prayer is essential to the life of a disciple. (p. 240)

- There are several definitions of prayer. One way to think of it is a *relationship* with God: Father, Son, and Holy Spirit. (pp. 241–242)

- The greatest benefit of prayer is that it deepens our relationship with the Triune God. (p. 242)

- Prayer is an act of love that can be enhanced by following "6 Ps": place, period of time, posture, presence, passage, and persistence. (pp. 243–244)

- Christian prayer expresses itself as vocal prayer, meditation, and mental prayer. (pp. 243–244)

- Expressions of prayer may be in several forms that are revealed in both Sacred Tradition and Sacred Scripture, including: blessing, adoration, petition, intercession, thanksgiving, and praise. (p. 245)

- Other ways for Catholics to pray are with icons, before the Blessed Sacrament, and by reciting litanies, novenas, and the Jesus Prayer. (pp. 248–249)

- Sacred Scripture is also a rich source of prayer; there are many models of prayer in both the Old Testament and New Testament. (p. 250)

- The Church prays with Sacred Scripture, especially in the Liturgy of the Hours, and also through practice of a prayer method called *lectio divina* or "sacred reading." (pp. 251–255)

- Two special Catholic prayers are the Our Father and the Hail Mary. (pp. 255–256)

- The Our Father has been called "a summary of the whole Gospel." (pp. 256–259)

- The Hail Mary helps the Church remain in communion with the Virgin Mary, "to magnify the great things the Lord has done for her." (pp. 259–261)

Terms, People, Places

Complete each sentence by choosing the correct answer from the list of terms below. You will not use all of the terms.

Blessed Sacrament

contemplation

contrition

Eucharist

Forty Hours' Devotion

Jesus Prayer

lectio divina

litany

Liturgy of the Hours

monasticism

transcendence

votive candle

1. Spending some time before the Lord in the _____ is another way to pray. Often, this practice is connected with an inter-parish celebration of _____.
2. After Christians were no longer regularly being martyred for their faith, _____ became the most extreme form of Christian witness.
3. Mental prayer often leads to _____.
4. You may wish to keep a _____ in the area you have chosen as a special prayer space.
5. The petition "in Heaven" in the Our Father refers to God's _____.

Primary Source Quotations

Meaning of Prayer

For me, prayer means launching out of the heart toward God; a cry of grateful love from the crest of joy or the trough of despair: it is a vast, supernatural force that opens out my heart, and binds me close to Jesus.

—St. Thérèse of Lisieux

Prayer reveals to souls the vanity of earthly goods and pleasures. It fills them with light, strength, and consolation, and gives them a foretaste of the calm bliss of our heavenly home.

—St. Rose of Viterbo

Necessity of Prayer

Nothing is equal to prayer; for what is impossible it makes possible, what is difficult, easy.

—St. John Chrysostom

Those who pray are certainly saved; those who do not pray are certainly damned.

—St. Alphonsus Liguori

The Lord's Prayer

The Lord's Prayer is the most perfect of prayers. . . . In it we ask, not only for all the things we can rightly desire, but also in the sequence that they should be desired. This prayer not only teaches us to ask for things, but also in what order we should desire them.

—St. Thomas Aquinas

Run through all the words of the holy prayers [in Scripture], and I do not think that you will find anything in them that is not contained and included in the Lord's Prayer.

—St. Augustine

Ongoing Assignments

As you cover the material in this chapter, choose and complete at least three of these assignments.

1. Research several prayers of saints. Transcribe into your prayer journal two of the most meaningful prayers that you found.

2. Read Isaiah 43:1–3. Write a short reflection about what it might mean for us today.

3. Look up each Gospel passage below. Write the names of the places where Jesus prayed. Then write and describe six places where you pray.

   • Luke 5:16

   • Luke 6:12

   • Mark 14:32

   • Matthew 21:12–13

   • John 17:1

   • Luke 23:34, 46

4. Read each Gospel passage below. Summarize Jesus' teaching on prayer in your own words. Rate how difficult each teaching is for you to follow in your own life.

   • Matthew 6:6–8

   • Luke 11:9–13

   • Matthew 21:21–22

   • Luke 11:5–8

   • Mark 11:25

   • Matthew 18:18–20

5. Write about or share an oral presentation about a friend, religion teacher, religious, or relative who is a model of prayer for you.

6. Translate and transcribe the Lord's Prayer in a foreign language you are studying.

7. Recite the Litany to the Sacred Heart of Jesus. Report on the history of this devotion.

8. Create a PowerPoint presentation to illustrate the Lord's Prayer. Choose appropriate visuals to accompany the text of the prayer.

9. Make a list of "daily bread" that you need to live a full, happy, holy, and healthy life. Consider these categories:

   • physical needs

   • psychological needs

   • spiritual needs

Prayer

St. Thomas Aquinas (ca. 1225–1274), one of the Church's most brilliant thinkers, is the patron saint of students. He composed the following prayer for students:

Prayer before Study

Creator of all things,
true source of light and wisdom,
origin of all being,
graciously let a ray of your light penetrate

the darkness of my understanding.
Take from me the double darkness
in which I have been born,
an obscurity of sin and ignorance.
Give me a keen understanding,
a retentive memory, and
the ability to grasp things
correctly and fundamentally.
Grant me the talent
of being exact in my explanations
and the ability to express myself
with thoroughness and charm.
Point out the beginning,
direct the progress,
and help in the completion.
I ask this through Christ our Lord.
Amen.

- *Reflection*: What do you need to do to become a better student?

- *Resolution*: Pray this prayer the next time you prepare for final exams.

CATHOLIC HANDBOOK FOR FAITH

A. Beliefs

From the beginning, the Church expressed and handed on its faith in brief formulas accessible to all. These professions of faith are called "creeds" because their first word in Latin, credo, *means "I believe." The following creeds have special importance in the Church. The Apostles' Creed is a summary of the Apostles' faith. The Nicene Creed developed from the Councils of Nicene and Constantinople and remains in common between the Churches of both the East and West.*

Apostles' Creed

I believe in God,
the Father almighty,
Creator of heaven and earth,
and in Jesus Christ, his only Son, our Lord,
who was conceived by the Holy Spirit,
born of the Virgin Mary,
suffered under Pontius Pilate,
was crucified, died and was buried;
he descended into hell;
on the third day he rose again from the dead;
he ascended into heaven,
and is seated at the right hand of God the Father
    almighty;
from there he will come to judge the living and the
    dead.

I believe in the Holy Spirit,
the holy catholic Church,
the communion of saints,
the forgiveness of sins,
the resurrection of the body,
and life everlasting. Amen.

Nicene Creed

I believe in one God,
the Father almighty,
maker of heaven and earth,
of all things visible and invisible.

I believe in one Lord Jesus Christ,
the Only Begotten Son of God,
born of the Father before all ages.
God from God, Light from Light,
true God from true God,
begotten, not made, consubstantial with the Father;
through him all things were made.
For us men and for our salvation
he came down from heaven,
and by the Holy Spirit was incarnate of the Virgin
    Mary,
and became man.

For our sake he was crucified under Pontius Pilate,
he suffered death and was buried,
and rose again on the third day
in accordance with the Scriptures.
He ascended into heaven

and is seated at the right hand of the Father.
He will come again in glory
to judge the living and the dead
and his kingdom will have no end.

I believe in the Holy Spirit, the Lord, the giver of
   life,
who proceeds from the Father and the Son,
who with the Father and the Son is adored and
   glorified,
who has spoken through the prophets.

I believe in one, holy, catholic, and apostolic
   Church.
I confess one Baptism for the forgiveness of sins
and I look forward to the resurrection of the dead
and the life of the world to come. Amen.

Gifts of the Holy Spirit

1. Wisdom
2. Understanding
3. Counsel
4. Fortitude
5. Knowledge
6. Piety
7. Fear of the Lord

Fruits of the Holy Spirit

1. Charity
2. Joy
3. Peace
4. Patience
5. Kindness
6. Goodness
7. Generosity
8. Gentleness
9. Faithfulness
10. Modesty
11. Self-control
12. Chastity

The Symbol of Chalcedon

Following therefore the holy Fathers, we unanimously teach to confess one and the same Son, our Lord Jesus Christ, the same perfect in divinity and perfect in humanity, the same truly God and truly man composed of rational soul and body, the same one in being (*homoousios*) with the Father as to the divinity and one in being with us as to the humanity, like unto us in all things but sin (cf. Heb 4:15). The same was begotten from the Father before the ages as to the divinity and in the later days for us and our Salvation was born as to his humanity from Mary the Virgin Mother of God.

We confess that one and the same Lord Jesus Christ, the only-begotten Son, must be acknowledged in two natures, without confusion or change, without division or separation. The distinction between the natures was never abolished by their union but rather the character proper to each of the two natures was preserved as they came together in one person (*prosôpon*) and one hypostasis. He is not split or divided into two persons, but he is one and the same only-begotten, God the Word, the Lord Jesus Christ, as formerly the prophets and later Jesus Christ himself have taught us about him and as has been handed down to us by the Symbol of the Fathers.

—From the General Council of Chalcedon
(AD 451)

Understanding the Paschal Mystery

This article by Rev. Paul Turner first appeared in the Institute Resource Packet of the North American Forum on the Catechumenate (2004), pp. 14–15.

> "Paschal mystery" is the expression we use for the suffering, death and resurrection of Christ, and for our participation in Christ through baptism and death.
>
> On the road one day with his disciples, Jesus took the Twelve aside to explain something to them in private (Mark 10:33–34).

"We are going up to Jerusalem, and the Son of Man will be handed over to the chief priests and the scribes, and they will condemn him to death and hand him over to the Gentiles who will mock him, spit upon him, scourge him, and put him to death, but after three days he will rise."

The Gospels say Jesus predicted his passion on numerous occasions, but the significance eluded even his closest followers. Once he suffered his horrible death and stunned the world with his resurrection, people understood his prediction.

The resurrection of Jesus became the centerpiece of early Christian preaching. In Acts of the Apostles 13:28–30, for example, Paul announced, "Even though [the inhabitants of Jerusalem] found no grounds for a death sentence, they asked Pilate to have [Jesus] put to death, and . . . they took him down from the tree and placed him in a tomb. But God raised him from the dead."

The Paschal Mystery also promises believers a share in the resurrection. Paul explains the benefit of faith (2 Thessalonians 2:14):

"To this end [God] has also called you through our Gospel to possess the glory of our Lord Jesus Christ." "Christ has been raised from the dead, the firstfruits of those who have fallen asleep" (1 Corinthians 15:20). To the Romans (6:5), he says, "If we have grown into union with him through a death like his, we shall also be united with him in the resurrection." Paul's words recall those of Jesus himself (John 14:3): "If I go and prepare a place for you, I will come back again and take you to myself, so that where I am you also may be."

Both words, *paschal* and *mystery*, are important. *Paschal* refers to Passover. The annual Passover recalls the day that the angel of death passed over Israel in exile, sparing the firstborn of God's chosen people, but visiting terror upon their enemies (Exodus 12). It was at Passover when Jesus mounted the cross at Calvary, freeing his own chosen people from sin and vanquishing death forever (John 19:14).

Mystery refers to our faith. We do not understand how God will save us, or even why God loves us so. We do not appreciate the joy that awaits us in eternal life. "What eye has not seen, and ear has not heard, and what has not entered the human heart, what God has prepared for those who love him, this God has revealed to us through the Spirit" (1 Corinthians 2:9).

Christians face the Paschal Mystery with every baptism and every death. Baptism ushers us into the Paschal Mystery, and death transports us to the threshold of its completion. "In the sacraments of Christian initiation we are freed from the power of darkness and joined to Christ's death, burial and resurrection. . . . Baptism recalls and makes present the paschal mystery itself, because in baptism we pass from the death of sin into life" (*Christian Initiation, General Introduction* 1, 6).

"In the face of death, the Church confidently proclaims that God has created each person for eternal life and that Jesus, the Son of God, by his death and resurrection, has broken the chains of sin and death that bound humanity" (*Order of Christian Funerals, General Introduction* 1).

The Paschal Mystery of Christ is the promise of life for Christians. This glory gives us hope and helps us face our fears.

One day long ago Jesus foretold his death, unveiling the Paschal Mystery to the Twelve. Mark describes the experience this way: "The disciples were on the way, going up to Jerusalem, and Jesus went ahead of them. They were amazed, and those who followed were afraid."

This still describes the experience of every Christian. We are disciples, on the way—the way of the commands of Christ, the way toward our own death, our own Jerusalem. Jesus is not exactly with us. He is ahead of us. This belief makes us amazed, but we followers remain afraid. We know not what lies ahead. It is all mystery. But we believe it is paschal, and therein lies our hope.

B. Faith in God: Father, Son, and Holy Spirit

Our profession of faith begins with God, for God is the First and the Last, the beginning and end of everything.

Attributes of God

St. Thomas Aquinas named nine attributes that seem to tell us some things about God's nature. They are:

1. *God is eternal.* He has no beginning and no end. Or, to put it another way, God always was, always is, and always will be.

2. *God is unique.* There is no God like Yahweh (see Isaiah 45:18). God is the designer of a one-and-only world. Even the people he creates are one of a kind.

3. *God is infinite and omniscient.* This reminds us of a lesson we learned early in life: God sees everything. There are no limits to God.

4. *God is omnipresent.* God is not limited to space. He is everywhere. You can never be away from God.

5. *God contains all things.* All of creation is under God's care and jurisdiction.

6. *God is immutable.* God does not evolve. God does not change. God is the same God now as he always was and always will be.

7. *God is pure spirit.* Though God has been described with human attributes, God is not a material creation. God's image cannot be made. God is a pure spirit who cannot be divided into parts. God is simple, but complex.

8. *God is alive.* We believe in a living God, a God who acts in the lives of people. Most concretely, God assumed a human nature in the

divine Person of Jesus Christ, without losing his divine nature.

9. *God is holy.* God is pure goodness. God is pure love.

The Holy Trinity

The Holy Trinity is the central mystery of the Christian faith and of Christian life. Only God alone can make it known to us by revealing himself as Father, Son, and Holy Spirit. Viewed in the light of faith, some of the Church dogmas, or beliefs, can help our understanding of this mystery:

*   *The Trinity is One.* There are not three Gods, but one God in three Persons. Each one of them—Father, Son, and Holy Spirit—is God whole and entire.

*   *The three Persons are distinct from one another.* The three Persons of the Trinity are distinct in how they relate to one another. "It is the Father who generates, the Son who is begotten, and the Holy Spirit who proceeds" (Lateran Council IV quoted in *CCC*, 254). The Father is not the Son; nor is the Son the Holy Spirit.

*   *The three divine Persons of the Blessed Trinity are related to one another.* While the three Persons are truly distinct in light of their relations, we believe in one God. The Three Persons do not divide the divine unity. They are inseparable in what they are and are inseparable in what they do. However each Divine Person reveals his own unique personal properties in the work that is done by the whole Trinity. Above all, the divine missions of the Son's Incarnation and the gift of the Holy Spirit show forth the personal properties of the Divine Persons. The Council of Florence taught: "Because of that unity the Father is wholly in the Son and wholly in the Holy Spirit; the Son is wholly in the Father and wholly in the Holy Spirit; the Holy Spirit is wholly in the Father and wholly in the Son" (quoted in *CCC*, 255).

St. John Damascus used two analogies to describe the doctrine of the Blessed Trinity.

Think of the Father as a root,
of the Son as a branch,
and of the Spirit as a fruit,
for the substance of these is one.

The Father is a sun
with the Son as rays
and the Holy Spirit as heat.

Read the *Catechism of the Catholic Church* (232–260) on the Holy Trinity.

Faith in One God

There are several implications for those who love God and believe in him with their entire heart and soul (see *CCC* 222–227):

*   It means knowing God's greatness and majesty.

*   It means living in thanksgiving.

*   It means knowing the unity and dignity of all people.

*   It means making good use of created things.

*   It means trusting God in every circumstance.

C. Deposit of Faith

"Deposit of Faith" refers to both Sacred Scripture and Sacred Tradition handed on from the time of the Apostles, from which the Church draws all that she proposes is revealed by God.

Canon of the Bible

There are seventy-three books in the canon of the Bible, that is, the official list of books the Church accepts as divinely inspired writings: forty-six Old Testament books and twenty-seven New Testament books. Protestant Bibles do not include seven Old Testament books in their list (1 and 2 Maccabees, Judith, Tobit, Baruch, Sirach, and the Wisdom of Solomon). Why the difference? Catholics rely on the version of the Bible that the earliest Christians used, the *Septuagint*. This was the first Greek translation of the Hebrew Scriptures begun in the third century BC. Protestants, on the other hand, rely on an official list of Hebrew Scriptures compiled in the Holy Land by Jewish scholars at the end of the first century AD. Today, some Protestant Bibles print the disputed books in a separate section at the back of the Bible, called the *Apocrypha*.

The twenty-seven books of the New Testament are divided into three categories: the Gospels, the letters written to local Christian communities or individuals, and the letters intended for the entire Church. The heart of the New Testament, in fact all of Scripture, is the Gospels. The New Testament is central to our knowledge of Jesus Christ. He is the focus of all Scripture.

There are forty-six books in the Old Testament canon. The Old Testament is the foundation for God's self-Revelation in Christ. Christians honor the Old Testament as God's Word. It contains the writings of prophets and other inspired authors who recorded God's teaching to the Chosen People and his interaction in their history. For example, the Old Testament recounts how God delivered the Jews from Egypt (the Exodus), led them to the Promised Land, formed them into a nation under his care, and taught them in knowledge and worship.

The stories, prayers, sacred histories, and other writings of the Old Testament reveal what God is like and tell much about human nature, too. In brief, the Chosen People sinned repeatedly by turning their backs on their loving God; they were weak and easily tempted away from God. Yahweh, on the other hand, *always* remained faithful. He promised to send a messiah to humanity.

Listed on the following page are the categories and books of the Old Testament.

How to Locate a Scripture Passage

Example: 2 Tm 3:16–17

1. Determine the name of the book.
   The abbreviation "2 Tm" stands for the book of Second Timothy.

2. Determine whether the book is in the Old Testament or New Testament.
   The book of Second Timothy is one of the New Testament letters.

3. Locate the chapter where the passage occurs.
   The first number before the colon—"3"—indicates the chapter. Chapters in the Bible are set off by the larger numbers that divide a book.

4. Locate the verses of the passage.
   The numbers after the colon indicate the verses referred to. In this case, verses 16 and 17 of chapter 3.

5. Read the passage.
   For example: "All Scripture is inspired by God and is useful for teaching, for refutation, for correction, and for training in righteousness, so that one who belongs to God may be competent, equipped for every good work."

The Old Testament

The Pentateuch

Genesis	Gn
Exodus	Ex
Leviticus	Lv
Numbers	Nm
Deuteronomy	Dt

The Historical Books

Joshua	Jos
Judges	Jgs
Ruth	Ru
1 Samuel	1 Sm
2 Samuel	2 Sm
1 Kings	1 Kgs
2 Kings	2 Kgs
1 Chronicles	1 Chr
2 Chronicles	2 Chr
Ezra	Ezr
Nehemiah	Neh
Tobit	Tb
Judith	Jdt
Esther	Est
1 Maccabees	1 Mc
2 Maccabees	2 Mc

The Wisdom Books

Job	Jb
Psalms	Ps(s)
Proverbs	Prv
Ecclesiastes	Eccl
Song of Songs	Sg
Wisdom	Wis
Sirach	Sir

The Prophetic Books

Isaiah	Is
Jeremiah	Jer
Lamentations	Lam
Baruch	Bar
Ezekiel	Ez
Daniel	Dn
Hosea	Hos
Joel	Jl
Amos	Am
Obadiah	Ob
Jonah	Jon
Micah	Mi
Nahum	Na
Habakkuk	Hb
Zephaniah	Zep
Haggai	Hg
Zechariah	Zec
Malachi	Mal

The New Testament

The Gospels

Matthew	Mt
Mark	Mk
Luke	Lk
John	Jn
Acts of the Apostles	Acts

The New Testament Letters

Romans	Rom
1 Corinthians	1 Cor
2 Corinthians	2 Cor
Galatians	Gal
Ephesians	Eph
Philippians	Phil
Colossians	Col
1 Thessalonians	1 Thes
2 Thessalonians	2 Thes
1 Timothy	1 Tm
2 Timothy	2 Tm
Titus	Ti
Philemon	Phlm
Hebrews	Heb

The Catholic Letters

James	Jas
1 Peter	1 Pt
2 Peter	2 Pt
1 John	1 Jn
2 John	2 Jn
3 John	3 Jn
Jude	Jude
Revelation	Rv

Relationship between Scripture and Tradition

The Church does not derive the revealed truths of God from the holy Scriptures alone. The Sacred Tradition hands on God's Word, first given to the Apostles by the Lord and the Holy Spirit, to the successors of the Apostles (the bishops and the pope). Enlightened by the Holy Spirit, these successors faithfully preserve, explain, and spread it to the ends of the earth. The Second Vatican Council fathers explained the relationship between Sacred Scripture and Sacred Tradition:

> It is clear therefore that, in the supremely wise arrangement of God, Sacred Tradition, Sacred Scripture, and the Magisterium of the Church are so connected and associated that one of them cannot stand without the others. Working together, each in its own way, under the action of the one Holy Spirit, they all contribute effectively to the salvation of souls. (*Dei Verbum*, 10)

D. Church

The Church is the Body of Christ, that is, the community of God's people who profess faith in the risen Lord Jesus and love and serve others under the guidance of the Holy Spirit. The Church is guided by the pope and his bishops.

Marks of the Church

1. *The Church is One.* The Church remains one because of its source: The unity in the Trinity of the Father, Son, and Spirit in one God. The Church's unity can never be broken and lost because this foundation is itself unbreakable.
2. *The Church is Holy.* The Church is holy because Jesus, the founder of the Church, is holy, and he joined the Church to himself as his body and gave the Church the gift of the Holy Spirit. Together, Christ and the Church make up the "whole Christ" (*Christus totus* in Latin).
3. *The Church is Catholic.* The Church is catholic ("universal" or "for everyone") in two ways. First, she is catholic because Christ is present in the Church in the fullness of his body, with the fullness of the means of Salvation, the fullness of faith, sacraments, and the ordained ministry that comes from the Apostles. The Church is also catholic because she takes her message of Salvation to all people. Put another way, the Church in this world is the Sacrament of Salvation, the sign and instrument of the communion of God and men. As Pope Paul VI explained, this is so because God desires "that the whole human race may become one People of God, form one Body of Christ, and be built up into one temple of the Holy Spirit" (quoted in *CCC*, 776).
4. *The Church is Apostolic.* The Church's apostolic mission comes from Jesus—"Go, therefore, and make disciples of all nations" (Mt 28:19)—and is directed by the Holy Spirit. It is from God's love for us that we receive both our obligation and vigor to proceed in forging God's mission that all will be saved and come to a knowledge of the truth. "Salvation is found in the truth" (CCC, 851). It is the Church's love for Christ that spurs this mission on. The Church remains apostolic because she still teaches the same things the Apostles taught. The Pope and bishops, who are successors to the Apostles, lead and guide the Church until Jesus returns.

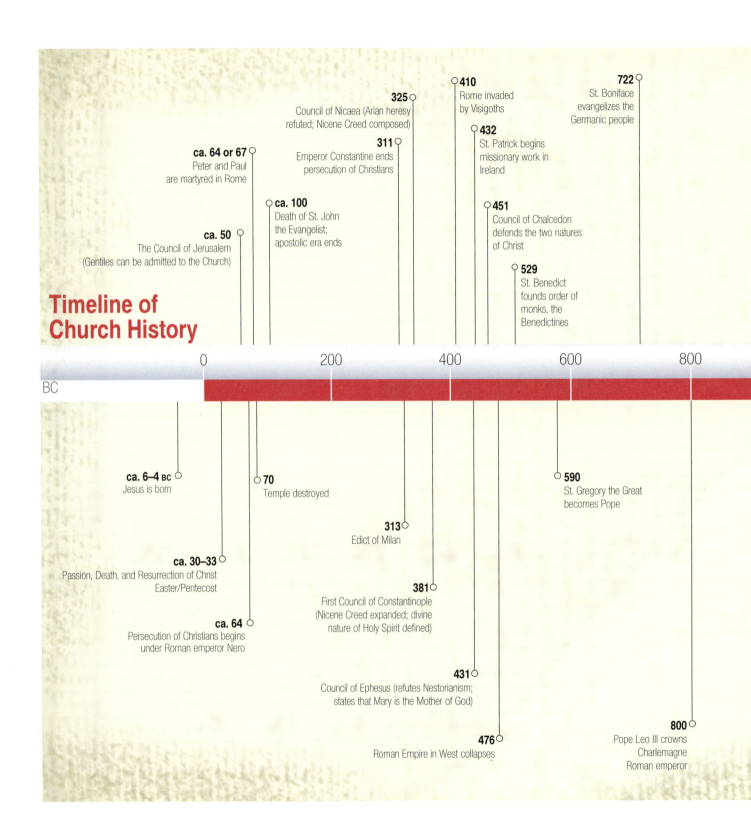

Timeline of Church History

410
Rome invaded
by Visigoths

722
St. Boniface
evangelizes the
Germanic people

325
Council of Nicaea (Arian heresy
refuted; Nicene Creed composed)

311
Emperor Constantine ends
persecution of Christians

432
St. Patrick begins
missionary work in
Ireland

ca. 64 or 67
Peter and Paul
are martyred in Rome

ca. 100
Death of St. John
the Evangelist;
apostolic era ends

451
Council of Chalcedon
defends the two natures
of Christ

ca. 50
The Council of Jerusalem
(Gentiles can be admitted to the Church)

529
St. Benedict
founds order of
monks, the
Benedictines

0   200   400   600   800

BC

ca. 6–4 BC
Jesus is born

70
Temple destroyed

590
St. Gregory the Great
becomes Pope

313
Edict of Milan

ca. 30–33
Passion, Death, and Resurrection of Christ
Easter/Pentecost

381
First Council of Constantinople
(Nicene Creed expanded; divine
nature of Holy Spirit defined)

ca. 64
Persecution of Christians begins
under Roman emperor Nero

431
Council of Ephesus (refutes Nestorianism;
states that Mary is the Mother of God)

476
Roman Empire in West collapses

800
Pope Leo III crowns
Charlemagne
Roman emperor

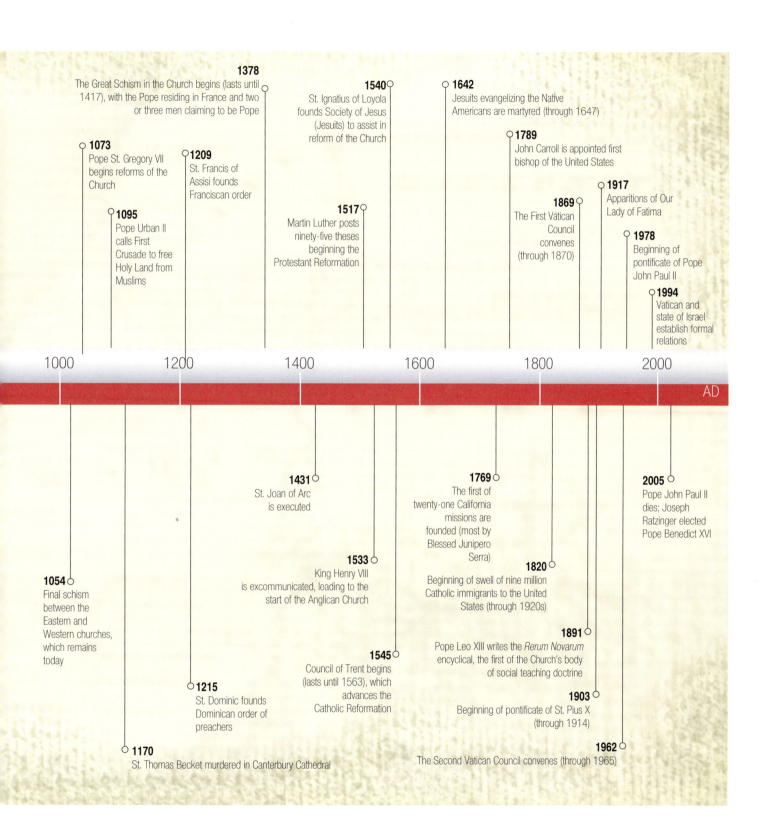

1378
The Great Schism in the Church begins (lasts until 1417), with the Pope residing in France and two or three men claiming to be Pope

1073
Pope St. Gregory VII begins reforms of the Church

1209
St. Francis of Assisi founds Franciscan order

1540
St. Ignatius of Loyola founds Society of Jesus (Jesuits) to assist in reform of the Church

1642
Jesuits evangelizing the Native Americans are martyred (through 1647)

1789
John Carroll is appointed first bishop of the United States

1095
Pope Urban II calls First Crusade to free Holy Land from Muslims

1517
Martin Luther posts ninety-five theses beginning the Protestant Reformation

1869
The First Vatican Council convenes (through 1870)

1917
Apparitions of Our Lady of Fatima

1978
Beginning of pontificate of Pope John Paul II

1994
Vatican and state of Israel establish formal relations

1000   1200   1400   1600   1800   2000

AD

1431
St. Joan of Arc is executed

1769
The first of twenty-one California missions are founded (most by Blessed Junipero Serra)

2005
Pope John Paul II dies; Joseph Ratzinger elected Pope Benedict XVI

1533
King Henry VIII is excommunicated, leading to the start of the Anglican Church

1820
Beginning of swell of nine million Catholic immigrants to the United States (through 1920s)

1054
Final schism between the Eastern and Western churches, which remains today

1891
Pope Leo XIII writes the *Rerum Novarum* encyclical, the first of the Church's body of social teaching doctrine

1545
Council of Trent begins (lasts until 1563), which advances the Catholic Reformation

1215
St. Dominic founds Dominican order of preachers

1903
Beginning of pontificate of St. Pius X (through 1914)

1170
St. Thomas Becket murdered in Canterbury Cathedral

1962
The Second Vatican Council convenes (through 1965)

The Apostles and Their Emblems

St. Andrew

Tradition holds that Andrew was crucified on an X-shaped cross, called a *saltire*.

St. Bartholomew

Bartholomew was flayed alive before being crucified. He was then beheaded.

St. James the Greater

James the Greater, the brother of John, was beheaded by Herod Agrippa. It is the only death of an Apostle mentioned in Scripture (Acts 12:2). The shell indicates James's missionary work by sea in Spain. The sword is of martyrdom.

St. James the Less

James the Less is traditionally known as the first bishop of Jerusalem. The saw for his emblem is connected with the tradition of his body being sawed into pieces after he was pushed from the pinnacle of the Temple.

St. John the Evangelist

John was the first bishop of Ephesus. He is the only Apostle believed to have died a natural death, in spite of many attempts to murder him by his enemies. One attempt included his miraculous survival after drinking a poisoned drink.

St. Jude

Some traditions have Sts. Jude and Peter martyred together. It is thought that he traveled throughout the Roman Empire with Peter.

St. Matthew

Matthew's shield depicts three purses, reflecting his original occupation as tax collector.

St. Matthias

Matthias was the Apostle chosen by lot to replace Judas. Tradition holds that Matthias was stoned to death and then beheaded with an ax.

St. Peter

Simon Peter was the brother of Andrew. The first bishop of Rome, Peter was crucified under Nero, asking to be hung upside down because he felt unworthy to die as Jesus did. The keys represent Jesus' giving Peter the keys to the Kingdom of Heaven.

St. Philip

Philip may have been bound to a cross and stoned to death. The two loaves of bread at the side of the cross refer to Philip's comment to Jesus about the possibility of feeding the multitudes of people (Jn 6:7).

St. Simon

The book with fish depicts Simon as a "fisher of men" who preached the Gospel. He was also known as Simon the Zealot.

St. Thomas

Thomas is thought to have been a missionary in India, where he is thought to have built a church. Hence, the carpenter's square. He may have died by arrows and stones. It is then thought that he had a lance run through his body.

The Pope

The bishop of Rome has carried the title "pope" since the ninth century. Pope means "papa" or "father." St. Peter was the first bishop of Rome and, hence, the first pope. He was commissioned directly by Jesus:

> And so I say to you, you are Peter, and upon this rock I will build my church, and the gates of the netherworld shall not prevail against it. I will give you the keys to the kingdom of heaven. Whatever you bind on earth shall be bound in heaven; and whatever you loose on earth shall be loosed in heaven. (Mt 16:18–19)

Because Peter was the first bishop of Rome, the succeeding bishops of Rome have had primacy in the Church. The entire succession of popes since St. Peter can be traced directly to the Apostle.

The pope is in communion with the bishops of the world as part of the Magisterium, which is the Church's teaching authority. The pope can also define doctrine in faith or morals for the Church. When he does so, he is infallible and cannot be in error.

The pope is elected by the College of Cardinals by a two-thirds plus one majority vote in secret balloting. Cardinals under the age of eighty are eligible to vote. If the necessary majority is not achieved, the ballots are burned in a small stove inside the council chambers along with straw that makes dark smoke. The sign of dark smoke announces to the crowds waiting outside St. Peter's Basilica that a new pope has not been chosen. When a new pope has been voted in with the necessary majority, the ballots are burned without the straw, producing white smoke and signifying the election of a pope.

Recent Popes

Since 1900 and including the pontificate of Pope Benedict XVI, there have been ten popes. Pope John Paul II was the first non-Italian pope since Dutchman Pope Adrian VI (1522–1523). The popes of this era with their original names, place of origin, and years as pope:

- Pope Leo XIII (Giocchino Pecci): Carpineto, Italy, February 20, 1878–July 20, 1903.
- Pope St. Pius X (Giuseppe Sarto): Riese, Italy, August 4, 1903–August 20, 1914.
- Pope Benedict XV (Giacomo della Chiesa): Genoa, Italy, September 3, 1914–January 22, 1922.
- Pope Pius XI (Achille Ratti): Desio, Italy, February 6, 1922–February 10, 1939.
- Pope Pius XII (Eugenio Pacelli): Rome, Italy, March 2, 1939–October 9, 1958.
- Pope John XXIII (Angelo Giuseppe Roncalli), Sotto il Monte, Italy, October 28, 1958–June 3, 1963.
- Pope Paul VI (Giovanni Battista Montini): Concessio, Italy, June 21, 1963–August 6, 1978.
- Pope John Paul I (Albino Luciani): Forno di Canale, Italy, August 26, 1978–September 28, 1978.
- Pope John Paul II (Karol Wojtyla): Wadowice, Poland, October 16, 1978–April 2, 2005.
- Pope Benedict XVI (Joseph Ratzinger): Marktl am Inn, Germany, April 19, 2005–present

Fathers of the Church

Church Fathers, or Fathers of the Church, is a traditional title that was given to theologians of the first eight centuries whose teachings made a lasting mark on the Church. The Church Fathers developed a significant amount of doctrine that has great authority in the Church. The Church Fathers are named as either Latin Fathers (West) or Greek Fathers (East). Among the greatest Fathers of the Church are:

Latin Fathers	Greek Fathers
St. Ambrose	St. John Chrysostom
St. Augustine	St. Basil the Great
St. Jerome	St. Gregory of Nazianzus
St. Gregory the Great	St. Athanasius

Doctors of the Church

The Doctors of the Church are men and women honored by the Church for their writings, preaching, and holiness. Originally the Doctors of the Church were considered to be Church Fathers Augustine, Ambrose, Jerome, and Gregory the Great, but others were added over the centuries. St. Teresa of Avila was the first woman Doctor (1970). St. Catherine of Siena was named a Doctor of the Church the same year. The list of Doctors of the Church:

Name	Life Span	Designation
St. Athanasius	296–373	1568 by Pius V
St. Ephraim the Syrian	306–373	1920 by Benedict XV
St. Hilary of Poitiers	315–367	1851 by Pius IX
St. Cyril of Jerusalem	315–386	1882 by Leo XIII
St. Gregory of Nazianzus	325–389	1568 by Pius V
St. Basil the Great	329–379	1568 by Pius V
St. Ambrose	339–397	1295 by Boniface VIII
St. John Chrysostom	347–407	1568 by Pius V
St. Jerome	347–419	1295 by Boniface XIII
St. Augustine	354–430	1295 by Boniface XIII
St. Cyril of Alexandria	376–444	1882 by Leo XIII
St. Peter Chrysologous	400–450	1729 by Benedict XIII
St. Leo the Great	400–461	1754 by Benedict XIV
St. Gregory the Great	540–604	1295 by Boniface XIII
St. Isidore of Seville	560–636	1722 by Innocent XIII
St. John of Damascus	645–749	1890 by Leo XIII
St. Bede the Venerable	672–735	1899 by Leo XIII
St. Peter Damian	1007–1072	1828 by Leo XII
St. Anselm	1033–1109	1720 by Clement XI
St. Bernard of Clairvaux	1090–1153	1830 by Pius VIII
St. Anthony of Padua	1195–1231	1946 by Pius XII
St. Albert the Great	1206–1280	1931 by Pius XI
St. Bonaventure	1221–1274	1588 by Sixtus V
St. Thomas Aquinas	1226–1274	1567 by Pius V
St. Catherine of Siena	1347–1380	1970 by Paul VI
St. Teresa of Avila	1515–1582	1970 by Paul VI
St. Peter Canisius	1521–1597	1925 by Pius XI
St. John of the Cross	1542–1591	1926 by Pius XI
St. Robert Bellarmine	1542–1621	1931 by Pius XI
St. Lawrence of Brindisi	1559–1619	1959 by John XXIII
St. Francis de Sales	1567–1622	1871 by Pius IX
St. Alphonsus Liguori	1696–1787	1871 by Pius IX
St. Thérèse of Lisieux	1873–1897	1997 by John Paul II

Ecumenical Councils

An ecumenical council is a worldwide assembly of bishops under the direction of the pope. There have been twenty-one ecumenical councils, the most recent being the Second Vatican Council (1962–1965). A complete list of the Church's ecumenical councils with the years each met:

Nicaea I	325
Constantinople I	381
Ephesus	431
Chalcedon	451
Constantinople II	553
Constantinople III	680
Nicaea II	787
Constantinople IV	869–870
Lateran I	1123
Lateran II	1139
Lateran III	1179
Lateran IV	1215
Lyons I	1245
Lyons II	1274
Vienne	1311–1312
Constance	1414–1418
Florence	1431–1445
Lateran V	1512–1517
Trent	1545–1563
Vatican Council I	1869–1870
Vatican Council II	1962–1965

E. Morality

Morality refers to the goodness or evil of human actions. Listed below are several helps the Church offers for making good and moral decisions.

The Ten Commandments

The Ten Commandments are a main source for Christian morality. The Ten Commandments were revealed by God to Moses. Jesus himself acknowledged them. He told the rich young man, "If you wish to enter into life, keep the commandments" (Mt 19:17). Since the time of St. Augustine (fourth century), the Ten Commandments have been used as a source for teaching baptismal candidates.

I.   I, the Lord, am your God: you shall not have other gods besides me.

II.   You shall not take the name of the Lord, your God, in vain.

III.   Remember to keep holy the sabbath day.

IV.   Honor your father and your mother.

V.   You shall not kill.

VI.   You shall not commit adultery.

VII.   You shall not steal.

VIII.   You shall not bear false witness against your neighbor.

IX.   You shall not covet your neighbor's wife.

X.   You shall not covet your neighbor's goods.

The Beatitudes

The word *beatitude* means "happiness." Jesus preached the Beatitudes in his Sermon on the Mount. They are:

Blessed are the poor in spirit, for theirs is the kingdom of God.

Blessed are they who mourn, for they will be comforted.

Blessed are the meek, for they will inherit the land.

Blessed are they who hunger and thirst for righteousness, for they will be satisfied.

Blessed are the merciful, for they will be shown mercy.

Blessed are the clean of heart, for they will see God.

Blessed are the peacemakers, for they will be called children of God.

Blessed are they who are persecuted for the sake of righteousness, for theirs is the kingdom of Heaven.

Cardinal Virtues

Virtues—habits that help in leading a moral life—that are acquired by human effort are known as moral or human virtues. Four of these are the cardinal virtues, as they form the hinge that connects all the others. They are:

- Prudence
- Justice
- Fortitude
- Temperance

Theological Virtues

The theological virtues are the foundation for moral life. They are gifts infused into our souls by God.

- Faith
- Hope
- Love

Corporal (Bodily) Works of Mercy

1. Feed the hungry.
2. Give drink to the thirsty.
3. Clothe the naked.
4. Visit the imprisoned.
5. Shelter the homeless.
6. Visit the sick.
7. Bury the dead.

Spiritual Works of Mercy

1. Counsel the doubtful.
2. Instruct the ignorant.
3. Admonish sinners.
4. Comfort the afflicted.
5. Forgive offenses.
6. Bear wrongs patiently.
7. Pray for the living and the dead.

Precepts of the Church

1. You shall attend Mass on Sundays and on holy days of obligation and rest from servile labor.
2. You shall confess your sins at least once a year.
3. You shall receive the Sacrament of Eucharist at least during the Easter season.
4. You shall observe the days of fasting and abstinence established by the Church.
5. You shall help to provide for the needs of the Church.

Catholic Social Teaching: Major Themes

The 1998 document *Sharing Catholic Social Teaching: Challenges and Directions—Reflections of the U.S. Catholic Bishops* highlighted seven principles of the Church's social teaching. They are:

1. Life and dignity of the human person
2. Call to family, community, and participation
3. Rights and responsibilities
4. Preferential option for the poor and vulnerable
5. The dignity of work and the rights of workers
6. Solidarity
7. God's care for creation

Sin

Sin is an offense against God.

Mortal sin is the most serious kind of sin. Mortal sin destroys or kills a person's relationship with God. To be a mortal sin, three conditions must exist:

- The moral object must be of grave or serious matter. Grave matter is specified in the Ten Commandments (e.g., do not kill, do not commit adultery, do not steal, etc.).

- The person must have full knowledge of the gravity of the sinful action.

- The person must completely consent to the action. It must be a personal choice.

Venial sin is less serious sin. Petty jealousy, disobedience, and a sarcastic word may be examples of venial sins. Venial sins, when not repented, can lead a person to commit mortal sins.

Vices are bad habits linked to sins. Vices come from particular sins, especially the seven capital sins: pride, avarice, envy, wrath, lust, gluttony, and sloth.

F. Liturgy and Sacraments

The Sacraments and the Divine Office constitute the Church's liturgy. The Mass is the most important liturgical celebration.

Church Year

The cycle of seasons and feasts that Catholics celebrate is called the Church Year or Liturgical Year. The Church Year is divided into five main parts: Advent, Christmas, Lent, Easter, and Ordinary Time.

Holy Days of Obligation in the United States

1. Immaculate Conception of Mary
   December 8

2. Christmas
   December 25

3. Solemnity of Mary, Mother of God
   January 1

4. Ascension of the Lord
   Forty days after Easter

5. Assumption of Mary
   August 15

6. All Saints Day
   November 1

The Seven Sacraments

1. Baptism
2. Confirmation
3. Eucharist
4. Penance and Reconciliation
5. Anointing of the Sick
6. Matrimony
7. Holy Orders

How to Go to Confession

1. Spend some time examining your conscience. Consider your actions and attitudes in each area of your life (e.g., faith, family, school/work, social life, relationships). Ask yourself, Is this area of my life pleasing to God? What needs to be reconciled with God? with others? with myself?

2. Sincerely tell God that you are sorry for your sins. Ask God for forgiveness and for the grace you will need to change what needs changing in your life. Promise God that you will try to live according to his will for you.

3. Approach the area for confession. Wait at an appropriate distance until it is your turn.

4. Make the Sign of the Cross with the priest. He may say: "May God, who has enlightened every heart, help you to know your sins and trust his mercy." You reply: "Amen."

5. Confess your sins to the priest. Simply and directly talk to him about the areas of sinfulness in your life that need God's healing touch.

6. The priest will ask you to express your contrition or sorrow and to pray an Act of Contrition. Pray an Act of Contrition you have committed to memory. See page 290 for a prayer of contrition.

7. The priest will talk to you about your life, encourage you to be more faithful to God in the future, and help you decide what to do to make up for your sins—your penance.

8. The priest will then extend his hands over your head and pray the Church's official prayer of absolution:

   God, the Father of mercies, through the Death and Resurrection of his Son, has reconciled the world to himself and sent the Holy Spirit among us for the forgiveness of sins; through the ministry of the Church may God give you pardon and peace, and I absolve you from your sins in the name of the Father, and of the Son, and of the Holy Spirit.

   You respond: "Amen."

9. The priest will wish you peace. Thank him and leave.

10. Go to a quiet place in church and pray your prayer of penance. Then spend some time quietly thanking God for the gift of forgiveness.

Order of Mass

There are two main parts of the Mass, the Liturgy of the Word and the Liturgy of the Eucharist. The complete order of Mass is as follows:

The Introductory Rites

> The Entrance
> Greeting of the Altar and of the People Gathered
> The Act of Penitence
> The *Kyrie Eleison*
> The *Gloria*
> The Collect (Opening Prayer)

The Liturgy of the Word

> Silence
> The Biblical Readings (the reading of the Gospel is the high point of the Liturgy of the Word)
> The Responsorial Psalm
> The Homily
> The Profession of Faith (Creed)
> The Prayer of the Faithful

The Liturgy of the Eucharist

> The Preparation of the Gifts
> > The Prayer over the Offerings
> > The Eucharistic Prayer
> > > Thanksgiving
> > > Acclamation
> > > Epiclesis
> > > Institution Narrative and Consecration
> > > Anamnesis
> > > Offering
> > > Intercessions
> > > Final Doxology
> The Communion Rite
> > The Lord's Prayer
> > The Rite of Peace
> > The Fraction (Breaking of the Bread)
> > Communion
> > Prayer after Communion

The Concluding Rites

Communion Regulations

To receive Holy Communion properly, a person must be in the state of grace (free from mortal sin), have the right intention (only for the purpose of pleasing God), and observe the Communion fast.

The fast means that a person may not eat anything or drink any liquid (other than water) one hour before the reception of Communion. There are exceptions made to this fast only for the sick and aged.

Three Degrees of the Sacrament of Holy Orders

There are three degrees of the Sacrament of Holy Orders: the ministries of bishop, priest, and deacon.

The bishop receives the fullness of the Sacrament of Orders. He is the successor to the Apostles. When he celebrates the Sacraments, the bishop is given the grace to act in the person of Christ, who is the head of the Body of the Church.

Priests are ordained as coworkers of the bishop. They, too, are configured to Christ so that they may act in his person during the Sacraments of Eucharist, Baptism, and the Anointing of the Sick. They may bless marriages in the name of Christ and, under the authority of the bishop, share in Christ's ministry of forgiveness in the Sacrament of Penance and Reconciliation.

Deacons are ordained for service and are configured to Christ the servant. Deacons are ordained to help and serve the priests and bishops in their work. While bishops and priests are configured to Christ to act as the head of Christ's body, deacons are configured to Christ in order to serve as he served. Deacons may baptize, preach the Gospel and homily, and bless marriages.

G. Mary and the Saints

The doctrine of the Communion of Saints flows from our belief that we Christians are closely united as one family in the Spirit of Jesus Christ. Mary is the Queen of the Saints. Her role in the Church flows from an inseparable union with her Son.

Mother of God

Mary, the Mother of Jesus, is the closest human to cooperate with her Son's work of redemption. For this reason, the Church holds her in a special place. Of her many titles, the most significant is that she is the Mother of God.

The Church teaches several truths about Mary.

First, she was conceived immaculately. This means from the very first moment of her existence she was without sin and "full of grace." This belief is called the Immaculate Conception. The feast of the Immaculate Conception is celebrated on December 8.

Second, Mary was always a virgin. She was a virgin before, in, and after the birth of Jesus. As his Mother, she cared for him in infancy and raised him to adulthood with the help of her husband, Joseph. She witnessed Jesus' preaching and ministry, was at the foot of his cross at his crucifixion, and present with the Apostles as they awaited the coming of the Holy Spirit at Pentecost. With her whole being, she is as she stated: "I am the handmaid of the Lord" (Lk 1:38).

Third, at the time of her death, Mary was assumed body and soul into Heaven. This dogma was proclaimed as a matter of faith by Pope Pius XII in 1950. The feast of the Assumption is celebrated on August 15.

The Church has always been devoted to the Blessed Virgin. This devotion is different from that given to God—Father, Son, and Holy Spirit. Rather, the Church is devoted to Mary as the first disciple, the Queen of All Saints, and the Church's own Mother. Quoting the fathers of the Second Vatican Council:

> In the meantime the Mother of Jesus, in the glory which she possesses in body and soul in Heaven, is the image and the beginning

of the Church as it is to be perfected in the world to come. Likewise she shines forth on earth, until the day of the Lord shall come, a sign of certain hope and comfort to the pilgrim People of God. (*Lumen Gentium*, 68)

Marian Feasts throughout the Year

January 1	Solemnity of Mary, Mother of God
March 25	Annunciation of the Lord
May 31	Visitation
August 15	Assumption
August 22	Queenship of Mary
September 8	Birth of Mary
September 15	Our Lady of Sorrows
October 7	Our Lady of the Rosary
November 21	Presentation of Mary
December 8	Immaculate Conception
December 12	Our Lady of Guadalupe

Canonization of Saints

Saints are those who are in glory with God in Heaven. *Canonization* refers to a solemn declaration by the pope that a person who either died a martyr or who lived an exemplary Christian life is in Heaven and may be honored and imitated by all Christians. The canonization process first involves a process of beatification that includes a thorough investigation of the person's life and certification of miracles that can be attributed to the candidate's intercession.

The first official canonization of the universal Church on record is St. Ulrich of Augsburg by Pope John XV in 993.

Some non-Catholics criticize Catholics for "praying to saints." Catholics *honor* saints for their holy lives but we do not pray to them as if they were God. We ask the saints to pray with us and for us as part of the Church in glory. We can ask them to do this because we know that their lives have been spent in close communion with God. We also ask

the saints for their friendship so that we can follow the example they have left for us.

Patron Saints

A patron is a saint who is designated for places (nations, regions, dioceses) or organizations. Many saints have also become patrons of jobs, professional groups, and intercessors for special needs. Listed below are patron saints for several nations and some special patrons:

Patrons of Places

Americas	Our Lady of Guadalupe, St. Rose of Lima
Argentina	Our Lady of Lujan
Australia	Our Lady Help of Christians
Canada	St. Joseph, St. Anne
China	St. Joseph
England	St. George
Finland	St. Henry
France	Our Lady of the Assumption, St. Joan of Arc, St. Thérèse of Lisieux
Germany	St. Boniface
India	Our Lady of the Assumption
Ireland	St. Patrick, St. Brigid, St. Columba
Italy	St. Francis of Assisi, St. Catherine of Siena
Japan	St. Peter
Mexico	Our Lady of Guadalupe
Poland	St. Casmir, St. Stanislaus, Our Lady of Czestochowa
Russia	St. Andrew, St. Nicholas of Myra, St. Thérèse of Lisieux
Scotland	St. Andrew, St. Columba
Spain	St. James, St. Teresa of Avila
United States	Immaculate Conception

Special Patrons

Accountants	St. Matthew
Actors	St. Genesius
Animals	St. Francis of Assisi
Athletes	St. Sebastian
Beggars	St. Martin of Tours
Boy Scouts	St. George
Dentists	St. Apollonia
Farmers	St. Isidore
Grocers	St. Michael
Journalists	St. Francis de Sales
Maids	St. Zita
Motorcyclists	Our Lady of Grace
Painters	St. Luke
Pawnbrokers	St. Nicholas
Police Officers	St. Michael
Priests	St. John Vianney
Scientists	St. Albert
Tailors	St. Homobonus
Teachers	St. Gregory the Great, St. John Baptist de la Salle
Wine Merchants	St. Amand

H. Devotions

Catholics have also expressed their piety around the Church's sacramental life through practices like the veneration of relics, visits to churches, pilgrimages, processions, the Stations of the Cross, religious dances, the rosary, medals, and many more. This section lists some popular Catholic devotions.

The Mysteries of the Rosary

Joyful Mysteries

1. The Annunciation
2. The Visitation
3. The Nativity
4. The Presentation in the Temple
5. The Finding of Jesus in the Temple

Mysteries of Light

1. Jesus' Baptism in the Jordan River
2. Jesus Self-Manifestation at the Wedding of Cana
3. The Proclamation of the Kingdom of God and Jesus' Call to Conversion
4. The Transfiguration
5. The Institution of the Eucharist at the Last Supper

Sorrowful Mysteries

1. The Agony in the Garden
2. The Scourging at the Pillar
3. The Crowning with Thorns
4. The Carrying of the Cross
5. The Crucifixion

Glorious Mysteries

1. The Resurrection
2. The Ascension
3. The Descent of the Holy Spirit
4. The Assumption of Mary
5. The Crowning of Mary as the Queen of Heaven and Earth

How to Pray the Rosary

Opening

1. Begin on the crucifix and pray the Apostles' Creed.
2. On the first bead, pray the Our Father.
3. On the next three beads, pray the Hail Mary. (Some people meditate on the virtues of faith, hope, and charity on these beads.)
4. On the fifth bead, pray the Glory Be.

The Body

Each decade (set of ten beads) is organized as follows:

1. On the larger bead that comes before each set of ten, announce the mystery to be prayed (see above) and pray one Our Father.
2. On each of the ten smaller beads, pray one Hail Mary while meditating on the mystery.
3. Pray one Glory Be at the end of the decade. (There is no bead for the Glory Be.)

Conclusion

Pray the following prayer at the end of the Rosary:

Hail, Holy Queen

Hail, holy Queen, Mother of Mercy,
our life, our sweetness, and our hope.
To thee do we cry,
poor banished children of Eve.
To thee do we send up our sighs,
mourning and weeping in the valley of tears.
Turn then, most gracious advocate,
thine eyes of mercy toward us;
and after this our exile,
show unto us the blessed fruit of thy womb, Jesus.
O clement, O loving, O sweet Virgin Mary.

Pray for us, O holy Mother of God,
that we may be made worthy of the promises of Christ.
Amen.

Stations of the Cross

The Stations of the Cross is a devotion and also a sacramental. (A sacramental is a sacred object, blessing, or devotion.) The Stations of the Cross are individual pictures or symbols hung on the interior walls of most Catholic churches depicting fourteen steps along Jesus' way of the cross. Praying the stations means meditating on each of the following scenes:

1. Jesus is condemned to death.
2. Jesus takes up his cross.
3. Jesus falls the first time.
4. Jesus meets his Mother.
5. Simon of Cyrene helps Jesus carry his cross.
6. Veronica wipes the face of Jesus.
7. Jesus falls the second time.
8. Jesus consoles the women of Jerusalem.
9. Jesus falls the third time.
10. Jesus is stripped of his garments.
11. Jesus is nailed to the cross.
12. Jesus dies on the cross.
13. Jesus is taken down from the cross.
14. Jesus is laid in the tomb.

Some churches also include a fifteenth station, the Resurrection of the Lord.

Novenas

The novena consists of the recitation of certain prayers over a period of nine days. The symbolism of nine days refers to the time Mary and the Apostles spent in prayer between Jesus' Ascension into Heaven and Pentecost.

Many novenas are dedicated to Mary or to a saint with the faith and hope that she or he will intercede for the one making the novena. Novenas to St. Jude, St. Anthony, Our Lady of Perpetual Help, and Our Lady of Lourdes remain popular in the Church today.

Liturgy of the Hours

The Liturgy of the Hours is part of the official, public prayer of the Church. Along with the celebration of the Sacraments, the recitation of the Liturgy of the Hours, or Divine Office (office means "duty" or "obligation"), allows for constant praise and thanksgiving to God throughout the day and night.

The Liturgy of Hours consists of five major divisions:

1. An hour of readings
2. Morning praises
3. Midday prayers
4. Vespers (evening prayers)
5. Compline (a short night prayer)

Scriptural prayer, especially the Psalms, is at the heart of the Liturgy of the Hours. Each day follows a separate pattern of prayer with themes closely tied in with the liturgical year and feasts of the saints.

The Divine Praises

These praises are traditionally recited after the benediction of the Blessed Sacrament.

> Blessed be God.
> Blessed be his holy name.
> Blessed be Jesus Christ, true God and true man.
> Blessed be the name of Jesus.
> Blessed be his most Sacred Heart.
> Blessed be his most Precious Blood.
> Blessed be Jesus in the most holy sacrament of the altar.
> Blessed be the Holy Spirit, the Paraclete.
> Blessed be the great Mother of God, Mary most holy.
> Blessed be her holy and Immaculate Conception.
> Blessed be her glorious Assumption.
> Blessed be the name of Mary, Virgin and Mother.
> Blessed be St. Joseph, her most chaste spouse.
> Blessed be God in his angels and his saints.

I. Prayers

Some common Catholic prayers are listed below. The Latin translation for three of the prayers is included. Latin is the official language of the Church. There are several occasions when you may pray in Latin; for example, at a World Youth Day when you are with young people who speak many different languages.

Sign of the Cross

> In the name of the Father,
> and of the Son,
> and of the Holy Spirit. Amen.

> In nómine Patris,
> et Filii,
> et Spíritus Sancti.
> Amen.

Our Father

> Our Father
> who art in Heaven,
> hallowed be thy name.
> Thy kingdom come;
> thy will be done on earth as it is in Heaven.
> Give us this day our daily bread
> and forgive us our trespasses
> as we forgive those who trespass against us.
> And lead us not into temptation,
> but deliver us from evil.
> Amen.

> Pater Noster qui es in celis:
> sanctificétur Nomen Tuum;
> advéniat Regnum Tuum;
> fiat volúntas Tua,
> sicut in caelo, et in terra.
> Panem nostrum
> cuotidiánum da nobis hódie;
> et dimítte nobis débita nostra,
> sicut et nos
> dimíttimus debitóribus nostris;
> Et ne nos inducas in tentatiónem,
> sed libera nos a Malo.
> Amen.

Glory Be

> Glory be to the Father
> and to the Son
> and to the Holy Spirit,
> as it was in the beginning,
> is now,
> and ever shall be,
> world without end. Amen.

Glória Patri
et Filio
et Spiritui Sancto.
Sicut erat in princípio,
et nunc et semper,
et in sae'cula saeculórum.
Amen.

Hail Mary

Hail Mary, full of grace,
the Lord is with thee.
Blessed art thou among women
and blessed is the fruit of thy womb, Jesus.
Holy Mary, Mother of God,
pray for us sinners now
and at the hour of our death. Amen.

Ave, María, grátia plena,
Dóminus tecum.
Benedicta tu in muliéribus,
et benedíctus fructus ventris
tui, Iesus.
Sancta María, Mater Dei,
ora pro nobis peccatoribus
nunc et in hora mortis nostrae.
Amen.

Memorare

Remember, O most gracious Virgin Mary,
that never was it known
that anyone who fled to your protection,
implored your help,
or sought your intercession was left unaided.
Inspired by this confidence,
I fly unto you,
O virgin of virgins, my Mother,
To you I come, before you I stand,
sinful and sorrowful.
O Mother of the Word Incarnate,
despise not my petitions,
but in your mercy hear and answer me. Amen.

Hail, Holy Queen

Hail, holy Queen, Mother of Mercy,
our life, our sweetness and our hope!
To you do we cry,
poor banished children of Eve;
to you do we send up our sighs,
mourning and weeping in this valley of tears.
Turn then, O most gracious advocate,
your eyes of mercy toward us,
and after this exile,
show us the blessed fruit of your womb, Jesus.
O clement, O loving, O sweet Virgin Mary.
V. Pray for us, O holy Mother of God.
R. that we may be made worthy of the promises
of Christ. Amen.

The Angelus

V. The angel spoke God's message to Mary.
R. And she conceived by the Holy Spirit.
Hail Mary . . .
V. Behold the handmaid of the Lord.
R. May it be done unto me according to your
word.
Hail Mary . . .
V. And the Word was made flesh.
R. And dwelled among us.
Hail Mary . . .
V. Pray for us, O holy Mother of God.
R. That we may be made worthy of the promises
of Christ.
Let us pray: We beseech you, O Lord, to pour
out your grace into our hearts. By the message of an angel we have learned of the Incarnation of Christ, your son; lead us by his
Passion and cross, to the glory of the Resurrection. Through the same Christ our Lord.
Amen.

Regina Caeli

Queen of Heaven, rejoice, alleluia.
The Son you merited to bear, alleluia,

has risen as he said, alleluia.
Pray to God for us, alleluia.

V. Rejoice and be glad, O Virgin Mary, alleluia.
R. For the Lord has truly risen, alleluia.
    Let us pray.
    God of life, you have given joy to the world by the Resurrection of your son, our Lord Jesus Christ. Through the prayers of his Mother, the Virgin Mary, bring us to the happiness of eternal life. We ask this through Christ our Lord. Amen.

Grace at Meals

Before Meals

Bless us, O Lord,
and these your gifts,
which we are about to receive from your
  bounty,
through Christ our Lord. Amen.

After Meals

We give you thanks, almighty God,
for these and all the gifts
which we have received
from your goodness
through Christ our Lord. Amen.

Guardian Angel Prayer

Angel of God, my guardian dear, to whom God's love entrust me here, ever this day be at my side, to light and guard, to rule and guide. Amen.

Prayer for the Faithful Departed

V: Eternal rest grant unto them, O Lord.
R: And let perpetual light shine upon them.
    May their souls and the souls of all faithful departed, through the mercy of God, rest in peace.
R: Amen.

Morning Offering

O Jesus, through the Immaculate Heart of Mary, I offer you my prayers, works, joys, and sufferings of this day in union with the holy sacrifice of the Mass throughout the world. I offer them for all the intentions of your Sacred Heart: the Salvation of souls, reparation for sin, the reunion of all Christians. I offer them for the intentions of our bishops and all members of the apostleship of prayer and in particular for those recommended by your Holy Father this month. Amen.

Act of Faith

O God,
I firmly believe all the truths that you have
  revealed
and that you teach us through your Church,
for you are truth itself
and can neither deceive nor be deceived.
Amen.

Act of Hope

O God,
I hope with complete trust that you will give me,
through the merits of Jesus Christ, all necessary
  grace in this world
and everlasting life in the world to come,
for this is what you have promised
and you always keep your promises.
Amen.

Act of Love

O my God, I love you above all things, with my whole heart and soul, because you are all good and worthy of all my love. I love my neighbor as myself for the love of you. I forgive all who have injured me, and I ask pardon of all whom I have injured. Amen.

Act of Contrition

My God,
I am sorry for my sins with all my heart.
In choosing to do wrong
and failing to do good,
I have sinned against you
whom I should love above all things.
I firmly intend, with your help,
to do penance,
to sin no more,
and to avoid whatever leads me to sin.
Our Savior Jesus Christ
suffered and died for us.
In his name, my God, have mercy.

Prayer for Peace
(St. Francis of Assisi)

Lord, make me an instrument of your peace.
Where there is hatred, let me sow love;
where there is injury, pardon;
where there is doubt, faith;
where there is despair, hope;
where there is darkness, light;
where there is sadness, joy.
O Divine Master,
grant that I may not so much seek to be
    consoled as to console;
to be understood, as to understand,
to be loved, as to love.
For it is in giving that we receive,
it is in pardoning that we are pardoned,
and it is in dying that we are born to eternal life.

GLOSSARY

allegory
A story involving a sustained comparison in which people, things, and events symbolically represent something else.

Annunciation
The announcement of the birth of Jesus that takes place when the angel Gabriel tells Mary that God has chosen her to be the Mother of the Lord.

anti-Semitism
Unfounded prejudice against the Jewish people.

Ascension
Jesus' passage from humanity into divine glory in God's heavenly domain forty days after his Resurrection. It is from this domain that Jesus will come again.

ascetic
A form of strict self-denial as a means of spiritual discipline. Christian ascetics imitate Christ's life of self-sacrifice in order to live the Gospel more faithfully.

Assumption
The Church dogma that teaches that the Blessed Mother, because of her unique role in her son's Resurrection, was taken directly to Heaven when her earthly life was over. The Feast of the Assumption is on August 15 and is a holy day of obligation.

Beatific Vision
Seeing God "face to face" in Heaven; it is the source of our eternal happiness and final union with the Triune God for all eternity.

Beatitudes
Beatitude means "supreme happiness." The eight Beatitudes preached by Jesus in the Sermon on the Mount respond to our natural desire for happiness.

Beloved Disciple
The Fourth Gospel refers in several places to the "disciple whom Jesus loved." Church Father St. Irenaeus attributed the Gospel of John to the Beloved Disciple. Church tradition identified this John as one of the Apostles.

blasphemy
Any thought, word, or act that expresses hatred or contempt for Christ, God, the Church, saints, or holy things.

Blessed Sacrament
"A name given to the Holy Eucharist, especially the consecrated elements reserved in the tabernacle for adoration, or for the sick" (*CCC*, 1330).

cardinal virtues
The four hinge virtues that support moral living: prudence, justice, fortitude, and temperance.

Charisms

Special gifts the Holy Spirit gives to individual Christians to build up the Church.

chastity

The moral virtue that enables people to integrate their sexuality into their stations in life.

circumcision

A sign of incorporation into Judaism. Jesus is circumcised on the eighth day after his birth as a sign of his submission to the Law.

common priesthood

The priesthood of the faithful. Christ has made the Church a "kingdom of priests" who share in his priesthood through the Sacraments of Baptism and Confirmation.

Communion of Saints

The unity of Jesus Christ with all those he has redeemed—the Church on earth, in Heaven, and in Purgatory.

conscience

A person's most secret core and sanctuary that helps the person determine between good and evil. It moves a person at the appropriate times to make specific choices, approving those that are good and rejecting those that are evil.

contemplation

Wordless prayer whereby a person's mind and heart rest in God's goodness and majesty.

contrition

Heartfelt sorrow and aversion for sins committed along with the intention of sinning no more. Contrition is the most important act of penitents, necessary for receiving the Sacrament of Penance.

corporal works of mercy

Charitable actions that include feeding the hungry, clothing the naked, visiting the sick and the imprisoned, sheltering the homeless, and burying the dead.

Decalogue

Literally, "ten words," it describes the Ten Commandments given by God to Moses on Sinai.

Deposit of Faith

"The heritage of faith contained in Sacred Scripture and Tradition, handed on in the Church from the time of the Apostles, from which the Magisterium draws all that it proposes for belief as being divinely revealed" (*CCC*, Glossary).

discipleship

The life of following Jesus Christ. The word *disciple* comes from a Latin word that means "learner."

Divine Revelation

The way God communicates knowledge of himself to humankind, a self-communication realized by his actions and words over time, most fully by his sending us his divine Son, Jesus Christ.

dogma

A central truth of Revelation that Catholics are obliged to believe.

domestic Church

A name for the Christian family. In the family, parents and children exercise their priesthood of the baptized by worshipping God, receiving the sacraments, and witnessing to Christ and the Church by living as faithful disciples.

Emmanuel

A name for Jesus that means "God is with us." Quoting Isaiah 7:14, Matthew uses Emmanuel to show that God's promise of deliverance is fulfilled in the birth of Jesus.

Epiphany

The feast that celebrates the mystery of Christ's manifestation as Savior of the world.

eschatology

A study of and teaching about the "last things" (death, judgment, Heaven, Hell, Purgatory, the

Second Coming of Christ, and the resurrection of the body).

Eucharist

The source and summit of Christian life, the Eucharist is one of the Sacraments of Initiation. The word *eucharist* comes from a Greek word that means "thankful." The Eucharist commemorates the Last Supper, at which Jesus gave his Body and Blood in the form of bread and wine, and the Lord's sacrificial Death on the cross.

evangelical counsels

Vows of personal poverty, chastity understood as lifelong celibacy, and obedience to the demands of the community that those entering the consecrated life profess.

evangelization

Sharing the Good News. Evangelization involves proclaiming the Gospel in such a way that people's hearts and lives are changed.

exegesis

A Greek word meaning "to lead." It is the study or the explanation of a biblical book or passage.

Forty Hours' Devotion

A prayer devotion made for forty continuous hours in which the Blessed Sacrament is exposed. It begins with a Solemn Mass of Exposition, which concludes with the exposition of the Blessed Sacrament and a procession. The forty hours models the time that Jesus spent in the tomb from Death to his Resurrection.

free will

The "power, rooted in reason and will . . . to perform deliberate actions on one's own responsibility" (*CCC*, 1731).

fruits of the Holy Spirit

Perfections that result from living in union with the Holy Spirit.

Gentiles

A term that means "non-Jews."

gifts of the Holy Spirit

God-given abilities that help us live a Christian life with God's help. Jesus promised these gifts through the Holy Spirit, especially the Sacrament of Confirmation. The seven gifts are wisdom, understanding, knowledge, counsel, (right judgment), fortitude (courage), piety (reverence), and fear of the Lord (wonder and awe).

grace

A free and unearned favor from God, infused into our souls at Baptism, that adopts us into God's family and helps us to live as his children.

Guardian Angel

Angels are messengers with free will and naturally superior intellect to humans. Since the third century, the Church has maintained, though not officially, that all the baptized have Guardian Angels who personally watch out for them. The Feast of Guardian Angels is October 2.

Heaven

Our final communion with the Blessed Trinity, Mary, the angels, and all the saints.

high priest

In Jewish history, the priest in charge of the Temple worship. The high priest shared in the general priestly duties, however, he was the only one allowed to enter the holy of holies, and only then on the Day of Atonement. He was a descendent of Aaron.

idolatry

Worshipping something or someone other than the true God.

Immaculate Conception

The belief that Mary was conceived without Original Sin. The Feast of the Immaculate Conception is on December 8.

Incarnation

The dogma that God's eternal Son assumed a human nature and became man in Jesus Christ to save us from our sins. The term literally means "taking on human flesh."

infancy narratives

Stories in the Gospels of Matthew and Luke about the early life of Jesus.

inspiration

The guidance of the Holy Spirit that enabled the human authors to record faithfully, and without error, what God wanted revealed to us for our beliefs.

Jesus Prayer

A prayer that may have originated with the Desert Fathers in the fifth century, it is a short, formulaic prayer that is said repeatedly.

Judges

In ancient Israel, those who acted as temporary military leaders, as well as arbiters of disputes within and between tribes. The judges were also expected to remind people of their responsibilities to God.

justification

The Holy Spirit's grace that cleanses us from our sins through faith in Jesus Christ and baptism. Justification makes us right with God.

kerygma

The core teaching about Jesus Christ as Savior and Lord.

Kingdom of God

The reign of God proclaimed by Jesus and begun in his Life, Death, and Resurrection. It refers to the process of God's reconciling and renewing all things through his Son and his will being done on earth as it is in Heaven. The process has begun with Jesus in the Church, and will be perfectly completed at the end of time.

Last Judgment

Jesus Christ's judgment of the living and the dead on the last day when he comes to fully establish God's Kingdom.

lectio divina

Literally, "divine reading." This is a prayerful way to read the Bible or any other sacred writings.

litany

From the Latin word *letania*, meaning prayer or supplication, a litany is a form of prayer used in liturgies that includes prayers with responses.

Liturgy of the Hours

The official daily prayer of the Church; also known as the Divine Office. The prayer offers prayers, Scripture, and reflections at regular intervals throughout the day.

Liturgy of the Word

An essential part of the celebration of the Sacrament of the Holy Eucharist that draws on readings from the Old and New Testaments and features a reading from one of the Gospels and a homily that is an exhortation to accept these readings as the Word of God.

Magisterium

The official teaching office of the Church. The Lord bestowed the right and the power to teach in his name to Peter and the other Apostles and their successors. The Magisterium is the bishops in communion with the successor of Peter, the Bishop of Rome (Pope).

Magnificat

The Latin title for the Canticle of Mary in Luke 1:46–55 that begins *Magnificat anima me Dominum* ("My soul proclaims the greatness of the Lord").

martyrdom

The word *martyr* means "witness." Martyrdom applies to a person who bears witness to the truth of his or her faith even unto death. Jesus died the death of a faithful martyr. St. Stephan is recognized as the first Christian martyr.

ministerial priesthood

The priesthood of Christ received in the Sacrament of Holy Orders. Its purpose is to serve the common priesthood by building up and guiding the Church in the name of Christ.

monasticism

A style of Christian life that stresses communal living and communal worship along with private prayer, silence, poverty, chastity, and obedience.

mortal sin

A serious violation of God's law of love that results in the loss of God's life (sanctifying grace) in the soul of the sinner. To commit mortal sin there must be grave matter, full knowledge of the evil done, and deliberate consent.

myth

Symbolic stories that express a spiritual truth or a basic belief about God.

natural law

God's plan for human living that is written in the very way he created things. Binding on all people at all times, it is the light of understanding that God puts in us so that we can discover what is good and what is evil.

New Adam

Announced in the Protoevangelium, a name for Jesus Christ who through his obedience in Life and Death makes amends for the disobedience of Adam.

New Covenant

The climax of Salvation History, the coming of Jesus Christ, the fullness of God's Revelation.

Original Holiness and Original Justice

The state of man and woman before sin. "From their friendship with God flowed the happiness of their existence in paradise" (*CCC*, 384).

Original Sin

The fallen state of human nature into which all generations of people are born. Christ Jesus came to save us from Original Sin.

pantheism

The belief, in opposition to Christian doctrine, that God and nature are one and the same.

parable

A favorite teaching device of Jesus in which he told a short story with a striking, memorable comparison that taught a religious message, usually about some aspect of God's Kingdom.

Parousia

The Second Coming of Christ when the Lord will judge the living and the dead.

particular judgment

The individual's judgment immediately after death, when Christ will rule on one's eternal destiny to be spent in Heaven (after purification in Purgatory, if needed) or in Hell.

Paschal Lamb

In Jewish history, the Paschal Lamb was what the Israelites were commanded to eat as part of the Passover celebration. Jesus is the new Paschal Lamb because he shed his blood for the Redemption of the world.

passion narratives

The name for the four separate accounts of the Passion of Christ. The passion narratives of the Synoptic Gospels follow a general literary and thematic plan. The passion narrative of John's Gospel provides an independent version.

patron saint

Saints that are chosen as special intercessors or protectors for our lives.

Pentateuch

A Greek word meaning "five scrolls." It is used to refer to the first five books of the Bible—Genesis, Exodus, Leviticus, Numbers, and Deuteronomy. The books contain the Jewish Law, the Torah.

Pentecost

The day when the Holy Spirit descended on the Apostles and gave them the power to preach with conviction the message that Jesus is risen and Lord of the universe.

philosophy

The investigation of truths and principles using human reason.

polytheism

The belief, in opposition to Christian doctrine, that there are many gods.

prejudice

An unsubstantiated or preformed judgment about an individual or group.

primeval history

Stories or myths about the origins of the earth, humans, other creatures, languages, and cultures.

Protoevangelium

A term that means "the first gospel," which is found in Genesis 3:15, when God revealed he would send a Savior to redeem the world from its sins.

Purgatory

The state of purification that takes place after death for those who need to be made clean and holy before meeting the all-holy God in Heaven.

Real Presence

The presence of Jesus Christ in the consecrated species of bread and wine.

Redemption

A word that literally means "ransom." Jesus' Death is ransom that defeated the powers of evil.

religion

The relationship between God and humans that results in a body of beliefs and a set of practices: creed, cult, and code. Religion expresses itself in worship and service to God and by extension to all people and all creation.

Sacred Scripture

The inspired Word of God; the written record of God's Revelation.

Sacred Tradition

The living transmission of the Church's Gospel message found in the Church's teaching, life, and worship. It is faithfully preserved, handed on, and interpreted by the Church's Magisterium.

Salvation History

The story of God's saving actions in human history.

Sanhedrin

The seventy-one-member supreme legislative and judicial body of the Jewish people. Many of its members were Sadducees.

Satan

A fallen angel or the devil; the Evil One (*CCC*, 391, 395, 2851).

Son of David

A title for Jesus that indicates his ancestry can be traced to King David, as foretold in Scripture.

Son of God

In the Old Testament, a title used for angels, kings, and others who had an intimate relationship with God. In the New Testament, through his actions and teachings, the title reveals the divinity of Jesus as the only Son of God.

soul

The innermost or spiritual part of a person. The soul is the subject of human consciousness and freedom. Body and soul together form one human nature. The soul does not die with the body. It is eternal and will be reunited with the body in the final resurrection.

spiritual works of mercy
Seven practices of Catholic charity directed toward the soul of our neighbor; based on the teaching of Christ and the Tradition of the Church from the time of the Apostles. They are: counsel the doubtful, instruct the ignorant, admonish the sinner, comfort the sorrowful, forgive injuries, bear wrongs patiently, and pray for the living and the dead.

synagogue
A meeting place for study and prayer.

Talmud
A collection of rabbinical teachings collected after the destruction of the Jerusalem Temple in AD 70.

theological virtues
Three important virtues bestowed on us at Baptism that relate us to God: faith, hope, and charity.

Torah
The Law handed down to the Chosen People by God that they were to live in response to his covenant with them. A summary of the Torah is found in the Ten Commandments.

transcendence
A term that means "lying behind the ordinary range of perception." Because of God's transcendence, he cannot be seen as he is unless he reveals his mystery to our immediate contemplation.

Transfiguration
The mystery from Christ's life in which God's glory shone through and transformed Jesus' physical appearance while he was in the company of the Old Testament prophets Moses and Elijah. Peter, James, and John witnessed this event.

Venial sins
Actual sins that weaken and wound our relationship with God but do not destroy divine life in our souls.

vice
A bad habit, such as laziness, that inclines us to choose the evil rather than the good.

virtue
A firm attitude, stable disposition, and habitual disposition of our intellect and will that regulates our actions, directs our passions, and guides our conduct according to reason and faith.

vocation
A word that means "call." For Catholics the primary call is to be disciples of Jesus Christ. This call, given at Baptism, requires Catholics to bring God's love to others and to share the Good News.

votive candle
A prayer candle typically placed before a statue of Jesus or the Virgin Mary that is lit for a prayer intention.

Subject Index

Scripture Index

Photography Credits

Megan Meier Foundation
page 37

Corbis
page 20, 23, 35, 68, 84, 176, 205, 214, 228, 231, 251

SuperStock
cover; page 4, 5, 28, 33, 42, 44, 49, 54, 60, 62, 71, 73, 75, 86, 108, 100, 112, 117, 120, 122, 124, 125, 126, 132, 138, 140, 142, 145, 150, 152, 160, 167, 178, 184, 189, 190, 192, 193, 195, 196, 200, 210, 215, 217, 221, 226, 238, 247, 253, 256, 257, 258, 259, 260

Art Resource
page viii, 7